NATURE'S
ALCHEMIST

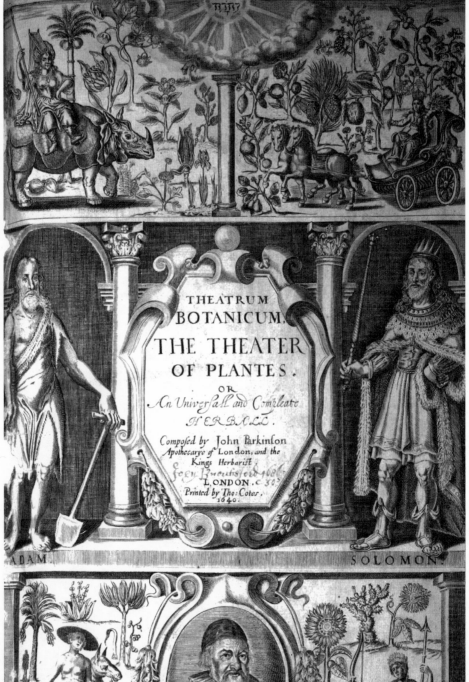

THEATRUM
BOTANICUM.
THE THEATER
OF PLANTES.
OR
An Universall and Compleate
HERBALL.

Composed by John Parkinson
Apothecarye of London, and the
Kings Herbarist
London. C
Printed by Tho: Cotes.
1640.

ADAM.   SOLOMON.

W. Marshall sculpsit

NATURE'S ALCHEMIST

JOHN PARKINSON, HERBALIST TO CHARLES I

ANNA PARKINSON

F

FRANCES LINCOLN LIMITED
PUBLISHERS

FOR *DAISY* AND *CLARA*
WHOSE NAMES IMPLY
THE EARTH AND THE SKY

Frances Lincoln Ltd
4 Torriano Mews
Torriano Avenue
London NW5 2RZ
www.franceslincoln.com

Nature's Alchemist: John Parkinson,
Herbalist to Charles I
Copyright © Frances Lincoln 2007
Text copyright © Anna Parkinson 2007
Photographs copyright © Anna Parkinson except for
those listed on page 336

First Frances Lincoln edition: 2007

A catalogue record for this book is available from the
British Library.

ISBN: 978-0-7112-2767-5

Printed and bound in Singapore

2 4 6 8 9 7 5 3 1

Commissioned and edited by Jane Crawley
Designed by Michael Brunström

Title page: Frontispiece from Theatrum Plantarum, 1640, *showing John Parkinson aged 73, engraved
by William Marshall.*

CONTENTS

Frontispiece from Paradisus Terrestris, Paradisi in Sole, *1629, with the Hebrew word for God, Yahweh, at the top, engraved by Albert Switzer.*

PROLOGUE

This story began as a personal quest. I was fascinated by a mystery that has lain dormant in my family for several generations. I never lived with my father, so he and his possessions were never as completely familiar to me as my mother and hers. Yet I loved, as he did, the most precious of these, which was a book he would occasionally fetch from the drawer where it was kept, saying casually as he did so, 'This is the Parkinson book'. He would keep his hands firmly clasped around the smooth brown leather end-boards as he spoke, so that only if you displayed persistent interest would you glimpse the treasures inside. The tale, which my father told at least as often as he showed the book itself, was that he was directly descended from the author, John Parkinson, who had been Charles I's herbalist.

The front cover of the *Paradisus Terrestris*, published by John Parkinson in 1629, opens to reveal a fantastic frontispiece, a black and white dream of Heaven on Earth. My grandmother's tapestry copy of this picture hung in my bedroom as a child, so I knew the details intimately. The lilies, the chequered fritillary and the cacti grow all together, each one the size of a small tree. An enormous pineapple grows straight out of the ground, magnified in her needlework into glorious orange that clashes with giant purple and white crocuses. The flowers tower over the figure of Eve, who looks as though she is rushing towards them. Behind her, Adam is preoccupied with an apple tree, and in the middle distance a curious sheep-wolf seems to be impaled, prevented from grazing by a trunk that grows straight from the earth into its belly. The book's full title at the foot of this picture is *Paradisi in Sole: Paradisus Terrestris*, promising that the reader will find inside:

> a garden of all sorts of pleasant flowers which our English air will permit to be nursed up, with a Kitchen garden of all manner of herbs, roots and fruits used with us, and an Orchard of all sorts of fruit-bearing trees and shrubs fit for our land, together with the right ordering, planting and preserving of them, and their uses and virtues, collected by John Parkinson, Apothecary of London.[1]

The *Paradisus* was valued, I knew, as the book that brought decorative gardens to England, but it was not until my father died, in 1995, that it took on a new lease of life. I took the *Paradisus* home and did something

not many people do to old books. I read it. I was immediately startled by
the freshness of the voice I encountered. From the six hundred pages, a
description of the finest fruits and flowers that the author could lay his
hands on, emerged what felt like a friendly whisper from someone I might
encounter wandering in my own garden. That strange sheep-wolf and the
Latin title on the frontispiece had given me the impression that this book
was the product of an ancient, primitive and superstitious world, a long
way from my own present reality.[2] Quickly I realized that nothing could
be further from the truth.

Beyond the fragile-looking title-page were more dramatic illustrations of
tulips, lilies, daffodils and melons. These were black and white, squarely
drawn with the solid lines of a woodcut, but each one recognizably a plant
that grows in our gardens today. The text between them revealed a deeper
knowledge of the origins and properties of those plants than I had ever
encountered, and refreshingly direct instructions for making them bloom.
John Parkinson wrote the way he spoke, and since the fundamentals of
gardening have not changed much in four hundred years, you can almost
hear him having a lively discussion with gardeners of our own time.
The man of the soil shines through when he writes about the best way to
deal with heavy clay. This was something he knew with the intimate
appreciation of bitter experience. 'The stable dung of horses [as opposed
to cow dung] is best for cold grounds [clay] to give them heat and life,' he
writes optimistically. Yet, with the special relish that old men reserve for
bad news, he goes on to point out the backbreaking preparatory work:

> Of all other sorts of grounds, the stiff clay is the worst for this purpose
> [of making a garden]. For though you should dig out the whole
> compass of your garden, carry it away, and bring other good mould
> [soil] in instead... the nature of clay is so predominant, that in a small
> time it will eat out the heart of the good mould and convert it to its own
> nature, or very near.... To bring it to any good there must be continual
> labour bestowed... by bringing into it a good store of chalk, lime or
> sand, or else ashes of wood or sea-coal (which is the best for this
> ground) well mixed and turned in with it.[3]

There will be no instant garden on unworked clay. The *Paradisus* is, in
its author's own words, 'a speaking garden'. Its colloquial tone brings
us very close to an age that is more famous for its civil wars and the
literary giants, William Shakespeare and John Donne, who were John's

contemporaries. While they held up a mirror to man's emotions, this portrait of plants reflects minute details of seventeenth-century daily life. It shows us the favourite food of the rich and the poor, their notions of beauty and personal decoration, the illnesses that were common as well as the remedies. Through this book we glimpse gardens and their creators, long after both have been covered in concrete. It is a guide to a lost world but also to a world that can still be found, quite literally, beneath our feet.

The more I read, the more I felt compelled to discover what drove the author to create such a startlingly original book. The bare facts of John Parkinson's life that I could establish quickly were that, from humble beginnings as an apprentice in the Company of Grocers, he came to be named as Britain's first official Royal Herbalist by a king who, at that moment, had a reputation for holding the most splendid court in Europe. John also served Charles I's father. As an apothecary he was part of a radical group that formed the first society dedicated to producing pure medicines and sponsored by King James. He crowned his career in 1640 at the age of seventy-three by publishing the most detailed and searching account of the chemical properties of plants in the English language, the *Theatrum Botanicum*. This book would become a key source for doctors and pharmacists for the next hundred years.

Beyond this, I was frustrated by the repeated assertion that not very much was known. A typical comment was published by Eleanour Sinclair Rohde, a lively writer with a thorough knowledge of early gardening, in 1924:

> But who would venture to describe that most lovable of all gardening books – the Paradisus? Of John Parkinson, the author, we can learn very little. He was born in 1567, probably in Nottinghamshire. Before 1616 he came to London and set up as an apothecary in St Martin-in-the-Fields, and had a garden in Long Acre.[4]

John Parkinson's work has been used extensively as a key to the lives of other men, most notably his close friend the gardener John Tradescant, but no one has ever told his story. His books have been well thumbed by generations of gardeners, chemists and doctors, yet none has explored why he dedicated his life to developing his vast understanding of plants. I began to find it strange that the life of a leading member of his society was so shrouded in silence. Was there a reason why this man kept so much to himself?

I turned to the family history of the Parkinsons to see if I could find out more, and it was amongst these genealogical sources that I uncovered the first clue to the story that unfolds in this book.

My initial encounter with genealogical records was daunting. I quickly discovered that most of what was 'known' about John Parkinson was wrong, and while this encouraged me to search deeper, finding the true story was not easy. As a journalist by training, I am used to trawling through original sources, but this was a little like not knowing your alphabet in a class of fluent primary readers. The obvious start was to try to discover a will, but my diary from those early encounters charts a muddled world of sixteenth- and seventeenth-century records.

Spent a breathless, hopeless day pursuing a Parkinson will, bewildered by the strangeness of it all and my own inability to operate. I looked through wills proved in the Middlesex Archdeaconry court. No Parkinsons between about 1610 and 1660. Then all through the wills proved at the Parochial court of Canterbury in 1651. All sorts of fascinating wills – these were people with money – but no Parkinson will. It's so hard to concentrate. You feel driven by a sense of escaping time.

Then Heraldry – couldn't make much sense of it. Then, just as I was leaving [the Society of Genealogists' Library in London] I found (a) a box of documents about Parkinsons from Lancashire and (b) a huge book about said Parkinsons and I think they have the same crest as (i) John Parkinson, botanist, and (ii) Dad's family.

This crest turned out to be the first piece in the jigsaw I have since fitted together.

As my research developed, I realized that John's story is a powerful universal tale. It tells of a poor man born into a community of outsiders. His lifelong passion for plants became the vehicle that steered his course through the fierce political factions dividing his age. He survived overwhelming obstacles long enough to win respect and honour from his society, leaving an unprecedented collection of botanical knowledge as his legacy to the world. He made a significant contribution to the scientific revolution that was stirring in England. The achievements of John and his contemporaries were obscured by the dramatic political shifts that followed, but his generation pioneered the scientific exploration of the material world that has been under way ever since. The life of this humble man is an untold tale of the English Renaissance in operation.

When John was born in 1567, Elizabeth I was still a young queen. He witnessed the beginning of an English empire and the union of Britain under the first Stuart king. He lived long enough to see that king's son and heir beheaded on the scaffold outside his own palace. When John died in 1650, the state he had served all his life was in utter collapse. Yet almost every salient achievement of our recent cultural history had begun during his lifetime: the first English settlers in North America; the foundations of parliamentary government; the first English bank and the maiden voyage of the East India Trade Company.

John's generation is particularly fascinating to us because he lived, as we do, in a time of transition. As we plunge into the beginning of another technical revolution that has already changed the face of science and business, we can appreciate the excitement and the fear of a world revolutionized by rapid and easy communication in the form of printed books.

The sources I have used to trace this story of John's life are universal. The parish and guild records that reveal the bare bones of his existence are a testament to the stability of the state his generation was in the process of overturning. John's own published books and some others put flesh on the bones, and a few letters fill in key details. All of these sources are available in public libraries. Very few diaries written by John's contemporaries have been discovered. We have to wait for the next generation for gentlemen, like Samuel Pepys and John Evelyn, who had the wealth and leisure to keep the detailed records of their domestic lives that have so intrigued us subsequently. Yet John and his contemporaries performed the labour and took the risks that created this wealthy society. His own work, as you will see, reveals the triumph of patience over prejudice, of industry over show, of determination over luck.

In the closing pages of this book you will find the resolution of my own family mystery. Yet it was clear by the time I came to it that John's real legacy was not his family, but his work. He would be rewarded to discover that he had left for future generations a link in the continuity of human knowledge that remains vital hundreds of years after his death.

Note: In John Parkinson's day the year changed on 25 March. I have used the old division between the years in citing dates. 26 January 1567 would be, in modern terms, 26 January 1568.

Portrait of John Parkinson, aged 52, from inside the Paradisus, *engraved by Albert Switzer, 1629.*

CHAPTER ONE

THE BLESSED PLACE

John Parkinson's God was in the flowers at his feet. By the time he published his famous gardening book in 1629, it was conventional wisdom that God was to be found in a garden. Every educated man knew that 'Paradeza' was the Persian word for a cultivated enclosure, barely altered in Greek or Latin. When John called his book *Paradisi in Sole: Paradisus Terrestris*, he placed himself at the centre of his garden by the English translation: Park in Sun's Earthly Paradise. The pun was a familiar literary device of the kind his contemporaries relished in John Donne's poetry. Yet this description of his work was more than a matter of convention for John. His title was an expression of his life and his soul.

This English apothecary devoted everything he had to plants. He sought them from every corner of the world he could reach. He studied their chemical values and experimented with them for medicine. He crossed their seeds and cultivated them patiently to develop new varieties. He nurtured new arrivals at home and catalogued their habits. He gave his life to describing their beauty, scent and purpose. He valued even humble weeds, comparing them in all their variety to his fellow men.

When he wrote in the introduction to his book 'God's purpose was that man should know and understand plants – not just their scents and pleasure for beauty, but also their uses and properties for meat and medicine', John was stating his position in a debate about the true nature of divinity that had dominated his life. He had come to see humanity as a part of the heavenly order that he could best understand through comparison with the flowers he grew in his garden. 'We can learn', he wrote, 'from the less beautiful plants which are useful to man, just as some men's uses to their fellows be hidden!'

John was sixty-two by the time he published the *Paradisus*. He had been in London for over forty-five years. His friends, his business, his reputation and his garden were all rooted in this community of about 100,000 people, small enough for everyone to know the principal players in town. In the thousands of pages he wrote about plants, he mentioned friends, their houses, their gardens and their livelihoods, throwing light on his society. Yet John referred directly to his own family only twice.

The first reference was a small shield displayed discreetly beneath his portrait in the *Paradisus*. This shield reveals his birthplace, a long way from London. It was a ten-day journey from the capital, and John was never a keen traveller. But there was more to his silence about his people than geographical distance or poor memory. From his earliest days he had learned that his family spelled danger, and though he expected that danger to diminish as he grew older, it continued to haunt him even at the height of his fame. The reason why this apothecary chose to keep his personal life safe from the public eye and pursue his God privately through the miraculous power of plants was a secret known only to John's closest friends.

The wood engraver commissioned to illustrate the *Paradisus* was a German called Albert Switzer.[1] He was considered 'the most exquisite and curious hand' of the age and certainly studied John Parkinson's face carefully before setting pencil to paper for the portrait to be published with his book. Switzer had worked for many months with the man who sat before him, but as he held unusually still for his portrait to be taken, the artist began to pick out significant details.

He saw hooded eyes that gazed sharply back at him, while the small ears sticking out of the short cropped hair told him this man's body was smaller than his puffed-up clothes would suggest. Such slight discordance echoed the difference between the man and his apparel. He wore a starched lace collar over a lavishly embroidered waistcoat, with capped sleeves and pearl buttons. The padded jerkin beneath was slashed to reveal a beautiful lining of contrasting silk. His knickerbockers were parti-coloured in two shades of velvet. Every detail of this immaculate court dress Switzer faithfully reproduced, though he knew this gentleman was no follower of fashion. In the time of King James, many courtiers had imitated the king's short trousers, stuffed with horsehair to give them more 'bottom'. But the old king had been dead for five years and fashions at court had changed completely when his son Charles had taken the throne.

Switzer's subject evidently saw no reason to follow fashion and replace a perfectly good set of clothes. Judging by the lack of wear in this suit, he crammed himself into it as seldom as possible. His book was dedicated to 'The Queen's Most Excellent Majestie', the young Henrietta Maria, so court dress was essential, yet the artist took care to complete a drawing whose tiny details showed the man in front of him was as far from being a courtier as he could be.

With deft strokes of his knife in the finished portrait, Switzer reproduced the coarse hair on the back of the author's square hands; the wiry tufts of whisker on his cheek that refused to lie flat; the ruddy weather-beaten skin that came of hours in the sun and rain, and the dark fingernails that were the result of his daily work with medicines and plants. A conventional oval frame around the finished work declared this was:

Ioannis Parkinsoni Pharmacopoei Londinensis Effigies. LXII Aetatis Annum Agentis. A Nato Christo CICDCXXIX [A Portrait of John Parkinson, Apothecary of London, Aged 62. In the Year of Christ, 1629]

Switzer filled out the space below with two further badges of his subject's identity: the shield of the Apothecaries, and the heraldic badge that the man said belonged to his family.

The coat of arms that John Parkinson chose to display in his book has three stars on a red chevron between three silver ostrich feathers. It can be seen today, stripped of its colours, carved into the stone wall of a farm-house in Lancashire, less than three miles from the road between Preston and Lancaster. This farmhouse at Higher Fairsnape, one of two standing together on the side of the hill, was built by John's cousin, Robert, in 1637, nearly ten years after the portrait was drawn. Yet its presence clearly shows that this range of peaty hills, known as the Bleasdale Moors, is the wild and windswept country John knew as a child.

The moors of this region tower 700 feet above the populated dale below, catching the lowering clouds that sweep in from the Atlantic. Beneath the peaty moss and heather of the surface the soil is heavy clay, so that the rain drains slowly from the rugged terrain. When John was a child, untamed marshes lay to the west, separating this rough moor from the waters of the Irish Sea. To the north and east is Bowland Forest, where the land climbs more steeply, up to another 700 feet in places, and the hills were then covered in scrubby trees of alder, holly, hazel and thorn that could withstand the gusting winds. The river Ribble in the dale to the south, and its tributary, the Calder, was the only gentle route between one place and another.

By the middle of the sixteenth century there were Parkinsons scattered all over these Pennine moors, in Lancashire, neighbouring parts of Yorkshire and the county of Durham. The three richest families claimed descent from the Featherstonehaughs of Featherstone Castle in Northumberland. A third son in the fourteenth century, Peter or Perkin,

Robert Parkinson's coat of arms on the farmhouse at Higher Fairsnape on Bleasdale, Lancashire, photographed by the author in 2002.

had inherited their Lancashire lands. Perkin's heir went by the name of John-le-Perkinson.[2]

Henry VIII had revived the old medieval tradition of coats of arms. He saw it as an opportunity to capitalize on family pride and to register potential sources of wealth in the country at the same time. His appointed heralds made self-financing tours of the nation during which the local grandees would bring them written or verbal proof of their ancestry. If they could show they were descended from gentry they were allowed to pay for a coat of arms that was regarded thereafter as belonging to the family, although, strictly speaking, arms were awarded to individuals. The descendants of John-le-Perkinson or Parkinson presented their credentials to the king's heralds, and chose shields that differed significantly from one another.[3] The one John used in 1629 links him decisively with the clan of farmers on Bleasdale.

It was hard country to farm, but the Parkinsons had stuck to these hill-sides for many generations before John was born. In 1350 the Abbot of Whalley said the human inhabitants of Bleasdale were 'few, intractable and wild'.[4] Above the level where the family's sheep and cattle grazed, deer roamed the area, as well as their predators, wild boar and wolves. The wilderness of Bowland was good hunting country, retained as royal hunting ground by the kings of England. Some Parkinsons in the region held their leases direct from the crown. The Bleasdale branch had theirs in long leases from the Stanleys, hereditary earls of Derby, who had owned most of Lancashire since 1485 when it was given them by the man whom they helped to win the English throne and found the Tudor dynasty, Henry VII.

The king's power in the north depended on this bond with the Earl of Derby and on the earl's links with his tenants in turn. Under the terms of their tenancy, the Bleasdale Parkinsons were obliged to join the earl's militia when called for. They were the first line of defence against the other main predators in this part of the kingdom: marauding Scots from over the border. By the time John was born, these battles with the Scots were history. Military service to your lord was considered a feudal arrangement, and rarely called on, but the Parkinsons kept their weapons waiting in the barn. They were conscious that the security of the throne depended on their loyalty.[5]

The bitterest fights in this area were all about access to land, or to water. On the face of it there was plenty of both. England's population had suffered so severely from the ravages of the Black Death in the four-teenth century that an Italian visitor during Henry VIII's reign wrote home: 'The population of this island does not appear to me to bear any proportion to her fertility and riches'.[6] Here in Lancashire, the struggle to keep back the wilderness, clear the land and feed the family, in the face of corn harvests that could fail and the bitter onslaught of the wet wind from the west, was a grinding task. Every member of the family was needed, particularly every male member, and it is clear from the wills these Parkinsons left that their family ties were essential. The preoccupations of the male line were their tenancies, their rights to their farmland, their sons and their livestock.

The Parkinsons kept their precious leases in the family by passing them always to their eldest son at their death, or their nephew, if there was no direct male heir.[7] They increased their wealth by marrying widows and heiresses who brought lands with them, and they acquired at least one extra advantage. They had a corn mill at Admarsh, the old name for the lowlands of Bleasdale, which became a great source of wealth but also of continuing disputes within the family and with their neighbours. Others who did not have the 'right of soke' (permission to take water from the river that drove the mill) were forced to pay the Parkinsons a fee to grind their corn. This monopoly significantly increased the family's wealth, until it began to break down in family rivalries.

In the second half of the sixteenth century, peace and a growing population meant there were more hands for the backbreaking labour of living off the land. Prices for meat, leather and wool began to rise from about 1540 as the population grew, and, with secure tenure on their lands and relatively fixed costs, the Parkinsons were in a good position to make money. Nevertheless, the increasing value of the land drove more intense competition for it. Farmers in this area fought in the courts over a hillside that hitherto had been more than enough for them. They forced out strangers encroaching with their sheep, calling them 'foreigners'. When Richard Parkinson of Fairsnape died around 1540, the farm passed to his brother Ralph. But Richard's widow married again and her second husband, Anthony Richardson, took the new owner of Fairsnape to court. He accused Ralph Parkinson of driving his cattle out of Admarsh common. In the end the land was enclosed and divided between them in 1548.[8] Richardson built another corn mill because Ralph Parkinson refused him 'right of soke'. This is the story of the two farmhouses that stand side by side at Higher Fairsnape today: two feuding families locked into the same remote stretch of land.

John's father belonged to a branch of this Bleasdale clan who farmed further to the east, at Hazlehurst, close to the gentler lowlands of the Ribble. When Robert Parkinson, the head of this family, died rich in 1562, he left his farm, the tenancy of a corn mill on the river Calder, the lease of a farm called Blindhurst, and a blacksmith's or 'smoke'.[9] He chose to endow two kinsmen besides the immediate family: Thomas Richardson, who must have been a relative of Anthony Richardson, feuding with the other Parkinsons at Fairsnape, and Richard Hodgson. John's father, James, had married Joan Hodgson two years before. The parish priest in Whalley nearby had registered the marriage of 'Jacobus Parkinson et Jona Hodgeshon, primo die Feb. 1560'.[10]

The shield that John displays in his book is the same as the one at Fairsnape in all respects, except that its little bird in the centre at the top denotes the fourth son, so John's father could have been the fourth son, mentioned in Robert's will, who received money instead of one of the precious land tenancies. Younger brothers were forced into towns and villages to make their living, to keep the size of farms intact. There is no record of James Parkinson's trade in Whalley. One of his sons became a glover, so he may have traded in the skins that were produced on the family farm. They were used locally for saddles and shoes, but there was also a growing market for other products from the farm. English wool, finished, dyed and woven, was valued throughout Europe. Goods would travel down the Ribble to Preston, and ships carrying international exports embarked from the port of Lancaster nearby. By 1567, when John was born, sheep farmers and provincial merchants were thriving on this trade.

The pattern of John's immediate family reveals a steadier domestic influence than the feuding Parkinson farmers at Fairsnape. John's mother, Joan Hodgson, clearly knew how to manage childbirth and contraception. Joan and James waited five years after their marriage before having their first child, and the couple's seven children born thereafter came at intervals of almost exactly two and a half years, allowing their mother time to recover her strength before starting to feed the next baby.

Before John there was Richard, baptized by the parish priest, George Dobson, on 15 November 1565. John himself was christened next, a few days after his birth, on 26 January 1567. John's younger brother, Robert, the one who became a glover, was entered in the parish register in the priest's neat Latin on 2 June 1570. The first daughter, Alice, was born on the last day of September 1573, then another, Agnes, on 5 February 1575. Lawrence, his mother's sixth child, was her first sickly baby. He arrived on 13 February 1577 but died only six days later, on the 19th. Elizabeth was born on 26 March 1579 and Jean on 13 May 1581. The baby Jean was the last family birth witnessed by the old priest. By the time the eighth child, Katherine, was christened on 7 October 1583, a new vicar, Robert Osbaldeston, had taken his place.[11]

The parish where John was born was rich and gentle compared to his cousins' land. Nestled between the rivers Ribble and Calder, it was the site of a huge Cistercian abbey, which had been the most powerful establishment for miles around in the time of his grandparents. It was then about two hundred years old, and outshone an even more ancient Cistercian abbey at Sawley in Clitheroe, a short distance upriver. The monks had chosen their territory with care. There was flat pasture and corn land fed by the river Calder, sheltered by steep wooded hillsides that provided oaks for building, and quarries of grey stone. The abbey's parish was exceptionally large, almost thirty miles north to south and fifteen miles wide. The monks prospered on the tithes they drew from the population of this large endowment, as well as from their own careful farming. So great were the abbey's riches that the country where John grew up had come to be known as 'Locus Benedictus', the blessed place.

As soon as he was able to wander about on his own, John was aware of how his family used this rich natural environment to survive. It is unlikely that these Parkinson children ever went short of food, since their cousins and uncles farmed all the hillsides round about. Even so, they were sent out to gather what they could from the moors to supplement the family meals.

> If I should set down all the sortes of herbes [plants] that are usually gathered for Sallets [Salads] I should not only speak of Garden herbes, but of many... that grow wild in the fields, or else be but weeds in a garden, for the usual manner of many is to take the young buds and leaves of everything almost that groweth, as well in the garden as in the Fields, and put them all together, that the taste of the one may amend the relish of the other.[12]

John wrote this more than half a century later, throwing light on the unwritten traditions of his country childhood. When he was young, knowledge was passed on verbally or not at all. It seems likely that it was John's mother, who managed the birth of her children so neatly, who also taught them carefully how to gather herbs from the hillsides. John learned quickly that his family's health and wealth depended partly on his ability to select the right plants and observe where they were found.

Peas and beans were the most common staple at his family's table, grown in fields to meet the demand. Beans were 'boiled in fair water and a little salt, and afterwards stewed with some butter, a little vinegar being put unto them', but the broad bean was valued in the country as more than just a food. The water from the distilled flowers was used to 'take away spots, and clear the skin'. Peas were so popular and various that the names of pea varieties roll off the tongue like players on a stage: the 'Rouncivall'; the green or white 'Hasting'; 'the Scottish or Tufted peas which some call the Rose peas'; 'spotted peas'; 'gray peas'; 'sugar peas'; 'the Pease without skins'. 'There is a very great variety of manured peas known to us', wrote John, 'and I think more in our Country than in others.' These peas were 'much used... For them that go long voyages, ... because it is fresh, a welcome diet to most persons therein.' This was the food that would fortify the discovery of a world beyond the sea.[13]

Most people cultivated long narrow plots around the house, and the family dug in the contents of their privy to boost the crop. The most nourishing and delicious vegetables they grew there, in John's view, were the turnips:

Being boiled in salt broth, they all of them eate most kindly, and by reason of their sweetness are much esteemed and often seen as a dish at good men's tables: but the greater quantitie of them are spent at poor men's feasts.[14]

It was essential to have a patch of onions. The white ones shone out of the ground at the end of the summer like 'chalk stones lying upon the ground, when they are ripe and fit to be gathered'. They were an ingredient in almost every dish 'sliced and put into a pottage, or boiled and peeled and laid in dishes for salads at supper, or sliced and put into water for a sauce for mutton or oysters'. They were needed also for emergency medicine:

The juice of onions is much used to be applied to any burnings with fire or with Gun-powder, or to any scaldings with water or oil, and is most familiar for the Country, where upon such sudden occasions they have not a more fit or speedy remedy at hand.[15]

Even when cultivated vegetables were plentiful, wild plants were an important part of most meals. The red variety of dock, known as blood-wort, was used as a principal 'pot-herb', thrown in together with other leaves and roots to make a broth to accompany meat or bread. John was particularly wary of its incidental effects, since it had more of a 'binding' effect on the bowel than 'patience', another kind of dockweed whose leaves went into the pot.[16]

The children would collect the field variety of parsnips as the best source of seed from which to grow a crop for the table. John considered 'Goatsbeard', or salsify, a delicacy. He found it

wild abroad in many places, but is brought into many gardens.... If the roots of these kinds being young be boiled and dressed as a Parsnip they make a pleasant dish of meat, far passing the parsnip in many men's judgments, and that with yellow flowers to be the best.[17]

In early spring, during the season of Lent, people would purify their bodies with great quantities of herbs. The cleansing potion took its name from tansy leaves, eaten

> while they are young, either shred small with other herbs, or else the juice of it and other herbs fit for the purpose, beaten with eggs and fried into cakes which are usually called Tansies, and are often eaten, being taken to be very good for the stomach to help to digest from thence bad humours that cleave thereunto: as also for weak raines and kidneys, when the urine passeth away by drops.[18]

Other herbs could be used, like garden clary, or clear eye, a variety of which, known as 'Christ's eye', 'groweth in many places'around Britain:

> the most frequent and common use of clary is for men and women that have weak backs, to help to comfort and strengthen the raines [the region of the kidneys] being made into Tansies and eaten.

The seed was 'to be put into the corner of the eye' to heal obstructions and injuries, but John thought the best medicine came from the wild. The garden variety, 'may peradventure do some good, yet the seed of the wild kind will do much more'.[19]

Many families managed to keep essential herbs, such as thyme, sage, winter savory, hyssop, mints and pennyroyal, around the house, though few could afford the time to keep a garden. John's choicest meals were spiced with quantities of these. The best use he knew for sage was

> boiled... with a Calves head, and being minced, to be put with the brains, vinegar and pepper, to serve as an ordinary sauce thereunto. Or being beaten and juiced, rather than minced as many do, is put to a roasted Pig's brain, with Currants for sauce thereunto.

Thyme was also used in handfuls: 'to stuff the belly of a goose to be roasted, and after put into the sauce'.[20]

Later, John would encounter people who despised 'hearbes' as food for the poor, or for fast days, which they repudiated along with the

Catholic Church. English prejudice against fancy vegetables in preference for meat surfaced in 1642, when a Puritan named Thomas Fuller wrote in praise of the good plain cooking to be found in an English farmer's house:

> You shall have... no meat [there] disguised with strange sauces; no straggling joynt of a sheep in the midst of a pasture of grass, beset with salads on every side, but solid, good, substantial food.[21]

Yet John maintained for the whole of his life that eating quantities of 'hot' herbs like thyme, hyssop and pennyroyal was the key to health and strength:

> The former age of our great Grandfathers, had all these hot herbs in much and familiar use, both for their meats and medicines, and therewith preserved themselves in long life and much health; but this delicate age of ours, which is not pleased with anything almost, be it meat or medicine, that is not pleasant to the palate, doth wholly refuse these almost, and therefore cannot be a partaker of the benefit of them.[22]

There were some extraordinary tales of longevity in the wider Parkinson clan. One old man from Eastburn, twenty miles to the east of where John was born, died in January 1600. The parish register noted the event: 'John Parkinson, commonly called Lord of Eastburne, who lived one hundred years and almost five more'. When John Parkinson the herbalist was born, his namesake was already 72 years old, claiming to have been born in 1495. This, perhaps, was the 'great Grandfather' John had in mind.[23]

The self-reliant traditions that John grew up with formed the basis of his family's strength, and, within his community, he was secure. His name alone carried status. On his father's side he was connected to generations of tenant farmers who had tales to tell of their ancestors' close relationship with nobles and kings. His mother's knowledge of herbs and medicines made her essential, not just to her family, but to her neighbours. Yet, even as a child, it was impossible for John to be unaware that danger lurked just over the horizon. His community was, in a sense, under siege. Within living memory his people had suffered a shattering defeat, and neither they, nor the country's rulers, would ever let him forget it.

CHAPTER TWO

'THE RUDE PEOPLE
OF THE NORTH'

John had barely learned to walk when the fourth Duke of Norfolk
proclaimed a 'Northern Rebellion' against Elizabeth I, and called on
the people to take up arms for the cause. Norfolk's revolt in 1569 was
the result of a long intrigue to restore his family fortunes by unseating
the young Protestant queen and putting her prisoner and cousin, the
Catholic Queen of Scots, on the English throne instead. Norfolk was
even planning to marry the Scots Queen Mary, who had been through
two husbands by this time, the second despatched in notoriously
dubious circumstances. Norfolk was backed by two of the most powerful landowners in the north, the earls of Northumberland and
Westmoreland, but not, fatally, by the people. The men and women
of Lancashire still remembered that this duke's uncle had been the principal instrument of their defeat a generation before, when they had lost
the one rebellion that they would willingly have died for. For nearly forty
years now, they had been picking up the pieces.

In the 1560s, when John was sent to learn his catechism, the farmers'
children chanted their Latin prayers in the gatehouse that led to Whalley
Abbey. The horses and carts that rumbled beneath them as they learned
headed now only for the barns and private house of a local landowner
called Sir Richard Assheton. Out of the window they could see the
ruined walls that had, in living memory, supported the vaulting roof of
a magnificent church. Their parents and the priest told them how once
it had echoed with the sound of hundreds of monks glorifying God.
Their teachers were all that was left. The king's men from the south had
long since beheaded the abbot.

John's mother could tell him the story of the great rebellion in 1536
that local people were so proud of they named it the 'Pilgrimage of
Grace'. Her family had looked upon the abbey as the centre of their
lives. She had almost certainly learned her skill with plants from her
relative, John Hodgson, who had been chaplain of the church of St
Michael at Clitheroe nearby, appointed by the executed abbot.[1] As a

Cistercian monk, Father Hodgson's role in the community was to offer medical as well as spiritual help. Most monasteries had an infirmary able to treat the population round about, especially those who worked on Church lands. Each order had its educated monks who had travelled to study with the mother order in Italy or France, and many learned from the oldest medical schools in Europe. There had been a school of herbal medicine in Montpellier in France since the thirteenth century, and the school of medicine at Salerno in Italy was almost as old. Priests and physicians were often looked on as one and the same thing,

Growing up close to Father Hodgson, Joan had a thorough grounding in the use of the herbs of the countryside to pass on to her son. But her medical knowledge came mixed with the message that the monks were essential to the people's souls. She also believed, quite firmly, that the king who had robbed the people of their priests had committed a mortal sin.

For as long as anyone could remember, the abbey had been a vital hub of life on this side of the Pennines. It had been the only tangible presence in their midst of order and government. In 1526 the Abbot of Whalley, John Paslew, presided over the local ecclesiastical court that reprimanded Richard Parkinson for branding his neighbour a 'poller' or plunderer – the court being only one of the many functions of the abbots and priors in the community. Paslew was also an international politician. He needed the express permission of the Pope, far away in Rome, to take any major decision, but he had to balance papal commands against the growing demands of King Henry VIII.

The abbots were powerful, but not remote. The monastic orders provided a clear route for anyone, including clever sons of poorer families, to reach the top. Paslew came from a family in West Yorkshire, that had been landowners for at least three generations, as it happened, although by becoming abbot he assumed a power in the community far greater than the legacy of his birth. However, the Augustinian prior of the beautiful Bolton Priory near his birthplace, Richard Moone, was the son of 'poor people' from Airedale.[2]

There was palatial splendour inside this wealthy abbey, befitting its political status. Hospitality for important guests was as lavish as that of any noble house at the time. Its accounts show regular imports of delicacies that travelled a long way to titivate the palates of visitors to Whalley. Delights such as figs, almonds, dates, ginger, cloves, cinnamon, liquorice and sugar passed through the abbey kitchens on a regular basis.[3] The ordinary monks rarely shared in this luxury. They came from the local community and each played their part in it. Their establishment combined the functions of a farm, a hospital, a school, a library, and the court of appeal with a hostel for travelling pilgrims, to say nothing of daily spiritual leadership. Their presence was the cement that held the community together.

In the winter of 1536, a great change came to Whalley, which would have indelibly marked John's parents' lives though they were still babes in arms when it happened. The roads had frozen hard that February, so that a man could ride swiftly over them, when the abbey received a visit from two of King Henry VIII's men. They were on the final leg of a tour of about a hundred northern monasteries with a mission, as one of them wrote, to 'beat the King's authority into the heads of the rude people of the North'.[4]

The people of northern England were considered in the south to be 'more superstitious than virtuous, long accustomed to frantic fantasies and ceremonies, which they regard more than either God or their Prince, right far alienate from true religion'. The best way for the king to assert his authority, therefore, was to take control of their abbeys.

At first the interference was minimal. The abbot was obliged to deliver a daily lecture on the Holy Scripture for an hour to the monks, who were all confined to the main abbey site and ordered to sleep in the common dormitory. A short time later these new rules were relaxed. The king was more interested in the abbey's wealth than the monks' spiritual practice. Very soon afterwards, the Speaker of the House of Commons proposed that 'where there was vice and immorality' the king should take charge of the monks' resources to devote them to charitable and educational purposes. Commissioners were appointed once more to visit each county and take a record from each abbot, abbess, or prior 'on oathe' of their house's property, livestock and income.

While the northern people paid for their abbeys' splendour, there was no sign that they resented it. Their clever sons joined the monasteries and were sent south to the great university of Oxford to study. They were obliged to give the monks a tenth of their income each year in tithes, but they also left them their money when they died, in return for prayers for their souls. When the king's policy forced them to choose between their loyalty to him and their loyalty to the Church, the impact was shattering. No battle ever before had put their landowner, their sovereign and their God on different sides. When the confrontation came, the landowners equivocated. The king was far away in the south. The people in the north of England chose, very emphatically, their God and the Church as they knew it.

The commissioners who arrived at Hexham Abbey in Northumberland found the door barred against them. A monk wearing armour climbed on the roof and declared that their charter had been granted by King Henry VIII, 'God Bless him', and there were twenty monks inside all armed and ready to resist. The king's men left, faring better than their colleagues who, a few days later, at Louth in Lincolnshire, were lynched. One was hanged. The other was sewn up in a cow's skin and given to the dogs to eat. Over the next three weeks the rebellion blazed like a forest fire across Lincolnshire, Yorkshire and Lancashire.[5]

For three months in 1536, from the beginning of October to the end of December, Henry VIII was powerless in the north of England. He asked his friend, the Earl of Derby, to raise an army by summoning his tenants and servants, and march it to the Sally Abbey at Sawley where he was to hang the monks in their habits. This army would have brought the Parkinsons down from their hillsides, but the Earl of Derby knew the king's orders would outrage them. He explained to Henry that he could not muster a large enough army 'because of the general support for the rebels in the countryside'.[6] So the king sent the Duke of Norfolk to deal with the rebels at Doncaster with an army of 7,000 men. The duke found himself facing 40,000, and was forced to negotiate.

The rebels' petition, presented to the king on 6 December 1536, made it clear why the people were fighting for their monks. The monasteries, they said, provided all their social support. They gave alms and relief to the poor, they were the only educational establishments, they gave hospitality to travellers in a district where roads were bad, distances long and the climate severe. They pleaded that the monasteries should be maintained and that there should be some adjustment to the Act of Supremacy that established the king as 'Protector and Supreme Head of the English Church, so far as the law of Christ allows'.

While seeming to listen, the king sent Norfolk back to Yorkshire weeks later with secret instructions to hang the rebel leaders without trial. Seventy-four were hanged in Cumberland. Henry explicitly singled out the monks for blame:

Forasmuch as all these troubles have ensued by the solicitation and treacherous conspiracy of the monks and canons of these parts: ... you shall without pity or circumstance cause all the monks and canons that be in any wise faulty, to be tied up [hung], without further delay or ceremony, to the terrible example of others.[7]

That was the final nail in the coffin of Whalley Abbey. John Paslew, the abbot, was arrested and taken to Lancaster to stand trial, with a couple of the monks from his abbey. To the surprise and relief of the court, the seventy-year-old abbot pleaded guilty when he was accused on five counts of treason. In fact, he appeared to have taken very little part in the rebellion. The Earl of Sussex, who was in charge of the trial, wrote to Henry's secretary of state, Thomas Cromwell, that with so much local support, 'it would have been hard to find anything against him in these parts' if he had been determined to defend himself. But the abbot appeared to believe his time had come.[8] 'On Saturday 10th March, 1537, there died then Sir John Paslew, Bachelor of Theology, the twenty-fifth and last abbot of the House of Whalley'.[9]

Thirty years later, when John was born, nothing had erased these bitter memories from people's minds. Weeks after the abbot's execution, they had watched the treasures that once lit up their feast days disappear under armed guard to the south. There were processional crosses of silver and gold, silver chalices and cruets for the frankincense that had filled the abbey. The abbot's mitre, all of silver and gold, and set with rubies, turquoise and emeralds, and his gloves, embroidered with roses of gold and encrusted with pearls and sapphires, were bundled away. The beautiful ceremonial vestments, worn for High Mass, one of green velvet embroidered with an image of St Michael on the back, one of black velvet with a cluster of letters of gold delicately laid across, and others made of satin from Bruges, silk from Baghdad, and cloth of gold, all were lost.[10]

These glittering objects had expressed for the people the beauty and power of God in a world where daily life was harsh. Nothing, certainly not the death of their abbot, could dislodge their belief that as God directed life on earth, so men could intercede with God in Heaven, through the Mass and prayer. The Latin-speaking priests and monks were most closely connected to the Universal Holy Roman Church and were chosen to intercede on their behalf. This was what their tithes and gifts paid for. Did the king have the legal right to take this away, and with it the teaching, medical care and charity that the monks provided, leaving nothing in its place? The outrage was deeply felt.

The community was left to pick itself up as best it could. The king claimed the abbey and its lands, inviting the monks 'to go to other houses of their cote', other Cistercian monasteries, or renounce their vows, 'and so receive secular habit'.[11] Of course, 'other houses' of all the monastic orders in England were suffering the same fate as Whalley. The king knew that 'it cannot be holsom for our common wealth to permit them to wander abrode', but this, with few exceptions, is exactly what they did.

Some monks obtained appointments as parish priests, and in Whalley the people continued to worship in the way they had always done. Other monks returned to the local families they had sprung from, married and had children. They became farmers and were able to rent or later, buy, abbey lands. Most of this scholarly Cistercian order were skilled in reading and writing Latin and could teach the local children. Some, like John's relative, John Hodgson, were valuable in the community because they had special knowledge of medicine. The abbey buildings stayed empty for another eighteen years. The monks were reputed to be hanging on, clinging 'to the old hive like surviving bees'.[12] The secure society the abbey had dominated began to melt away, and in John's childhood the loss was palpable.

The poor roamed the countryside in ever-increasing numbers, many of them made homeless by the trend towards enclosing common farmland. Although the people of Whalley kept the old faith, they could not maintain the system for taking care of the poor and the sick after the monasteries had gone. Gradually the church registers became a record of wandering paupers, since the parish now bore the expense of burying them. Ten miles up the Ribble valley and over the pass into Yorkshire, the great Bolton Priory had suffered the same fate as Whalley. Its ruined skeleton overshadowed the landscape for miles around. In Kildwick, nearby, Brother Whixley, the parish priest, was one of its former canons. He continued to say Mass and dispense absolution at his church for another sixty years, in spite of the disaster that had overtaken his priory. His register recorded paupers buried together in one coffin, since they could not afford the charge of thirteen pennies for each adult burial, or five pence for a child. Every vagrant whipped in the market place was entered. 'Unlicensed beggars' were now outlawed, but however many they whipped, more kept coming. In one year alone there were forty-five whippings in Kildwick.[13]

Even those who grew rich at the abbey's expense felt the impossible burden of replacing its charity. The biggest purchaser of the Whalley lands that were gradually sold off was John Braddyll, a local man who had been given the job of surveying the king's newly acquired possessions there. He and his family became part of the new landed gentry that was emerging all over the country, nourished on the body that the king had taken from the Church. Yet when John Braddyll lay dying early in April 1578, forty years after the collapse of Whalley Abbey, he felt he was only a caretaker of land that by right belonged to the community. He asked his son and grandsons to take on the responsibility of care that came with the wealth he left them:

> for the most part of the lands that I do leave unto them was given and came to me by special gift and sufferance of Almighty God without any desert by me at all, by reason of buying and selling of landes that I bought of King Henry the Eighth [that had once belonged to Whalley Abbey], and thereby got gaines to the intent that I should distribute to the poor and be myself for a common wealth and all my succession likewise.[14]

The disappearance of the monasteries left a question for John's society that demanded solution from his earliest days until his last. How to replace the charity, medicine and education that had once been given by the monks? The monks were by no means perfect, but the system of which they were part had cared for the poor, and brought knowledge deep into the countryside. Such a network was hard to replace.

In the beginning, the king's seizure of monastic property had nothing to do with Roman Catholic doctrine. Roman Catholic beliefs were affirmed and reaffirmed by a royal act of 1539, except that the king, and not the Pope, would be the head of the Church. Breaches of this act were punishable by burning at the stake.[15] When Henry VIII's ten-year-old son, Edward, became king in 1547, however, the country came under the Protectorate of the Calvinist Duke of Somerset. John Calvin was in Geneva teaching that only those educated or born into Calvinism could be 'saved'. The mission of any true English Christian was to free his country from the self-serving intercession of Catholic priests who had held it in check for so long. The Mass was suddenly abolished in England. Latin was outlawed in church services.

Chantries, the chapels endowed to say prayers for the dead, which had survived this far, were closed on the grounds that they perpetuated the belief that Masses could reduce the time souls spent in purgatory which was a 'hellish papist perversion'.[16] Their assets were seized and used, in Whalley as in other places, to fund grammar schools to replace the teaching function that most of them had held.

The Calvinist assault unleashed on Catholicism by the Duke of Somerset was violent in the south of the country. In Lancashire no one took much notice. Rich and poor were unified in their belief that God's presence on earth was wrapped up in the mystery of the communion, the drifting smells of incense, the whisper of confession and the priests' Latin prayers, breathed over a memory of gold and silver plate. They were forced to close their abbeys and chantries but the old monks remained their priests. Nowhere was this fidelity to the old religion more pronounced than in Whalley. The rectory was granted to the Archbishop of Canterbury, but he was a long way away in the south. The biggest power in the region, now that the monasteries were gone, was Lord Stanley, the Earl of Derby, who was loyal to the Tudors and the king's ecclesiastical commissioner. Even he was devoutly Roman Catholic. Within a radius of ten miles of the old abbey there were at least a dozen families who grew rich in the new order of things, but whose primary loyalty was to the Catholic faith. Most attempted to carry on the style of the old abbot to some degree: giving alms, sheltering priests and arranging for Mass to be said in their private chapels for themselves and their household.

Soon the event they must all have been expecting occurred. The sickly young king died, and Henry VIII's eldest daughter, Mary, came to the throne: a devout Roman Catholic committed to restoring the Pope's domain in England with a vengeance. For five years from 1553 everyone expected that monastic property would be returned to displaced monks and abbots. Leading Protestants, among them the Cambridge bishops, Latimer and Ridley, and Archbishop Cranmer, the author of the English prayer book, were brutally burned at the stake. In fact so terrifying was Mary's zeal that the new owner of Whalley Abbey, Richard Assheton, actually destroyed it rather than be found living in a recognizably ecclesiastical building, Roman Catholic though he was.[17]

George Dobson, the vicar of Whalley who baptized the infant John, was appointed to the parish in Mary's time. When the country swung back to an Anglican Church in 1558, with the accession of Elizabeth I as queen, George Dobson stayed in the parish, continuing to conduct services and say Mass as though nothing had changed. He was the only priest for miles around who kept all the church records in Latin. In 1564 the new Bishop of Durham, Dr Pilkington, wrote to Archbishop Parker in Canterbury to complain about the pernicious influence of this unreformed Roman Catholic: 'Whalley hath as ill a vicar as the worst.' He hoped very much that the archbishop would do something about it, but, much to his disgust, twenty-five years later when the Anglican service was firmly established in the south of the country, Father Dobson was still the vicar of Whalley.[18]

Father Dobson remained in spite of the fact that in 1562, the so-called 'Thirty-Nine Articles' had been introduced, aimed at preventing 'papists' from exercising influential positions in society. From then on, schoolmasters and all other clerics, as well as midwives and surgeons, were supposed to swear recognition of the sovereign's supremacy over the Church, which, of course, Catholics could not do. But the system was slow to get started. Archbishop Young of York did not record his first 'examinations' in the Thirty-Nine Articles until 1605. So John Parkinson was educated, at home and at school, in the full doctrine of the Roman Catholic Church.

The young Duke of Norfolk's rebellion, mounted with the aim of dislodging the new Queen Elizabeth when John was a two-year-old, was a political failure. Having no appeal to the hearts and minds of the people he turned to for support, the duke was easily overcome and he was executed with his followers. Yet, curiously, this uprising had a decisive effect on John's community and his own future career, because it branded him and all his associates with the taint of suspicion. The penetrating gaze of another powerful Calvinist, Elizabeth's secretary of state, William Cecil, was suddenly focused on the Lancashire Catholics. Cecil denounced the Catholic Lancastrian nobility, calling them 'worse than Jews and infidels'. And he dramatically increased his scrutiny of the county.[19]

Cecil married his eldest son, Thomas, to a Yorkshire heiress and began to buy land across the region. Meanwhile he commissioned a Yorkshireman called Christopher Saxton to make the first accurate map of Lancashire, using the new mathematical surveying techniques. He had a copy made when he received it. On it he picked out in black ink and marked with a cross the house of every single Roman Catholic gentleman, including every one of John's landowning neighbours.[20]

As John grew older he would find the religion of his childhood increasingly dangerous. It became clear to him that the world order outlined by his parents and grandparents could not accord with the service to his king and country that his family also held dear. There were many reasons to think again about how a pious man could communicate with God on this earth. His study of plants and his devotion to gardens would become a delightful, and far safer, way of celebrating God's miraculous creation than the Catholic Masses he was now forced to attend in secret.

CHAPTER THREE

'IDLE TALES'

John's first schoolmaster was a priest to whom Father Dobson had given refuge after he was driven out of another parish. His crime, no doubt, was his unrepentant loyalty to the Catholic Church. In Whalley, such a man was safe, for the time being. 'There is one come thither that hath been deprived [had his parish taken away from him] or changed his name,' fumed the bishop to the archbishop,'and now teacheth school there, of evil to make them worse. If your Grace's officer's list they might amend many things.'[1]

In general, the priests dispensed their learning in small measures. The aim of education was to teach the true religion. Farmers' children were taught to read, and only 'when fitting or desired, to write'.[2] The 'ABC with the catechism', printed in London in 1555, when Mary was on the throne, would have been the first book John handled. This book was sent out 'to be learned of every chylde before he be broughte to be confirmed'.[3] By the time John was prepared for his first Communion in 1574, it had been superseded many times by Anglican versions, but the Whalley priests would have resisted the change.

Almost as a by-product of the Catholic teaching he imbibed from the priests, however, John acquired what would prove to be a golden ticket to his future. Perhaps he was particularly zealous as a young boy, or perhaps his mother's connection to the Church made the priests pay him special attention. It came about that he learned to read, write and speak Latin exceptionally well for someone of his social background. As religion was the fundamental purpose of education, so Latin was the key to Catholic religious instruction. It was the language that unified the faithful with the head of the Church in Rome. Meanwhile, although the reformed Protestant churches had discarded the Latin Mass, Latin was still the language of scholarship that bound Europe together. For so long, monks and scholars had been indistinguishable. John's skill in the language put him on a level with the sons of gentlemen who had been privately tutored before studying at Oxford or Cambridge. It opened up for him the cream of European knowledge contained in the Latin manuscripts and rare printed books that had, until recently, been confined to the libraries of monks.

Since the destruction of the abbey libraries, books belonged generally only to the nobility. John would have had access to very few as a child, yet even those few presented an astonishingly different view of the world he knew. Though books were rare, and nature plentiful, John's teachers believed that only books contained real understanding of God's creation on earth. Direct observation of nature, of the kind that was essential to John and his family, was considered to have no scholastic value. For over 300 years, the Church had seen nature through the lens of moral interpretations of Greek and Latin classics.

One of the classic texts, *De Civitate Dei* (The city of God), written by St Augustine, contained the visionary statement that the world around us is only a corrupted version of the heavenly reality of God. Over time, this was interpreted to mean that all creatures, all forms of life on earth, must contain a symbol of Christian truth. The study of nature for itself was less important than uncovering the inherent message it was hiding. The moral authority of this attitude, and the danger of diverging from it, when thought was so strictly controlled by the Church, had led to some surprising interpretations of Roman classics. Virgil's *Aeneid*, in which he tells of the hero's journey from Troy to Italy, was seen as an inspired prophecy of the coming of the Messiah. Even Ovid's lascivious poetry in *The Art of Love* came to be considered the product of a transport of spirituality, and an acceptable part of a monastic or convent library.

By 1530 the standard encyclopaedia of God's natural world in England was the work of a thirteenth-century Franciscan monk, Bartholomew. This book had been popular for 300 years, and its worldview was still unchallenged. It was based on the populist Roman writer Pliny, and a classic seventh-century text by Isidore, Archbishop of Seville, and included wonderful creatures amongst its list of the world's 'fauns and satyrs'. There were Cyclopes, with one eye, and some with 'closed mouths and in their breasts only one "hole"', and creatures with ears so large as to cover their whole bodies which came from 'Sithia'.

Even plant and vegetable life, on which food and medicine depended, was described in a similar mixture of fact elaborated through successive accounts into fable. Aristotle had observed: 'wild goats in Crete are said, when wounded by arrows, to go in search of dittany [wild oregano: *Oreganum dictamnus*] which is supposed to have the property of ejecting arrows from the body'. By the time this account reached Pliny, the goats had become deer. 'The value of dictamnus for extracting arrows was shown by stags when wounded by that weapon and ejecting it by grazing on that herb.' The medieval monk, Bartholomew, took up Pliny's tale uncritically: 'Bestes smitten with arrows eat thereof [dittany] and drive the yren out of the body', he declared.[4]

Another book of natural history, of the kind read to boys, was written by a thirteenth-century English Augustinian monk who was abbot at Cirencester. Alexander Neckham's book on the natures of things, *De Naturis Rerum*, drew on a range of Latin and Greek scholarship to spread knowledge of a wide world that must have seemed miraculous to those who had never been out of Lancashire. The world's fishes include mermaids and a hippopotamus. The catalogue of animals has a dragon that fights an elephant, a bird called the 'Grips' that digs for gold, and a story of a knight and his hawk that shows the medieval taste for finding a moral in everything:

> There was once a king in Great Britain who was very fond of his hawking and particularly admired the skill and speed of one of his Goshawks. One day this Goshawk was chased by an Eagle, and, to save himself, crept into a wattled enclosure made for sheep. The Eagle went peeking round this enclosure, trying to find a way in, and while doing so put his head through one of the wattles and got his neck stuck there; the Goshawk took advantage of this predicament and killed him. By this time the courtiers had come up and begun to extol the Goshawk for his victory over a much stronger enemy; but the King would have none of this, deeming that the Goshawk was guilty of treason and lèse-majesté for killing the king of his own tribe, and ordered the unfortunate victor to be hung![5]

John may have learned something from this tale about the insecurity of kings, but it was obvious that the writer had never looked, as he had done, to see how an eagle flies.

Only one book emerged from the new printing presses at the end of the fifteenth century with a different outlook on nature. This was a book intended to help impoverished convents and monasteries catch enough fish for fast days. Results were essential, so its text was closely observed from life. The *Boke of St Albans* was one of the first books written by a woman, reportedly assembled by Juliana Barnes, the Prioress of Sopwell Nunnery in that city. The section on fishing contained detailed descriptions of the freshwater fish that could be caught in England. The trout is a 'right fervent byter' and carp are scarce: 'there ben but few in Englonde'. It described methods of making effective bait and line, plaited from horsehair and dyed for different waters, and it was written with an understanding of the countryside: 'fisch not in no poor man's... water,' it admonished, nor 'breke noon man's hegges... ne open noo man's gates'.[6]

Still no book, anywhere, could be found to supply the one over-whelming need that had arisen since the monks' social network had disappeared. Practical medical knowledge was essential to replace the care they had once offered. John knew from experience that some understanding of medicinal herbs still existed in the country. His own mother apparently had the skills of a midwife. Yet in the vacuum caused by the lack of better teaching, he saw many people return to ancient superstitions. Ignorance, poverty, and the pressure to conform to an alien 'Anglican' doctrine only encouraged the growth of private beliefs and personal worship behind closed doors. Some of the old country lore people turned to was helpful, but other beliefs were undoubtedly harmful.

Even the monks' treatment had often been mystical, and those old remedies were current when John was young. An early fourteenth-century cure for toothache was retained to 1595 when the English medical treatise that contained it was reprinted at Augsburg. It was written by a monk called John of Gaddesden whose treatment was the Paternoster. First the words 'Rex Pay in Christo Filio' were to be 'written' on the jaw, then: 'when the Sunday gospel is read, let the man sign his tooth and his head with the sign of the cross and say a Paternoster and an ave for the souls of the father and mother of St Philip without stopping'.[7] This method was said to work because illness itself was a punishment for past sins, and recovery entirely in the hands of God and his saints.

Superstitions now blossomed in Lancashire beside the Catholic trad-itions. Most of these came from old magical rituals. The planets were said to influence particular plants so that the phases of the moon would change the efficacy of a herb. Iron vessels were believed to leach away the healing 'vertues' of plants, destroying their power. There were people who fashioned mandrake roots into voodoo dolls. Women who eked out a living alone might gain more power in the community from this than from gathering herbs from the hillside, and they were now unchecked by the Church. Mandrake boiled in a cauldron with henbane and animal fats induced hallucinations. This effect gave its users magical powers and they warned non-magical people they would suffer pain and punishment if they dared to pick a mandrake root from the earth.

John learned quickly to be wary of superstition. When he was growing up, his community was still at peace with itself, comprehensively Catholic, and unified in its conservative ways. But it was beginning to splinter under pressure from the south. Prominent Catholics were already being punished for their faith with hefty fines and spells in Lancaster prison. As the old establishment grew weaker, a forest of accusations broke out that threatened John's childhood home. Women who used herbs, like John's mother, were especially vulnerable to charges of witchcraft. By the time he reached middle age, John had no doubt that myth and superstitions brought nothing but danger. He had nailed his colours to the mast of truth. Only scientific observation could save people from such nonsense as surrounded the mandrake root:

> many idle tales have been set down in writing, and delivered also by report, of much danger to happen to such as should dig them up or break them; ... I [have not] seen any form of man like or woman like parts in the roots of any... but many cunning counterfeit roots have been shaped to such forms, and publicly exposed to the view of all that would see them, and have been tolerated by the Chief magistrates..., notwithstanding that they have been informed that such practices were mere deceit and insufferable.[8]

By the time John was ten years old, Elizabeth's Calvinist councillors had found an effective means to break up the religious solidarity of the north. In 1577, a key instrument of change arrived in the region in the shape of a seventeen-year-old bride. The Catholic Earl of Cumberland, Henry Clifford, who owned huge tracts of land across West Yorkshire, Westmoreland and Cumberland, almost encircling Lancashire, had seen the writing on the wall. He remained a Catholic himself, but arranged for his son and heir, George Clifford, to be brought up in one of the most staunchly Calvinistic households of Elizabethan England. Francis Russell, the second Earl of Bedford, whose ward George became, had spent the reign of the Catholic Queen Mary in exile in Geneva, studying with John Calvin. Nevertheless he arranged for one of his daughters, Margaret Russell, to become George Clifford's wife, agreeing with the Earl of Cumberland that this was the best way of cementing the Clifford family's position in the north with political power in the south.

Lady Margaret Russell, Countess of Cumberland. The portrait is in the collection at Skipton Castle in Yorkshire, still a complete medieval fortress, where she lived as a young bride.

For Margaret, the product of this agreement was a joyless existence. She came to live in the castle at Skipton, which guarded the pass between the high moors leading from Lancashire into Yorkshire, less than twenty miles upriver from John's home. The huge semi-fortress of the Cliffords' ancestral seat was unlike any house she had known. The thick grey stone walls of Skipton Castle were softened inside only by the brightly coloured tapestry arrases that hung on them. Sweet-smelling rushes on the floor and thick woollen undergarments were a thin defence against the bitter cold of the damp winter air. The open fires sucked in the draughts. The wild dales and moors, the forbidding forests, and the people's accent and speech were strange to her. The arrases on the walls celebrated her husband's ancient family colours in battle. Romantic feats of the past meant nothing to this girl, brought up to play her part in a new future. In the south it had long been out of fashion to live in castles. When her husband went back to London to attend at court soon after they arrived in Yorkshire, she was left alone with his mother, a Catholic Lancastrian lady who took pride in the fact that she had never been south. Margaret lamented that she had only 'one servant, rather for trust than wit, about me..., in a country contrary to my religion, his mother and friends all separate in that opinion, himself not settled but carried away with young men's opinion'.[9]

Miserable though she was in the northern atmosphere of rosaries and incense, and at being regarded, herself, as a heretic, Margaret had a core of steel. She profoundly believed it was her duty to help herself. Her father was not only a Calvinist but also a self-made man. She and her three sisters had been tutored carefully, by which her father meant ample instruction in religion and philosophy.[10] The greatest influence on Margaret, her daughter wrote later, was the teaching of Seneca, the stoic philosopher who preached indifference to pain and pleasure. She was 'truly religious, devout and conscientious' from childhood, growing up accustomed to reading the scriptures and other good books and spending her days 'in heavenly meditations, and in prayers, fastings, and deeds of charity'.[11] Faced with this environment that she disliked so much, Margaret set about changing it.

She brought friends to teach her and preach her Gospel in the north. A young man called Robert Moore, who had studied Puritan doctrines at Cambridge, came to Skipton Castle at Lady Margaret's special request. He stayed as rector at Guiseley for the rest of his life, and over sixty years did a great deal to convert the region to Protestantism. From this small beginning, the new religion and the old began to live side by side.

Meanwhile, despite herself, Margaret's surroundings gradually effected a change in her. For distraction from her loneliness she turned to the books she loved, and in this respect she stumbled upon unexpected treasure in the castle. Her new home had a library, built up and cared for by her husband's father, with some manuscripts that had been acquired by his grandfather. These Cliffords had devoted much of their time to private study and experiment, which they had shared, so it was said, with the monks of Bolton Priory nearby. A library was not, in itself, a novelty to Margaret, but the manuscripts she found here were quite unlike the books in her father's house.

She could not read the Latin in which they were written, since her father had believed, in common with many Puritan Englishmen, that learning any foreign language would lay his daughters open to corruption. Yet she could see from the titles and the diagrams that these dusty old papers related to the ancient art of alchemy. Amongst many other old papers, she found:

An old book of Chemistry and Alchimy, no title, unbound
The practise of the Great work etc. by the Monk of Berye
Another book of Alchimy entituled a Dialogue between Nature and a
Disciple of Philosophie, a stitched folio... Part of a very old, imperfect
Manuscript of Alchimy[12]

The goal of alchemy was to synthesize precious metals from base ones, to create something entirely new. Its chemical processes combined with astrology and the application of magical symbols to achieve what no one had so far managed. Converting lead or mercury to gold was such a great prize that princes and sovereigns fought jealously for information that could not be allowed to fall into the hands of the ignorant masses, and its methods were shrouded in tempting mystery. As if the goal of making gold was not enough, alchemists also promised to be able to deliver the elixir of life, answering all the dreams of an age in one miraculous transformation. Elizabethan England was unable to tear itself away from the appeal of this possibility. Inspired by greed and fear, even the country's intellectuals steered an uncomfortable course between the danger of witchcraft and the potential of this magic, most people believing in both. As a Calvinist, Margaret regarded the miracle of transubstantiation during Mass, in which the communion wine and bread were believed to become literally the blood and body of Christ, as a wicked papist superstition. Yet she was quite prepared to entertain the possibility that lead could be turned into gold. Margaret soon commissioned translations of the documents so that she could begin her own experiments, and she became so addicted to the practical processes of heating the base metals, cooling them and distilling the liquids in exactly the right way, that she sought out more books on the art to add to the library at Skipton.

Margaret already knew something of alchemy. She was a close friend of the most prominent practitioner in the country, Dr John Dee, to whose daughter she was godmother. Dr Dee was a scholar of Trinity College, Cambridge, and mathematics, astronomy and alchemy were his areas of special learning. Once, in 1572, he was summoned to Windsor Castle, and spent three days explaining the appearance of a new star to Queen Elizabeth 'alarmed by a comet'. He believed that the study of mathematics, just becoming fashionable in England now that Arabic numerals had replaced the unwieldy Roman ones, was 'next to theologie, most divine, most profound, most subtle, most commodious and most necessarie'. The beauty of numbers sent him into such transports of delight that he echoed Plato by saying 'it lifts the heart above the heavens by invisible lines'.[13] One of the pupils he had inspired with his love of the subject was Margaret's husband, George, whom he tutored at Trinity between 1571 and 1576. Through George, John Dee met Margaret and became a regular visitor at their house.

Despite his devotion to mathematics, alchemy was the study for which Dr Dee was famous. When he went to Prague as Elizabeth's ambassador in 1584, he reported quite a lot of success. People said that his son, Arthur, 'used to play at Quoits with the plates of gold made by Projection in the Garrett of Dr Dee's Lodgings in Prague and... had more than once seen the Philosopher's Stone'.[14] Such reports led William Cecil to write to him and his laboratory partner in 1591, begging them to return to London. He asked them to share their secret of making gold, 'not to keep God's gift from your natural country, but rather help make Her Majesty a glorious and victorious power against the malice of hers and God's enemies'. Strangely, none of this gold was ever seen outside Prague, and when Dr Dee did return to London, he was forced to practise medicine to keep his family from starving.[15]

In the late 1570s Margaret had high hopes for the 'old instruments', a collection of stoves, glass stills and mortars that she discovered in her father-in-law's workshop in Barden Tower. This isolated old watchtower on the property, close to the remains of Bolton Priory, contained tools that were rarely found outside an apothecary's shop. She moved the equipment to the castle and began to experiment in her own stillroom, and eventually this activity led to some practical results. Margaret soon found a more immediate need for herself, her family and her neighbours in Yorkshire than this elusive gold. She was often ill in her first year at Skipton, and there was little help on hand to restore her to health. Household physicians and apothecaries' supplies were almost non-existent in the north, and she would never have gone, as other people did, to a Catholic priest for help. Through necessity, her alchemy began to metamorphose into 'chymistry': distilling and synthesizing compounds from plants for a practical purpose. She learned 'some knowledge of most kinds of minerals, herbs, flowers and plants'. In time, 'She found excellent medicines which did much good to many people.'[16]

Sadly, Margaret's medicines failed her when she needed them most. For all her skill in the stillroom, she could not prevent the deaths of her sons, who both died in Skipton before they were seven.

The record of survival in John Parkinson's family was much more robust. Yet the desire to discover effective medicines was the one thing this Catholic farmer's boy from Whalley had in common with the young aristocrat at Skipton. Just as she was a catalyst for change in the north, bringing with her a Calvinist outlook that she used her wealth and position to promote, so his practical outlook would prove a catalyst for change in the south.

When John was fourteen, his sister Jean died, aged two, the only one of this large family to die in childhood. There was also an outbreak of plague in the surrounding area. These events may have shaped his ambition to learn more about the healing power of plants than his family could teach him, and the only route open to him was to become an apprentice apothecary. The apothecaries were a new profession in England, scarcely existing outside a handful of specialists in the royal household before the dissolution of the monasteries. There had been no need for them, so long as the monks' skills were available. When Elizabeth came to the throne in 1558, there were no more than about fifteen skilled apothecaries in the whole country, and nearly all of these were members of the Company of Grocers in London.[17]

It was already late for John to become an apprentice, and the journey to London was expensive. He would be the only one of his family to go south, and they must have struggled to find the money to send him there. But the Bleasdale Parkinson cousins were connected to a wealthy and influential Lancashire clan. Their mother had been a Houghton from Pendleton. Some branches of this family were well established in London. Peter Houghton was a successful grocer apothecary and citizen. Roger Houghton, from Winwick in south Lancashire, was a steward for none other than the queen's secretary of state, William Cecil. Connections such as these probably helped this clever young boy to move on from the 'rude north' of his birth.[18]

John set out to study the metamorphosis of plants into medicine with a distinctly different approach from that of most scholars and aristocrats of his day. He had no inclination to follow their example and mix his facts with philosophy. Nothing dimmed his expectation that his results would come through direct observation of nature in action, since that was the way his family had always learned. As a child of farming folk, his world-view was quite unclouded by such scholarly mysteries as the magic of alchemy. He was never diverted by the notion that adding magic to his experiments would bring him gold. On the contrary, he had seen in his own community the dangerous power that myth and superstition and blind belief could exert over uneducated people. From the very beginning, he was inclined to believe that the evidence of his naked eye would bring him the knowledge he needed. He cannot have known it then, but his attitude was exactly the one that was beginning to overturn the world of scholarship.

So it was a curious irony that the trade he would learn in London did indeed lead him to a kind of alchemy. Experimenting with the plants that so fascinated him, he began to fuse varieties and discover how to create something entirely new, in a mysterious, almost magical, process that he never tired of. Ultimately it was this natural alchemy that first made him famous.

CHAPTER FOUR

'THE NEW FOUND WORLD'

The story of Dick Whittington, a poor farmer's son who left his family in the country and set out for London in search of success, could have been written for John Parkinson. There were hundreds like him: boys whom the family fields could not support, who could not aspire to university and service in a noble household like the sons of gentlemen, whose only option was to learn a trade and succeed by their wits. When John left the north there was little luxury in the Parkinson family. Every surviving will lists only fields, animals, husbandry tools and cash, until Janet, the wife of Robert Parkinson of Chipping, died in 1592, leaving her servant 'three shillings and fourpence', and her sister Margaret her 'best gown and petticoat'.[1]

Most travellers from Whalley began their journey south by water, carried downriver to Preston. Once in the market town near the mouth of the Ribble, the journey to London took nine or ten days. Travelling by easy stages of twenty miles or so each day, sometimes on horseback, sometimes on foot, people still journeyed in groups, for safety and companionship, just as they had in Chaucer's day. The potential threats were vagrant robbers and, occasionally, wild boar, but the biggest hazard was the ground under their feet. In south Lancashire the way led through boggy marshes or 'mosses' which had a tendency to expand and burst in foul weather. They had a reputation for swallowing up unwary strangers. In the eighteenth century the marshes were drained, and became hugely fertile peat moss fields, but at the end of the sixteenth century they were a haven for fugitives, and the few residents were said by William Camden, the contemporary historian, to make use of a strange fuel they found half buried in the marshes, blackened trees that burned 'as bright and clear as a torch, which is perhaps caused by the bituminous earth they have laid in'.[2]

There were still no maps generally available. Christopher Saxton's survey of the country that he had begun in 1577 was in the palace rooms of William Cecil, Lord Burghley. Burghley's copy of the Lancashire map,

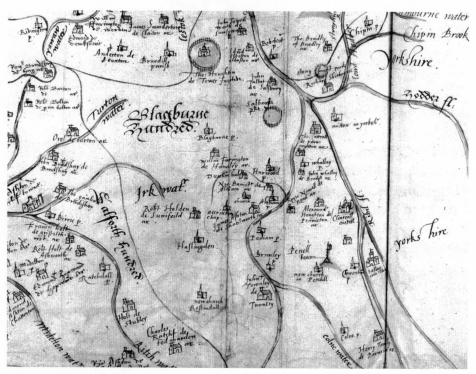

A section of Lord Burghley's personal sketch map of Lancashire, showing John's birthplace of Whalley north of the tower at 'Pendell' in the angle between the rivers Ribble and Colne, just over the border from Yorkshire. Some neighbours' land is marked with a cross, to indicate suspicion of their Catholic loyalties. Some estates, like Thomas Houghton's, are marked 'fugitive'.

now busy with the names of Catholics who had fled or been arrested, showed how even his own steward's family was splintered by religious differences: 'Thomas Houghton de Tower... fugitive'. 'Thomas Houghton de Lea... fugitive... now arr. [arrested]'; 'John Talbot de Salsbury, arr'. (Salesbury Hall was just south of Whalley along the Ribble)

The arrest of prominent Catholics was widely known, but the map on which their names were marked was a state secret. It would be another fifty years before maps were available to the public. But Saxton's map shows the route people took from this remote part of the queen's realm to her capital. The usual stages of John's journey are written in longhand on the front of Cecil's copy: 'From Preston to Wigan: 14 miles, From Wigan to Warrington 20 miles'.[3]

Carts and carriages were impossible on roads like these. Changing horses and sleeping at staging inns on the way, avoiding places where the floor was strewn with scented rushes as they were known to attract fleas, the traveller came after two nights to the edge of Lancashire. With plenty of time to study the surrounding countryside, John could have observed at close quarters a world startlingly different from the one he was used to.

When John travelled in 1584, the forests of southern Lancashire and Cheshire had grown thin, compared to the protected royal hunting grounds he knew around Bowland and Bleasdale. The country's oaks, birch and ash were in such demand for building, for ships and for fuel that great swathes of forest had disappeared in a generation. In 1629 a single Durham woodsman was said to have felled more than 30,000 oaks in his lifetime. Timber had become more valuable than land.[4]

John would have been familiar with the way new owners of monastic property used the wealth it generated to build grander homes. In Lancashire, many gentlemen were still building houses in oak and plaster, keeping to the defensive semi-military style of their fathers and grandfathers.[5] Further to the south, on the other hand, the mansions were planned with another view entirely.

The new fashion was for large open houses in the Italian style, with the most important rooms, on the first floor, looking out over the surrounding land through imposing windows. The simple symmetry of these houses with their decorative turrets at each end would soon dominate the landscape, in the style of the earliest example in the country, the queen's palace at Hampton Court. When John travelled, most of these houses were still in the planning stage. The Earl of Shrewsbury's wife, Bess of Hardwick, waited until she became a rich widow in 1590 before spending her inheritance on Hardwick Hall, in Derbyshire, a little way to the east of John's road to Coventry. When it was finished this house prompted an anonymous wit to quip 'Hardwick Hall – more glass than wall', indicating the need for another innovation that would shape John's career: a grand, decorative garden to look down upon.

The steady transformation of the old traditions was already evident on the road. The destruction of church buildings had released a large amount of cut stone, and the high price of wood increased the attractions of stone and brick as building materials. Towards the end of the century, William Harrison, the queen's Dean of Windsor, observed:

The ancient manors and houses of our gentlemen are yet... of strong timber, in framing whereof our carpenters have been and are worthily preferred before those of other nations. Howbeit, such as be lately builded are commonly either of brick or hard stone or both, their rooms large and comely. Those of the nobility are likewise wrought with brick and hard stone... but so magnificent and stately as the basest house of a baron doth often match in our days with some honors of princes in old time.[6]

Here and there, John saw gardens that showed how many women in country districts were beginning, like Margaret Clifford, to keep a garden of medicinal plants 'to serve for the especial uses of a family'. They were taking over the monastic tradition of an infirmary herb garden, just as their husbands had taken over the monks' land. The plants grew like weeds in plots around their houses: angelica, rue, snapdragons, feverfew, chamomile, *Cardus benedictus* (the Blessed Thistle), valerian, smallage (a kind of parsley) and tobacco. No special care was needed to cultivate these, but the women had learned to use them

> to help to cure such small diseases as are often within the compass of the Gentlewomen's skills, who, to help their own family, and their poor neighbours that are far remote from Physicians and Chirurgions [surgeons], take much pains both to do good unto them and to plant those herbs that are conducing to their desires.[7]

In the town of Shrewsbury, where travellers spent the night on their way to the old episcopal capital of Lichfield, there was a draper called Richard Gardiner who sold, amongst the linen and thread in his shops, vegetable seeds for kitchen gardens. This draper was also an enthusiastic grower, who became known for feeding the poor with his produce.

> The poore which late were like to pine,
> and could not buy them bread;
> In greatest time of penury
> Were by his labours fed.[8]

Gardiner tried to spread his love of vegetables, so often derided, and he was especially keen on carrots. He believed they could be the key to feeding the poor and saving whole communities if ever they came under siege:

Carrets are good to be eaten with salt fish [he wrote in the pamphlet he published in 1597], Therefore sowe Carrets in your Garden and humbly praise God for them, as for singular and great blessing.... Admit if it should please God that any city or towne should be besieged with the Enemy, what better provision for the greatest number of people can bee, than every garden to be sufficiently planted with Carrets?[9]

A besieging enemy in Shrewsbury seemed a remote possibility in the early 1580s. England was at peace. The country labourer's greatest battle was with the relentless drive to complete land enclosure, as those who owned farmland took steps to drive up its profitability. Cattle and wood fetched far higher prices than corn, and needed less labour. The rich men's houses were hard to see from the road, encircled as they were by their protective estates. In contrast, groups of displaced people and the remains of abandoned settlements were visible everywhere. They were the evidence that the new economics of the land were driving rich and poor apart.

Everywhere arable land, which needed intensive labour, was being replaced by enclosed pasture, 'which could be easily rid by a few herds-men', as Francis Bacon put it in his seventeenth-century biography of Henry VII. That king had introduced a law intended to prevent farms with over twenty acres from being swallowed up by large landowners. The law had helped secure the existence of John's own family. He came from exactly the type of self-reliant yeoman stock that Francis Bacon considered the unique strength of his country, a result of this law ruling that farms big enough to support 'middle-people, of a condition between gentlemen and cottagers or peasants' should be retained.[10]

Yet, as John journeyed through 'the deep country where Warwickshire and Northamptonshire meet',[11] it was clear that this law was now widely flouted. They passed close to the estate of a certain John Spencer, who bought his land in 1506. Spencer had been accused of ignoring the enclosure law in 1517, evicting the tenants of twelve farms and three cottages to make a new estate. He defended himself on the grounds that these tenants had been

so poor and lived so poorly... they had no books to sing services on in the church. And where they never had but one priest, I have had and intend to have two or three.... And where there is no wood or timber growing with twelve or fourteen miles of the same lordship, the said John Spencer hath there set trees and sown acorns for timber and wood, and double ditched and set with all manner of wood both in the hedgerows and also betwixt hedges.[12]

Although Spencer lost his argument with the Royal Commission, and was ordered to restore the lands, he managed to continue driving his fat cattle to wealthy buyers in London, whose markets were near enough to make him rich. Eventually his family built a grand manor at Althorp in Northamptonshire, and from there sprang the Dukes of Marlborough, as well as their most famous descendant in the twentieth century, Diana, Princess of Wales.

From this point in John's journey, he would have been able almost to smell the wealth generated by the city of London. South of Daventry, the ancient Roman road, Watling Street, pointed straight as the crow flies to his destination. From Stony Stratford to Dunstable, farmers and traders travelled to London along fourteen miles of paved road. As they approached the city, the road grew busier: drovers herding cattle and merchants with carts; poor people heading to London to find work; groups of heralds in the bright colours of their master's household livery; noblewomen wearing silk and lace, fur and velvet, who sometimes rode on horseback, sometimes in litters borne on the shoulders of liveried pages. 'The English are lovers of show', wrote a German lawyer who came to England at this time. He was struck by their 'liking to be followed wherever they go by whole troops of servants, who wear their master's arms in silver fastened to their left arms'.[13]

From Barnet in the county of Middlesex it was only ten miles down-hill to 'the ancient and famous city of London',[14] which the travellers must have watched approaching with the awe and fascination that inspires people who see Manhattan rising out of the Atlantic. The densely packed city, glittering with the spires and pinnacles of churches built so close together, would dazzle a country boy whose parish church had been the only one for miles around. A map of London attributed to Ralph Agas in the mid-sixteenth century described this city of which Englishmen were inordinately proud:

at this present it flourisheth, that it containeth in length from East to West about 3 English miles, from the north to south about 2 English miles. It is also so plentifully peopled that it is divided into a hundred and twenty two parishes (within the Liberties) besides sixteen parishes that are in the suburbs. It is planted on very good soil: for on one side it is compassed with corn and pasture grounds, and on the other it is enclosed with the river of Thames, which not only aboundeth in all kinds of fresh-water fish, but also is so navigable, that it as well bringeth abundance of commodities from all parts of the world, as also conveyeth forth such commodities as the plentifulness of our country doth yield us... God prosper it at his pleasure. Amen.[15]

The road into London from St Albans ran via the wooded hills of Highgate, from where one could see the whole city spread out below, the glint of the Thames curving round it, and the Kent countryside beyond. On the river there was a constant flow of masted ships heading to and from the sea, which grew ever more visible and enticing to a boy whose experience so far had been almost entirely inland.

The press of traffic now was intense, although the road was broad. In London there were opportunities for every man. There was work for vagrants: rowing barges or cleaning ditches. There were markets for farmers; wares for merchants; sponsorship for scholars and potential promotion or office at court for the nobility. At Islington the road split, and the drovers taking cattle to market would take the road west, known as St John's Street, heading downhill towards Smithfield market. Travellers with a mission in the city, like John, carried on towards Aldersgate, one of the four original gates in the city's walls.

They passed by Charterhouse to the west, a huge burial plot with a church in the middle. Someone might have pointed out that this had been the London home of the old Duke of Norfolk, the third, who, despite his Catholicism, had not scrupled to build 'large and sumptuous buildings' there, 'both for lodging and pleasure'.[16] From horseback, it was possible to glimpse over the wall and see what was left of land that had been richly cultivated by the white-robed Carthusians until it was taken from them in 1537.

The Carthusians were a silent order, who lived in detached cottages with their own gardens where they grew the vegetables they lived on and transcribed manuscripts. When these monks were driven out, their treasure consisted of plants and trees, which the king and his men nevertheless seized as riches. As yet few noblemen had the evergreen beauty of a cypress, a bay, or a yew to show in their own gardens. Three loads of bay trees, ninety-one fruit trees, rosemary and other shrubs and hay were taken to the king's garden at Chelsea. Two gardeners were sent to gather 'cypers, bays and yews' for his palace at

Hampton Court. The secretary of state, Thomas Cromwell, sent his gardeners to take 'all such bay trees and grafts' as they could, as well as a bundle of rose trees and four loads of timber. The Lord Privy Seal even took '3 baskets of herbs'.[17] Such gardening skills as these monks possessed were rare. Only roses, vines and rosemary were left behind, flourishing still in 1584, when John passed this 'fayre Garden' on his way into the city.[18]

From here to Aldersgate, houses fronted the road and began to shut out the countryside. The smells became gradually more oppressive. Alongside the city walls there were dyers' frames where their coloured cloth was hung to dry. The mordant used to fix the new bright red dyestuff that Elizabethan Londoners loved above all was urine, and the stench from the dyers' vats was almost as bitter as the smells from the pigsties to the side of the road here and there.

The travellers came to the town ditch, where water from the river Thames ran around the city walls. The ditch was cleaned periodically by a scratch force of labourers, hired by the city tradesmen, but since this had not been done for fifteen years, and it received daily all the waste dyestuffs, pigswill, human waste and rubbish the city could produce, there were, at this point, few nastier stretches of water in the country. It had been vaulted over in places to build houses and, ironically, to create gardens, so that its original defensive purpose was no longer recognizable. Within ten years this ditch was no more than 'a verie narrow and... filthie channel, or altogether stopped up for Gardens planted and houses builded thereon, even to the verie wall, and in many places upon both ditch and wall, houses to be builded'.[19]

Once they were through the city wall, even the sky seemed to retreat. The road was suddenly narrower, and the throng of horses, people, carts and little passages was confusing. Never before would a boy from the provinces have seen houses pressed so close. The timber-framed buildings were four storeys high in some places, each storey projecting slightly above the floor below, so that they seemed almost to shut out the air above.[20]

John had no time then to consider the loss of the countryside. He needed to find an apprenticeship, and the sooner he did so the less he would have to pay for expensive city lodgings. His experience was very like that of John Sadler, a friend of Shakespeare's who had come to London a year or two before from Stratford-on-Avon. Sadler set out from Stratford on horseback. Once he arrived in the city he sold his horse at the Friday market at Smithfield, and applied to various grocers to be taken on as an apprentice, offering the proceeds from the sale of his horse as a fee. This was ten pounds, the minimum a master would expect to take him on and feed, clothe, teach and lodge him for the length of his term.[21]

By 9 November 1584, John had struck a deal with Francis Slater, a twenty-four-year-old grocer with a shop near St Mary Colechurch, one of the tiny parishes into which the city was divided. Francis had become a freeman himself only three years before, and John was his first apprentice. The boy was older than most, but Francis could consider himself lucky to have one whose exceptional skill with Latin would prove so useful in the shop, deciphering the physicians' scrips and the notes that came in with imported bundles of herbs. For the next eight years, John would live and eat with Francis and his family, and work in the shop.

On this particular day, John would have followed slightly behind his master on their way to attend his first important ritual at the Grocers' Hall. They left the wide city thoroughfare called Poultry and darted into a narrow alley that was crowded with men and boys bound for the same destination. Emerging from the dark overhang into a courtyard, John came face to face with striking evidence of the wealth of the guild he was about to join. One of the finest medieval halls in the city formed the centre of the Grocers' Company headquarters, its stone walls lovingly carved with decorations befitting the place of worship it had once been.[22]

John was about to become a member of one of the twelve richest guilds in the City of London. Its members had had the exclusive right to their trade in the city and seven miles around for over 200 years. They had been given their first royal charter on 9 May 1345, when 'a fraternity was founded of Companions Pepperers of Sopers Lane'.[23] Those Pepperers had developed an impressive self-governing society which administered its own rules for the control of trade, settled disputes between members, and diverted a considerable share of funds to pensions and charity. They raised money from their members by annual subscription, but as a 'brotherhood' that encouraged a lifetime of loyalty, a large part of their property came from bequests. By 1584 the Grocers had become a very rich company indeed.

The London trade institutions, whose internal democracy was founded on Christian principles of cooperation and mutual support, mimicked the structure of the monastic life that was gone. Their discipline and cooperation were the foundation of the capital's strength and their wealth underpinned the wealth of the nation. Kings and queens looked enviously at their treasure chests.

On this November morning, the courtyard in front of the Grocers' Hall would have been thick with the azure blue gowns of freemen Grocers greeting each other as they headed for one of the regular quarter-day meetings. The crowd milled into 'the Great Chamber', where the rich banners on the walls dazzled young apprentices entering for the first time.

'A great new banner of red and blue farcenett of the Queen's arms, gilt'; two blue banners carrying the arms of masters of the Grocers' Company who had also been Lord Mayors of the city; a 'great new banner in crimson taffeta with the Grocers' arms', and a banner in 'crimson and white taffeta with the City arms', were proudly listed in the Grocers' inventory. On the many ceremonial occasions when the Grocers loved to show off their wealth, the banners were paraded in the streets, with 'great new streamers' bearing the Grocers' arms, one 'wrought with silver and garnished with charnelled griffins', another with the arms of the city 'wrought with charnelled gold and flowers'.[24] There was more glitter in this hall than in many noblemen's houses, and John had seen nothing like it.

Beneath such splendour on the walls, the semi-religious atmosphere of these quarter-day meetings had a powerful effect. It was impressed on the Grocers that they bore a joint burden of loyalty to their company and responsibility to their brethren. These meetings resembled the church services they were also obliged to go to, not least because the freemen were often reluctant to leave their other business and attend.[25]

Every year they elected one of their members as master to manage the business of their 'court', together with the second and third warden. These three had a heavy burden of work, attending every Tuesday, to sort out the finances of the company, applications for charity, disputes between members or between masters and apprentices, appointments, rentals of the company's property, as well as the busy calendar of festive and ceremonial events that peppered the year. They were helped by a couple of dozen 'assistants', experienced grocers who might aspire to become wardens, and who were invited to pay a fee and form part of this 'livery'. It was a great honour to be chosen, but costly to join; at the same time, there was a stiff financial penalty for refusing.

The current master, Hugh Morgan, had in fact attempted to decline the honour. On 19 July 1584, after the aldermen, wardens and assistants had returned from evening prayer, which they had attended 'in decent and comlye order', a letter was read from him. He explained that since his appointment as the Queen's Apothecary he was 'in daily attendance at the court upon her Majesty's service, and so cannot be here to keep the courts and follow the affairs of the Company'. His letter was considered and the Grocers decided to ignore it and appoint him anyway, 'he being known a very sufficient man to take [this] place, it fell out by scrutiny that he was chosen to be the Master Warden of the Company for this year next ensuing'. A reply was written, 'praying him to take the place upon him and bear the charge of the same, and be here when he may so as Her Majesty be not hindered in any wise'.[26] So the 'Father of the Company' when John Parkinson advanced to take his oath this quarter-day was, coincidentally, the one person in the Company of Grocers he would come to emulate. Hugh Morgan was not only the Queen's Apothecary, he was known to the queen as her 'Philobotanicus', lover of plants.

The assembled livery of the company presented a powerful impression of authority. They faced the freemen with their faces half hidden under the white damask hoods they wore over their blue gowns. Only the lambskin facings peeping from their chests proclaimed their superior positions. Hugh Morgan wore a gown faced with marten fur, white spotted with black. Beneath their gowns, the three senior wardens showed glimpses of 'russet satten in their doublets', whereas ordinary grocers were expected to wear 'only black and white, their doublets to be of black satin'.[27]

When John's turn came to step forward and be presented to this group, he might have reflected that he could one day join their ranks, even though such an advance on his social status was almost inconceivable. He was about to take an oath that would surely lead to his becoming a free merchant of the City of London. This alone would give him privileges in the law of the land that none of his family had ever enjoyed. He had indeed travelled a long way from Lancashire. With this prize in prospect, he swore to accept its price: complete obedience to the impressive hierarchy ranged in front of him.

I, John Parkinson, swear to be good and true to our sovereign Lady, Queen Elizabeth, and to her heirs, and well and truly to serve my master for the term of my apprenticeship, and in all lawful and honest causes to be obedient to the Wardens and all them that be of the clothing [livery], and to have the same in due reverence. The lawful secrets of the said fellowship I shall keep, and give none information nor instruction thereof to no person but of the said fellowship. In all these things I shall well and truly behave and surely keep this said oath by my power. So help me God, and His saints, and by that Book.[28]

With the warning singing in his ears that 'if it fortune that you depart from your master' he could not serve anyone else without the permission of the wardens, John then handed over two shillings and two pennies. The clerk entered his name in the book of accounts: 'John Parkinson apprenticed with Francis Sclater for viii years from Christmas next, appointed the 9th day of November'.[29]

Once the ceremonies were over, the quarter-day cakes and casks of beer were brought into the hall. Each bite of the soft rich cake, made with finely milled flour, was a reminder of the privileged future John was now bound for. The next eight years were in the hands of his master, it was true, but as John washed the cake down with ale, he could be forgiven for believing he had secured a comfortable home in the Company of Grocers.

CHAPTER FIVE

WEAPONS FOR
THE NEW AGE

Copperplate map made shortly before 1561, when St Paul's spire was destroyed by lightning, showing St Paul's Cathedral and the area around Ludgate where John Parkinson would have his shop.

John's apprenticeship began in a way he never anticipated. The spring came to London. The fields and woods round about became swathed in the wild daffodils for which they were famous. Yet, in April, John found himself tramping up and down the common outside the city at Mile End, being forced into line by the shouts and commands of a certain Captain Tibbett.

For just over three weeks, on Mondays, Tuesdays and Wednesdays, the captain's band of apprentices marched up and down, training to use the new weapons the Grocers had bought for their armoury. They had thrown out the old swords and daggers that were 'considered not serviceable' and bought two dozen new ones.[1] The boys were learning to use these along with the pikes, black bills and halberds already in the company armoury. So John found himself thrusting and parrying in the muddy ground, preparing to protect his new company from an invading army.

John had none of the combative genes of his Parkinson relatives at Fairsnape. Later events in his life would show how he hated confrontation. One of the privileges of becoming a citizen of the City of London was that he would be exempt from being pressed into military service. So he was entitled to feel indignant that he should find himself undergoing military training at the very start of learning his new trade in London.

Hugh Morgan's premonition that being master warden would take more time than he could afford was correct. His year as master turned out to be a particularly demanding one. The national crisis began in the summer of 1584, when an exceptionally nasty plot to kill the queen by members of her own household was revealed. The ringleader was a rich young Derbyshire Catholic called Antony Babington, who was admitted at court, where the queen refused to discriminate against Catholics. In the circumstances, this was a risky policy, as the Pope had not only excommunicated her but also announced that year the 'Enterprise of England', with the aim of removing her and restoring Catholicism to her country. This was yet another plot with Elizabeth's most troublesome prisoner at its heart, her cousin Mary, the Catholic Queen of Scots.

Elizabeth believed she could outwit Mary and her schemes. She said she knew:

> all that goes on in my kingdom. I myself was a prisoner in the days of the Queen, my sister [Mary I], and am aware of the artifices that prisoners use to win over servants and obtain secret intelligences.[2]

Yet this plot, uncovered by her ministers' ingenious spy network, shook her so severely that she eventually gave in to pressure to have her cousin executed. Her first response, however, was to call on the city to help her, asking the guilds to swear 'to protect their own Queen's person, and to revenge to the uttermost all such malicious actions and attempts against Her Majesty's most Royal Person'.[3]

The Grocers responded enthusiastically, with an oath they put to their members soon after Francis Slater had sworn John in. 'It hath been manifest', Hugh Morgan announced, 'that the life of our gracious Lady Sovereign hath been most treacherously and devilishly sought.' The company reiterated its loyalty to the queen with a ringing declaration:

> We do voluntarily and most willingly bind ourselves everyone of us to the other jointly and severally in the bond of one firm and loyal society and do hereby vow and promise before the Majesty of Almighty God that with our whole powers, bodies, lives, lands and goods and with our children and servants we and every of us will faithfully serve and humbly obey our said Sovereign Lady Queen Elizabeth against all estates, dignities and earthly powers whatsoever.[4]

They swore this 'upon the Holy Evangelist', and added an oath that tied them even more closely to each other:

> No one of us shall for any respect of persons or causes for fear or reward separate ourselves from this Association or fail in the preservation thereof during our lives, upon pain to be by the rest of us persecuted and suppressed as perjured persons and as public enemies of God, our Queen, or native country.[5]

John was spared from being swept into this passionate vow, as he was still an apprentice. Swearing his loyalty to the queen, or to the Company of Grocers, would have presented no problems for him at this moment. Yet as time went on, he had reason to be thankful that he had never been forced to commit himself quite as deeply to the company as his master had.

The plot against the queen had a decisive effect on John, however, though he cannot have known it at the time. Because of it, and the assassination of the Protestant prince of the Dutch States, William the Silent, Elizabeth agreed to declare war on the country that most aggressively promoted the policy of a united Catholic Europe: Spain.

The exercises at Mile End were a minor consequence of her decision. On 20 April 1585 the Grocers were asked by the Lord Mayor, 'on her Majesty's commandment', to train 'three hundred and ninety six men whereof one hundred and ninety seven shot, one hundred and fifty nine rowlett with pike and thirty nine douslett with halbert'. The Grocers'

court discussed which of their members had enough military experience
to do this and agreed to choose 'sufficient citizens of this company to
be Captains'. In the end no one volunteered, so the full burden of the
exercise fell on the company beadle. He hired Captain Tibbett. This was
the force, to be deployed 'within the Citie only,' for the defence of the
citizens and their goods, of which John found himself a part.[6]

The drill culminated in a display before the queen: 'a very brave show
at grooming before Her Majesty,' on 18 May at St George's Field.[7] This
would have been the closest John had ever come to the queen, though
not in quite the circumstances he had imagined. The Grocers were
considered to have the most disciplined Trained Band of any trade in
London and the master, Hugh Morgan, would have been proud, as her
Apothecary, to show off his company in front of her. Patriotic fervour
was so strong at this point that the Grocers could never have foreseen
that just over half a century later they would put their military skills to
use against their sovereign.

Their display of loyalty was expensive. The 'charges in training' filled
four pages of the year's accounts, but there was more to come. They
were asked, in a way that was hard to refuse, to contribute individually
to a lottery devised by the palace. 'It is her Highness' pleasure that every
man to adventure some money into the Lotterye, being lots of 5s.' Then,
on 23 July, came the request to raise thirty-seven soldiers to send to the
Netherlands. An army on the move required a different approach, as
citizens were exempt from such service. The Cripplegate beadle was
paid, 'for his paine in spoking of soldiers, and for his pains in pressing
others when some failed'. Some of the men were unsuitable and money
had to be found for 'six other humble men pressed in place of some
misliked' and also for 'bread, drink and sundry items to keep the
souldiers together'. On 27 July the soldiers were 'trained, armed and
unarmed at the hill until they were fit and shipped at the Tower on 13
August'.[8]

Once this unhappy bunch of men had embarked to meet the Spanish
at the Flemish port of Flushing, John was free to concentrate on more
interesting matters. He was about to discover that there was a silver
lining to the war with Spain.

Under the agreement with his master, John's needs for food, clothing
and shelter were taken care of while he was 'set awork, and sufficiently
instruct[ed] as apprentices ought to be instructed and learned'. It was a
carefree existence, so long as he observed the City rules. London's alder-

men had taken steps to impose discipline on apprentices of every trade, since there were now so many arriving in the city. The Grocers alone took on 133 apprentices in the same year as John. The most obvious restrictions to which he was subject concerned his clothes. Apprentices were not allowed to indulge the fancy for extravagant colours and silks that their contemporaries loved. It was stipulated that John should wear:

> no hat, nor anything but a woollen cap, without any silk in or about the same... neither ruffles, cuffs, loose collars, nor other than a ruff at the collar and that only a yard and a half long... To wear no doublets [waistcoats] but what was made of canvas, fustian [cotton and flax cloth from Italy], sackcloth, English leather or woollen, without any gold, silver or silk trimming.... To wear no other cloth or jersey in hose or stockings than white, blue or surret [russet].

For eight years John was obliged to show his lowly status by walking without a weapon and wearing no gold, silver or silk.[9] This was no hardship for a boy from the country. Far more exciting was the main source of the goods his master traded: the Port of London. The broad river Thames with the quays and harbours that made up the port quickly became the focus of John's new life. This marvel of the city gave it a cosmopolitan vigour startlingly different from any community John had known in rural Lancashire.

It became clear that he had arrived in London at a critical time for its development as a port. The pre-eminent northern European port had been Antwerp, but the English and Dutch forces were unable to prevent it from being sacked by the Spanish at the start of the war. London merchants at once spotted new opportunities for trade that the fighting had delivered into their hands. The destruction of Antwerp was so complete that it never recovered. It was now the turn of London and Amsterdam to compete for its crown. Spanish and Portuguese merchant ships still traded in these ports in spite of the war, and London's trade was growing at dazzling speed.

A wonderful variety of imports fuelled the daily lives of the 90,000 people who lived in the city. Merchandise such as this hardly ever reached the country districts or northern counties. The twenty-four quays that lined London's river frontage, from Queenhithe, just south of St Paul's Church in the west, to Tower Dock at the Tower of London in the east, landed riches from all over the world. From Italy came fustian, the cotton and flax cloth, and silk taffeta. Ostrich feathers and sugar arrived in Spanish ships from Africa and the West Indies. Gunpowder, nails and steel came from Antwerp, and wine and lace from France. But the ships also brought many extraordinary curiosities: dolls, tennis balls, hatbands and harp strings, spectacles, straw hats and Scotch salmon.[10]

The Grocers handled many of the most exotic imports, which they landed at Billingsgate. This quay had a deep-water mooring, where masted ships would tie up after the timber section of London Bridge had been drawn up to let them through. London's chronicler, John Stow, described it as:

> a large Watergate, port or Harbrough for Shippes and boats, commonly arriving there with fish, salt, Oranges, Onions, and other fruits and roots, wheat, rie, and graine of divers sorts for service of the Citie and the parts of the realm adjoining.[11]

The precious oranges that John could not afford would capture his imagination, but the mundane was equally astonishing. Whole ships devoted to cargoes of onions came in from France. The French ships were admittedly small, but it was amazing to see a vegetable that was so commonly and easily grown at home carried into London in the holds of foreign boats. Strangest of all, to this country boy's eye, were the shiploads of apples that came in from the Low Countries: Holland, Belgium and northern France. What was it that made a worthwhile business out of importing into England crops and vegetables that the native soil was so readily suited to grow? These crops were grown everywhere in the country, though variable harvests made it necessary for the City guilds to store corn against times of famine, and some of the imported corn was destined for these stores. Yet the imports must have made John curious to learn more about the special horticultural skills of these Flemish lowlanders whose produce Londoners found so irresistible.

The Flemish merchants traded on Sommers Quay, which adjoined the west side of Billingsgate, so John's master's business brought him into regular contact with them. Flemish families had been settled in the southeast of England for several generations. In London, East Anglia and Kent they were known for silk-weaving and growing fruit. But the Flemish John now met were overwhelmingly travelling merchants based across the Channel, trading in the goods John's master needed for his shop. There were cargoes of vegetables, as well as sugar; molasses; vegetable dyes, such as rose madder for red; commonly imported spices, such as nutmeg, ginger, mace, cloves and caraway, which the Grocers had the exclusive right to handle in England. As an apothecary his master imported ingredients such as fenugreek for making medicine; oak apples for ink; gum arabic for medicine and paint; calamine, made from zinc; lignum vitae, a wood from the guaiacum tree in the West Indies; rhubarb; turmeric and a wide range of plant seeds. So, while the Flemish were intriguing, John's new environment presented him with a tantalizing array of unfamiliar sources of knowledge.

An apothecary's studies began with the theoretical basis of his art: medical principles that were nearly 2,000 years old. Apothecaries, physicians and surgeons learned theory from the Greek doctor Galen, whose commentaries on Hippocrates' writings had formed the basis of medicine for the Romans. The text John used was the one freshly translated only a century before by 'English Thomas', the monk Thomas Linacre, who had worked for the Vatican in Rome, painstakingly translating classics from original manuscripts, stripping them, in the process, of centuries of crusty medieval distortion.

Galenic theory identified physical and mental health with a balance between wet and dry, hot and cold, the so-called 'four humours'. The physician associated a patient's complaint with a deficiency of heat or moisture, or a combination of 'humours', and looked for a remedy with the right properties to redress the balance. The Indian tradition of ayurveda would have been quickly recognized in Elizabethan London.

As an apothecary, John's primary role was to know and understand the properties of plants that could then be placed at the physician's disposal. It was the physician's job, in principle, to diagnose the imbalance that caused a patient's illness. Yet John soon saw, in practice, that many apothecaries prescribed treatments directly to patients who visited their shops. Some London apothecaries ran a mini-hospital service, giving board and lodging to the sick.

As far as plants were concerned, the classic text was by another Greek: Dioscorides. This book was also freshly translated by Thomas Linacre, and it became his most influential legacy. Dioscorides had been the personal physician of Antony and Cleopatra and this text was based on his experience as a doctor in the Roman army in the first century AD. In his preface, Dioscorides addressed his patron: 'having travelled much (for you know I led a soldier's life) I have by your advice gathered together all that I have commented hereupon'.[12] Fifteen centuries after he died, Dioscorides' confident, dispassionate observations on the plants he used were followed all over Europe. His work on vegetables and other drugs was based on simple observation and experiment, free of the welter of quotations and rhetorical argument that had come to characterize European scholarship in the intervening ages. Perversely, respect for his ancient authority was so great that his name – associated with the medicinal values of plants – had come to have almost magical connotations.

As before, John found that most books were disappointing sources of knowledge. There was only one useful herbal, or encyclopaedia of plants, that had been published in English. This book, by William Turner, had appeared posthumously in 1568. Coincidentally, Turner, who had garnered and published more knowledge of plants than any Englishman so far, was also a country boy from the wild north like John. He grew up in Morpeth, Northumbria, and his herbal was peppered with memories of how his neighbours had used the plants around them: 'The boys in Northumberland scrape the root of the herb [*Scilla nutans*, the field hyacinth] and glue their arrows and books with that slime that they scrape off.'[13]

Turner had also garnered most of his knowledge in a busy port. A generation before, it had been Antwerp that had dazzled all visitors, and when, during the reign of Elizabeth's sister, the Catholic Queen Mary, Turner was forced into exile for his Protestant convictions, he picked up a rich seam of knowledge in that city. He found Dutch merchants importing sugar from the East Indies, and was particularly fascinated by the wrappings they used: 'I have seen Papyrus divers times in Antwerp wherein was sugar and divers other merchandise wrapped.' There were also unusual plants whose medicinal properties were tantalizingly unexplored: 'I have seen herb Aloe also in Antwerp in shops and there it endureth long alive as houseleek doth.'[14]

Like John, Turner was impressed by the sophistication of the Flemish apothecaries, and fascinated by their gardens. 'A faithful and learned apothecary' of Antwerp was Pieter Coudenberg, who by 1568 had been a gardener for twenty years, and grew 'six hundred kinds of exotic plants'. Turner was particularly struck by *Artemisia arborescens*, the silver-grey-leaved frost-hardy plant that Coudenberg had received from Rome and grew in his Antwerp garden 'with many other strange and wholesome herbs, hard to be found in any other place of Germany beside'. Coudenberg gave the enthusiastic Englishman a sprig, a picture of which Turner included in his herbal, examining it fully and tasting its leaves. This plant, he said, has 'longer, whiter and bitterer leaves than the common'. Some time afterwards, Coudenberg wrote sadly to his friend in Zurich: 'I gave a sprig of Roman wormwood formerly to William Turner who inserted its picture in his English Herbal: but then the plant died for me without seed, nor could I with all my care recover it.'[15]

What Turner had stumbled upon in Antwerp and John now encountered in London was a network of traders whose business was fuelled by their exploration and discovery of new materials. The revolutionary tool of these sixteenth-century explorers was not so much the information given them by the Greeks, but their method. For the first time in hundreds of years these men, who were turning the medicinal use of plants into a science, began to add to the knowledge of the past by recording direct observations of their own.

When John arrived in London, few people thought of knowledge as something gained through personal experience. Wisdom was considered to belong to those who had learned the classics at Oxford or Cambridge, and social status was reserved for its 'gentlemen' graduates. Only the sharpest minds of the day recognized the restrictive limits of academic instruction. Francis Bacon quipped that 'the universities of Europe at this day' did little to advance wisdom. The new sciences progressed slowly there, in the teeth of dogma and entrenched argument. 'Alas, they learn nothing there but to believe: first to believe that others know that which they know not, and after [that they] themselves know that which they know not'.[16]

Yet, in his lively new home, John found knowledge all around him, not in books, but in the people he met and their merchandise. Among them were exceptional scholars who made clear that it was not a university education that was called for in this new project of studying the natural world, but the power of honest and accurate observation. John's childhood had taught him this skill in abundance. He left the north with very little, but he was equipped with two essential weapons for the new age of science: practical knowledge of native plants and familiarity with Latin. He found he was fully prepared to join the new scientific adventure.

The process under way in Europe, of identifying native plants and matching them to descriptions revealed in the fresh translations of Greek classics, ran parallel to the reinterpretations of the Christian message that

had begun with new translations of the Bible. While the reformed
Protestant Church was essentially conservative, however, seeking inspiration
from the old texts so as to return to the simple faith of the early doctrine,
the re-examination of the natural world that had begun would bring about
a radical reassessment of man's relationship to his environment.

The apothecaries and physicians of Europe were taking the first steps
in a continuous chain of discovery of the planet that has lasted to this
day. Whether or not John as a young man glimpsed the immensity of the
task that lay ahead, even within the span of his lifetime, it is hardly
surprising that he was gripped by the thrilling prospect of the undiscovered potential of plants. His short life so far had taught him that the
inter-relationship between man and plants was wholly beneficial. Now,
here in London, he met scholars who indicated a vast field in which an
enthusiastic young man, with the right method and equipment, could
make a valuable contribution.

John found that the Company of Grocers opened up a network of rare
city gardens to him. Hugh Morgan, the master of the Company, had 'a
garden neere Colman Street' in the north-east corner of the city, where
the houses were spaced thinly enough to let in the sunshine. Morgan was
known as 'a curious conserver of simples', a collector of rare plants, and
he used his planted specimens to teach the apprentices.[17] In the
European tradition, students were made welcome and invited to learn
directly from the plants at their feet. The specimens intrigued John, but
the people he met in these gardens fascinated him more. Jacques Garret
was a Flemish grocer, originally from Lille in northern France, who had
moved to London to practise as an apothecary. His business was in Lime
Street, on the eastern edge of the city, and he had a garden there where
John often went. John de Franqueville was another skilled Flemish
plantsman working as a London merchant, 'from whose care', wrote
John later, 'is sprung the greatest store [of rare plants] that is now flourishing in this kingdom'.[18]

There was one man, above all, whose presence in the city inspired
him. He found a reason to be grateful for the weeks spent tramping up
and down the common at Mile End. The war that had forced John's
military training had also delivered Matthias de l'Obel to London. The
assassination of William the Silent, which had brought England into the
war, had also cost the prince's personal physician his job. For John,
whose friend and mentor that physician became, Matthias de l'Obel's
safe haven in London was a wonderful piece of luck.

Matthias de l'Obel aged 76 from a portrait by Francis Dellarame, 1615. The lines beneath him from the Roman poet Julian read: Melius a limpidissimis fontium scaturiginibus haurire, quam turbidos confectari rivulos.

Matthias de l'Obel was Flemish, from Lille, like his friend Jacques Garret. He was nearly thirty years older than John, born the son of a lawyer in 1538. He travelled through Europe as a young man, and it was at the mature age of twenty-seven that he settled down to study medicine at Montpellier, one of the great European universities of the day. His teacher was the French botanist Rondelet, who was writing his own pharmacology, updating the observations of Dioscorides. Rondelet was so impressed by his new student that, at his death only a year after his first meeting with Matthias, he left him his unpublished papers. It was the tradition amongst European scholars to choose a younger man to further their work, by ensuring that he bought or inherited their papers after their death.

De l'Obel quickly established his reputation as a scornful critic of earlier scholars. His books lambasted the best-known European authority, a German called Matthiolus, for writing about plants he had never seen. Matthias' own uncompromising approach was the botanical equivalent of puritan Christianity: the original should be sought out, dispassionately re-examined and then proclaimed as a new truth that displaced the old. John met de l'Obel at Jacques Garret's house but Matthias was also a regular visitor to Hugh Morgan's garden and had drawn heavily on plants he saw there for the book that had made his name. This was his *Stirpium Adversaria*, the botanical commentaries that he published in 1571 under the sponsorship of an English aristocrat named Edward St Loo. It seems likely that when John first met Matthias he already possessed the imposing presence he had in old age. The portrait of him taken then gives him the beady ferocity of an eagle: a high forehead, a big nose and penetrating eyes under quizzically raised brows. Beneath it is a line from the Roman poet Julian which expresses the guiding principle of his life. In translation it says,'Better to drink from the clearest springs at source than to trust in muddy brooks.' This man became John's greatest teacher and had a profound influence on the whole of his career.[19]

In the pleasant atmosphere of Jacques Garret's garden, John could listen to these Flemish experts' tales. He would have heard them talk about Garret's regular correspondent, their friend and countryman Charles de l'Ecluse, who was the most famous herbalist in Europe at that time. Clusius, as he was known, had a reputation for exceptional skill with flowers, especially tulips, of which he claimed to have bred fifty varieties. English gentlemen on a tour of Europe for pleasure or political reasons would visit Clusius' shop in Lille to collect one of his curiosities. He was also in the last stages of compiling a comprehensive herbal for which he had travelled all over the continent collecting specimens.

John was only thirteen when Clusius made his last visit to London as Sir Walter Raleigh's guest. The Flemish scholars found that English aristocrats were particularly receptive to their skills. Like Lady Margaret Clifford, Sir Walter had grown fascinated by plant chemistry. His earlier passion for alchemy had begun to transmute into something more productive. He needed effective medicines to use at sea, just as she, isolated in Yorkshire, was forced to help herself. Raleigh's favourite laboratory was his cabin at sea, wrote John Aubrey:

> He studied most in his Sea-Voyages, where he carried always a Trunk of Books along with him, and had nothing to divert him. He made an excellent Cordiall, good in Feavers, etc.; Mr Robert Boyle haz the recipe, and makes it and does great Cures by it.[20]

When Clusius came to London, he and de l'Obel were greeted by Sir Walter's glittering circle of friends. There was Francis Drake, just back

The oldest teaching garden in northern Europe, established by Clusius in Leyden in the 1590s. Hortus Academicus, *Johannes van Meurs, Leyden, 1625.*

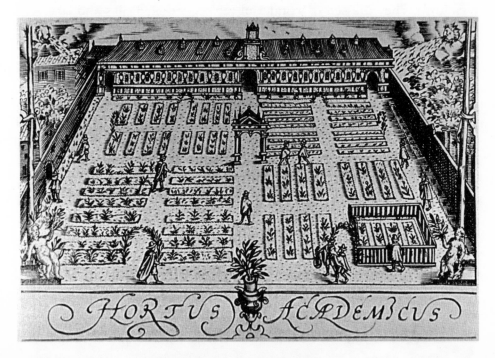

from sailing around the world, and the handsome romantic poet Sir Philip Sidney. Just as attractive was Sidney's sister Mary, keenly interested in literature and science, and fluent in Latin, Greek and Hebrew. This clever woman was 'a beautifull Ladie [with] a pretty sharp-ovall face [and] haire of reddish-yellowe,'[21] who had recently married the Earl of Pembroke's heir. Her wit and beauty were so distrusted by her new father-in-law that he advised his son to keep her safely buried in the country.

The Flemish scholars found that there were many women in this circle who were, if anything, more interested in the pursuit of knowledge than were the men. De l'Obel received some Spanish beans from 'an illustrious lady, Dame Catherine Killigrew' who had found them on the coast of Cornwall.[22] No ships had been wrecked there at the time and she guessed they must have travelled from Spain to the English coast on some current that carried them so far: an early record of the Gulf Stream in action. Catherine Killigrew and her three sisters were known as 'the learned ladies'. One of them had married William Cecil, Lord Burghley, and her sister Anne was the mother of Francis and Anthony Bacon.

It is not surprising that de l'Obel found England appealing. These English aristocrats offered hospitality in the best homes in their beautiful country. Many of them had travelled widely, in exile or on government service, and they were familiar with the cities of Europe, including his own town. They dressed in wonderful velvets, jewelled silks and lace, and could often converse, like their queen, in Latin, French or Greek. Most important of all, they approved his religious background. In London he was no longer a heretic, but a foreign expert whose views were championed as a standard for the new religion.

It is much more surprising that Matthias struck up a friendship with John. When de l'Obel first set eyes on him, he was hardly a striking figure. Dressed in the dull buff uniform of a fustian doublet and breeches, this young man who turned up in the gardens of his friends appeared to have little that set him apart from scores of other rough London apprentices. Yet there was something that emerged when John opened his mouth. Unperturbed by his broad Lancashire accent, de l'Obel would have been impressed that this boy could speak, read, and write Latin.

This legacy, inherited from John's Lancashire Catholic teachers, unlocked the cosmopolitan world he found in London. Latin allowed him to appreciate these Flemish scholars' work, which was unlike any of the old books in English he had come across so far. John read and was inspired by Matthias de l'Obel's second book, *Stirpium Observationes*, or *Observations on the History of Plants*, which he had published in 1576, much of which was devoted to garden plants. Over time John covered his copy in annotations of his own, written in the margins in his neat Latin script. They testify to his fascination with de l'Obel's work and the powerful influence of this man over him. De l'Obel's approach was entirely in tune with John's own frankly practical nature. This internationally recognized scholar, who insisted on personal and accurate observation as the only route to knowledge, gave John confidence in the methods within his reach, and hope for the future.[23]

The two men had one other thing in common. They were professionally concerned with the medicinal value of plants, but they shared a passion for their beauty. Many of the plants in Matthias' second book were included solely for their decorative value. The older man's account of the beautiful royal gardens of Brussels and France would have awoken John to the potential of garden flowers.

Matthias de l'Obel had a son called Paul who practised as an apothecary in London, but nevertheless he came to look upon John as the natural successor to his own investigations into the nature of plants. There was something else about this young apprentice that may have softened the Flemish physician's usually magisterial manner. John had arrived at his trade later than most, coming to the apothecary's profession at sixteen, without the support of his family's precedent or connections. His eagerness to learn came of his fascination with the material and a desire to make up for lost time. So it had been with Matthias. Though he was born into a lawyer's family, he had, by his own account, fallen in love with plants and *materia medica* (the study of their medical properties) at sixteen. It had taken over ten years before he could settle down and pursue the subject properly, and he must have seen in John's dedication a reflection of himself as a younger man.

It was a paradoxical fact that so many of John's friends came from Europe. He was different from them in class, race, background and religion, yet they had one thing in common, over and above their interest in plants. They were all foreigners in a rapidly expanding cosmopolitan city that was none the less founded on systems designed to keep foreigners out. There was scarcely a trade that a foreigner could practise, no matter what his knowledge or experience might be, without being accepted into one of the City guilds. Foreigners might buy a place in a guild, or serve an apprenticeship, but London's rules were deliberately restrictive. While the English were generally xenophobic, considering themselves superior to all foreigners, Londoners considered themselves above all other Englishmen.

John was as much an outsider in the city as the Flemish. His Lancashire accent would have been a subject of mockery and his Catholic background a matter for mistrust. The Huguenots in London understood what it was to be persecuted for your religion. They respected John's right to keep his faith to himself and, untroubled by his accent, proved more sympathetic friends than his fellow countrymen.

After three years of this busy new life, John received news that underlined his isolation in the city, and significantly changed his circumstances. In November 1587 both his parents died suddenly, within eight days of each other.[24] His older brother, Richard, just past his twenty-second birthday, was now responsible for John's five younger brothers and sisters. The family could no longer afford to give John any extra financial support, and John, whose twenty-first birthday was only weeks away, was forced to consider how to survive on his own in London.

CHAPTER SIX

ELIZABETHAN GOLD

The time-honoured method of increasing your wealth amongst the Parkinson farmers of the north was to marry a rich widow. An opportunity for John to follow the family's example arrived almost at once. He was still only twenty when he met Mary Hutchens, the young widow of a coppersmith. William Hutchens, Mary's first husband, left no will, but as his widow she possessed, briefly, everything that had been his. His house and shop and the land around it at Cripplegate, just north of the city, would belong to her until she married a second time. Then, once again, everything she owned would become her husband's.

John's situation was awkward. Apprentices had no right to marry, and he still had over three years of his term left to serve. Moreover, until he attained his majority at twenty-one, his master had the authority of a father over him. Yet, whether through romance or practical need, John was determined enough to bring about this marriage to Mary to overcome these obstacles.

Apprentices did sometimes marry without their master's consent, but it always brought trouble. Not long before, an apprentice grocer called John Greenwood had been turned out by his master, Richard Walston, because he 'did entangle or contract himself in marriage contrary to the tenure of his indenture without his master's knowledge'. Greenwood had begged the Grocers' court for forgiveness, and they were inclined to be lenient, but his master would not take him back. Eventually Greenwood was allowed to find another master to finish his apprenticeship.[1]

John did not want to jeopardize his future career as an apothecary. His marriage was meant to secure it. Mary's money would give him the capital to open his own shop when there was no other way to obtain one. Without it he would be condemned to work indefinitely as an employee, a journeyman apothecary in some other man's business, a prospect that fell far short of his ambition. He would be in a stronger position if he waited until he was twenty-one, because until his majority he had no right to take possession of Mary's goods anyway. Yet there was a chance that if he waited so long in the hurly-burly of London life, the bird would fly from his hand.

The solution John found was an early form of engagement that suited them all. His master, Francis Slater, would have been loath to lose his useful apprentice at this stage, when he was trained to take up many duties in the shop, so he accepted John's proposal. For Mary the arrangement meant she could continue to own her former husband's home until John was free to marry and support her. So John paid for a legal notice of engagement, issued by the Bishop of London on 8 July 1588 to 'Parkinson, John (Parkynson) of St Sepulchre, London, yeoman and Mary Hutchens, of the city of London, widow of William Hutchens, late of St Giles, Cripplegate, London "stannarius", deceased'.[2]

With this piece of paper John's marriage to Mary was a legal fact even before it took place. Most couples simply had the banns read in church and were married. Getting a bishop's licence seemed an expensive and unnecessary duplication of a legally binding church service. There was a growing fashion for licences amongst the gentry and wealthier merchants' families, precisely because they were too expensive for ordinary people. John's circumstances hardly allowed him to indulge in expense for fashion's sake. But for him, a licence not only secured Mary as his bride, it served a further purpose. Once it had been issued, any form of holy blessing could solemnize their union – even one performed in private by a Catholic priest.

From Mary's point of view, this union meant that she had the prospect of joining a profession in which she could become a useful partner in her husband's business. Widows often thrived as the owners of their husbands' grocers' and apothecaries' businesses – no women were coppersmiths. Moreover, she must have recognized the spark of ambition in this bright young apothecary.

John was already toying with the idea that would one day make him famous. He was planning to write an encyclopaedia in English that would accurately describe all the known plants and their medicinal properties. The only book of this kind in English so far was William Turner's herbal, which John scarcely referred to, finding that it had been overtaken by many discoveries in the twenty-five years since Turner's death. His aim was to devise a book fit for the modern age, and he talked about it freely with his friends. When, at last, John came to publish the *Theatrum Botanicum* in 1640, as an old man of seventy-three, there were some who remembered the beginning of this lifelong dream. One of them, John Harmer, chose verse to celebrate the long slow maturing of this precious work over half a century:

Phoebus hath fifty times lash't through the signes
Since thou intend'st this jubilee of lines
And now tis extant and shall swifly scour
Through dark oblivion to the world's last houre.[3]

John's learning and vision were already exceptional in the circles in which he worked. For Mary his youthful optimism and striking ability outweighed the disadvantages of his Catholic northern background. When, in August, the news came that a Spanish armada, sent to destroy the English ships, was in flames off the coast at Tilbury, Mary and John were already bound as a couple and able to join the general rejoicing together.

The destruction of almost the whole Spanish fleet in English waters was the beginning of rich opportunities for the English. It also marked the start of a new era for John. Curious plants and objects began to pour into England from all corners of the world, as English sailors and merchants sought untapped sources of wealth. Each import was examined for opportunities by John's contemporaries, distinguished from their fathers and grandfathers by their enthusiastic exploration of all things new. John had arrived in London at a perfect time to become both student and storyteller of this modern era. He was not only willing but able to meet the challenge.

The most tangible expression of English enthusiasm for new opportunities at this time was the planting of colonies in America. Many Englishmen had dreamed for years of riches beyond the sea, akin to the South American gold that had given Spain and Portugal their overwhelming power. As early as 1527 the potential wealth of North America – at least that part not controlled by indomitable foreign forces – was painted as a treasure trove waiting to be seized. According to one enthusiast, English adventurers would find Paradise waiting for them in Florida:

There is no doubt that the islands are fertile of cloves, nutmeg, mace and cinnamon; and that the said islands with other there about, abound with gold, rubies, diamonds, balasses, jacints and other stones and pearls, as all other lands that are under or near the equinoctial.... As our metals be tin, lead, and iron, so theirs be gold silver and copper. And as our fruits and grains be apples, nuts and corn, so theirs be dates, nutmeg, pepper, cloves and other spices. And as we have jet, amber, crystal and jasper ... so they have rubies, diamonds, balasses, sapphires, jacints and other like.[4]

Sir Walter Raleigh did more than any other Englishman of his day to seize that dream. His natural arrogance and fierce patriotic pride were offended by Spanish imperialism. While many Englishmen shared his hatred for Spain, which was the paymaster of the Pope, Sir Walter's views were coloured less by religion than by envy. He devoted most of his life to seeking a way to emulate or steal Spanish wealth. He helped to stoke a propaganda campaign to promote the riches waiting for the English in America. Privately he dreamed about the fabulous Inca gold that he had heard lay ready for the taking in Guyana (then called Guiana). These stories of treasure that the Spaniards had not been able to reach tantalized him. For a long time he nursed the prospect of an expedition to unearth it from the jungle, high up near the source of the Orinoco river, on the borders of Venezuela and Peru.

In the 1580s, before open war with Spain began, Sir Walter focused his energy on the shores of North America. He believed that annexing territory there gave his country the best chance of matching the Spanish and Portuguese wealth and stalling French ambition. There were reports from sailors like John Walker who had reached Carolina in 1580, and spoke of a silver mine on the bank of a good deep river and 'a country that was most excellent both for the soil, diversity of sweet woods and trees'.[5]

On the strength of such reports Sir Walter backed an expedition that sailed in March 1583, led by his half-brother, Humphrey Gilbert, and persuaded the queen to give him her patent. In Newfoundland, Gilbert's men discovered a small international community of fishermen, who planted seeds for vegetables at the settlement round St John's harbour in May, and harvested them when they left in August. Theirs was a self-governing body like the formidable trade guilds in London. They elected one of the English captains amongst them as 'admiral' for the season, to keep order. But when Gilbert arrived they allowed him to claim the colony 'on behalf of the crown of England and the advancement of Christian religion in those Paganish regions'. On 5 August 1583, he set up 'the arms of England ingraven in lead, and fixed upon a pillar of wood', which had been brought along for the purpose.[6]

Few of Gilbert's expedition survived a shipwreck while exploring the coast further south. Still, Sir Walter did not give up. He sent two of his household servants, Amadas and Barlow, to prospect America. They took with them the mathematician and alchemist John Dee and returned in August 1584 with skins, pearls and two Indians on board named Manteo and Wanchese. Delighted, Sir Walter put a bill into Parliament almost at once to stake his claim to the lands they had found, which he called Virginia in honour of the queen.[7] He had already employed a mathematician from Oxford University, Thomas Harriot, to tutor his household in astronomy and navigation. Now he commissioned Richard Hakluyt as propagandist to publish an account of the next expedition and whip up support for the potential of English colonies in America.

In August 1585, 140 men had landed on the Florida coast, including Harriot, Hakluyt and John White, a soldier who would become famous for his account of his American adventures. The 'colonizers' had no food at first, although they planted corn, and they were dependent on friendly Indians for food. They learnt to eat local starches, including cassava (golden club) and chyna root (*Smilax officinalis*, better known as sarsaparilla). Their native hosts, however, grew hostile after supporting so many strangers, who were described even by their leader as 'wild men of mine own nation', through the winter. After eight months of bare survival Francis Drake appeared offshore with a welcome invitation to take them all home, and the 'colony' was no more.[8]

While English settlements in North America lurched a step closer to reality, the gold the colonizers sought was not immediately apparent. The men who survived this first settlement found the experience tougher than they had hoped. Harriot thought their city ways had made them soft.

> Some also were of a nice bringing up, only in cities or towns, or such as never, (as I may say) had seen the world before. Because there were not to be found any English cities, not such fair houses, nor at their own wish any of their accustomed dainty food, nor any soft beds of down and feathers, the country was to them miserable.[9]

By the time this account was published in 1588, the defeat of the Spanish armada, and open war with Spain, had exposed a far more obvious source of gold to English eyes. People like Margaret Clifford's husband, the Earl of Cumberland, diverted their attention from colonies and pursued a new path. George Clifford was soon to become the most famous English pirate, or 'privateer', as they were euphemistically called, of his day.

George was inspired by the great achievements of English sailors such as Francis Drake and Thomas Cavendish, both of whom had, by 1588, sailed round the world. At twenty he had watched Francis Drake prepare to set sail from Plymouth, and he was there to greet him when he returned, victorious, from the first successful circumnavigation. Drake complained to the queen, as late as 1592, that accounts of this spectacular journey 'hitherto have been silenced'. It was true that Drake's voyage was a badly kept secret for more than ten years after his ships returned to England, because the queen was unwilling to admit that she knew her sailors were pirating Spanish ships and stealing their gold. Drake had managed this more than once as he made his way across the oceans.[10]

Once the open war with Spain began in 1585, all that changed. Spanish and Portuguese merchant ships returning from the West Indies, heavily laden with gold and spices, were now fair game. In fact, before the queen sent even one soldier to the Netherlands, she sent Drake to the Azores to prey on Spanish fleets on their way home to the motherland.

George was one of the biggest landowners in England, but hungry for cash. His tenant farmers thrived on fixed rentals and rising prices, while he had no other source of income. George could not persuade the queen to give him any kind of commission, despite his frequent presence at court and his direct protestations of poverty. So he gambled his fortune on the adventures he craved. In 1586, two years before the defeat of the armada in English waters, George Clifford mortgaged his estate to buy two ships and began what became twelve years of 'private anti-Spanish enterprise at sea'.[11] In that time he fitted out twelve expeditions, buying or building his own fleet, and sailed himself with nearly every one.

In the first glory years after the defeat of the Spanish armada, the prizes the privateers brought home utterly dazzled the English. The captured cargoes were laid out on the quays of the south-west ports to be assessed by the queen's inspectors. One prize unloaded in Falmouth yielded:

Jewels, stones, pearls, musk and ambergris, 8,500 quintals of pepper; 900 of cloves, 700 of cinnamon, 500 of cochineal.... Of white small diamonds, 200; of small rubies, 1,027; of great rubies, 358; of sparks of diamonds, 1,972; of great diamonds, 96; of other diamonds, 551; of orient pearls, 880; of pieces of gold, 7; of cinnamon 3 bags; of Indian hides, 100; of gold rings, 10: one fashioned as a dragon, with four rubies, a sapphire, and a pearl, six with rubies and one with five large rubies.[12]

The description of the cargo was precise down to the number of 'sparks of diamonds' because the queen and the lord chancellor were entitled to ten per cent of the value. Every part of the captured treasure was sized up: 'Elephants' teeth, porcelain, vessels of china, coconuts, hides, ebon wood as black as jet, bedsteads of the same; cloth of the rinds of trees very strange for the matter and artificial in the workmanship...'.

As these treasures reached the market in London their impact was profound. Richard Hakluyt proclaimed them as a sign from God:

I cannot but enter into the consideration and acknowledgement of God's great favour towards our nation, who by putting this purchase into our hands hath manifestly discovered those secret trades and Indian riches, which hitherto lay strangely hidden, and cunningly concealed from us.[13]

The English now understood what it meant to be a colonial power. They saw for themselves the extent of the wealth that had poured into Spain and Portugal for over a hundred years through those countries dominance of Central America and the West Indies.

The sense of the immense wealth to be found at sea grew steadily year by year. In 1592, George Clifford's private fleet brought home a Portuguese cargo that cast all the others in the shade. A huge merchant ship called the *Madre de Dios*, with seven decks full of passengers and cargo bound for Lisbon, was sailing unprotected in the waters off the Azores when she was caught and surrounded by George's ships. After ten hours of harrying her, the English streamed on board her to find, between decks so thick with bodies they could barely walk, undreamed-of wealth.[14]

They brought the conquered ship and cargo back to Dartmouth, where

They unladed and discharged about five millions of silver all in pieces of eight or ten pounds great, so that the whole quay lay covered with plates and chests of silver, beside pearls, gold, and other stones which were not registered.... The spices were pepper, cloves, maces, nutmegs, cinnamon, green ginger; the drugs were Benjamin; frankincense, galingale, mirabolans, zocotrine, and camphire; The silks: damasks, taffetas, sarcenets, altobassos (counterfeit cloth of gold), unwrought China silks, sleaved silks, white twisted silk, curled cypress. The calicoes were book calicoes, calico lawns, broad white calicoes, fine starched calicoes, coarse white calicoes, brown broad calicoes, brown coarse

Gathering cinnamon bark in India, illustration from Les oeuvres, *Ambroise Paré, ed., Gabriel Buon, Paris, 1579.*

calicoes. There were also canopies, and coarse diaper towels, quilts of coarse sarcenet and of calico, carpets like those of Turkey, whereunto are to be added the pearl musk, civet and ambergris.[15]

London merchants won both ways during this war with Spain. Their regular trade with Spanish merchant ships continued, and even grew, in the absence of competition from Antwerp. But they also discreetly backed their country's privateers. If these expeditions succeeded, they were rewarded with rich prizes that they could resell. If they failed, then the merchants' loans were still due.[16]

Wealthy Elizabethans soon found themselves deluged in a shower of rare delights: sweet-smelling herbs, foreign sweets and spices, precious silks and glittering jewels. Some of the richest parts of the pirates' prizes were exhibited in the grocer/apothecary shops in the city. While still an apprentice, John was now handling, on a daily basis, exotic substances that had been uncommon to behold. Musk was a rarity for the English. The true musk, John knew, was left by deer rubbing their sacs against trees, leaving a mixture of blood and mucus which hardened in the sun and became a substance of 'perfect, sweet scent,... and this is the best and choycest Muske to be had and gotten by great persons'.[17]

There was a counterfeit version, made by mixing the ordinary blood of the deer with a small amount of genuine musk, which was sold in little purses made of the deer's skin. Its desirability came from its power to consume 'all the ill scent' that abounded in London. Musk was also used as an aphrodisiac

> very beneficiall to comfort the heart and fainting spirits, and taketh away the passions and trembling thereof, maketh it merry and joyful, helpeth to expel sadnesse, it comforteth, warmeth and refresheth the brain and senses, quickening the dullness thereof, and is a help unto Venery.[18]

Almost as precious was ambergris, heated in a warm mortar and mixed by the apothecaries with a little ointment of orange flowers to rub on the temples and ease a headache. They knew it to be 'hot and dry in the second degree' so they used it to treat 'barennesse proceeding from a cold cause' and 'it is conducible to Epilepticke persons, to smell often there-unto, which causeth their fits to be both less violent and permanent'. None of John's contemporaries knew the origins of this substance. It was

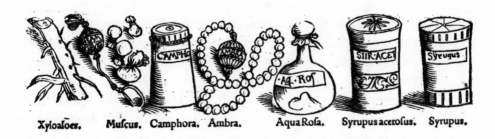

Xyloaloes.   Muſcus. Camphora. Ambra.   Aqua Roſa.   Syrupus acetoſus. Syrupus.

Herbal medicines from a sixteenth-century German text, Argentorati, Johannem Schottum, 1531.

found on the shores of tropical seas and brought to Europe by merchants who knew its value there. Some said it was the spawn of a whale, others that it came from the belly of 'the true whale (that hath no teeth and eateth soft fishes [blue whale]) which it casteth forth at certain times and by the great agitation of the sea is cast ashore'.[19]

John was particularly fascinated by rare substances like camphor resin. Even as an old man he marvelled at its properties:

> It is such a subtle thing, both in substance and nature, that although it is the gum or liquor [sap] of a great vast tree, partly distilling forth of its own accord, but chiefly by incision, which cometh forth cleer and white, and hath no spot therein, ... yet what we have and use seemeth plainely to be made by art, being cast as it were, into broad round pannes or dishes, and little above the thicknesse of one thumb, cleere, white, and transparent.[20]

John would take this substance in his hands, patiently learning to break it down by grinding and binding it with the oil that held it emulsified. Camphor wood was often made into boxes, because the wood was 'a preserver from putrefactrion', but the resin John handled was used as a potent ingredient for preparations to resist 'venom, poysons, and infection of the plague'. It was also sold as a cosmetic: 'of much use' with female customers 'that desire to preserve their beauty, by adding a luster to the skinne'.[21]

Nutmegs and mace had to be pressed between round copper plates and the medicinal oil carefully drawn off, and there were bundles of herbs to be dried or correctly identified and steeped in boiling water to make a decoction of the greatest efficacy. John would have been familiar with the process of drying, storing and decocting herbs and roots, but now there were so many strange new plants, seeds and gums to be understood. He discovered there were at least four varieties of cardamom seed alone. He would set to work with the pestle and mortar, grinding cardamom seeds, 'used in many of our compositions, cordials, Antidotes and others'.[22] John used the seed to:

> Provoke ... urine when it is stopped or passeth with pain ... it is good against the falling sickness [epilepsy], the broad wormes, and the torments of griping pains in the guts, or bowels, and expelleth wind powerfully, both from the stomach and entrails ... easeth those that have loose and weak sinews, and the pain of Sciatica or hip gout, and used with vinegar is good against scabbes.[23]

The gum, which was usually called 'Benjamin' and which we know as benzoin, was a novel rarity:

> Benzoin ... was not knowne to the Ancients.... [It] is not used inwardly in Physicke, neither by the Indians nor us that mistake it not, but is wholly spent in perfumes either water or oyle, pouther [powder], Pomanders, burning perfumes or the like, and is of excellent sent, where or howsoever it is used.[24]

Frankincense was also used for rich perfumes but was more highly valued for its medicinal properties. As a kind of antiseptic anti-depressant, it matched all the miseries of sixteenth-century Londoners wealthy enough to pay for it.

> It restraineth bleedings, stoppeth the laske [diarrhoea] and the Gonorrhoea, helpeth the memory, avoideth sadness and melancholy, and comforteth the heart mixed with other things for that cause.[25]

Even for the grocers who specialized in confectionery there were special riches in the pirates' ships. They included galingale, a form of ginger root that usually arrived in Europe through Persia from China, and was popular to season a dish with and 'to warm a cold stomach'. George Clifford's Portuguese prize included 'Mirobalans', white plums that were much sweeter than the common French variety known as damask that were 'dried in France in great quantities, and brought over unto us in Hogs-heads'.[26]

Eager merchants examined every herb and spice for its potential. Sailors carefully carried home curious seeds and twigs amongst the profits of their voyage. No one knew which might be found to have golden properties. It was customary to present rare plants and roots first to the queen, but soon they were displayed proudly in the windows of apothecaries' shops. The London apothecaries became the European champions of curious treasures from the 'new-found world'.

Amongst these curious herbs was the Indian coca leaf, which was brought from the West Indies. John later explained that it was:

> generally used by the Americanes to be chawed [chewed], as well in their long journeyes to preserve them from hunger and thirst abroad, as for pleasure at home ... if they would have them [the leaves] to be stronger, able to intoxicate their brains like unto drunkennesse, or to be as it were senseless, they put the leaves of tobacco to it and take great pleasure in those courses.[27]

While the fierce narcotic effects of the coca leaf remained a curiosity that Europeans at that time preferred to disdain, another American herb was much more warmly welcomed. The milder intoxication of tobacco, which 'maketh a man as it were drunke by taking the fume only',[28] was already popular in England, and 'Indian' tobacco from the Americas rapidly became a staple of the London apothecary's trade.

In France, tobacco was known as Herba Regina, or Nicotiana, after the French sailor Jacques Nicot came across it in Portugal and sent some to his queen. But only in England did the practice of smoking it catch on. Visitors to London found the natives strikingly devoted to bear-baiting, theatre, and tobacco:

> At these spectacles and everywhere else the English are constantly smoking tobacco; and in this manner – they have pipes on purpose made of clay, into the farther end of which they put the herb, so dry that it may be rubbed into powder, and putting fire to it they draw the smoke into their mouths, which they puff out again through their nostrils like funnels, along with it plenty of phlegm and defluxion from the head.[29]

Smoking was prescribed as medicinal, even against 'asthmatical or pectoral griefs', although John despaired of the English addiction to smoking to the end of his life. He suspected the herb could have a potent medicinal use 'if it were rightly ordered and applied, but the continual abuse thereof in so many, doth almost abolish all good use in any'.[30] The London apothecaries' customers became so enamoured of this curled brown leaf that within thirty years the profits from its sale were enough to sustain English colonies in America. In this unlikely form, the English adventurers at last found the gold hidden in Virginian soil.

A few months after the treasure of the *Madre de Dios* was disgorged on to the city, John's long apprenticeship ended. He finally qualified as an independent apothecary at the peak of the excitement over the arrival of so many intriguing novelties from the 'new world'. A week or so after his twenty-fifth birthday, on 30 January 1592, he went to the Grocers' Hall to be examined and swear the oath that would bind him to the Company of Grocers for life. His master, Francis Slater, was obliged to come with him, since no apprentice could be admitted 'until his master and the wardens of the Company testify his good condition'. After eight years of study in the small circle of London apothecaries, John's character was well known, but the Company of Grocers was now so large that this personal testimony was a serious matter. As an apothecary he also had to pass an oral examination of his knowledge of medicine and the use of drugs by the College of Physicians.

Four fellows from the Physicians' College came to the Grocers' Hall in their capacity as examiners of everyone who wished to practise medicine in and around London. These examinations were soon over on the day John became a freeman, since only a few of the seventy-one other grocer apprentices due to be freed were apothecaries. In the great hall where, as a boy, he had sworn allegiance to his master, he then took his place to swear loyalty for the rest of his life, using an oath that had barely changed in centuries.

Ye shall swear to be good and true to our sovereign Lady the Queen and her heirs, and to be obedient to the Wardens in lawful manner. Ye shall also keep secret all the lawful counsels of the said fellowship, so help you God and all saints and by that Book. And ye shall not serve out of the same fellowship, whiles ye may have sufficient salary within the said fellowship, without licence of the Wardens. And all manner rules, impositions and ordinances that be made, or hereafter shall be made and lawfully ordained for the ordering of the said fellowship ye shall truly obey to your power, upon pain to forfeit for the use of the said fellowship such penalty as shall be forced upon you by the Warden and associated of the said fellowship.[31]

The clerk wrote John's name in the warden's accounts and John handed over the three shillings and fourpence he had saved from his wage.[32] He was now not only a full member of the Grocers' Company, but also a freeman of the City of London. His new status was recognized everywhere in the country and meant that he had an inalienable right to have his own ground at all the fairs in England. The queen's officers could not seize his goods, even when he owed money, unless he used them to pay his debts, and he could travel 'toll free' wherever he wished. He could not be pressed into any army, on land or sea. He and his goods had the right to protection from the constable of the Tower on journeys to and from the city. Any non-freeman, including all foreigners, who wished to sell anything in London had in theory to act through the agency of a freeman, though the market in London was growing so rapidly that this rule was frequently broken.

John had already achieved a status that no one in his family had ever possessed. His marriage had given him a stable financial footing, and he had a profitable skill with which to secure his future. More exciting than this, though, was the sense that he had arrived in a city that was on the threshold of a great adventure. London was becoming the centre of the civilized world. As the English scoured the world for discoveries like those that had made the rest of Europe rich, London buzzed with possibilities. The war in Europe and opportunities in England attracted 'men of science' to the city. Those 'men of science' encouraged John to believe that he could one day proudly join their number.

He had already begun taking notes of all the exceptional specimens that came his way. Jacques Garret showed him a little star anise that Sir Thomas Cavendish had brought him from the distant Philippines. The sample was 'of the toppes only, with the husks and seed in them'. Once Jacques had shown it to his friends in London, he sent it to Clusius, who included a description in the herbal he was preparing. Jacques carefully added the name it went by in the Philippines, 'in China characters, which as Clusius saith he could not imitate, but was Damor, every letter being written under the other downwards'.[33]

This little star indicated to John the myriad of mysterious plants around the world waiting to be explored. The speed and skill of English sailors, equipped with new mathematical charts, seemed to make this task possible for a London apothecary for the first time. It was a task that captured his imagination from now until the end of his life. John's courage might have failed him had he travelled beyond Europe and gained any idea of the complexity of the world's vegetation. Asia, Africa and the Americas were vast beyond his imagining, and, tied to his trade in London, John was at the mercy of dried relics delivered from abroad. Yet he was a patient and persistent man, who put his faith in diligent work. He began to collect these samples to build as comprehensive a picture as he could of the world's vegetation.

Snippets of discovery came back to England in the most unlikely hands. George Clifford returned that year from an expedition to Puerto Rico, where he had carried out a daring capture of the Spanish base at San Juan. It had been a complete victory, but a hollow one. By the time his fleet returned, 700 men had been lost, and only forty of them had died fighting. They found the port of San Juan empty when they took it. The gold mines were worked out and the English sailors began to die of dysentery. So George freed the negro slaves who had worked the mines, and planned to leave. The only treasures he could take were the oranges, lemons, sugar and ginger with which he filled his ship. On 11 August, as the fleet was preparing to weigh anchor, George potted up a curious plant that grew wild on the promontory of San Juan, the sensitive *Mimosa pudica*.[34]

The variety of seeds and roots that were now being carried to London conveyed to John 'the many wonderful Workes of God in nature'.[35] Here was a religion more profound than the arguments between Catholic and Protestant that had dominated his life so far. Uncovering the secrets of these plants was a way to bring God's blessings to his fellow human beings. This was a private and uncomplicated worship that he could devote himself to and share with the network of like-minded men he had discovered in this city.

CHAPTER SEVEN

BROTHERHOOD

The election day dinner at the Grocers' Hall in June 1593 was John's first as a free citizen of London. A young man of twenty-five, suave in the new blue gown that indicated his status as a freeman grocer, he would have walked out of the shadow of Grocers' Alley with his wife upon his arm. For the first time, Mary and John took their seats with the others in the fine hall, where the trestle tables had been laid out with white cloths ready for a feast. As they surveyed the glittering splendour of their surroundings, it was evident that John's new social position promised rich opportunities. But there were also many obligations.

The next few years would make it clear to John that he was only 'free' in a relative sense. Between him and the realization of his dream there was a political minefield to cross. He had no choice but to attend and pay for this sumptuous dinner, which far excelled their own at home. The price was two shillings and sixpence for each of them, and John ran the risk of being required to pay double or be expelled from the Company if he refused. This dinner was only one of the steep costs he now faced. In a few hours he would pay his brotherhood money to the clerk. At least this year he would pay only the twelve pennies that jangled in his purse rather than the full two shillings. The Grocers allowed the younger men to pay only half the brotherhood money every other year for the first five years, while they were getting established.[1]

John's financial obligations to his Company were intertwined with moral ones that threatened to ensnare him. Some areas of the Grocers' moral authority presented no problems for him: their firm stand on homosexuality, for instance. Private homosexuality was common and tolerated in the upper classes, but two men of the tradesmen's class living together upset the guilds' tradition. Wives were also members of the company by marriage. No business could be founded on the basis of two separate trades in the same household. A freeman called Lewis Sympsone was summoned to the Grocers' court 'for occupying with a yonge man free of the lettersellers'. Lewis was told to 'avoyde reoccupying with hym, otherwise he is lyke to feel the smarte thereof'.[2]

This sixteenth-century German apothecary was already displaying exotic curiosities, like the stuffed body of a crocodile dangling from his ceiling. From Thesaurus pauperum, *H. Braunschweig, Frankfurt, 1537.*

The company's stance on religion was another matter for John. He must have known that he would encounter powerful Protestant pressure in the south of England, but the Company of Grocers was particularly puritanical. The tiny church of St Antholin's which they patronized was dominated by priests who were paid to give a 'morning lecture' there. This was a practice the Grocers had adopted during the regency of the Protestant Duke of Somerset in the middle of the sixteenth century, and the lectures were aggressively puritan in tone. One of the Company's scholars at Oxford had recently fallen victim to their evangelizing spirit. This was Edmund Campion, who had an exceptional reputation for wit and talent that had attracted the sponsorship of the queen's favourite, the Earl of Leicester. Campion was maintained by an annual scholarship from the Company of Grocers under the terms of which he was 'charged with

the education of divers worshippfull men's children'. Catching wind of
the Catholic sympathies that their scholar kept barely concealed in
Oxford, the worshipful Grocers took steps to force him to reveal himself
publicly. An open declaration of Catholic conviction would put Campion
in breach of the Thirty-Nine Articles of Faith, recently confirmed by the
Anglican bishops and designed to keep Catholics out of influential positions. He was told to preach at 'Pawll's Crosse' in London to make his
views clear, or else lose his scholarship. Eventually he was forced to
refuse, confess his Catholic beliefs, and resign as a Company scholar.[3]

Now that he was no longer an apprentice, there was pressure on John
to attend services at the Grocers' church. He was not obliged to attend
every member's funeral as he would have been in the past: 'the fraternity
to attend the dirge and funeral of every brother on forfeiture of 12d'.[4] The
company was now so large that this rule had grown impractical. Still, the
religious unity of the brotherhood was considered an integral part of its
commercial strength. The assumption remained that the company would
worship together and this fact was intensely uncomfortable for John.

His primary need at this point, however, was to establish his business.
His trade had become increasingly competitive. Now that the practice of
medicine in England was accepted as permanently divorced from the
monastic traditions that still dominated it in Catholic Europe, more and
more apprentice apothecaries were coming forward. The handful of
skilled apothecaries in London when Queen Elizabeth took the throne
had been replaced by more than a hundred by the time she died in
1603.[5] John's options, as he contemplated his future, were either to work
as a journeyman, in another man's shop, or rent and fit out his own.
There was no halfway house, such as a stall in the market place. The
Grocers' Company forbade such cheap expedients. 'Grocerie wares
should not be sold in the streets, figges onlie excepted'.[6]

Rents in this crowded, thriving, cosmopolitan city were high. The
Company owned many properties themselves, but they rented them
outside the brotherhood for commercial returns. Rents ranged from
twenty shillings a year for one of their little tenements on Cornhill to
twelve times that amount for grander houses. Only a few were retained
for almsmen and women dependent on the Company. There was a
system for lending young freemen money at preferential rates to meet
the steep costs of starting out. They had to apply for a loan from the
next legacy left to the Company by former members or their widows.
Legacies arrived so frequently that an application could be entered in the

company accounts one year and a loan received the next. But John seems to have found enough money in Mary's property to set up a shop on his own. He never approached the Company for a loan.

Mary's Cripplegate property was outside the north wall, where there were gardens, open fields and cows. Appealing though that environment was to John, an apothecary's business had to be in the heart of London. The most obvious place for a shop was close to the market at Bucklesbury, just south of the Grocers' hall, where the air was rich with the scent of herbs and spices. There was an old chapel at the corner of Grocers'Alley that had once been endowed with £20 a year to distribute to the poor. Now it was a kind of shopping mall owned by a haberdasher called Thomas Hobson, who 'turned this Chapell into a faire Warehouse and shoppes, towardes the streete, with lodgings over them'.[7] This is the kind of place where John could set himself up initially, and he would continue to trade in this part of the city for the first ten years of his career as an apothecary.

London was growing dramatically. Its international reputation now attracted educated Europeans as tourists. Paul Hentzner, the German lawyer who travelled through Europe in 1598, noted that Britain in general, but London in particular, produced 'a great number of men of learning, distinguished for their writings'. Hentzner was impressed by the natural wealth of England and its capital city. The river Thames, he wrote, 'is everywhere spread with nets for taking salmon and shad'. The 'swans, swimming in flocks' on the river were a captivating sight. He was even more impressed by the quantity of gold he saw. The main streets of the city were now 'very handsome and clean', and Hentzner found the wares displayed in the shops in Goldsmiths' Street extraordinary.

> There are besides to be seen in this street as in all others where there are goldsmiths' shops, all sorts of gold and silver vessels exposed to sale, as well as ancient and modern medals in such quantities as must surprise a man the first time he sees and considers them.[8]

Years of uninterrupted merchant trade, assisted by more than a decade of English piracy, had made London rich even by the standards of continental Europe.

> The wealth of the world is wafted to it by the Thames swelled by the tide and navigable to merchant ships through a safe and deep channel

for sixty miles from its mouth to the city: its banks are everywhere beautified with fine country seats, woods and farms.[9]

With all this wealth around, John was able to ensure that his business was immediately successful. Less than two years after becoming a freeman, he took on his own first apprentice in 1594. He undertook to feed, clothe, lodge and train Richard Bragge for eight years,[10] and the apprentice's customary fee allowed him to look for a larger shop in the rapidly expanding western suburb of the city. Keeping a foothold in the centre at Bucklesbury, John established an apothecary shop on the south side of Ludgate Hill, just outside the newly restored city gate. This area was described as a ward of the city even though it was outside the walls. It was known as Faringdon Without and, together with Holborn to the north, it marked the western border between the rural county of Middlesex and the city.

There was huge pressure on land for development in this suburb of London. The fields and meadows that John had seen when he first arrived in the city were disappearing fast under rows of new terraced houses, or tenements, built to rent to the press of courtiers, scholars and tradesmen who found this area convenient.

Between it and the city was Smithfield, traditionally an open space where the cattle market, joustings and tournaments were held and horses watered at the large pond called Horsepool that was shaded by elm trees. But the elm trees had gone, and the market itself:

> remaineth but a small portion for the old uses, to wit, for markets of horses and cattle, neither for military exercises, as Justings, Turnings and great triumphes which have been there performed before the princes and nobility both of this Realm and forreigne countries.[11]

The former St Bartholomew's fairground next door, once protected by royal decree, had been swallowed up by the powerful demand for houses, though the fair was still held annually 'in a field around London'. Six or seven years after John first settled on Ludgate Hill, John Stow chronicled the disappearance of the last traces of the farmyard from this district. 'At the bottome of Oldbourne hill is Gold Lane, sometime a filthy passage into the fields, now both sides builded with small tenements.'[12]

The frantic pace of settlement brought benefits for John and Mary, despite the drawbacks of noise and smoke from Limeburners Lane where building lime was slaked. The streets were paved and had been recently relaid. There was a new conduit in Fleet Street, pumping sweet water to street level, built by the City in 1582 and the inhabitants had paid for another conduit to take away waste water, so it was a clean and comfortable area to settle in.[13]

A burgeoning class of medical and literary men lived in the neighbourhood. It was ideally placed between the rich aristocratic sponsors who had their 'palaces' on the Strand, running alongside the Thames to the Palace of Whitehall and Westminster, and city commerce. John's and Mary's near neighbours included many of the best men in London. There was the family of John White, well known for his pioneering journey to Virginia. There was Dr Henry Atkins, one of the examiners or Censors from the London College of Physicians. Dr William Harvey settled in the neighbourhood after marrying the daughter of another doctor there in 1604. The poet and preacher John Milton lived in the churchyard of St Bride's on Fleet Street. Added to this were the countless sons and daughters of gentlemen who served the nobility in their establishments dotted around, like Thomas Sackville in Salisbury House on Fleet Street, or Sir Christopher Hatton in Ely Place in Holborn. All in all, there were plenty of prosperous customers for an apothecary's perfumed waters, cosmetics and medicines.[14]

Ironically, in such a neighbourhood, John found his contacts with 'men of science' weaker than they had been in his days as an apprentice. His mentor, Matthias de l'Obel, who had become household physician to the English Lord Zouche, had left London in 1592, when his master was appointed ambassador to the court of Denmark. The English doctors were not so friendly.

The relationship between the apothecaries, the barber-surgeons and the physicians in England was a tortuous one. Together they represented the complete range of medical treatment available, and each was dependent, to some extent, on the other. But most English physicians had studied at Oxford or Cambridge. They came from a wealthier social class than either the apothecaries or the barber-surgeons, who were apprenticed. The European tradition was for apothecaries and physicians to train together. When the German doctor Felix Platter studied medicine in Montpellier in 1552, he was sent to a wealthy apothecary who was the son of a wholesale pepperer from Spain. Other German boys were learning the apothecary's trade there at the same time and they, Felix Platter wrote, 'shared his bed at different times'.

Such close proximity as students diminished the class divisions that persisted between the professions in London.[15]

Recently the twenty-four fellows of the London College of Physicians had taken steps to maintain their social superiority by deciding to penalize applicants who had cut financial corners. Their power lay in examining candidates who wanted to practise as doctors in London. They tested for knowledge of Galen, the Greek authority, for elegant or at least adequate Latin and Greek, and for evidence of a university education. In 1585 they voted to triple the membership fees for those

> who have left their own universities before the end of their courses to go abroad, where in unknown countries, in a shorter time and with less expense they take the doctorate degree which they were unable to follow at home in their own universities....[16]

Every fortnight the fellows would meet in a room at their house in Knightrider Street, near Smithfield Market. This house was used for meetings but also rented out to one of their members as a family home. It was an irony not lost on the Grocers that for all their education and individual wealth, the august body of doctors could not even afford its own hall. The College of Physicians had established the right to be the watchdogs of medical standards in London only in 1518. Compared to this, the Grocers could look back on 200 years of political manoeuvring and fundraising, and they now had far greater influence over City affairs than the doctors. Every year the Grocers' wardens and the Physicians' censors co-operated to tour the apothecary shops and check the quality of the goods being sold. Afterwards the apothecaries clubbed together to entertain the doctors to a dinner at their hall 'for such as did assist Mr Wardens when they searched simples and confections'. So it was there, once in the year at least, that the apothecaries enjoyed the precious satisfaction of showing off their Company's glittering silver plate to their guests, otherwise so quick to assume their social superiority.[17]

It was not only in the matter of City politics that the Grocers considered the Physicians irrelevant. Amongst themselves the apothecaries agreed that most physicians had little to do with tending the sick in the City of London either. Their care was too expensive. Although technically it was against the law, most people went to the barber-surgeons or to an apothecary's shop and bought a remedy over the counter when they were sick. John's early years in business, however, coincided with a concerted effort by the physicians to reassert the law that gave them control over medicine in the capital. In the summer of 1595, John's neighbour, Dr Henry Atkins, was one of the team of censors who checked the apothecary shops. He inspected John's shop and met him again as his guest at the Grocers' Hall dinner afterwards. So it was embarrassing for them both when, the following summer, John was peremptorily summoned to appear before the Physicians on a charge of 'practising'.

John was forced to leave his shop and make his way to Knightrider Street to answer the charge. The doctors had elected to wear scarlet gowns for the fortnightly meetings of their *Comitia*, instead of their usual purple ones, and black woollen or silk caps, to effect a more imposing presence. They insisted on using Latin throughout to further dignify their judgements and confound the miscreants who appeared before them. Arrayed in a group of twenty or so, they crammed together in the small front room to face their summoned victims.

When John was asked to stand up before them the clerk summarized the charge: 'Illicit practice against the law and equity; [and] of having extorted money from a woman who charged him even with the homicide of her husband.'

John had, of course, been mixing medicines for patients who came to his shop. One of these patients had died and his widow demanded the return of the money she had paid for his medicine. When John had refused, she reported him to the College of Physicians, forcing him to defend himself before the doctors.[18]

No one doubted that John had broken the letter of the law, but most apothecaries faced a charge of 'practising' at some point or another. In 1563, even so distinguished an apothecary as Hugh Morgan was fined for being an 'empiric', although this was before he became the Queen's Apothecary.[19] In the end the encounter did John's reputation no harm amongst the Physicians. On the contrary, this meeting with the senior doctors in the capital gave him a chance to show off his Latin and his thorough knowledge of the treatments he administered. Since his manner was courteous with everyone, the fellows' reaction to the charge against him was muted. Exceptionally, they recorded no discussion in the register, no fine and no punishment. John left the *Comitia* without shame and was never summoned to appear before them again.

The doctors were inclined to be lenient if the person before them showed any knowledge at all. At his first summons, a young man called Stephen Bredwell said he never practised medicine for money, but only for love of his sister and other close family. When he appeared again he confessed:

> that he has practised medicine here in London for four years. He was examined and his behaviour was unassuming and his answers were not without learning. He was fined 40s for his illegal practice ... and was advised to gain the good will and favour of the college by suitable and honest means in order that later he might be admitted as a Licentiate.[20]

Stephen Bredwell reappeared a month later and was licensed to practise as a doctor in London.

The Physicians had many far more serious cases, which frustrated their efforts to keep the extravagant side-effects of their remedies under control and establish public respect for their profession. A month earlier they had seen Nicholas Kelway, who confessed that he had applied ointment to a tailor, called Worcall, suffering from paralysis and a swelling of the feet.

> The wife of the man whose treatment he had undertaken said that he had given her husband one pill of mercury and, as he himself said, of powdered roots of Bryony and Laurel. The woman declared that her husband had vomited to such an extent that his basin became so full that it could not be rinsed out and kept dry; moreover due to this medicine his mouth had had an unpleasant smell, his tongue had become swollen, his teeth had fallen out and his saliva was forever running out of his mouth.... When he was examined regarding the ointment he denied that it had been mixed with mercury; it appeared however quite clearly when it was tested with gold that it had been made from mercury. Not only had he applied the ointment externally but he had administered it internally through the anus.[21]

Nicholas Kelway was fined and sent to prison.

Time and again the censors found themselves faced with toughened practitioners who refused to allow fines and the occasional spell in prison to get in the way of a profitable business. A woman called Scarlet declared she would by no means desist from practising medicine. When she was fined £10 and sent to the house of correction at Bridewell, she treated one of the wardens there, who in due course brought to the doctors his own complaint against her. Katherine Chaire forced the *Comitia* to communicate in English when she was summoned. She agreed with all the doctors' charges:

> She confesseth Mrs Bridgeman's husband gave her V li [five pounds] for a Tansy, and a purge with Sene [senna], and she gave I oz of that Sene.... she confesseth moreover that she has practised physick ever since Mrs Saunders was hanged. She confesseth likwyse that she had three cloths of Mrs Bridgeman; and sayth she can tell whether wemen be with child or no by washing clothes with red rose water and sope etc.[22]

Yet Katherine Chaire knew that the doctors had little power to stop her. The Physicians' personal influence with the aristocrats who were their patients and chief customers was a double-edged sword. They were cravenly submissive when their aristocratic customers intervened in their efforts to impose medical standards. Leonard Poe, who came before them described as a 'deacon from Lincoln', sought a licence in 1589 to practise in 'the French disease [syphilis], in fevers and in rheumatism. He was examined and found to be a completely ignorant man'. Nevertheless, he was able to summon an astonishing number of noble names to back his medical practice and soon afterwards the College received a letter from Lord Essex recommending him. They replied that they found him ignorant but, out of deference, re-examined him ten months later, even though it was known that such 'recommendations' were easily bought. This time Dr Poe 'replied to examiners' questions in English, which they made a point of, noting his unlearned status', and confessed to having practised in London for two years, saying he had cured many epileptics. When asked what epilepsy was he 'replied in English: It is a certaine water gathering about the cells of the hearte'. The doctors decided he should either pay a £20 fine or legal proceedings would be started immediately. But Poe was not easily beaten. He persuaded the College to give him 'a limited licence for these diseases only'. When further charges and complaints brought him back many times before the *Comitia*, they sentenced him to prison, but on 24 November 1598 they discovered that in spite of all their efforts and legal expenses, 'Dr Poe' had obtained a letter of protection from the queen's councillors which he 'had shown ... to each keeper of the prisons; he was bringing it out in public and as he walked about in the streets so that not one of the apparitors or prison officials dared to molest him'. This was not to be the last they heard of Dr Poe.[23]

Meanwhile John was facing similar problems with his own Company of Grocers. His business was growing fast enough for him to swear in a second apprentice, Thomas Nicoll, for nine years on All Saints' Day in 1597.[24] He was careful from here on to avoid complaints that would lead him into conflict with the Physicians, but he could not escape the wilful ignorance of his own fellow grocers.

It was much easier to become a confectioner or a general grocer than an apothecary. Robert Croggatt was fined 'for serving a part of his apprenticeship with a haberdasher, and also being made free before his time', but he was still able to become a grocer.[25] There were at least six or seven widows active in the Company at this time, who had not served any apprenticeship but like Mary Parkinson had simply been married to a freeman. All these people had the right to sell medicines. They made too much money from this practice to allow it to be restricted to the apothecaries in their Company. They could charge huge prices for effective medicines, and for plenty of ineffective ones. In 1602, John Clerk was selling 'one pint of cinnamon water at the price of five pounds'.[26]

Apothecaries were frustrated that the leaders of their Company seemed deaf to their appeals to restrict sale of medicines. Properly practised, their trade was the most scholarly and least profitable of all those the Grocers embraced, so they tended to have little impact within the Company. They were rarely invited to join the livery, or become wardens. By the 1590s, the influence of the former Queen's Apothecary, Hugh Morgan, within the Grocers' court had waned.

In 1588, four senior apothecaries had come up with the idea of a self-monitoring apothecaries' 'corporation' within the Company, which would keep a close check on standards. They presented a draft of this corporation to the wardens which was apparently 'well liked', but deferred for discussion 'until considered by the court of Assistants'. 'Long debating' of the issue led to a decision that some of the Company would meet to 'devyse the best meanes they can for reformation'.[27] This was an effective means of burying a thorny problem, and nothing more was heard of reform for over twenty years.

While the Grocers refused to take action, the need for controls had become acute in the face of a growing flood of imported plants. There was, for example, the question of the popular cure-all 'Venice or Genoa treakle'. Treacle had been imported for a long time, ready-made, from

Italy or Constantinople. Its principal ingredient was an allium called *Scilla alba*, which John called sea onion or squill. It was used, he said, 'wholly physically with us, because wee can receive no pleasure from the sight of the flowers'. Pythagoras dedicated an entire volume to the medical benefits of the sea onion, which has been lost, according to Hugh Morgan, who wrote a pamphlet in 1585 boasting that he could make 'treakle' as good as any from Venice or Genoa. It was widely acknowledged to be an effective remedy for toothache and running sores and for the general benefit of the lungs, head, heart, liver and spleen:

> therefore it is used as a principall ingredient into the Theriaca Andromachi, which we usually call the Venice Treakle. The Apothecaries prepare hereof, both Wine, Vinegar and Oxymel or Syrup, which is singular to extenuate and expectorate tough flegme, which is the cause of much disquiet in the body.[28]

Many English apothecaries sought to make their own 'Venice Treacle' in the 1580s, complaining that the imported variety was defective. The problem was that there was another kind of sea onion, the red squill, so deadly in its effects that when Clusius came across it in Spain he was forbidden to taste it, according to his custom when examining unfamiliar plants. This red squill was 'a most strong and present poison'. So any mistake in the composition of this popular medicine, whether innocent or deliberate, could be fatal. Eventually treacle was controlled. After 1587, the College of Physicians co-operated with the Grocers and produced a recipe that just one grocer apothecary, William Besse, was licensed to produce. Yet the cases that rolled in every fortnight for the Physicians to consider made it plain that many more controls were needed.

The Physicians' attempts to impose standards were resisted as much by their own members as by the Grocers. On 10 October 1589, the *Comitia* 'proposed, discussed and resolved to publish one uniform Pharmacopoeia or Dispensary of Prescriptions to be followed by shops'. The doctors agreed to split the vast range of usual medicines into groups, with several physicians in charge of each:

> 'Syrups, Juleps and decoctions' were to be compiled by 'Drs Atslowe, Browne, Farmery and Preest, Oils by Drs. Fryer, D'Oylie, Distilled waters by Drs Smith: Oxon, and Taylior; Liniments, Ointments,

Plasters & Cerates by Drs Forster and Atkins; Juices, Robs, Conserves, Medicated wines and Confections by Drs Smith, Cantab, Osborne, Hector Nones, and Dodding; Extracts, Salts, Metallic Chemicals by Drs Johnson, Langton, Muffet [Mouffet]; Powders and Marmalades by the Royal Physicians; Pills by Dr Gilbert, Dr Turner; Electuaries, Opiates and Eclegmas by the President [Dr Smith] and Dr Wilkinson; Lozenges and Eye Salves by Drs Marbeck and James.[29]

The doctors were confident the Dispensatory could be ready by the following Christmas. They intended to keep these medical recipes safe from the ignorant public by publishing in Latin, but even so there were problems. The first was that each prescription was a commercial secret. All the medical professions knew there was profit in compounding and mixing medicines for sale, and these profits proved too attractive to resist. Later that same year, the Physicians simply overturned one of their own statutes to make it legal for doctors to sell medicines that had hitherto been licensed only to apothecaries.

The second problem was that the apothecaries knew more about the ingredients of many medicines than the doctors did. The doctors agreed to broach this carefully: 'Since with regard to the apothecaries there would be certain points needing correction and amendment, all the Fellows were enjoined to give careful consideration to this matter.'[30]

However, the apothecaries were unwilling to cooperate. On his very first day as a freeman John had sworn, like all the rest, to keep the 'arte and mysterye' of his profession secret. 'The lawful secrets of the said fellowship I shall keep, and give none information nor instruction thereof to no person but of the said fellowship'. Given this situation, it was to be another thirty years before the first London Pharmacopoeia appeared.[31]

In spite of all the politics that surrounded his profession, John was busy establishing his business, and his family. By the turn of the century he and Mary felt secure enough to have a child, having waited eight years since their marriage, even longer than John's own parents. In the hundreds of pages that John wrote about the medicinal uses of plants, he showed a particularly profound knowledge of gynaecology. His familiarity with a vast range of remedies for women may have been gleaned initially from his mother, and added to in the course of his career, so that he became a known specialist in women's problems. Certainly he was able to put what he knew at the service of his own wife when she gave birth to their first child. The simplest remedy was the distilled water of lily flowers, used to bring on delivery, or horehound which was used as a poultice 'to speed delivery and the afterbirth'. For certain situations there was dried cyclamen, known as sow-bread root, which would accelerate the birth if the delivery turned out to be long and hard or dangerous. To prevent disasters afterwards, John used dried leaves of crowsfoot, or geranium, which was 'effectual to stay bleedings'.[32] Mother and baby emerged successfully from this birth, so that in February 1601, John's first-born son was delivered into his arms. They named the child Richard, after John's own brother and many of the elder sons in the Parkinson family.

Such a major family event finally drove John into the arms of the priests at the Grocers' church. He chose to attend regularly and to have Richard christened there, so that his son would be officially registered as the son of a freeman, with an automatic right to freeman status himself when he reached twenty-one. John had now not only achieved a status that no one in his family had held before him, but by sacrificing the niceties of his personal religious conviction, he would be able to pass this status on to his son.

John knew plenty of Catholics who worshipped in the Anglican Church, as the law now stated they must. Those who still refused to attend were called 'recusants' and forced to pay a fine for the privilege of staying away. Yet there were many others who were dubbed 'Church papists' who

> dissented from the Reformed Establishment in many points of doctrine, and still acknowledged the Pope's infallibility and supremacy, yet they looked not upon these doctrines to be fundamentals without which they could not be saved; and therefore continued to assemble and baptise and communicate ... in the Reformed Church of England.[33]

With this in mind, John could clearly see the benefit that joining the congregation of the Grocers' church would have for his reputation in the Company and for his family.

That year, and the next, he paid the churchwardens three shillings towards the puritan 'morning lecture'. He also paid a tithe, traditionally a tenth of his income. If John's dues were a true representation of the strength of his business, they meant that his income was £48 in 1602, a very decent sum for a young man in his early thirties.

However, worshipping at St Antholin's was not easy for John. It was useful politically, and he may have been genuinely interested in exploring the Protestant faith of his French and Flemish friends, but the vehement speech of these Puritans was intolerable. They spoke of Catholics as having 'given their names to Baal [the Devil]'. John's own mother, father, sisters and brothers were no devil-worshippers. The differences between Catholic and Protestant were drifting towards vicious extremes that John could not bridge. He stuck it out for another year until his second child, his daughter Katherine, was born.

In June 1603, John and Mary took Katherine to St Antholin's to be christened. But now everything was on the point of change. Later that year, when the churchwarden came to make his account, John Parkinson had gone. He would never again show his face in that parish church or any other church in London. Against his name in the accounts, the churchwarden entered nothing: 'nihil'.[34]

John had found a new interest that offered him an escape from the political problems hedging him in. His fascination with plants had taken a new turn, into the novel field of growing beautiful flowers for gardens. The more he learned about the skill of manipulating magnificent blooms, the more this delightful study fascinated him. The results he achieved brought him closer to the mysteries of God than did the rantings of any Protestant preacher.

CHAPTER EIGHT

THE GARDEN LABORATORY

The tiny *Mimosa pudica* that fascinated the English sailors when its leaves recoiled in response to their rough fingers succumbed to the jolting wind and waves on the long journey back to England. In London, George Clifford delivered it, dried and lifeless, into the hands of Jacques Garret, who kept it as a curiosity.

The new plants that flooded into London from all corners of the world came most often in the form of dried twigs and seeds, roots and bulbs. They presented John and any other conscientious medical practitioner in London with a challenge. The old master, Dioscorides, advised that 'it behoves anyone who desires to be a skilfull herbalist, to be present when the plants first shoot out of the earth, when they are fully grown and when they begin to fade'.[1]

It was clearly essential for any serious apothecary to keep a garden, where he could attempt to grow the plants he used and study them. Establishing a garden was an important part of John's plan for the future when he married Mary, and he began to keep one almost immediately. When he came to publish the *Paradisus* in 1629, he could look back on forty years of experience, or 'forty yeares of travaile', as he put it.

At first John's garden was a laboratory where he could explore for himself the truth of the fundamental tenets of Dioscorides. The master had advised:

We ought to gather herbs when the weather is clear, for there is a great difference whether it be dry or rainy when the gathering is made... Before all else it is proper to use care both in the storing up and in the gathering of herbs each in its due season, for it is according to this that medicines either do their work or become quite ineffectual.[2]

John could not effectively provide medicines without putting these principles to the test, and so far his ambitions were no different from those of the best apothecaries of his day, such as Hugh Morgan or Pierre Coudenberg.

Yet the range of plants John could experiment with was continually expanding, with the arrival of many from parts of the world that Dioscorides had never heard of. While John duly carried out experiments in the methodical way that de l'Obel had taught him, there were new skills he learned from his Flemish friends that filled him with excitement. John's garden had begun to capture his imagination and take over his life. He glimpsed in it the possibility of innovations that would bring about a revolution in English gardens.

When John was young, English gardens were not the spaces filled with tumbling natural colours that we associate with them today. They were nevertheless cherished, and in the overcrowded city of London brutal methods were sometimes used to acquire one. John Stow remembered how Henry VIII's secretary of state, Thomas Cromwell, had treated his own family. In the 1530s Cromwell built a house near Stow's father, by the London wall at Moorgate. When the house was finished he had, according to Stow:

> some reasonable plot of ground left for a garden, [but] he caused the pales [fences] of the gardens adjoining to be taken down, 22 foot to be measured right into the north of every man's ground, a line then to be drawn, a trench to be cast, a foundation laid, and a high brick wall to be builded. My father had a garden there, and there was a house standing close to his south pale; this house they loosed from the ground, and bare upon rollers into my father's garden 22 foot ere my father heard thereof.[3]

Thomas Cromwell had the kind of reputation that allowed no protest. Traitors' heads were still displayed on London Bridge. 'No man durst goe to argue the matter, but each man lost his land,' wrote Stow.

Though the English valued their gardens, their love of flowers was associated primarily with flowers in the wild. Roses and lilies had long held religious significance through the whole of Christendom, but in their homes the Elizabethans favoured the strange flowers of the humble borage plant, for example. They took it into their gardens to admire, put it in their food, and worked its multiple shades of blue and curious horned shapes into their needlework, so they could see it on their walls and wear it in their clothes.

The natural beauty of the English landscape was very striking, and the English allowed nature to run almost to their door, even around their palaces. Paul Hentzner was deeply moved by the view from Windsor Castle on his tour of England in 1598:

A walk of incredible beauty, three hundred and eighty paces in length, set round on every side with supporters of wood, which sustain a balcony, for when the nobility and persons of distinction can take the pleasure of seeing hunting and hawking in a lawn of sufficient space; for the fields and meadows, clad with variety of plants and flowers, swell gradually into hills of perpetual verdure quite up to the castle, and at bottom stretch out in an extended plain that strikes the beholders with delight.[4]

As the countryside receded from the expanding city, London's citizens put increasing amounts of their wealth into nurturing a private green space of their own. With so much natural abundance, a garden in sixteenth-century England was a place where nature was forced into clipped formality. Within its walls the wilderness of the countryside, which their parents and grandparents had struggled to control, was kept fiercely trimmed. The topiary at the royal garden in Hampton Court astonished visitors from abroad. Felix Platter, the physician from Basle, had a younger brother, Thomas, who came to England to complete his education. At Hampton Court Thomas saw plants treated in a way he had never encountered before:

There were all manner of shapes, men and women, half men and half horse, sirens, serving maids with baskets, French lilies and delicate crenellations all round made from dry twigs bound together and the aforesaid evergreen quick set shrubs, or entirely of rosemary, all true to the life, and so cleverly and amusingly interwoven, mingled and grown together, trimmed and arranged picture-wise that their equal would be difficult to find.[5]

Paul Hentzner found the English way of clipping and training rosemary just as remarkable. 'We were led into the gardens which are most pleasant; here we saw rosemary so planted and nailed to the walls so as to cover them entirely, which is a method exceeding common in England.'[6]

In these grand gardens, privet, hyssop, rosemary and lavender, so familiar everywhere, were also planted in tight knots in the centre. The pattern they made, filled in with coloured stones or sand, was designed to be admired from above, from the large first-floor windows of the new Renaissance mansions, or from the more traditional raised walk that ran alongside. Many grand Elizabethan gardens were sterile places. The colour in them came not from flowers but from painted wooden statues and railings, or the soot and pebbles that filled the spaces between the shrubs.

The style of most urban gardens was much simpler and more familiar. A popular pamphlet by a Londoner called Thomas Hyll was printed in 1563. It was the first to appear in English:

Teachyng how to dress, sowe and set a Garden, and what properties also these few herbs here spoken of have to our comodytie: with the remedyes that may be used against such beasts, wormes, flies and such lyke, that commonly noy gardes [gardens].[7]

Hyll's text was printed again, in an enlarged version called *The Proffytable Arte of Gardening*, in 1568 with 'a number of Secrettes with the Phisick helpes belonging to eche herbe', a treatise on the care of bees, as well as a calendar of tasks 'meete for husbandmen to knowe'. This, and a later version called *The Gardener's Labyrinth*, was so popular that it was reprinted every six or seven years until 1608, appearing for the last time as late as 1651.

The pictures in these books show the London gardens John saw around him. They have a simple outside border, a quickset hedge, or, in later books, a brick wall. Inside, there is an arbour built into one side and plant-covered walks echoing the reflective cloisters of the monks' gardens that had now disappeared. Hyll calls this 'the vine herber'. The ideal gardens of his illustrations offered private householders a simple monastic close combined with the satisfying yield of a farmer's field.

Hyll's gardeners sit contentedly at benches and tables in the sunshine beside the trellis, sharing a jug of wine and the fruits from their trees with friends (see page 145). A circle of bowls lies abandoned in the shade of the vine herber after a game, while two men set to work digging and raking the small square beds. The plants they grow reflect the household cook's needs: 'Lettis; Endive; Bleet; spinage; ...leeke; onions; garlicke; great garlicke', and many herbs, including 'Parcelye; Savery;

'The maner of watering with a Pumpe by troughes in a Garden', from Thomas Hyll, Gardener's Labyrinth, 1577.

Alisander; Fennell; Annis; Cummine; Coriander'. A few flowers besides are treasured for their scent: lilies, violets, roses, carnations, and the gilliflowers that we would call pinks.[8]

The chief attraction in the garden, whether large or small, was a fountain. In an age before piped water, the business of getting enough water to the plants took careful thought and expense. In one of Thomas Hyll's books, a couple preside calmly over a garden that has been given over almost entirely to irrigation. The lady of the house sits breastfeeding her baby, while her husband proudly displays a standing pump, erected exclusively to feed the network of channels surrounding every bed in the garden.

John now glimpsed the possibility of another kind of garden. He saw in the skills he was learning from the Flemish a potential feast of colour and form. If he could develop varied blooms that were adapted to the English climate, he could light up the sterile formality of Elizabethan flowerbeds.

When John began to garden, English knowledge of horticulture was in its infancy. Thomas Hyll, who called himself 'simple and unlettered', 'never having tasted of the learned laake but always rather rudely taught', quoted a lot of country lore for managing plants. If artichoke seeds were soaked in rose water, or lily juice, or oil of bays before planting, for example, then 'the fruits will yelde the same savour as the licuor in which the seedes were soked'.[9] 'Sowing, planting and grafting' were governed by astrological positions, much as Dioscorides had advised in his herbal.

John's childhood experience contradicted this accepted piece of folklore, and he was inclined to subject it to the experimental methods that he applied to medicinal herbs. He sympathized with Fulke Greville who, even in 1566, published a pamphlet castigating Hyll's advice: 'Good dayes to sowe and plant, I thinke be when the earth is moderately moistened, and gentilly warmed with the heat of the sonne.' If those conditions were met, he argued, then the position of the constellations was 'as much healpe unto the sedes as it was ease for the Camell when the Flye leapt of from his backe'.[10] The truth, one way or the other, had so far not been proved, but John thought it was important to put this and a host of other 'old wives' tales' to the test.

The experiment that most fascinated John, which he had learned from Jacques Garret and John de Franqueville, was the long and painstaking process of growing tulips from seed. He discovered that after four or five years of patient work with the seed from the mother flower he could produce tulips with a fantastic variety of colour and display.

John's method was to sow the seed at the end of October, 'after they be thorough ripe and dry'. Each of the first few years, an ever thicker leaf would appear from the seed, until in the fourth or usually the fifth year after planting the seed, a second leaf breaking out from the first came as 'a certain sign that it will bear a flower'.[11] In the 1590s John's family and friends shared the excitement of waiting for those first seeds to flower. His years of care and patient experiment were rewarded with a glimpse of perfectly unique blooms, quite unlike their mother flower, since tulips never grow true from seed. The special beauty of these flowers was the first fruit of the natural alchemy that John was learning to master.

By the time John wrote the *Paradisus*, in 1629, he could list 125 'varieties' of tulips, many of which he had grown personally in this way. He was confident that he had matched and excelled the skills of Clusius, famous in the 1580s for his fifty varieties of tulip. John was still an apothecary, but he had become by then also a famous florist, renowned for the 'miracles' he achieved with flowers. He had developed similar methods to create new varieties of daffodil, fritillary, auricula, and his personal favourite, French anemones.

Like most of his generation, John loved colour. The wealthy noblemen and merchants he knew commissioned hangings of bright colours to hang on their walls, and wore their wealth in coloured silk or velvet waistcoats and dresses delicately embroidered with trailing roses and honeysuckle. John admired those coloured cloths that shone in the winter sun like the beautiful stained-glass windows of St Paul's Church at the top of the hill above his shop. But he was working on another

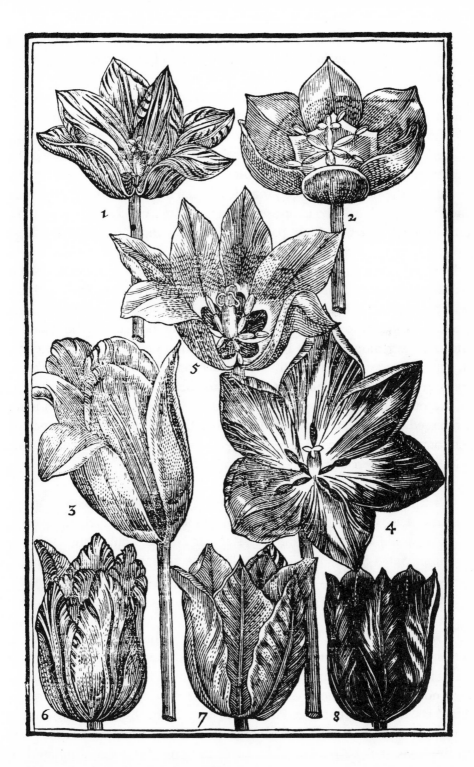

Tulips, illustration from Paradisus, *1629*

source of colour. He was beginning to grow a tapestry in the garden. All the natural shades available in plants seemed to him miraculous in their variety, and he was just discovering their range.

He was working on a method of extending the flowering season of anemones, planting some of his 'roots' in February, instead of the usual planting month of August, so that he could have anemones continuously flowering for several months before their usual season. And he crossed the seed to increase the range of colours: 'There is so great diversity in the colours of the flowers of these broad leaved anemones or windflowers that their range can hardly be expressed.' There was the violet purple anemone, and another violet 'a little paler and tending more to redness whose flowers have many white lines and stripes'. There was 'rich crimson red'; 'blood red'; 'scarlet'; 'another whose flower is of a pale whitish colour, tending to gray, such as the monks and Friars were wont to wear with us, and this we call A Monk's Grey' and 'another whose flower is of a lively flesh colour, shadowed with yellow, and may be called The Spanish Incarnate Anemone'.[12] Such intense appreciation of the subtle differences in their colours was as though he saw each one through one of the novel magnifying lenses that had just come into use.

No other Englishman pursued the business of raising prize anemones from seed with such dedication. To his irritation, John could not persuade his countrymen to take pains in sowing anemone seed 'as divers hath done with Tulips', whereas in the Low Countries, he pointed out:

> Their industry hath bred and nourished up such diversitiès and vari-
> eties, that they have valued some Anemones at such high rates as
> most would wonder at, and none of our Nation would purchase, I
> think. And I doubt not, if we would be as curious as they, but that
> both our air and soil would produce as great a variety as ever hath
> been seen in the Low Countries.[13]

It was Matthias de l'Obel who had opened John's eyes to the possibilities for English gardens. De l'Obel lamented the damage that the wars had brought to his country, because, he enthused in an outburst of patriotic nostalgia, his fellow countrymen were so clever and industrious. Matthias believed that the Flemish occupied the highest rung of the botanical arts 'in excolenda re herbaria'.[14] He had expressed this view in the book that he published in 1576, the one that John annotated so copiously, which featured many plants solely for their beauty in gardens. In spite of the poor climate, it was impossible to find any kind of plant his countrymen could not raise and grow. Moreover his friends and compatriots, Clusius and Pierre Coudenberg, had brought plants at great personal expense from Greece, Spain, Italy, from different parts of Asia and Africa, from Constantinople and even from the New World.

No one had so far assembled such a great collection in England. The few samples that William Turner had brought back from Europe seemed scanty beside the riches that were now available. It seemed as though history had handed John a great opportunity. His own love of plants was deepened and enriched by his Flemish friends, who had been driven to London by political circumstances. The war with Spain had opened up the world to English sailors and turned the port of London into the most important destination in northern Europe, beside Amsterdam. Moreover, as John's fellow countrymen grew wealthier they seemed prepared to invest more and more of their riches in creating beautiful gardens. John discovered a mission to add to his apothecary business that filled him with joy. It would be to supply these wealthy new gardeners with the finest flowers that could be grown.

A few Englishmen had already created spectacular gardens. The most famous private estate of the day was Lord Burghley's, the house called Theobalds that he built in Hertfordshire. Theobalds captured the imagination of his contemporaries because its fantastic structures perfectly expressed Elizabethan national pride. Paul Hentzner's party made a special detour from London 'in order to see the remarkable places in its neighbourhood. The first was Theobalds, belonging to Lord Burleigh, the Treasurer. In the gallery was painted the genealogy of the Kings of England.'[15]

William Cecil's 'gallery' was a long covered walk that echoed the cloisters of the old monasteries from which the English nobility had taken so much of their wealth. The English were now turning to their gardens to supply the spiritual peace they had lost in the Reformation. Cecil was a self-made man and a Puritan. He kept the 'walk', but replaced the religious themes of the past with his nation's history, having no remarkable family history of his own to look back on. His gallery led through to a wonderfully extravagant summerhouse, his tribute to the statecraft of ancient Rome:

We were led by the gardener into the summer house, in the lower part of which, built semi-circularly, are the twelve Roman emperors in white marble, and a table of touchstone; the upper part of it is set round with cisterns of lead, into which the water is conveyed through pipes, so that fish may be kept in them, and in summer-time they are very convenient for bathing. In another room for entertainment, very near this, joined to it by a little bridge, was an oval table of red marble.[16]

The summerhouse was used for the open-air feasts and entertainments that were a regular feature of English life in the summer. Hentzner's party arrived on 4 August, but found no feasting. The whole estate was deserted. The household was in London, attending the old man's funeral.

Paul Hentzner was a lawyer, with a dim appreciation of flowers, so he could only hint at the fact that Lord Burghley's garden was also a testament to his lifelong interest in plants. 'Bookes he loved, but after bookes, his Garden was his chiefe pleasure',[17] wrote one contemporary account of him. As a young man, Cecil had learned from William Turner when they both worked for the Duke of Somerset at Syon Park. His interest in collecting rare plants was apparent from the variety that grew in the garden at Theobalds, between the summerhouse and the gallery. Hentzner's vague account is the only description that survives.

The garden [was], encompassed with a ditch full of water, large enough for one to have the pleasure of going in a boat and rowing between the shrubs; here are a great variety of trees and plants, labyrinths made with a great deal of labour, a jet d'eau, with its basin of white marble, and columns and pyramids of wood and other materials up and down the garden.[18]

William Cecil passed on his enthusiasm for plants to others in his circle. Lord Edward Zouche, who had hired Matthias de l'Obel as his household physician, was a former ward of Cecil's. His purpose in recruiting the distinguished scholar was that he should supervise the 'Botanical Garden' he wished to establish at Hackney. In 1585, when de l'Obel settled his family in Highgate and began to work for Lord Zouche, his employer was twenty-five, and four years into spending the large fortune his father had left him. He had travelled through Europe, like many young English gentlemen, but, unlike most he also went to Constantinople as the queen's ambassador. The formal Muslim gardens he saw there captivated him, particularly their dense beds of tulips, irises and lilies, glittering like scented jewels beside the fountains that formed their centrepiece, and he wanted to transplant the whole effect to London. The bulbs were well known in western Europe, though still hardly grown in England. There were other delicate beauties that Lord Zouche had never seen before, such as the early blue-flowered hyacinth that he carefully carried from Constantinople to flower in his garden in England.

Lord Zouche's estate near London was then close to the pleasant village of Hackney on the hills to the north of the city, fast becoming one of its most sought after country suburbs. Wealthy London merchants settled their families there to protect them from the smells and fumes of the overcrowded city that they feared might otherwise ruin their health. In the last fifteen years of the sixteenth century the village acquired what must have been the first Muslim-style garden in the country. Lord Zouche was not a patient man. While John Parkinson and Jacques Garret laboured for years over tulip seed to produce a single variety, he, with de l'Obel's help, specialized in transplanting mature trees. He was reputed to have successfully transplanted fruit trees, probably pomegranate and crab apples, as much as thirty and forty years old.[19]

In the first years of the seventeenth century, de l'Obel recorded the exotic imports from Constantinople that Lord Zouche had brought into this garden. In retrospect they seem a small beginning: the hyacinth; two small white tulips, a winter crocus and a *colchicum*. There were a number of lilies, however, which were dazzling harbingers of what was to come. What de l'Obel called 'the radiant lily', on account of its 'blazing beauty', delighted owners and visitors alike by producing 200 flowers in the first season that it was grown in Hackney, according to de l'Obel, although 'in subsequent years it returned to its nature'. John Parkinson was one of the onlookers who took careful note of this plant's remarkable charm.[20]

Plans for the Hackney botanical garden were interrupted in 1592 when Lord Zouch left England as ambassador to the court of Denmark, with de l'Obel by his side. When they returned four years later, the garden was revived and the few exotic species it sheltered were the first signs of a spectacular garden revolution that was approaching.

Lord Zouche's gardeners must have withered under the direction of the superior Flemish scholar whom their master had put in charge. Not many of John's English contemporaries found de l'Obel as engaging as he did. John was not alone in his ambition to hold the most intriguing collection of plants in England, and many of his competitors were unimpressed by

John Gerard holding his symbol of modernity, the 'Potato's of Virginia', from an engraving by T. Berry, frontispiece to his Herbal, 1597.

de l'Obel's claim that Flemish horticultural knowledge was superior to English.

The individual who held the crown for the best garden of exotic rarities in London in the 1590s was John Gerard. Gerard was about twenty years older than John. He was established as a citizen and surgeon of the city by the time John was starting out. He had travelled abroad as a naval surgeon. The barber-surgeons were proud of the way their members gave medical care to men on royal ships, unlike the city's physicians, who refused to sail. Gerard had travelled to Finland and Moscow including 'Denmark, Swenia, Poland, Livonia, or Russia, or any of those cold countries'. When he returned he became a *protégé* of William Cecil, supervising his gardens for over twenty years.[21]

Gerard had much in common with John. He came from Nantwich in Cheshire, only two days' ride south of John's birthplace. Like John, he retained the accent of the north-west of England and had grown up steeped in the distinct politics of the region. John Gerard was just as closely familiar with the tensions between Catholic and Protestant as John Parkinson. His family was related to the Gerards of Ince in Lancashire, their Catholic household clearly marked on Lord Burghley's notorious map. One of the Lancashire Gerards later became a famous martyr for the faith, but by then his gardening cousin was long dead.[22]

Just as for John, plants were John Gerard's business, as well as his passion. A barber-surgeon was allowed to apply external medicines in his practice, although, in theory, only apothecaries were allowed to prepare them. In fact, Gerard's medical business depended on his knowledge of effective remedies to staunch bleeding and heal wounds, and he prided himself on his familiarity with native plants.

Gerard was also keen to be the first in England to grow exotic imports. He could often be seen down at the Exchange, haggling with the international crowd of merchants for new rarities to plant in his garden. One day he bought a root known as 'skirrets of Peru', or 'Batata': 'The potato's grown in India, Barbary, Spaine and other hot regions; of which I planted divers roots (which I bought at the Exchange in London) in my garden where they flourished until winter, at which time they perished and rotted.'[23]

The root was a sweet potato, not so uncommon in London by the late sixteenth century, but what distinguished Gerard from the merchant's other customers was his desire to plant it. Working for Lord Burghley, Gerard had access in other ways to the most exotic plant specimens to enter the country. He had much more success in his garden with another kind of potato, the common or garden variety, which came to him direct from Virginia: 'It groweth naturally in America, where it was first discovered, as reporteth Clusius, since which time I have received roots hereof from Virginia, which grow and prosper in my garden as in their own native country.'[24]

Gerard must have had this potato from the man who led the third British attempt to settle a colony in America, Captain John White, who set out in May 1587. To ensure the success of an American colony, Raleigh now offered each man who ventured his money or his life 500 acres of land there. A hundred and fourteen would-be colonists sailed with White that year. When he left them there and returned to London, he carried Virginian potatoes with him as a curious gift for the queen and the man who was always at her side, her chief counsellor, Lord Burghley. Naturally Burghley's garden caretaker, John Gerard, was eager to try them. His planting showed they increased wonderfully in a single season, and Gerard proudly chose this exotic plant to be his badge of honour.

For Gerard was steadily building his own collection of rarities in his private garden in Holborn, where Matthias de l'Obel, Jacques Garret and John Parkinson were frequent visitors. When de l'Obel came back from Denmark he went to see Gerard in his garden, and together they counted 1,033 species growing there, many of them previously unknown English plants. Gerard listed them in a *Catalogus* for publication, but he knew that a garden would hardly outlive him, and he was seeking something more enduring through which to make his name.

> Because gardens are private and many times finding an ignorant or a negligent successor, come soon to ruin, there be that have solicited me, first by my pen, and after by the Press to make my labors common and to free them from the danger whereunto a garden is subject.[25]

Gerard was an ambitious man. His ideas were ahead of his time, even if they were also sometimes ahead of his abilities. After publishing his catalogue, he chanced upon what he knew was a historic opportunity.

He was famous in London for his knowledge of native plants. His friend George Baker, the queen's chief surgeon and master of the Company of Barber-Surgeons, once sent him out with a French visitor, scouring the fields for plant samples, or 'simples', in a sort of patriotic trial of strength:

> I do not think for the knowledge of plants that he is inferior to any: for I did once see him tried with one of the best strangers that ever came into England.... He being here was desirous to go abroad with some of our herbarists ... and one whole day we spent therein, searching the most rarest simples, but when it came to the triall, my Frenchman did not know one to his fower.[26]

Naturally, the Frenchman was at a disadvantage, being on unfamiliar soil, but when a printer called Dr Norton found himself with an unfinished book on plants, Gerard seemed the right man to turn to. Norton had commissioned a translation of a herbal by Rembert Dodoens, a Dutchman who published it in Latin in 1552; it was translated into Dutch in 1587. The English translation was almost completed by the physician in charge of 'Syrups, Juleps and decoctions' for the proposed *Pharmacopoeia*, Dr Priest, when he died suddenly, so Dr Norton asked Gerard to finish it.

Gerard took on the job with enthusiasm, adding touches that were the outcome of his own personal experience and that of his wife, whose snippets were 'mainly for women'. This combination spiced up many of the entries and ensured the book's popularity. The medicinal qualities of monk's rhubarb (*Rumex sativus*), for example, included a glittering description of its cosmetic attributes:

> If you take the roots of Monks Rhubarb and red madder, each half a pound, Senna four ounces, Anise seed and Licorice of each two ounces, Scabious and agrimony of each one handful; slice the roots of the Rhubarb; bruise the Anise seed and Licorice, break the herbs with your hands and put them into a stone pot called a stean with four gallons of strong ale, to steep or infuse the space of three days, and then drink this liquor as your ordinary drink for three weeks together at the least, though the longer you take, so much the better, ... being always careful to keep a good diet: it purifieth the blood and makes young wenches look fair and cherry-like.[27]

Gerard's *Herball* was published in 1597, and he was pictured for the frontispiece holding the flowering potato in his hand. In spite of its 1,630 pages, the book was an instant success. In a foreword George Baker marvelled at the range of plants that Gerard had been able to include:

> There you shall see all manner of strange trees, herbs, roots, plants, flowers, and other such rare things that it would make a man wonder, how one of his degree, not having the purse of a number, could ever accomplish the same.[28]

There had been no complete herbal in English since the work of William Turner thirty-five years before. The variety of plants and vegetables that had become available or that had been rediscovered in England since then had grown out of all recognition. More and more people, particularly women, had, like Margaret Clifford, seen how they needed to take responsibility for growing and distilling their own plants for the household's use. This book gave them the knowledge they needed, much of it with charming descriptions of places and plants that were familiar to them. Best of all, it was in English, and opened a world of knowledge to 'gentlewomen' and their untutored husbands, the many newly prosperous merchants and farmers.

There was only one problem. Much of the information in the book was untrue. The enthusiastic reception and later fame of the book concealed some fundamental flaws. The reason that Gerard had been able to conjure the variety his friend George so admired was that many of the plants were specimens he had not seen. Gerard had little respect for Dodoens's methods and was personally more inclined to fantasy than truth. He broke the cardinal rule of this age of discovery, that truth must be tested through personal experience or experiment, and reverted instead to the medieval method of mixing fact and fable, which proved extremely popular and repaid him handsomely.

He never revealed to his readers that his book was a translation of work by a well-known Flemish scholar. He himself admitted that he did not know enough Latin to do a translation, and the initial results must have been very strange. Jacques Garret read the opening chapter on grasses when Gerard had it ready for the printer and found it full of serious mistakes. At Garret's suggestion, Dr Norton brought in Matthias de l'Obel to supervise and save the book.

This should have been a perfect combination, the scholarly Flemish botanist and the experienced English gardener. They had worked together before and were on cordial terms. But the relationship quickly turned explosive and ended abruptly in furious acrimony. De l'Obel corrected the manuscript 'in a thousand places', he wrote later, but there were many other mistakes that Gerard would not allow him to alter, 'alleging it was sufficiently correct and that de l'Obel had forgotten the English language'.[29]

When the book was published, de l'Obel decided for some reason to keep his feelings to himself. In fact he contributed an enthusiastic foreword in Latin to sit beside Gerard's other tributes. But he never forgot or forgave him. It was most likely that Gerard's stubborn refusal to pursue truth offended him more than the man's slurs on his inadequate English, but, for the time being, de l'Obel kept his powder dry.

John would have been intensely interested in Gerard's book, which so closely mirrored his own ambitions. Since he was close to everyone involved, he was able to follow the arguments blow by blow, and found himself caught in the middle. He was personally committed to de l'Obel's approach, having long ago adopted the principle that empirical truth was the only way to advance knowledge. Yet he must also have admired Gerard's practical gardening skills, and seems to have been fond of the older man. He never attacked Gerard in print, except with gentle hints that he was not entirely truthful. By the time John wrote the *Paradisus*, Gerard was long dead and the story of his clumsy plagiarism was widely known. Yet, unusually for his day, John proffered only the mildest criticism, such as this comment on a mysterious double white clematis that made its first appearance in Gerard's herbal. 'Master Gerard in his herball maketh mention of one of this kind [clematis with double white flowers], which he saith he recovered from the seed was sent him from Argentine ... but I never saw any such with him.'[30]

More important for John was the fact that Gerard's book blazed a trail. Its popularity showed him what a great opportunity had been missed. There was a powerful market for the latest information about botany and horticulture in English. A book like this needed to be written by someone who understood and respected the new scientific method, unlike Gerard. The author should be an English native, in touch with the public, and an experienced gardener, not a remote scholar, like de l'Obel. The author should be, in fact, someone exactly like himself.

The appearance of Gerard's herbal at the close of the sixteenth century deepened John's ambition to lead this English horticultural revolution in the right direction. As a first step in establishing his credentials, it was essential for him to make a bigger and better garden.

The city had grown so fast by 1597 that its polluting air stifled the garden behind his shop on Ludgate Hill. He found that his beloved anemones, in particular, 'will never thrive well [if] annoyed with the smoke of Brewers, Dyers, or Maltkilns'.[31] Even John Gerard's garden, in the fashionable suburb of Holborn, was quickly becoming engulfed by the city overspill. Hugh Morgan had a country house and garden by this time, in the village of Battersea on the other side of the river, and John envied the way his plants flourished in the clean atmosphere. He even saw there, on one of his infrequent visits, a rare and precious Judas tree that Morgan was able to grow.[32]

The area John had his eye on for a new garden was the fertile seven-acre field to the west of the city, known as Convent Garden. The place was perfect for him. It had fertile soil and it was close to his home and shop on the western edge of London. It was even closer to the rich households that lined the Strand, a 'continual row of palaces belonging to the chief nobility of a mile in length' whose gardens ran down to the river's edge.[33] Such fine gardens needed the unique and curious plants that John intended to supply.

Convent Garden was still named after the Dominican nuns who farmed it before 1536, when Henry VIII gave it to his friend John Russell, the second Earl of Bedford. At the beginning of the seventeenth century, the Russell household used the field as pasture for their horses, and it was not available for rent. However, on its northern edge, separated from the Convent Garden field by a lane called Long Acre, was Elmfield. This field was held on a long lease from the Mercers' Company by William Cecil, Lord Burghley, Francis Russell's next-door neighbour. In 1597, Lord Burghley took out a new twenty-one year-lease that, when he died less than two years later, passed to his eldest son, Thomas Cecil.[34] John was aware of this because his kinsman, Roger Houghton, now had the important post of steward to the Cecils' London household. The Cecil and Russell families had a plan to develop the area jointly, and Roger Houghton was leading the negotiations.

Most likely this family connection was the key that delivered to John the use of two acres of Elmfield for his garden. John Parkinson and Roger Houghton were only distant cousins, but they had a common experience that made the bond between them stronger than simple kinship. Both had family members who were openly and defiantly Catholic. Each was distantly related to a notorious Catholic exile called Thomas Houghton from Preston in Lancashire. He had fled to the Jesuit College at Liège, in

French Flanders, which had a policy of training English Catholic priests before sending them home to operate underground as 'masse priests'. Each man was aware that this kinship implied to some that they were themselves potential traitors.

Antagonism towards Catholics in England was gradually deepening. Even in Lancashire, Catholics now stayed away from parish churches. Sir Richard Sherburn of Stoneyhurst served the queen there as a Justice of the Peace, but an intelligence report to the Privy Council in 1591 rudely described him as 'a temporizer' because 'his wife, children and family, for the most part, seldom come to church, and never communicate [take communion], and some of his daughters marryed and not knowne by whom, but suspected by masse priests'.[35]

Moderate or 'auncient' Catholics like John, who had grown up with the religion, kept to the old faith but were at the same time intensely loyal to the throne. It cannot have been easy for them to express the delicate balance of their patriotism in a society where religious extremes were so rapidly polarizing. No one would have understood John's dilemma better than Roger Houghton. He had also grown up in a Catholic environment, but for the last twenty years he had faithfully served an employer who, as secretary of state, pursued a ruthless policy of depriving intransigent Lancashire Catholics of their lives and estates. Roger Houghton would have been inclined to look beyond John's religion and promote his evident talents. Since Thomas and Robert Cecil both valued horticultural skills as highly as their father did, Houghton's recommendation of John's ability as a gardener must have helped him secure the plot of land that eventually made his name.

CHAPTER NINE

THE WORLD
IN A GARDEN

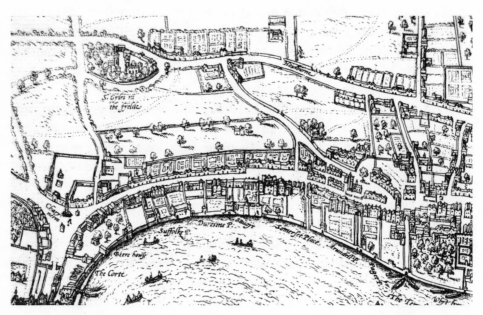

Map of Whitehall and Covent Garden showing 'the great field anciently called Long Acre' referred to by John Stow in his Survey of London. The map, by Braun & Hogenberg, was published in Cologne in 1572 but drawn before 1561.

John reached his new garden by turning north at Charing Cross at the end of the Strand, between St Martin's church in the fields to his right, and the royal stables on his left, then turning right again along the neglected country road known as Long Acre that led out to the north-east. His garden plot was two acres of the field a little way along on his left.

The first task he faced was to turn these two acres of virgin pasture into ground suitable for a delicate range of exotic plants. He would hardly achieve this in a hurry, but he was a persistent man. To keep the plot safe from cattle and other marauders and shelter it from 'many injurious cold nights and dayes, which else might spoyle the pride thereof in the bud', John preferred 'such helpes of bricke or stone wals to defend it, or by the helpe of high grown and well spread trees, planted on the North side thereof, to keepe it the warmer'.[1] However, this was an expensive way to begin, and he could not wait until he had the funds to build a wall. When his garden was mature, it would be enclosed by a wall, but meanwhile there was a cheaper way to protect it: a hedge of whitethorn and dog rose, 'enterlaced together, and Roses of one, two or more sorts placed here and there amongst them'.[2]

The new planting beds would be separated from the orchard with rows of household shrubs like 'Lavander, Rosemary, sage, southernwood', or plashed cornelian cherry trees. One innovation for making partition hedges in the garden particularly excited him. The *pyracantha*, or 'prickly Corall' tree would, he discovered, be

> an ornament to a Garden or orchard ... [making] an evergreene hedge or border, and when it beareth fruite, which are red berries like unto Hawthorne berries, make a glorious shew among the greene leaves in the Winter time, when no other shrubbes have fruit or leaves.[3]

The fundamental nature of the soil in his new plot made the task of turning it into a garden much easier. It was not the very best, which he considered to be the soil of parts of his native Lancashire: 'No man will deny, but the naturall blacke mould is not only the fattest and richest, but farre exceedeth any other either naturall or artificiall, as well in goodness and durability.' But he had the next best, that he held to be 'little inferiour', which was 'the sandy loame which is light and yet firme, but not loose as sand, nor stiffe like unto clay'. This kind of ground was easily improved with well-rotted horse manure, 'when it is old and almost converted to mould', while other, more tricky grounds needed very careful manuring.[4]

Like most of his contemporaries, John considered manure the essential beginning of any garden, and it could be surprisingly expensive to obtain. In 1598, when the Company of Grocers decided that their garden was inadequate, they paid as much as £3 8s 8d, more than three years' rent for some people, for '106 loads of dung used in the said garden'.[5] Considering that the stables and pens that produced this dung were all over the city, it was a substantial sum.

Garden plants, as opposed to wild ones, were described as 'manured' varieties. One of John's experiments was to work with different types of manure on different soils, so that eventually he developed the process of manuring into a science. This was another skill inspired by his Flemish friends. As late as the mid-nineteenth century, the English were learning from the Flemish how to manage manure. The Flemish counted ten sorts of manure and conserved 'anything that could be sold for profit'. The human variety was managed by a network of sworn brokers, who could 'evaluate the condition of night soil including the exact period of fermentation proper to each stage of a crop's growth'.[6]

John made a distinction between just two types of manure for gardeners, but the difference between the two was critical. Grounds that are 'over dry loose and dustie', like chalk and sandy soils, must have 'the manure of stall-fedde beasts and cattell, being buried and trenched into the earth, when it is thorough rotten (which will require twice the time that the stable soyle of horses will)'. Horse manure was for 'cold' clay ground.[6a]

This principle, of taking the 'temperature' of a soil and feeding it with its opposite, was very similar to his Galenic methods of treating patients. The results of this treatment for plants were often spectacular. The 'great white Spanish daffodil' that John grew, which came from the Pyrenees, had 'a round strong stalke about two foote high'.[7] His fritillaries, either the common sort or the blood-red, great purple, double blush or chequered yellow varieties, had stalks 'a foote, or a foote and a halfe high'. And the 'white lily of Constantinople' was more vigorous than the 'ordinary white lily' that was 'so well knowne and so frequent in every Garden'. 'For I have seene the stalke of this Lilly turn flat, of the breadth of an hand, bearing neere two hundred flowers upon a head, yet most commonly it beareth not above a dozen, or twenty flowers'.[8] This was the 'radiant lily' (probably *Lilium candidum*, the Madonna lily) that had once been the unique charm of Lord Zouche's garden, so admired that over the next thirty years it came to occupy pride of place in every garden.

Before he could grow such triumphant plants, John had to raise beds of manured soil in which to cultivate them. In places he used simple 'dead materials' to outline his beds: 'oaken inch boards' which 'must serve rather for long outright beds, or such knots as have no rounds', and will not last long, or tiles. Some people had 'the shank bones of sheepe' to deck out their gardens, which 'although they look not white the first year, yet after they have abiden some frosts and heates will become white and prettily grace out the ground'. These bones had to be 'well cleansed and boyled to take the fat out of them' before they could be used, yet John considered them more acceptable than the Flemish fashion for 'jawe-bones, used by some in the Low Countries and other places beyond the Seas, being too grosse and base'.[9]

The overall design of John's garden interested him much less than the plants. He did not seek to differ from the convention of planting a decorative knot in each bed to contain the specimen flowers like jewels in a casket. Yet he devoted considerable effort to finding the best plant to create these gardens of knots.

The oldest tradition was to use thrift (*Armeria maritima*), which had many disadvantages in John's view, although it was 'most anciently received':

It will not only in a small time overgrow the knot ... in many places by growing so thick and bushie that it will put out the forme of a knot but also much thereof will dye with the frosts and snowes in Winter and with the droughte in Summer ... the thickness also doth hide and shelter snayles and other small noysome wormes so plentifully that Gilloflowers and other fine herbes and flowers being planted therein are much spoyled by them.[10]

Germander (sp. *Chamaedrys*) was popular for the same purpose because cuttings from it were taken into the house and strewn on the floor to absorb dirt and damp, emitting a 'pretty and sweete' smell. Otherwise the design of the knots was traditionally made with marjoram, savory, or thyme. By 1629, 'Lavander Cotton' (*Santolina chamaecyparissus*) was a novel introduction that was used for this purpose 'for the most part in the gardens of great persons'. Juniper or yew were sometimes used, although they 'will soon grow too great and stubbed'. Given all the disadvantages of the traditional varieties, John was particularly pleased with the innovation that his Flemish friends had taught him how to manage. The best shrub for outlining knots, he concluded, is the 'small, lowe or dwarf kind, called French or Dutch Boxe', despite 'the want of a good sweet scent with his verdure'.[11]

Later he would pass on to his English readers 'a secret knowne but unto a few', for taming the hungry roots of box that grow sideways and steal nutrients from the plants that the shrub shelters. He advised them to take 'a broad pointed Iren like unto a slice or a Chessil, which thrust down right into the ground a good depth all along the inside of the border of Boxe somewhat close thereunto, you may therby cut away the spreading rootes thereof...'. Yet it is fair to say that in the years during which John first planted the beds in his Convent Garden, box edging was a very rare sight in England.

The absorbing work of planting hedges and planning beds and walk-
ways for the new garden had only just begun when John was interrupted
by a series of crises. First, at the end of May 1603, he had to assist Mary
with the delivery of their second child, the little girl they named
Katherine. Then, almost immediately, there were further demands on his
medical skills because of a serious bout of plague. The 'sicknesse' this
year actually began where John's garden was, in the country parish of St
Martin's in the Fields, but it quickly engulfed the western part of the
city where he had his home and shop.

These frequent episodes of plague in London posed a dilemma for any
apothecary. This was the time when John's services were needed most,
yet his new young family was in the eye of the storm. John regularly
protected his household against the possibility of plague by ensuring that
they drank, every day in May before breakfast, 'the water distilled from
the greater Valerian both herbe and roote'. He knew it was 'a good and
safe medicine in the time of the plague' and this year he had reason once
again to be thankful for this bitter remedy which did indeed keep them
safe.[12] Apothecaries had a reputation for staying in the city, protecting
themselves with the valerian root that they held to their nose, and
dispensing its distilled water, known as the 'poor man's remedye', to
as many as they could supply, while the physicians fled town with their
wealthy patients. The outbreak of plague in 1603 was particularly
virulent. By July, they were burying six or seven in a day in the
parishes of St Bride's and St Martin's, near John's Ludgate shop,
numbers they usually buried in a month. All through August the
numbers climbed, until by mid-September the sextons at St Bride's
were burying, on average, twenty-nine people a day.[13]

'The sicknesse' did not die with the hot weather as usual, but drifted
on all through the winter and disrupted normal life. The grocers' market
at Bucklesbury was temporarily closed. John took the chance to shut his
shop there and withdraw from the City, and, as it happened, he never
did business inside its walls again. A fundamental change was coming,
which would have a direct effect on his life in a way he could never have
predicted.

The old queen was dying, and the people braced themselves for
'Commotions'. Her heir was expected to be King James VI of Scotland,
though there were Catholics and some Protestants who hoped for an alternative. But, on 24 March, the very last day of the old year of 1603, the
queen was pronounced dead and the accession of King James to the

English throne was proclaimed 'in Cheapside with great joy and triumph'. The streets were thick with the crowds that turned out to hear the proclamation. Margaret Clifford's daughter Anne, now thirteen, remembered the universal sense of relief that greeted James as king. 'I went to see and hear. This peaceable coming in of the King was unexpected of all parts of the people.'[14]

The official 'Reception of His Majesty' and his Danish Queen Anne was held at Theobalds, where they were greeted by 'the Nobility and Gentry ... in exceeding rich equipage'. Robert Cecil offered the house as a temporary haven from the residue of plague in London and the nobility turned out in all their finery to meet the new king, because his favour could make or break them. Almost at once came the dramatic news that the most charismatic and powerful nobleman of them all had met his downfall. Gossip about Sir Walter Raleigh had reached King James long before he arrived in England. So the story was that when he was introduced to the man, 'said the King, O my soule mon, I have heard rawly of thee'.[15] Within months Sir Walter was convicted of involvement in a plot to put Arabella Stuart on the English throne instead of James. His estates were confiscated and he and his wife removed to the Tower of London.

Though Sir Walter was out of the way, the ideas he had planted were springing forward in a new age of commerce and expansion that this king was eager to promote. James enjoyed innovation and considered himself an intellectual. He had already written two books. One, *De Daemonologie*, on the best way to identify witches, he wrote in 1597, after extensive 'witch-hunting' in Calvinist Scotland. The other, *Basilicon Doron*, was a tract on the philosophical position of kings, intended for his eldest son, Prince Henry, but ultimately used as instruction for the second son, the weaker Prince Charles. In the first year of his reign in England, James found time to write and publish anonymously a *Counterblaste to Tobacco*, disgusted, as Paul Hentzner was astonished, to find his new subjects 'constantly smoking tobacco'.

Surveying his rich new kingdom, the king was delighted, on the other hand, with the fine houses and gardens of the English nobles. The broad open facades of the late Elizabethan houses, with their formal gardens for walking and taking the air, were a spectacular contrast to the severe Scottish castles he was used to. James had not long since been held captive in one of those castles and the experience had left a deep impression. He had taken to marking the day of his deliverance, every Tuesday, with a special church service.

King James was especially pleased with the stately style of Theobalds: its grand classical summerhouse, its curious plants, and the choice hunting in the woods on its estate. This first little piece of England made such an impression on him that he was keen to secure Robert Cecil's home for himself. By 1607 James had persuaded Cecil to make Theobalds over entirely to Queen Anne, in exchange for a neglected old royal palace at Hatfield.[16]

One of the people the king met in those first months at Theobalds was the Cecils' now famous garden manager, John Gerard. For some time Gerard had, like John, been trying to establish another garden. England had no national physic garden, where the rarest plants could be grown and studied, whereas Italy and Germany had such gardens, and Clusius was now in charge of one in Holland. Henri IV of France had recently asked his gardener, Vespasian Robin, to plant a garden near the Louvre Palace that is still called the Jardin des Plantes. With considerable foresight, Gerard felt that England needed a garden of this kind, and, with characteristic self-confidence, that he was the man to run it.

Around 1595 Gerard sent a petition to the University of Cambridge, meant to be signed by Lord Burghley, though in fact it never was, recommending himself as Herbarist for a new teaching garden:

> By reason of his travaile into farre countries, his great practice and long experience [he] is thoroughly acquainted with the generall and speciale differences, names, properties and privie markes of thousands of plants and trees. So yt if you intend a work [a physic garden] of such emolument to yrselves and all young students I shall be glad to have nominated and furnished you with so excellent a Herbarist.[17]

This scheme came to nothing, any more than similar proposals Gerard discussed with the London College of Physicians and the Company of Barber-Surgeons. However, this new king, so enchanted with Theobalds, presented an excellent opportunity, and Gerard lost no time in exploiting it.

The king was prodigiously liberal with titles and honours in his early days on the English throne. By 14 August 1605, Gerard had secured a lease on a plot attached to the royal palace of Somerset House in the Strand in which he was described as 'herbarist to the King's Majestie'. The house was given to Queen Anne for her household, and Gerard, according to this lease, was allowed to rent a part of the garden, in return for supplying the royal family with flowers and fruit.

> In consideration of the sum of five shillings of lawful money in the name
> of a ffyne to us beforehand payde by John Gerrard of London Surgeon
> and herbarist to the King's Majestie ... We are pleased to graunt unto the
> said John Gerrard one garden plot or piece of ground belonginge and
> adjoining on the east part to our mansion house called Somerset howse
> ...Yeelding also and answering yearlie to and for our owne use onely at
> the due and proper seasons of the yeare a convenient proportion and
> quantitie of herbes flowers or fruite renewing or growing wh in the said
> Garden plot or piece of grounde by the art and industrie of the said John
> Gerrard if they be lawfully required and demanded.[18]

This piece of paper, probably drafted by Gerard himself, like Lord Burghley's letter to Cambridge, was a singular triumph for the old surgeon. But having established a written reference to himself as 'herbarist to the King's Majestie', Gerard was never able to build on it. Within months the plot he leased had been transferred to Sir Robert Cecil, and, not long after, the ground was used for a summerhouse. Gerard went on to become master of his own barber-surgeons' company in 1607, but he had no further contact with the royal family. In the background, it seems, his erstwhile collaborator, Matthias de l'Obel, was quietly easing him out of the way.

The appearance of a Danish queen of England was a magnificent opportunity for de l'Obel, and his employer Lord Zouche. De l'Obel and Zouche were among the few men in England familiar with the queen's homeland, although they had arrived at her brother's court two years after she married James and departed for Scotland. In London, Edward Zouche quickly became 'a courtier and drolling favourite of King James'.[19] De l'Obel, as former physician to Prince William of Orange, impressed the queen with his first-rate European credentials, and the king with his scholarship.

Matthias de l'Obel began work on another book, *Stirpium Illustrationes*, in the introduction of which he described himself as '*botanographi Regii eximii*', botanist to the most distinguished king. He was confident he had won favour on a higher level than Gerard. In his eyes, no doubt, a '*botanographus*' was a writer about plants, a scholar, rather than the mere gardener that the English 'herbarist' implied.

The king loved to entertain scholars, and regularly discussed their work. Matthias would have been on hand for consultation when he was considering how to use knowledge of plants to enrich the kingdom. In 1606, James ordered every county town to take delivery of 2,000 mulberry trees. The English countryside needed to replace its main export, as the woollen broadcloth that had once been sent all over Europe was losing favour. The imported mulberry trees were to be sold to the population cheaply, at the rate of three farthings the plant or six shillings the hundred, in an attempt to found a silk industry in Britain. This brave gesture was foiled by the English climate. White mulberry trees, favoured by silkworms, do not thrive in Britain. There was some confusion as to whether the king's order applied to white or to black mulberry trees, which were hardy and cheaper. 'Some are confident that the leaves of the black will do as much good as the white: but that respect must be had to change the seed, because therein lies the greatest mysterie',[20] wrote John diplomatically in 1629. It was clear to him then that silkworms have no use for black mulberries, and by this time, few remained of even the 500 trees that Robert Cecil had planted at Hatfield in 1608 to please the king.[21]

James must have seen the long and bristling footnote that destroyed Gerard's reputation in de l'Obel's manuscript of his new book.[22] In it he told the whole story of Jacques Garret's intervention in the preparation of Gerard's herbal, of his own role, and subsequent mistreatment. Gerard, said de l'Obel, is no more than an ignorant plagiarist. He never finished this book or published it, but it served his purposes. From this point until his death in 1612, John Gerard disappeared from public life.

Meanwhile de l'Obel refreshed his scholarly reputation by publishing at his own expense another edition of his famous book on plants, *Stirpium Adversaria*. It formed part of a complete edition of his works, *Opera Omnia*, which appeared in 1605. This volume was chiefly valuable for the fact that it was signed by the king, who referred to de l'Obel as '*botanographi nostri*', our botanist, on the title-page. Otherwise the only new material was in a few descriptions of new decorative plants. The 156 pages on the 'pharmacologie' of de l'Obel's teacher, Rondelet, harked back to the early sixteenth century and looked distinctly out of date, even though de l'Obel's central point, that the old herbal 'authorities' like the Italian Matthiolus had failed to observe nature directly, was still highly relevant.

From John's point of view, however, this edition possessed one feature that made it immeasurably precious. This international scholar, in such high favour with the king, now gave his young friend a great gift. He recognized John's collaboration with him in such glowing terms that he seemed to be crowning him his only worthy successor. De l'Obel called him '*D.I.Parkinson perbonus et honestissimus Pharmacopoeus Londinensis, Stirpium materiaque Medicae studiosissimus*', which translates as 'Master John Parkinson, the most excellent and honest of London apothecaries, and the most excellent scholar of the medicinal properties of plants'. John was credited with cultivating a yellow 'daisy' which he had had from Italy, studying its medicinal properties and distributing its seeds among his friends. This plant was one of the *trollius* species that John later described as a globe-flower from the mountains around Naples. John is also congratulated for contributing a picture of the 'Alexandrian bay' tree he has grown, a unique introduction that was the delicate rose-flowered oleander, cultivated from a seed he received from Pisa.[23]

No other official record confirms de l'Obel's claim that he was the king's botanist. He was now an elderly man of sixty-seven, unable or unwilling to write much, and preoccupied with fostering the fortunes of his family. He managed to do this remarkably well. The king had appointed a Scots apothecary, John Clavie, at a fee of forty pounds a year for life. However, de l'Obel's sons-in-law, Lewis Lamere and John Wolfgang Rumler, were able to 'sublet' the work at a fee of five pounds a year each.[24] Secure in the knowledge that he had all the connections he needed at court, de l'Obel retired to live at Highgate with his daughter by his English wife. This daughter was married to another of John's Flemish friends, the merchant named James Cole who had given him a bush of 'a most excellent shining green colour' that he had obtained from Constantinople. Cole protected this shrub from frost in the winter by wrapping it up in a blanket, and it adapted so successfully to the severe English climate that it lived to grace half the gardens in the country. John called it the bay or cherry laurel.[25]

Notwithstanding de l'Obel's flattering praises, John was barely a familiar of the royal court in 1606. He was much more absorbed in building the collection of plants in his garden and conscientiously noting their habits. One Sunday in May that year, as the weather grew warm and sunny, he set off along the Fleet canal towards the Thames on one of his many plant-hunting missions. He had heard news that Mr Richard Barnsley of Lambeth had a rare plant that was in flower. It was one that

John grew himself, but no one he knew had ever seen it flower. He hailed one of the ferry barges that plied back and forth from Blackfriars steps all day, and climbed out ten or fifteen minutes later on the opposite bank, just upstream of Lambeth Palace. The little village of Lambeth was in the opposite direction from the palace, and the Barnsley household would have been easy to spot by the press of curious visitors who had come to see Barnsley's flower.

Once in the Barnsley garden, John was treated to the sight of a long stem covered in clear blue flowers, 'every flower standing outright with his stalke, and spreading like a starre'. The plant flowered like a hyacinth and John grouped it with this species, calling it the Woolly Hyacinth or Eriophorus. It 'hath been sent divers times out of Turkie', he wrote. 'It continued a long time as well in my Garden as in others, but some hard frosty winters caused it to perish with me ... yet I have had it again from a friend and doth abide fresh and greene every year in my garden.' Luckily for Mr Barnsley his flower bloomed for a long time, so that many of his friends and neighbours were able to see it. Sadly, it was to be an isolated moment of glory. 'Neither he, nor anyone else in England that I know, but those that saw it at that time, ever saw it beare flower, either before or since.'[26]

'The woolly hyacinth', Scilla hyacynthoides, *illustration from* Paradisus, *1629*

John had many other friends on the south side of the river whose interesting gardens he could visit. Vincent Sion, another Flemish man, lived in the rough area round Bankside, where Londoners gathered for bear-baiting and the daily theatre performances that were so popular.[27] John knew Vincent as a friend of the de Franquevilles, and 'an industrious and worthy lover of faire flowers'. It was the characteristic industry and honesty of John's Flemish friends that so appealed to him. He would defend them at every opportunity against the bombast of his own countrymen, who so often belittled the Flemings contribution to England. When 'Mr George Wilmer of Stratford Bowe, Esq.', a merchant from the east side of London, laid claim to a new kind of daffodil, John set the record straight. This flower, which by 1629 was widely referred to as 'Mr Wilmers great double daffodil', was in fact grown by Vincent Sion, who

cherished in his garden for many yeares without bearing any flowers until the year 1620, that having flowred with him, (and he not knowing of who hee received it, not having seen the like flower before) he sheweth it to Mr John de Franqueville of whom he supposed he had received it (for from beyond Sea he never received any) who finding it to be a kind never seene or knowne to us before, caused him to respect it the more.[28]

Vincent Sion gave or sold some offsets of this bulb to John as well as to Mr Wilmer who 'would needs appropriate it to himselfe, as if he were the first founder thereof'.

John was filling his new garden with the wonderful decorative flowers that fascinated him. These plants had no medical use but 'serve[d] only to deck up the gardens of the curious'. Some were displayed in his shop, alongside the staples of an apothecary's trade, many of which he also grew in his garden. He sold the medicinal plants as roots or tinctures, plasters or ointments, but his particular passion at this time was the range of seeds and bulbs he grew 'for delight' that would brighten his customers' homes. For some time he had been sowing the seeds of anemones, daffodils, fritillaries and tulips in the autumn and nurturing the bulbs until they were big enough to harvest. 'Wee usually sow the same yeares seede', he would later advise his readers, and this practice was just beginning to generate an exciting variety of bulbs for sale.[29]

King James quickly settled into a restless pattern of visits to his royal hunting grounds and the route from Whitehall to Theobalds, his favourite palace, took him past John's garden. James took a keen interest in what he saw as he rode. This area was developing from open country into an aristocratic enclave built by the Cecils and the Duke of Bedford with 'good houses, well inhabited and resorted unto by gentry for lodging'.[30] Some of these houses were laid out with gardens that were 200 feet long, and James took care to ensure that nothing interfered with their stylish aspect.

When the king rode by, people tended to line the streets to wave and stare, which he hated. Avoiding their gaze, he could see into John's remarkable garden, over the hedge to the left as he progressed along Long Acre. Sometimes he would have seen the garden's creator, hunched over his experimental pots. Matthias de l'Obel had told the king about him, and John was also well known to Lord Edward Zouche, by now one of the king's regular riding companions. The king had no particular fondness for plants, but John's garden was unusual to behold, laid out like a nursery, with exotic blooms that grew in orderly rows. The low clipped box edgings that sheltered the flowers were not to be seen elsewhere. In this garden, plants flowered earlier than anywhere else and bloomed for longer. John had experimented to prove or disprove the boast Thomas Hyll had used, that plantings made 'on the change of the Moone, the constellations or conjunctions of Planets, or some other Starres or celestiall bodies' created the form of flowers. He had quickly found this to be a useless claim, but his experiments to extend the season of flowers with plantings at different times of the year, and different types of manure, were much more rewarding. By the time he came to write the *Paradisus* in 1629, he had plants flowering in every month of the year. This was the work in progress as King James trotted past.

Many of the king's courtiers had an interest in gardens. James's frequent companion, Sir Philip Herbert, was the younger son of the 'beautifull Ladie', Mary, the Countess of Pembroke. He had grown up at Wilton in Wiltshire, which Mary had turned into 'An Arcadian place and a Paradise'. Her husband's family had never managed to tame her. She still had a reputation as being 'very Salacious', entertaining herself with

a Contrivance that in the Spring of the yeare, when the Stallions were to leape the Mares, they were to be broughte before such a part of the house, where she had a vidette (a hole to peep out at) to looke on them and please herselfe with their Sport; and then she would act the like sport herselfe with her stallions.[31]

*An early seventeenth-century European garden, showing the
pride of place given to unusual specimen plants. Theodor de Bry,*
Florilegium Novum, Oppenheim, *1612.*

But Mary also used her husband's money to foster the new sciences.
She had sponsored Dr Mouffet, the first English doctor to use minerals
or so-called 'chemical medicines' to treat patients, who also wrote a
study of insects. Sir Walter Raleigh's half-brother, Adrian Gilbert, was
Mary's full-time 'Laborator'. He had trimmed the garden at Wilton to
express the spiritual ideas that were inspired by the constant discovery
of new physical forms.

He made walks, hedges and arbours, of all manner of most delicate
fruit trees, planting them and placing them in such admirable art-like
fashions, resembling both divine and moral remembrances, as three
arbours standing in a triangle, having each a recourse to a greater
arbour in the midst, resemble three in one and one in three.[32]

In this garden, nature's growth was clipped and twisted as before into unnaturally disciplined shapes. But now mathematical symbols began to replace the whimsical creatures and maidens of the Tudor period as garden creators explored the marvellous structure of the natural world. Alchemy seemed less absorbing now than the physical nature of the body; the relationship of the earth to the sun and stars; the forms and substance of earth, plants and animals. In 1600 Dr William Gilbert, one of Queen Elizabeth's physicians, published the results of his lifelong fascination with magnetism, in a text that introduced the terms 'electricity' and 'magnetic pole' for the first time.[33] Here were mysteries to be explored on the surface of the earth itself, and in a garden that quest to understand nature and to master natural forces was expressed.

John's practical nature, toughened by the circumstances of his childhood, made him wary of philosophy. He pursued his branch of science, the evolution and essence of plants, with simple dedication to the details he observed. He was more interested in the actual nature of plants than in the vision of cosmic order that some wealthy aristocrats chose to express in designs dwarfing the garden's living content. Increasingly there were many, outside the tiny circle of aristocrats who spent a fortune on palatial architecture, who came to share his fascination with natural forms and colours. While John continued to search for the best flowers, his compatriots and customers were gradually learning the art of planting them in their gardens. Sir Henry Fanshawe, a courtier and 'favourite of the Prince Henry', King James's eldest son, first attempted to create a garden at Ware Park in Hertfordshire around 1606. In his early enthusiasm he made, according to his house-guest,

> such a coil about gardening that a man cannot be idle though he do but look on – nor greatly well occupied, it goes so slowly forward; and yet there have been every day since my coming above forty men at work, for the new garden is wholly translated, new levelled, and in a manner transplanted, because most of the first trees were dead with being set too deep.[34]

Sir Henry was handicapped by his gardeners' ignorance. The following year the king inaugurated a Company of Gardeners, in an attempt to raise standards, but it was too late for Sir Henry's first trees.[35] His garden was also hampered at first by his somewhat idiosyncratic style, since in the midst of it he chose to make

> a fort in perfect proportion, with his ramparts, bulwarks, counter-scarps, and all other appurtenances, so that when it is finished it is like to prove an invincible piece of work.[36]

However, Sir Henry learned quickly. In 1613 he flattened the fort and replaced it with more fashionable fountains and watercourses.[37] His 'delicate and diligent curiosity'[38] about plants was slowly turning him into a skilled gardener. Sir Henry Wotton, who had visited the most famous gardens in Italy as England's ambassador to Venice, came to regard Fanshawe's skilful use of flowers as the finest garden style he had ever seen:

> He did so diligently examine the tinctures and seasons of his flowers, that, in their setting, the inwardest of those which were to come up at the same time should always be a little darker than the outmost, and to sow them for a kind of gentle shadow, like a piece, not of nature, but of art.[39]

Here is an echo of the praise that Matthias de l'Obel had showered on his Flemish countrymen. As the new century drew to the end of its first decade, the British were also becoming masters of decorative plants and bringing the craft forward to the status of an art. The knowledge and skills that were necessary for this transformation came largely from John. By 1608, he was the acknowledged leader in the field. John Gerard was dead. Matthias de l'Obel was an old man, while John was energetically innovating. He grew and sold a wide range of 'Out-landish flowers' that the English had never planted before:

> Fritillarias, Iacinthes, Saffron-flowers [Autumn Crocus], Lilies, Flowerdeluces [bulb Iris], Tulipas, Anemones, French Cowslips, or Bears Eares [Auriculas] and a number of other such flowers, very beautifull, delightfull, and pleasant ... whereof although many have little sweete sent to commend them, yet their earlinesse and exceeding great beautie and varietie do so farre countervaile that defect ... that they are almost in all places with all persons, especially with the better sort of the Gentry of the Land, as greatly desired and accepted as any other the most choicest....[40]

The showiness of these flowers was easing them into pride of place in gardens that the Elizabethans had reserved for plants with the rarest scent or the greatest medicinal value. Fragrant or medicinal plants were still cherished, but the new arrivals were gradually changing the meaning of a garden.

> The most part of these Out-landish flowers do shew forth their beauty and colours so early in the yeare, that they seeme to make a Garden of delight even in the Winter time, and do soe give their flowers one after another that all their bravery is not fully spent until that Gilloflowers [pinks], the pride of our English Gardens, do shew themselves.[41]

This great range of delightful introductions was only part of John's work. He knew that if he were to fulfil his long-term ambition of writing a comprehensive encyclopaedia of plants, he needed to take an active role in searching them out. He could not rely on the mislabelled bundles that the Turkish merchants put up for sale at the Exchange, or on other men's gifts. Many unusual plants circulated in Europe via a vigorous plant-swapping circle of friends. Sometimes, when plants were sent as a present to friends in England, they met a curious fate. The great beauty of tulip flowers was already extravagantly valued in Holland, but many English still knew so little of these exotic bulbs that they mistook them for food when they received them. John reported that tulip bulbs taste

> pleasant, or at the least no unpleasant taste ... for divers have had them sent by their friends from beyond Sea, and mistaking them to bee Onions, have used them as Onions in their pottage or broth, and never found any cause of mislike, or any sense of evill quality produced by them but accounted them sweete Onions.[42]

Luckily, John's circle included Lord Zouche, who had given him plants from Constantinople, and also the French king's gardener, Vespasian Robin. He had in his garden a yucca plant, such a rare and valuable possession that none of its owners had even tasted the leaves, as was customary when identifying a plant. 'They that have it are loth to cut any thereof, for fear of spoiling and losing the whole roote [plant].' John's yucca plant came to him by a remarkably circuitous route. Gerard said he had had the first one in England, from an Exeter apothecary named Thomas Edwards, whose servant had brought it from the West Indies.

Gerard sent an offshoot to Henri IV's gardener: 'by that plant, Vespasian Robin, the son of old Robin sent unto Master John de Franqueville, and now abideth and flourisheth in my Garden'.[43] Clearly, John's friendship with Gerard, and familiarity with his garden, never yielded any presents of plants. Gerard kept his collection to himself as energetically as he vaunted his knowledge. As the fashion for gardens took root with the English nobility, decorative plants were becoming a competitive business.

The glory of showing a plant's first flower could not be guaranteed by possessing it. That depended on luck, as John knew well from Richard Barnsley's 'woolly hyacinth'. There were now many eager amateurs cultivating curious plants in England. The first yucca to flower belonged to one of them. William Coys was 'a gentleman of good respect in Essex', who had a famous garden at Stubbers near North Ockendon, where the yucca flowered in 1604.[44] John never managed to travel to Essex to see the flower, but he had reason afterwards to remember William Coys.

It was impossible for John to travel to seek out plants as other men had done. He was busy maintaining his apothecary business, developing his garden, and conducting his experiments. He had neither the time nor the inclination to travel, and rarely even left London. So he solved the problem of establishing a truly international plant collection by employing 'roote gatherers' to search out unusual bulbs and seeds on his behalf. Most of the men and women who followed this trade came over from the Low Countries where their discoveries traditionally fetched a high price. John did business with a Frenchman called Francis le Veau, 'the honestest roote-gatherer that ever came over to us', who brought him the Pyrenean mountain daffodils.[45] Undoubtedly his most expensive commission, though, was to Dr William Boel whom he sent to the Spanish peninsula.

A particularly 'frosty violent' winter in 1607 killed a good part of John's collection. The losses spurred him to undertake the gamble of commissioning William Boel. Hiring 'roote gatherers' was a tricky business. Their journeys were long and expensive, and, just as with the English privateers, the returns they brought were uncertain. John was not a natural risk-taker, but, caught by the twin demands of his profession and his garden, he had no choice but to venture if he wanted to fulfil his ambition.

John knew Boel as 'a cunning, curious searcher' of plants who had supplied Matthias de l'Obel. He too was Flemish and had lived in Trier in Germany. He made regular trips to Africa, Spain and Portugal, from where he traded in bulbs, seeds and 'roots'. Clusius referred to him as a doctor who lived at Lisbon, but he travelled a lot. He went to Spain at

John's expense in 1608, and when he returned he was able to give John satisfyingly detailed notes on the plants he delivered.

Before the winter came, Boel returned with bulbs and seeds of more than a hundred species, many of which had never been cultivated in England before. John noted Boel's comments, complete with a geography he cannot have understood, in the detailed records he kept. Boel brought him a 'starry Iacinth of Peru': a wild hyacinth or bluebell which grew sometimes violet blue, sometimes white, sometimes pink. John was now able to explain that this plant grew wild in Spain, despite its name.

> These doe naturally grow in Spaine, in the Medowes, a little off from the Sea, as well in the Island Gades, usually called Cales [Cadiz], as likewise in other parts along the sea side, as one goeth from thence to Porto Santa Maria, which when they be in flower, growing so thick together, seem to cover the ground, like unto a tapistry of divers colours, as I have been reliably enformed by Guillaume Boel ... often before and hereafter remembered.[46]

As John set to work planting the seeds Boel had brought him, he made some delightful discoveries. One of his germinating seeds, he could tell by the leaves, would be a variety of a cherished plant called the 'marvel of Peru' that came from Trinidad and South America. This was extremely rare in England because it was so hard to keep over the winter, but it was a curiosity that greatly appealed to John's contemporaries. Its scented flowers opened and closed with the sun, giving white and red flowers on the same plant, or red and yellow, or purple or spotted, and sometimes wholly yellow. 'You shall hardly find two or three flowers in a hundred, that will be alike spotted and marked, without some diversitie' noted John enthusiastically.[47]

His joy was quickly tempered by disappointments. For a brief time he was the only possessor in England of a 'pale purple or peach colour' variety of this flower. But it was 'an unkindly year'. An early winter following a cold summer destroyed this and many of the other seedlings that Boel had brought him from Spain, and the expense of the trip was partly wasted. John's sadness at this was nothing, however, compared to his anger when he discovered later that Boel had given to other men some of the seed he had brought back. John would have had the only perennial pea in the country, a 'rare flower', had Boel not given some to William Coys, that genial amateur whose yucca had been the first to bloom. To add insult to

Posthumous portrait of John Tradescant the elder by Wenceslaus Hollar, for the
frontispiece of Musaeum Tradescantianum, 1656, the catalogue of Tradescant's
Ark. Hollar's original copper plate for this etching, with its partner portrait of
Tradescant's son, was discovered in 2005 in the collection of the central
museum in Northampton.

injury, he learned that Boel gave them to Coys, 'in love, as a lover of rare plants, but to me of debt, for going into Spaine almost wholly on my charge hee brought mee little else for my mony, but while I beate the bush, another catcheth and eateth the bird'.[48] He heard this unpleasant truth from William Coys himself. John's Long Acre garden had by 1610 become a noted London attraction. One of his early visitors was Mr Coys, who came eager to point out to his host how many of the unusual plants he grew himself at home. There was a a kind of sweet pea called a 'satin flower', for instance, with 'an excellent shining red or crimson colour', known, foolishly John thought, as French honeysuckle. This, 'Master William Coys ... a great and ancient lover and cherisher of these delights, and of all other rare plants, assured me he had growing in his garden at Stubbers by North Okenden'. Typically, John concealed any resentment he felt beneath a generous layer of gentlemanly praise when he came to tell the visitor's story.[49]

John's garden had become a focal point for men with similar interests. Here they could observe work in progress and exchange information and discoveries. He attracted a circle of friends and visitors who often brought him delightful gifts, and always information. Dr Robert Fludd, who had studied medicine at Pisa, brought him seed from a daffodil along with other seeds that he had gathered in the university garden there. Since his return to London, Fludd had been having trouble with the London College of Physicians because of his unorthodox Rosicrucian beliefs. They had already refused him a licence and he was forced to wait before being allowed to practise in London. John's garden was a welcome respite from London politics: an oasis of calm where new ideas about the nature of the material world could be freely discussed.[50]

One visitor to John's garden would become his lifelong 'especial good friend'. John knew John Tradescant slightly through his connection with John Gerard. Before 1597 Tradescant had given Gerard, and some 'other lovers of plants', a beautifully variegated 'painted sage' that he found 'in a countrey garden'.[51] John did not then know Tradescant well enough to receive one himself, but in 1607 Tradescant married, and John seems to have seen him more often in London. Tradescant was beginning to establish himself as a knowledgeable garden manager for the wealthy English aristocrats who were planting new gardens.

The two men found their characters complemented each other perfectly. Tradescant had all the skills of a root gatherer: a keen eye for plants, and a taste for travel and adventure. He could haggle for plants in all the capitals of Europe, obtain the best, manage their safe transport back to England and supervise their planting so that they survived and thrived. This he was soon to do for one of the most ambitious new gardens in the country, the one that Robert Cecil, the secretary of state, was making for the house he had built at Hatfield.

However, Tradescant lacked the essential qualities of a herbalist. He had no sense of smell. He could not, like John, inspect and describe in microscopic detail every aspect of a plant's colour, smell, taste, medicinal virtue and pattern of growth. Nor did he have the scholarship to research their history and provenance. Both men shared a fascination with the beauty of plants, and intense pleasure in cultivating them. But while Tradescant set off to scour Europe for the best fruit trees to 'furnish up the gardens of the great men',[52] John could nearly always be found in his shop or in his garden, patiently continuing his experiments with the new introductions.

John's persistence was beginning to yield spectacular results. He waited fourteen years for the seed from Dr Fludd's 'daffodil' to flower. When at last it did, the result was triumphant. The bulbs delivered no less than 'foure stalkes of flowers, with every one of them eight or ten flowers on them'. John had read about this miraculous white-flowered plant in the classics by Clusius and Matthiolus. What excitement he must have felt to see it bloom in his own garden! The Europeans called it the 'sea daffodil' because it flowered in the frost-free gardens near the coast and had been first found in Sardinia, but we would call it an amaryllis lily.

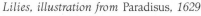

Lilies, illustration from Paradisus, *1629*

CHAPTER TEN

'The Art and Mystery of Apothecaries'

Matthias de l'Obel's ringing endorsement of John's abilities as a gardener and apothecary marked him out for success. In those first years of the new century, John's business was thriving. Yet there were dark clouds gathering on the horizon, which he could not entirely avoid, however much he sheltered behind his garden fence.

The position of English Catholics had taken a turn for the worse since James' arrival in England. The king's reign had hardly begun before a breathtaking plot to assassinate him in his parliament was uncovered. Guy Fawkes was found underneath the palace of Westminster early in November 1605, with enough gunpowder to have destroyed the whole edifice and seriously destabilized the nation. The outrage was shown to be an elaborate Catholic plot. Suspicion of Catholics was fanned to a flame of rage as Guy Fawkes was burnt at the Tower. Every year thereafter the incident was elaborately resurrected. Crowds marched through the streets on the anniversary, rekindling fear of the Catholic enemies of the state.

Anti-Catholic feeling was far more intense in the City and the House of Commons than it was at court. The king, whose background was a strange combination of his Catholic mother and a Calvinist upbringing, distinguished, like Elizabeth before him, between 'auncient papists' like John, and recent converts. The former he tolerated as fundamentally loyal. The latter he regarded as traitors. He was also hoping to arrange a Catholic marriage for his son that would reap from the Spanish throne, now at peace with England once more, a dowry large enough to keep his household afloat. Under pressure from the House of Commons, however, he devised new anti-Catholic legislation, including an oath of allegiance that became compulsory for all office-holders in 1610. James also found it convenient to increase the prosecution of Catholics for not going to church. Recusants now paid an annual fine and their estate was subject to a forfeit when they died. This brought the crown valuable revenue, so

Gardeners surrounded by the fruits of their labours, from Thomas Hyll, Gardener's Labyrinth, *1577.*

that prosecutions steadily climbed. John's younger brother, Robert, who had established a business as a glover in Whalley, died in 1612, and his estate was penalized because he was a recusant.[1]

There was no record so far of John having to pay such a fine, but he had not been to church since he withdrew from St Antholin's. It could only be a matter of time before he was included in the lists of recusants in London. It did not help that the name 'Parkinson' was often chosen as an alias by missionary Catholic priests trying to avoid capture, no doubt because of the prevalence of Parkinsons in the Catholic north. The way John chose to honour his God could not long be allowed to remain a personal matter.[2]

As the struggle between the old Church and the new began to bite, devastating news came from Lancashire. The Parkinson clan was dividing down the middle along religious lines. In many families, such a rift ended in fearsome accusations of witchcraft. In 1604 James had renewed an old English law making witchcraft punishable by death. Seeing himself as an experienced witch-hunter, he created a small army of like-minded followers by offering a bounty for every witch revealed. From now on denunciations for witchcraft became a regular feature of life in every community. In Lancashire, old superstitions mixed with a fierce religious struggle to create a particularly lethal combination.[3]

The story of Jane Southworth, a wealthy widow from John's parish of Whalley, shows how dangerous religious division within a family could become. Jane decided to join the Church of England in 1612. Not long afterwards she was accused of being a witch, and taken to the dungeons of Lancaster Castle. She was put on trial for having 'feloniously practised exercised and used diverse, devilish and wicked arts, called Witchcraft ... in and upon one Grace Sowerbutts, so that by meanes thereof her body wasted and consumed'. Jane was lucky that the case collapsed when she stumbled on the real reason why this child had accused her. Grace's tutor was an underground Catholic priest who was also the uncle of Jane's former husband. Jane had married into one of the staunchest Catholic families in the area. Her husband's grandfather, Sir John Southworth, had served the Catholic Queen Mary so boldly that he was imprisoned and fined when Elizabeth became queen. At her trial Jane was able to suggest that this tutor had encouraged Grace to accuse her and the other women because they had joined the Anglican Church. In this case, the 'witches' were released, the Catholic tutor fled, and Grace was sent to a Protestant, 'Mr Leigh, a very religious preacher', to finish her education.[4]

In London, John was committed to the scientific principles he had embraced in this cosmopolitan city, but he could not have failed to get the message. It was becoming dangerous for ordinary citizens to stand out from the crowd. Even leaving aside his preferred religion, the political tensions in his work were rising fast. The principle that John had learned from Matthias de l'Obel, his devotion to scientific truth, was becoming irreconcilable with the oath of loyalty he had given to the Company of Grocers. John's reputation as an apothecary was based on his use of known materials and measured quantities in his medicines. The Grocers' court meanwhile stubbornly refused to impose such standards on their members. The situation was particularly frustrating for any genuine doctor since, by law, physicians and surgeons depended on apothecaries to mix the internal medicines they used, so the apothecaries' knowledge and skill in preparing them was critical to every medical man's reputation.

However, after 1605, an energetic reformer had the ear of the king. John's neighbour, Dr Henry Atkins, had been chosen to bring the young Prince Charles from Scotland to his new home in England. Atkins seized the opportunity of his place in the bosom of the royal family to put the case for reform. When the Grocers submitted their royal charter for the new sovereign's approval, as they were bound to do, it was returned to them in 1607 with some unwelcome modifications.

The 1607 charter incorporated the dissident apothecaries' old proposal mooted nearly twenty years before. Apothecaries were to form a separate section of the company. The Grocers bitterly resented being commanded to change their internal government, but the momentum for reform was powerful and they were scarcely able to protest before a far more radical and damaging idea came forward.

This was a proposal to create a new and independent Society of Apothecaries, with its own court, or governing body, now put forward in a bill before Parliament. The bill's signatories were those same apothecaries whose attempt at reform had been frustrated by the Grocers all those years before, but the Grocers suspected that the ringleader was an apothecary who added insult to injury by being a foreigner.[5] Gideon de Laune was one of the many French Huguenots attracted to the court of the new English queen, Anne of Denmark. His royal appointment enabled him to practise in London without being a member of the Company of Grocers. The Flemish doctors and apothecaries in London all found it astonishing that the grocers were allowed to dominate the apothecaries' trade. In France and Germany, apothecaries had been separated from the 'épiciers' for over a hundred years.

When this bill was put before Parliament in June 1610, the Grocers immediately summoned the dissidents to their court. They made a point of refusing to admit Gideon de Laune because he was 'a stranger borne'. He was

> willed by the court to dep[art] into the Common Hall till the courte had conferred with the Free Brothers of this Company about the same Bill, telling him that after they has done soe they would speake with him. Whereupon the said de Laune returned into the hall, and there with great indignation and threatening terms against the said court and Company (as the court was informed) departed.[6]

Inside the Grocers' hall the separatist apothecaries were subjected to all the moral blackmail that ancient body could muster. They were asked to say openly:

> whether they were also devisors or furtherers of the sayd Bill or thought the same fitt to passe in Parliament to sever and devyde themselves from the Company and alter the government thereof, which hath continued many yeares of their forefathers in unity, love and concorde, or not?[7]

One by one they 'denyed themselves to have been any way authors or furtherers therein', though they begged once more for their grievances to be taken into account. The clerk recorded that they had chosen to drop the bill before the House of Commons, saying they 'utterly disliked thereof notwithstanding they thought fitt and prayed that the Wardens and the court would be pleased to raise some reformacion of some abuses committed'.[8] The wardens asked them to put their grievances in writing and believed they had successfully buried the matter once more. The summer recess of Parliament arrived and the bill disappeared into a black hole with other unfinished parliamentary business.

John made no contribution while this row was going on. He would have hated to break faith with old friends, including his master, Francis Slater, who was appointed a member of the Grocers' court in 1613, and Francis' son John, who had grown up alongside him and was also loyal to the company. John was faced with a challenge to his family's security as well as his sworn loyalty to the Company of Grocers. No thought had been given as to how a breakaway company of apothecaries could offer pensions and alms in the way that the wealthy Grocers did. John had worked hard to gain the status that membership of the Company of Grocers gave him. If he threw it all over, his position as a Catholic in the city would make him even more isolated than most, whatever his professional skill.

Yet he knew well that medicines had become infinitely more compli-cated in the last thirty years. The range of plants now imported into England had almost doubled, and several physicians had adopted the new fashion for 'chemical medicines'. There were now about 140 trained apothecaries in a company of over 700 grocers. Most of these grocers knew nothing about 'Argent Silver Vivum' or 'Lapis of all kinds' which the modern apothecary would be required to stock.[9] They had no experience of identifying one plant from another by taste, leaf, colour and smell. They could not read Latin and so would not be able to read a physician's 'receipt' or even the ancient recipes in Dioscorides that were tried and tested. Yet they all had a legal right to mix and sell medicines.

Reform was long overdue. All John's Flemish friends were accustomed to apothecaries operating independently, subject only to the guidance of physicians. John could not have denied that the rebels seemed to offer the best prospect of turning the apothecaries into the scientific profession he believed it should be. But he hated and feared politics. In the early years of the apothecaries' bid for freedom, he kept his head down. That autumn, when Parliament resumed, there was a tense standoff between the Lords and Commons over how the royal households should be financed. Powerful vested interests were at stake on both sides, and the apothecaries were forgotten.

Another key reformer had found a place at court, however, and after the failure of the apothecaries' bill he joined the battle to reform the medical profession. Francis Bacon's agile mind had never won him the place in politics he felt he deserved. Under Queen Elizabeth, he had stood uncomfortably on the sidelines at court, although his uncle, William Cecil, Lord Burghley, and later his cousin, Robert, were the two most powerful men in the country. Perhaps the old queen disapproved, as his mother did, of the fact that Francis and his brother Anthony were openly homosexual. After she was widowed, Francis' mother, Anne, grew increasingly frustrated that her efforts to push her clever sons forward seemed to lead to nothing but debt and despair. An ardent Puritan, she fulminated in her letters to Francis against the behaviour of his brother, but her comments were directed at both sons.

> Surely I pity your brother [his debts] but so long as he pitieth not himself but keepeth that bloody Percy ... yea as a coach companion and bed companion – a proud, profane costly fellow, whose being about him I verily fear God doth mislike ... surely I am utterly discouraged ... I will not have his cormorant seducers and instruments of Satan to him committing foul sin by his countenance, to the displeasing of God and His godly fear.[10]

His mother's fervently puritan views compromised Francis in his turn, and the frank expression of his penetrating logic in his early days as a young member of parliament did not endear him to the old Queen Elizabeth, who feared fanatical Protestants more than she feared Catholics. Unwisely, Bacon spelled out the reason for the moral anarchy that was perceived to be sweeping the country. The religious reforms unleashed at the Reformation could not be stopped at the limits prescribed by the queen, he said.

> If the will of God was not confided exclusively to Pope or priest, but revealed in the scriptures to all men, then it was the duty of all men to seek it there. Those who for that purpose searched and studied the Scriptures must come to their own conclusions ... To tell them to seek,

and yet to prescribe limits to what they should find, was to set human authority above the Word.[11]

Ironically, the righteous despair of Francis' mother deepened as the decadence of the new king's court unfolded, yet it was here that her son at last found a home. While Lady Bacon was appalled by the king's extravagance, by his courtiers' flamboyant arrogance and his openly homoerotic behaviour, her son found a man who shared his tastes and admired his ability. Francis Bacon was knighted in 1604 (along with 299

Sir Francis Bacon in an engraving by William Marshall, drawn thirteen years after Bacon's death, for the 1640 edition of The Advancement of Learning.

others in the gardens of Whitehall), appointed Solicitor General in 1607, and Attorney General in October 1613. That year, encouraged by these royal favours, Francis even gave vent to his whimsical side and wrote *The Masque of Flowers* for Queen Anne.[12]

The new Solicitor General happened to have particularly strong views about medicine. His own physical weakness as a teenage student in Cambridge meant that he often consulted apothecaries there. Bacon's illnesses had left him with a poor opinion of doctors. 'The physicians have frustrated the fruit of tradition and experience by their magistralities, in adding and taking out and changing quid pro quo [this for that] in their receipts [prescriptions], at their pleasures...'.[13]

In Francis Bacon, Henry Atkins found a powerful ally for reform. They both knew, however, how difficult it was to reform doctors, protected as they were by powerful clients who did not distinguish between good medicine and bad. Bacon had judged a case between Dr Leonard Poe and the College of Physicians on one of the many occasions when the notorious Poe had used letters from royal councillors to keep himself out of prison for practising medicine without a licence. A testimonial signed by Robert Cecil forced both doctors and judge to allow Poe to practise. 'Diseases are cured not by speech and letters,' complained old Dr Mouffet, who had pioneered work on new chemical medicines, on such an occasion, 'but by experience.'[13a] Complaints against Poe from dissatisfied patients continued to stream in, but Dr Henry Atkins himself reluctantly granted a full licence in 1605. Eventually Dr Poe became a full fellow of the College of Physicians, cheerfully entertaining the doctors and their wives to the lavish dinner in the college house that was customary on such occasions.[14]

Apothecaries were a much easier target than pseudo-physicians. In 1612, events took a turn that delivered Francis Bacon and Henry Atkins the power they needed. In June, Bacon's powerful cousin, Robert Cecil, died suddenly of cancer. The finishing touches to Cecil's great estate at Hatfield were still being made when he died. He left a vacancy at court as privy councillor and lord chancellor that Bacon was anxious to fill. Then, in November, Atkins joined the king's household as one of the Physicians in Ordinary, after his own royal master, the promising heir to the throne, Prince Henry, had died of typhoid fever. Widely viewed as national disasters, these two events nevertheless provided the reformers with the chance they were waiting for.

Their drive to liberate the apothecaries from the grip of the grocers was strengthened by yet another new arrival from France. Dr Theodore

Turquet de Mayerne came as royal physician to the queen in 1611 from the court of Henri IV of France. Like that other Huguenot, Matthias de l'Obel, he had been driven to the English court by the assassination of his royal master. After the massacre of the Huguenots in France on St Bartholomew's Day 1572, his family had fled to Geneva, where his father became known for his mastery of classical languages and his experiments with alchemy and the occult. Back in Paris as an adult, Theodore de Mayerne was banned by the university for his experiments with chemical medicines, but rescued by an appointment to the French king's household. By the time he arrived in London, he had weathered many political storms and was a skilled survivor. He endeared himself at once to his new royal mistress and her friends with recipes for cosmetics, such as the one for 'removing sunburn and wrinkled roughness of the skin' that he carefully recorded in his notebook.[15] The College of Physicians, where, as a royal physician, Dr Mayerne automatically became a fellow, was delighted meanwhile with his 'most excellent Latin, in which he promised and had high hopes of doing good in the future towards each of the Fellows and the whole College'.[16]

For all his urbane charm, Sir Theodore championed the new scientific method, and was seriously committed to improving medicine by experimental discovery. He was the only doctor in England at the time known to keep notes of his practice. Of course he believed that it was high time the London apothecaries were freed from the commercial influence of the grocers, as they were elsewhere in Europe.

Together these three men presented an overwhelming argument for change. John could no longer resist his friends' encouragement to join the battle for reform. So it was that in the spring of 1614 he met his colleagues in the garden outside the lawyers' courts at Gray's Inn for a meeting that would shape the future of their profession. The group was led by Edmund Phillips, Dr Atkins' apothecary for twenty years, and consisted of the most important apothecaries in the city. John's Flemish friends, Matthias de l'Obel's sons-in-law, Lewis Lamere and John Wolfgang Rumler, were both there. These two royal apothecaries were joined by Daniell Darnelly, Dr Mouffet's former apothecary, who was now working for Theodore de Mayerne, and some of the men behind the 1610 bill, Gideon de Laune, Thomas Fones and Stephen Higgins.

The men appeared to have raised a critical number of supporters. They had the names of seventy-five apothecaries, just over half the number practising in London, who were prepared to beg the king to create an independent Society of Apothecaries. This morning the representatives of the breakaway group, with John among them, walked through gardens that had been laid out by the man they were going to see. Sir Francis Bacon had been a resident or 'Bencher' at Gray's Inn since 1586. He had devoted time and money to making a garden there, enclosing 'a part of our back field', once used for archery and hunting, with a brick wall, and planting an avenue of elm trees to make a 'long walk' at the top of the garden. He had also planted three walnut trees, a young ash, and roses, with other flowers and ornamental trees to 'garnish the walkes'.[17] The trees were now nearly twenty-five years old, and the flowers in the garden had become part of its creator's flamboyant way of life. 'At every meale according to the season of the yeare, [Bacon was said to have] his Table strewed with Sweet Herbes and Flowers, which he sayde did refreshe his spirits and memorie'.[18] John would have been familiar with this garden, and may even have supplied some of the bulbs that were now in flower, but he was about to walk into wholly unfamiliar territory.

Every apothecary was well aware that the separation now proposed was a serious business. Breaking the oath to 'not serve out of the ... fellowship' was unprecedented, and possibly illegal. Some skilled legal sophistry would be needed to clear the way ahead. They were fortunate that a master of the art seemed to be driving their case forward. Guided by Sir Francis, the apothecaries drew up a 'Humble petition' that morning which they delivered to the king and his privy council on 2 April 1614, at the Palace of Whitehall. They explained that 'the Art of an Apothecary being also [as] essential to the Practick part of Physick' as the surgeons and physicians were, it was 'much more abused than their arts and hath more neede of reformation'. They asked the king 'by your letters patent to incorporate them and grant unto them thereby such power and authority as may best inable them to suppress the abuses of their Art'. Knowing the king's dislike of state affairs, the petition suggested he might refer the matter to his legal team. If 'your Highnesse would signify yr pleasure to your counsel at Law ... [Sir Francis Bacon, the Attorney General, and Sir Henry Yelverton, the Solicitor General] and also cause them to recommende the same to the house of Parliament for their confirmation therof', the matter could move swiftly forward. Their request was modelled on the letters patent that had granted the physicians their college a hundred years before.[19]

A few days later, Sir Francis and Sir Henry duly received His Majesty's request to confer with the king's physicians and the petitioning apothecaries to 'examine the disorder they complayne of' and report to his Majesty 'upon what points the sayd corporation it most consists and what rules for government to conteyne'. This was quickly accomplished, since much conferring had already been done. On 13 May, Sir Francis presented the king with their conclusion: 'Your majestie may by Law separate the Companie of Apothecaries'. There was no great argument to support this other than that the king would have good reasons for doing so:

> The Art of the Apothecaries which concearneth the health of many Bodie is fitter to be made subordinate and dependant to and upon the Physitians, which are professors of a science Liberall and hon'able and able to direct and in no wise interested in the corruption of the apothe-cary, than upon the Grocers, being but marchants and tradesmen.[20]

The reformers intended this new Society of Apothecaries to be a model scientific body, and took the precaution of writing the company's constitution before it came into being, in case the apothecaries' own efforts were inadequate. 'In this companye there bee a further case that some principall ordinances bee inserted in the Patente itself for which Purpose if your Majestie shall proceed I will advise with the physitians', wrote Sir Francis.[21]

The king was enthusiastic about the idea of rescuing the skilled apothecaries from the rich grocers who dominated them. Francis Bacon had appealed to his love of 'science Liberall and hon'able' over his mistrust of the wealthy citizens of London who opposed him in Parliament. On 16 May, only three days later, he issued instructions to draft a king's bill for the new charter, with a request to the City that the newly independent apothecaries should retain their standing within the city hierarchy. 'We are pleased upon their incorporatinge you consider of some such course, as that they retayne the reputation they formerly helde when as they were members of other companies.'[22]

If the king had understood the powerful mechanics of the City, he would have known that such a request was hollow. First, the apothecaries committed a cardinal sin by breaking their vows of loyalty en masse. Second, they were leaving a wealthy company that ranked fourth among the twelve largest guilds, and whose liverymen took their established place of precedence at every Lord Mayor's parade and public feast. Third, the breakaway apothecaries had no money or faction of the City behind them.

Still, the apothecaries' momentum seemed unstoppable. On 23 May the headings of a new charter were drawn up in Latin, including the names of seventy-six apothecaries, and witnessed by Dr Mayerne and Dr Atkins. The same day, belatedly, Dr Atkins raised the matter with the College of Physicians. Most of the doctors at this meeting of the *Comitia* agreed they were more likely to be able to control the apothecaries if they were self-governing than if they remained part of the Grocers, especially as it would be written into their constitution that they should sell only prescriptions listed in the *Pharmacopoeia* or *Dispensatory*, as they called it in English, that the doctors were now preparing. One small problem, however, was that the *Dispensatory* was still not ready. Dr Atkins raised the matter of completing it again at the *Comitia* on 26 June. Nine doctors were apparently busy with it, including Dr Harvey. Unfortunately one, Dr Herring, was engaged in a lawsuit with the president of the college, concerning 'insulting behaviour'.

Meanwhile three college members, Dr Lister, Dr Palmer and Dr Argent, delivered this letter of muted support for the apothecaries to Whitehall:

June 3 Letter to the King:
    From royal edicts ... the audacity of the quacks and the wickedness of the degraded were committed to our senate for correction and judgement. But now in such a way do they escape our judgement that neither the normal method of indictment nor the ancient way of punishment retain any force: now they fling scorn and all things are condemned. But we are not a little sustained by the knowledge that you most strongly consider the errors of the apothecaries ought to be corrected: for as we minister to the universe, so they are the attendants of the physicians.[23]

When everything was going smoothly, the king's lawyer-in-chief suddenly seemed to switch sides. The Grocers had been fighting a rearguard action to prevent the haemorrhage of their membership. They elected eight more apothecaries to the company livery, although two were separatists, Daniell Darnelly and William Quick, and refused the honour. Loyalist apothecaries spoke at meetings in the Grocers' hall, and to all who would listen in the City, about the 'emptiness and expenses with povertie and disgrace to them and their offspring'[24] that would result from the separatists leaving the company. So when Attorney General Bacon offered to hear their side of the story at his office in Gray's Inn, the Grocers' wardens accepted at once. With his help they drew up a counter petition to the king, arguing that the separatists were just 'a few discontented apothecaryes and tobacco sellers – no more than 28 in all', deliberately appealing to the king's dislike of smoking. The Lord Mayor of London that year, Sir Thomas Middleton, happened to be a grocer. He added a powerful protest from the City, and on 29 May 1614, the king instructed Bacon to delay the bill for further deliberations.[25]

What should have been a temporary delay seemed to turn into triumph for the Grocers. The proposed royal charter for the apothecaries could only be ratified by Parliament while it sat. James had called the second Parliament of his reign in an attempt to persuade the Commons to vote him a regular subsidy. But as soon as the members were assembled, they began to criticize the court's extravagance and question the king's right to impose taxes or 'impositions' on their trade.

After nine weeks of stalemate, James lost his temper. At a public assembly in the banqueting chamber in Whitehall he ripped up some of the bills that had not been passed, ordered four members of the Commons to be sent to the Tower, and dissolved Parliament, resolving to govern without it for as long as possible. Delighted at their unexpected victory over the apothecaries, the Grocers voted the king a 'free gift' of 500 marks.[26]

John and all the other apothecaries who had set their names to the petition were now in an impossible position. No longer welcome at their own Company hall, they still had no independent body of their own. Sir Francis Bacon, in another turnabout, came to their rescue. The king's privy council, of which he was now a member, pushed their case so successfully that James seized on the apothecaries' interests as a perfect example of the value of his personal rule. He announced a king's charter which, when it was read out in court on 30 May 1615, left no doubt as to the strength of his feelings. The skilful apothecaries were not only to be freed from the grasp of the mercenary Grocers, but also emancipated from all other ancient legal obligations:

We will [order] by these presents that the same apothecaries together withal and singular their aforesaid Apprentices, by virtue of these our Letters Patent be and remain from henceforth for ever discharged, acquitted, exonerated and wholly exempt ... as well from all Oaths, Jurisdictions, Powers, Authorities, Statutes, Ordinances, Constitutions, Supervisions, Scrutinies, Summons, Convocations, Conventions,

Government, Rule, Corrections, Impositions, Taxations, Collections of
Money, Payments, Charges, Fines, Amerciments, Imprisonments,
Distresses, Pains and penalties whatsoever.[27]

Suddenly the apothecaries were placed beyond the law, with privileges
that were otherwise only enjoyed by members of the royal household. The
king's charter went on to grant the separatists 'one body corporate and
politic in deed, fact and name'. It announced that Dr Atkins' apothecary,
Edmund Phillips, would be the 'first and present Master of the Art aforesaid' with Stephen Higgins and Thomas Fones as his wardens. John was
made one of the new company's 'livery' with twenty other men 'well
learned and educated and expert in the Art and Mystery of Apothecaries
to be the first and immediate Assistants'. His fellows included the king's
European apothecaries, John Wolfgang Rumler, Lewis Lamere, and Gideon
de Laune, as well as Daniell Darnelly. The English Royal Apothecaries,
George Shiers and Joliffe Lownes, were conspicuous by their absence. All
the apothecaries named in the charter were to take their oaths 'within forty
days after the date of these presents', and 'within fifty days after the date
of these presents' the master and wardens 'shall be sworn before the assistants'. With one stroke, the king had outlawed the Grocers' ancient rights.

It may not or shall be lawful henceforth ... for any Person or Persons
whatsoever now being Freemen of the said Art or Mystery of Grocers
aforesaid or of any other Arts, Faculties or Mysteries in the city to
furnish, hold or have any apothecaries' shop or warehouse or to make,
mix or put together, compound or administer any Medicines whatsoever.[28]

At this point there was a pause, and the separatists' triumphant victory
eluded them again. Objections from the City that the apothecaries were
'discharged of watch warde, jurors and office of Constable' were
accepted, and the charter was modified. More awkward objections came
from apothecaries who did not wish to leave the Grocers, and physicians
who compounded and sold medicines and recognized a threat to their
livelihood. These matters stopped the charter in its flow.

Yet, as the weather grew warmer that year, events were silently
unfolding that made the apothecaries' independence inevitable. In the
hot, dry summer of 1615 a great public scandal was brewing. When it
broke, in the autumn, it exposed a murky alliance between the king's

favourite and the deadly resources of a corrupt City apothecary. The affair made it a matter of urgency that the apothecaries be turned into a properly regulated scientific society.

Lady Frances Howard could never have intended to further modern science. She was the beautiful daughter of the Earl of Suffolk who shared control of the Treasury with his uncle Henry Howard, the Earl of Northampton, and the granddaughter of the Duke of Norfolk, who had been executed for trying to raise the northern rebellion in 1572. Her family was as notorious for soliciting bribes as they were for being

The famous beauty, Lady Frances Howard, Countess of Somerset, from the studio of William Larkin, 1615.

openly Catholic, which did nothing to enhance their popular appeal. Frances was married young to the fifteen-year-old third Earl of Essex, also descended from a nobleman who had lost his head for rebellion, but still immensely rich. For three years after the marriage, Essex travelled in Europe. When he came back to his bride, aged eighteen, he found she had fallen in love with a young Scotsman named Robert Carr, on whom the king doted. James had made him Viscount Rochester and granted him Sir Walter Raleigh's confiscated estates.

Frances set about freeing herself from her husband, and her lover from the restraining influence of his friend and adviser Sir Thomas Overbury. In removing Overbury she was helped by the fact that the king resented his influence over Rochester, while he was prepared to accept hers. The whole of London knew that Overbury had been offered a posting as ambassador to Muscovy, or France, or the Palatinate, indeed anywhere, but refused to go. A London lawyer named John Chamberlain recounted all the gossip in letters to a friend. 'He stood stiffly upon it that he was not willing to forsake his country, and at last gave them a peremptory answer that he hoped that the King, neither in law nor justice, could compel him to leave his country'.[29] This was the reason, said Chamberlain, that Overbury was sent to the Tower in April 1613.

Through the summer that followed, London society talked of the divorce proceedings against Essex instigated by his wife. The bishops appointed to decide the case heard the arguments behind closed doors at Lambeth, but details spread all over town. There were 'not more eyes upon the Earl's father losing his head than upon the Earl losing his wife'. Frances claimed that the marriage was unconsummated because Essex was impotent. 'He and I', said the Countess to the commissioners, 'have lain together in naked bed all night, but non potuit – he could not.' Her husband claimed in response that she had used magic and medicine to 'lessen and debilitate him'. She employed a notorious quack and astrologer, Dr Forman, to 'use all his subtlety and devise really to imbecillitate the Earl'. She had soaked his linen in camphor, which he believed had the same effect, though camphor was also a popular cosmetic. She had used 'an artifice too immodest to be expressed' to prevent consummation and 'so tormented him'.[30]

The sordid secrets of the rich were discussed in Latin and not released to the public, but John Chamberlain knew the gist from the lawyers, and spread the news. On 23 June 1613, the commissioners withdrew to make up their minds. 'In the meantime the Lady hath been visited and

A fig and vines, illustration from Paradisus, *1629*

searched by some ancient ladies and midwives expert in those matters, who both by inspection and otherwise find her upon their oath a pure virgin: which some doctors think a strange asseveration, and make it more difficult than to be discerned'.[31] In September the commissioners finally declared Frances Howard's first marriage null, to general public dismay. Preparations were made for a great wedding to Robert Carr, where at Westminster on 30 December, 'the Dean of the Chapel coupled them, which fell out somewhat strangely that the same man should marry the same person, in the same place upon the self-same day (after six or seven years...) the former party yet living', thought Chamberlain.[32]

Meanwhile, Sir Thomas Overbury died suddenly in the Tower. John Chamberlain queried the 'convenient' death of someone so bitterly opposed to Lady Frances. 'The manner of his death is not known, for that there was nobody with him, not so much as his keeper; but that the foulness of his corpse gives suspicion and leaves aspersion that he should die of the pox or somewhat worse.'[33]

What others suspected, the apothecaries could not deny, given the symptoms of a stinking corpse. John's friends were profoundly unsettled. Dr Theodore de Mayerne had been appointed to treat Overbury and one of his apothecaries was Matthias de l'Obel's son Paul. Paul de l'Obel's own son, William, had mixed and delivered the medicines given to Sir Thomas. How had the death of this man come about so suddenly? Their brother-in-law, Wolfgang Rumler, now the king's own apothecary on a salary of £80 a year, had also been asked to attend Overbury. What did he have to say about the affair? The de l'Obels were forced to ask anxious questions in private, and consider the implications of the position they were in, but the rumours died down, and Thomas Overbury, whose 'very friends' spoke 'but indifferently about him', appeared to be forgotten.[34]

The king left town that summer, soon after proclaiming the apothecaries' charter. The weather was so warm that the people of the west country, anticipating the expense of entertaining the royal household, begged James to delay his visit there 'in respect of the hard winter and hitherto extreme hot and dry summer, whereby our cattle are exceeding poor and like to perish everywhere'. The wealthy spent a pleasant month in their newly burgeoning gardens. John Chamberlain went to Sir Henry Fanshawe at Ware Park and enjoyed 'the best and fairest melons and grapes that ever I knew in England'.[35] Meanwhile, an apothecary's boy died at Vlissingen, in Flanders, confessing before he did so that he had given Thomas Overbury poison.

At court in Whitehall, Rochester, now the Earl of Somerset, heard
that one of the secretaries of state, Sir Ralph Winwood, was collecting
evidence against him come from Flanders. He took the precaution of
drawing up a pardon to himself for 'all manner of treason, misprision
of treason, murders, felonies and outrages, whatsoever', which he
persuaded the king to sign on his return from Dorset. The lord chancellor refused to put the king's seal to such a document, although
Somerset faced it out, 'leaning on the King's cushion' in public. Then
in September the lieutenant of the Tower admitted that he knew of two
attempts to poison Overbury before he finally died, and the king understood he could no longer save his favourite.

Just before the enquiry that followed, the de l'Obel family sent
William to France. In October his father, the 'outlandish doctor' as he
was called, though he was an apothecary, was summoned to testify in
court. Paul de l'Obel 'spoke hardly against those who tried to prove that
Overbury was poisoned, declared that he died of consumption, caused
by melancholy, and that the glister [suppository] prepared by his son
was made by the order of Dr Mayerne who', he added defiantly, 'was
the only physician in England worth anything'. A week later, however,
it was clear that Overbury had died from poison administered by an
apothecary's boy in Lime Street. The de l'Obel family were racked with
fear. The prosecuting lawyer, Edward Ryder, visited Paul l'Obel and
claimed, 'Madame Lobell explained to her husband, "That must be
William, whom you sent into France," on which he trembled violently.'[36]

Paul de l'Obel's nerves may have had more to do with Dr Mayerne's
chemical prescriptions than anything he knew about deliberate poison.
A suppository 'of corrosive sublimate' had been used, and such chemicals were largely unknown and untried. The case was looking bad for
him, until it emerged that Overbury had received plasters and waters
from another source. An apothecary named James Franklin, ironically
not even a freeman of the City, confessed to selling poison to the
Countess of Somerset's confidante, Mistress Turner, which she had
tested on a cat. This was the end for the beautiful Countess of
Somerset, who was forced to plead guilty to murdering Thomas
Overbury.

The apothecary, Mistress Turner, and the Somersets were condemned
to death, but the king pardoned his favourite, which 'the common
people did not take to be good payment'. So Somerset and his wife were
taken instead to the Tower of London where Lady Frances

did passionately deprecate and entreat the Lieutenant that she might not be lodged in Sir Thomas Overbury's lodging, so that he was fain to remove himself out of his own chamber for two or three nights till Sir Walter Raleigh's lodging might be furnished and made fit for her.[37]

For Sir Walter Raleigh the wheel of fortune had come full circle. The man who had been given his confiscated estates was now in the Tower in his place. Sir Walter had been released a week before on the king's orders with a last chance to pursue the great obsession of his life, an attempt to capture 'the large, rich, and beautiful Empire of Guiana; with ... the great and golden city of Manoa, which the Spaniards call El Dorado'.

'El Dorado' had been the focus of his dreams ever since he had stepped ashore there twenty years before. He was preparing now to sail to Trinidad, and from there up the Orinoco to the borders of Venezuela and Peru, where he hoped to find 'more quantity of gold, by manifold, than the best parts of the Indies, or Peru'.[38] King James was so desperate for sources of cash that he had gambled with Sir Walter. If he found the gold he promised, he would be pardoned. Even as he prepared his ships, Sir Walter knew the price of failure was death.

In the aftermath of the trial, the long-awaited apothecaries' charter was brought forward again. Conditions were inserted to ensure that the apothecaries' new privileges did not infringe the rights of the Physicians to 'exercise the Physical Art in all its parts'. It would still be unlawful for 'physicians to go to Grocers for medicines' but it was agreed that those apothecaries, such as John's old master, Francis Slater, who refused to leave the Grocers, could continue their business if they paid a penalty of £5 per month. Half of this money would go to the crown and half to the new Society of Apothecaries.

In such a form, the apothecaries' charter was finally signed and sealed by the king at the Palace of Westminster. The seceding apothecaries won their victory at the cost of the worst possible alienation of their former colleagues. John's old master must have rued the day he had taken John into his home. This Catholic northerner was now mixed up with a group of foreigners who had brought humiliation on Slater and his family. Henceforth the Slaters would have to pay a fine for practising their craft according to their ancient rights. Not surprisingly, the Grocers began plotting at once to strangle this new society at birth.

CHAPTER ELEVEN

A NEW FAMILY

The voice from the Grocers' hall that foretold nothing but 'povertie and disgrace to them and their offspring'[1] for the breakaway apothecaries must have echoed in John's ears all through the grim year that preceded its inauguration, and again in the years that followed.

First, the scandal of the Overbury trial seemed to hasten the death of John's old friend and mentor, Matthias de l'Obel. Matthias lived to see his family cleared, but the long pressure of the trial and the continuous slurs on their 'outlandish' origins were hard to bear. By the age of seventy-eight, when he died, the old man had put many good years into his adopted country, seeking to improve the national understanding of plants and medicines. All his children were now giving useful service as apothecaries. It was poor payment to have their skills condemned as foreign.

On 3 March 1616, Matthias' body was carried to the church at Highgate for burial. John would have cut rosemary from his garden to wear on his hat in remembrance, as was the custom, and ridden up the hill to walk in the old man's funeral procession. Matthias had few possessions to leave, having lived for so long with his daughter and son-in-law at Highgate. Still, it was quickly agreed that John should be allowed to buy his manuscripts and papers. The family knew that Matthias considered John the best hope of bringing his work to fruition. He had long ago selected John as the pupil with the intelligence and the dedication to take the science of plants forward. Significantly for this 'outlandish' doctor, who had put up with the xenophobic slurs of the English for so long, John was a native Englishman who would present the work in a form that his countrymen would accept.[2]

John hardly had time to grieve for his friend or consider how to use the baton that the old man had passed him, before calamity overtook his own family. Barely two months after the death of Matthias, John's wife, Mary, died. The burial record gives no clue to the cause of her death in early middle age. Tuberculosis, or consumption, was rife in London. The disease had claimed one of the most exotic visitors the city had seen only a few months before. The American Indian princess

Pocohontas had arrived from the new colony of Virginia with her English husband, John Rolfe, to a warm welcome from the king and queen and a fascinated public who were delighted by her story. In 1607, she had pleaded with her father, Chief Powhatan, to spare the life of his English captive, John Smith. Though she was feted everywhere she began coughing and spitting blood after a few months in England. She would die before the boat carrying her back to Virginia could leave the port at Gravesend.[3]

If Mary had died of tuberculosis, John's contemporaries would not have looked far for causes. They believed the disease was 'caused by melancholie', such as Mary might have felt at the 'disgrace' John had brought upon his family. Taunts about her husband's lack of faith, his religion, and his association with foreigners would have been harder for her to bear because she did not share the sense of mission that drove him. On the other hand, diseased lungs were a common consequence of the work she did. She had had a heavy role in managing the apothecary business, as well as feeding and caring for the household, while John was occupied with his garden experiments. Sorting and preparing the herbs was one among her continuous round of tasks in the vicinity of their shop on Ludgate Hill, and the dust she breathed in from this work could be fatal. Whatever the cause, John could do nothing to save her, for all his medical skill.

Mary was buried in the churchyard of St Bride's on 29 April, a month after the year of 1617 began. Her funeral was a quiet affair. The children, Richard and Katherine, aged fifteen and thirteen, would have been there. Some of Mary's first husband's family, the Hutchenses, also lived nearby. But John's own face was so little known at the church that the clerk – who was new – did not even know his first name to write in the register, though he had run a reputable business just a few yards away for over fifteen years.[4] Of course, no grocers came to pay their respects, and the 'Society of Apothecaries', which might have lent its support, did not yet exist. Once again, there was rosemary from the garden for the lonely mourners, and John was left to say his farewell in private to the woman who had helped him become the man he was.

However John felt about losing his wife, her death was a practical disaster. Mary had been not only the manager of his household but his partner in the business, and it would be hard to replace her. She had borne all the responsibility for the care of their children who were still young enough to need her. Moreover, this year above all John had other matters on his mind from which he could not allow domestic upsets to divert him. He was approaching his fiftieth birthday, and the death of Matthias de l'Obel would have made him acutely aware that his purpose was a long way from being fulfilled.

The old man's death left a vacancy at court as '*botanographus*', or botanist to the king. It was not an established role in England. De l'Obel seemed to have transplanted the idea from Europe. It did not carry a salary or the potential to make large sums from the exclusive supply of apothecary wares to the royal household. De l'Obel's sons-in-law, Lamere and Rumler, were making those sums. Rumler had even managed to secure a lucrative monopoly importing wines from Bordeaux for 'medicinal' purposes. There were other apothecary posts in the royal households. Hugh Morgan's apprentice, George Shiers, had succeeded his master, and become yeoman apothecary to the royal household for life in the time of Queen Elizabeth, with a fee of £10 a year and 22s.6d. for a livery coat. King James retained him for making 'all perfumes and sweet waters', increasing his salary to £40 a year, and allowing him to provide medicines for the king's poorest servants to an annual limit of £60. John's friend and 'neere neighbour' in St Bride's, Ralph Clayton, originally from Blackburn in Lancashire, had been apothecary to Prince Henry until the prince's death, and was still paid a pension, and Joliffe Lownes was apothecary to Prince Charles.[5]

Nevertheless, the position of Royal Botanist was what John wanted. He had worked hard for many years to become a worthy successor to Matthias de l'Obel, and he knew there was no other man in the country better qualified than he to take this title. It carried the glory of a scholar's status, infinitely desirable to a yeoman's son from Lancashire. But there was a problem. John still had not proved himself a scholar. His knowledge and skill were universally recognized in London, but the book he was planning was no more than a bundle of notes. His apothecary business and his studies in his garden kept him constantly busy. Writing a book, he was discovering, is a very different matter from intending to write one.

On the other hand there could be no turning back now from his commitment to the Society of Apothecaries. He had burned his boats with the Grocers and must do everything he could to ensure that the new society succeeded. This year was in many senses a turning point in John's life. He was facing more work than before, not less, but now he was without his wife to help him. Many men in his position would have remarried, but John chose not to do so. His decision seems to reflect his single-minded devotion to his work, which he valued now above all other relationships.

John chose to replace Mary by employing women to work for him in the household. Labour was certainly cheap enough. The population of the country grew almost as much in the first forty years of the seventeenth century as it had in the hundred years before that. As new patterns of farming drove ever more people off the land, wretched women and children offered themselves for casual work on every street corner in the city. When the Company of Gardeners applied for a renewal of their charter in October 1616, they listed the work they gave the poor as one of the benefits they conferred on the kingdom.

> They imploye thousands of poore people, ould men, women and children, in sellinge of their commodityes, in weding [weeding], in gathering of stones etc., which would otherwise be very burdensome to the cittie and suburbs thereof.[6]

So John could easily offer a living and a lodging to some suitable woman. He would have wanted fifteen-year-old Richard to follow him into his business. Richard had plenty of practical experience working in the shop and the garden, but John also needed to ensure that he had a good grasp of Latin. He had no time to teach him himself, but the best Latin tutors in London were the Catholic priests who worked clandestinely in and around the city, administering the sacraments in private homes. John expected much less of thirteen-year-old Katherine. There were female apothecaries in Germany, and two women had been royal apothecaries there in the sixteenth century, but such a thing was unheard of in England. Katherine would be expected to take her mother's place as far as possible. Inevitably she would leave to work in another man's household before long.[7]

John's apothecary business was healthy, despite all his personal and political problems. The grocers with whom he was fighting the battle for freedom were not his customers. He depended on the physicians who came to him for medicines, and the public. His reputation with them as a skilled apothecary and gardener was unaffected. Around this time, he took on William Orly as a servant to work in his shop. John had taught several apprentices, who had become freemen and left him, but he could not swear William in this way since he was no longer affiliated to the

Grocers, and the apothecaries' society had yet to be established. John's makeshift arrangement also happened to free him from the obligation for regular formal teaching that an apprentice's contract placed on his master.

While John grappled with these personal problems, he was constantly reminded that the great task of compiling his encyclopaedia of medicinal plants was as vital as ever. In the first two decades of the seventeenth century 'curiosities' flowed into London from sources that had never been tapped before. English horizons were expanding dramatically. James I caused confusion when he first became king by insisting that Scotsmen be treated as natives of England. While the king expected the London College of Physicians to approve his personal physician, Dr Craig, as a member, six months later the College was still discussing whether he could be a fellow since he was a Scot and a foreigner. James made clear he was 'astonished that anyone should have raised any question' so the Physicians decided to substitute the nationality 'British' for that of 'English' in all their business, endorsing a new nationality despite themselves.[8]

The British now possessed a colony of sorts. In Virginia, John Rolfe, with Pocohontas' help, had succeeded in crossing West Indian tobacco with the native North American strain. The result was a better crop and vigorous yields. The ships that now made their way to Virginia carrying settlers and supplies returned with their holds full of tobacco. At last the Virginian settlers had found a form of currency. James did his best to further the value of this crop to the colony in spite of loathing the detestable weed. At leisure in his favourite palace of Theobalds in 1619, the king sold the patent to inspect and grade imported tobacco to a Mr Nichols. Then in 1620, he eliminated competition by 'suppressing the planting' of tobacco in England.[9]

The new Virginia Company promoted the colony by a system of carefully controlled land sales. Only the desperate were keen to abandon Britain and settle in America, but by paying for a settler to sail with Captain Sam Argall's flotilla to Virginia in 1617, John's friend John Tradescant was entitled to a half share in fifty acres of land there. Under the system of 'headrights' that had been introduced, the settler whose passage he paid would farm the land and own equal rights with the investor. John Tradescant sent two settlers, at a cost of £12 10s. each, on this journey, while his friend Sam Argall settled there briefly as deputy governor, and built himself a house on three hundred acres of cleared forest. Everyone had heard magical stories of the great woods of Virginia, each tree 'with 20 yardes of usable timber', said John Smith. A few had also heard how bitterly the settlers struggled against disease, hunger and the country's existing inhabitants, the Paspaheg Indians. Not many people in England knew how hard the conditions were. The Virginia Company censored letters home.[10]

Since peace had been made with Spain, 'privateering' was no longer possible. Anyway it had long been deemed too expensive a venture for uncertain returns. On 7 October 1600, that old privateer, George Clifford, bought his last ship, the *Malice Scourge*. In December, he and some fellows from his Puerto Rican adventure managed to get royal approval for a new East India Company, and George invested £1,500 in stock. The *Malice Scourge* left Woolwich docks for South East Asia on 13 February 1601. It returned eighteen months later with a cargo that almost recouped the initial investment after the expenses of the trip. The prospects for a profit looked good. By the company's fifth voyage in 1608, Earl George was dead, but his brother Francis, who inherited the earldom in 1606, made a 234 per cent profit. George Clifford never made any money from his daring gambles, but a part of him lived on in these first steps towards a British Empire. His ship, the *Malice Scourge*, renamed the *Red Dragon*, became the East India Company flagship and sailed in pursuit of trade and exotic treasure for the next 200 years.[11]

The people of Britain had every reason to believe that the riches of the wider world were theirs for the taking, especially the virgin territories of the West. Much of this wealth continued to pour into England via members of the Grocers' Company. In the summer of 1617, disregarding their dispute with the apothecaries, the Grocers spent nearly £1,000 on a pageant in the streets of London to celebrate the election of another company member as lord mayor. The new incumbent, George Bolles, was entertained opposite Bow Church with 'a scean of drollery, in which were Americians, some of them pruning, others gathering, others planting several sorts of grocery, others disporting and throwing their fruit about, to show the abundance or profit of labour'. During the pageant, the wealth of nations was, literally, 'throwen about the streetes by those which sate on the griffins and camels'. Altogether they distributed '50 sugar-loaves, 36 lbs. of nutmeggs, 24 lb. of dates, and 14lb. of ginger.' The floats: 'the Island', the 'Indian Chariot' and the 'Castle of Fame' paraded the streets with 'severall beastes which drew them'. 'Green men' and 'dyvells' mingled with the crowds, inspiring fear and laughter, while spectacular 'fyer-works' burst from the 'Shipp' on the river.[12]

Exotic individuals were becoming as familiar a sight in London as these public pageants of wealth. In the parish of St Bride's, George Clifford's daughter, Anne, now the Countess of Dorset, employed Grace Robinson in her household. Grace was 'a blackamoor', who worked with the laundry-maids.[13] Some black people travelled, like Grace, from Britain's ports to their employers' country estates. Captain John Smith also brought Africans to London. Philip Behon and Anthony, both described as 'Blackmoor', died in St Bride's parish in December 1610.[14]

In his own sphere, John was working on methods of protecting 'exotics' from the ravages of the English climate. Since his disaster with the rare 'marvel of Peru' that William Boel had brought, John had developed various ways to preserve his precious plants through the fierce winters that froze the river Thames. His methods were essential to keep these plants, because the season of warm weather in their new home was not long enough for them to set seed. He would dig up the 'marvels of Peru' after the leaves had withered in autumn, and dry the roots for a few days. When this was done he would 'wrap them up severally [separately] in two or three brown papers and lay them by in a boxe, chest or tub, in some convenient place of the house all the winter time'. By preserving them like this until the spring, John could keep the plants going for two or three years. He was proud that his method was so much more effective than laying them away in sand or ashes, which always failed if the sand was even slightly damp.[15]

The results of his experiments were put to use in the royal gardens. Queen Anne had a penchant for keeping sweet scented orange and lemon trees on the terrace by Somerset House, part of a new garden laid out for her by the French engineer Salomon de Caus. The trees were to be kept on the terrace in the summer and housed in a vault below for the winter, but the winters of 1607 and 1608 were so severe that few could have survived. Orange trees were expensive even for the very wealthy, but fashionable English householders sought them out again, cherishing the sweet scent of the flowers in the open air outside their windows. When Robert Cecil built his new house and garden at Hatfield in 1610, he employed John Tradescant to cross the channel and bring back the best trees he could find. Tradescant found no orange trees until he reached Paris, where he bought '8 pots of orange trees of on [1] years grouthe grafted at 10s the pece: £4.0.0'. This made them five times as expensive as black mulberry trees and ten times as much as the pomegranate trees Tradescant bought in Rouen: '3 littill ons at 1s the pece'.[16]

At home, John found that nothing could be done to keep 'the Citron or Lemmon trees' alive for long in the English climate, although the 'Orange tree hath abiden with some extraordinary care'. They could be kept either 'in great square boxes, ... lift[ing] them to and fro by iron hooks on the sides ... to place them in an house or close gallerie for the winter time,' or planted against a wall, 'defend[ing] them by a shed of boardes, covered over with seare-cloth in the winter, and by the warmth of a stove ... giv[ing] them some comfort in the winter time, but no tent or mean provision will preserve them'.[17]

John shared his experiments with John Tradescant, who moved on from Hatfield after the death of his master to work for Henry Wotton's half-brother at Canterbury, Edward Wotton. John would visit his friend at these aristocratic houses when he could. This formidable pair of gardeners would inspect the planting and walk and talk in the fields nearby. As they walked they were 'simpling', collecting any rare samples they could find to add to their knowledge and understanding of plants. 'On Bushie Heath at Digswell pastures by Hatfield', John was pleased to find a sample of wild thyme, which he called 'mother of thyme', with white flowers but 'nothing so quick in smell or taste' as the ordinary garden kind. He took a sample of the plant and made a note in his records.[18]

Even when John was tied to relentless work in London, as he was for a few years after 1617, there were sometimes unexpected finds. He found a rogue seed in amongst the aniseed he was cleaning to sell, which turned out to be a rare yellow variety of perennial pea when he planted it in his garden.

At last, on 16 December 1617, the king's pet scientific society was ready for inauguration. John went to Sir Francis' apartments at Gray's Inn and waited with the other first officers to take his oath. It was a muted occasion by the usual standards of public ceremony, but these men knew that their Society of Apothecaries was a decisive step towards a scientific medical system. They had sacrificed a great deal for this belief, including the respect of their old colleagues. But for John more than any of the others, this new society was an essential step forward. When the wardens, master and thirteen of the 'livery' the king had named stepped forward one by one to swear the new oath of allegiance before 'Mr Attorney General [Francis Bacon], Mr Dr Atkins, Mr Dr Mayerne, the King's physicians', John found his chance, as an 'auncient Catholic', to swear publicly his loyalty to king and country. He became part of a society that embraced Englishmen, Flemings, Huguenots and Catholics alike in the interests of science. Moreover, from this moment, John was sheltered by the king. Had not James pronounced that these apothecaries were to be exempt from 'Impositions, Taxations, Collections of Money, Payments, Charges, Fines, Amerciments, Imprisonments, Distresses, Pains and penalties whatsoever'? This must include the penalties to which Catholics in England were normally subject. For the first time in his adult life, John was protected.

Each man swore the oath that had been devised for his office. John promised, as an assistant, to 'give in all things after your best skill and power, for ye good government and wealth and Common profit of ye said Corporation.... And kepe secritt all those things which for ye affairs of ye said Corporation shall be conferred.' These oaths were designed to resist the continuing hostility of the grocers. In an attempt to keep out spies, anyone joining as a freeman had to swear that he 'shall not bee party or privy in any Councill or Review that may bee to ye hurt or hindrance of ye same Company, or to ye overthrowing or breaking of ye good lawes or Ordinances of ye same'.[19]

At last the Apothecaries' Society had been formally inaugurated, but the dramatic display of royal backing that had brought them into being did nothing to help them in their early days. It was several months before they were able even to hold their first meeting. They had very little money, although John and the other assistants each put up £32 and posted a bond to allow the society to borrow more.[20] This should have been enough to assure them a reasonable base in the city, but they had unaccountable difficulty in finding a hall to rent or buy. Until they had one, they were forced to meet in taverns or each other's shops.

Another problem was that the promised band of forward thinking apothecaries failed to materialize. The society met for the first time on 15 March 1617, but there was only one man, Christopher Swidges, wanting to be accepted as a freeman. Two days later they made three apprentices full free members, but the field of new applicants was still depressingly thin. The London apothecary trade was still hedging its bets, refusing to believe that the king's proclamation would hold sway over the powerful ancient laws of the City. It was many months before the Apothecaries were swearing in new members in any numbers. On 7

June they swore in thirty men, including two friends of John's, Stephen Chase and Paul l'Obel, who were apothecaries of the kind of standing and reputation they had expected would join. Occasionally grocer apothecaries came along out of curiosity, but they balked at the oath they were asked to swear. On 7 June John Hide said, 'some of the oath was affeared. He desires time to consider of the oath'. On 18 June Mr Gwyn approached, 'but refuses to take the oath'. John's old master's son, John Slater, also stayed away, uncomfortable no doubt with the dual opposition to the new society from the Grocers' Company and from his father. The abstentions were hurtful, if not surprising to the pioneers.

There was further humiliation when the Apothecaries tried to give their society meetings the dignity worthy of a royal company. They decided that all the assistants should 'against 1st May following prepare for the compleat livery gowns, faced with Sattin and welted with Velvett'.[21] The City fathers refused to grant them their own livery colours, however, so long as the Grocers were questioning their existence in the courts. The City said they would award a new livery only to those who had worn it as Grocers, knowing very well that only one of the separatist apothecaries, William Quick, had been in that position, and he was now dead. Nevertheless, around this time, the fine clothes that John wore at court and on formal occasions were made, with striped velvet breeches, a slashed silk doublet, lace collar and embroidered surcoat. The suit would have been an appropriately defiant response to the City's refusal to grant the Apothecaries the status the king had awarded them.

Even the Physicians let them down. Dr Henry Atkins, who had agitated hardest to bring this society into being, assumed that the Apothecaries would rely on the Physicians' *'Pharmacopoeia'*, but the new 'Dispensatory', as it was called, had not appeared. At this stage, the apothecaries had no idea, even, what was in it. When Henry Atkins became president of the College of Physicians again in the summer of 1616 he gave his cherished project another push towards completion. On 13 September:

> It was decided that on the following day the papers gathered together should be brought and arranged in order for examination by Dr Ridley, Dr Lister, Dr Argent Dr Fox with the Registrar and referred by them to the Elects ... but when [they met the next day] it was ascertained that many were missing from those which had been collected by the men who first discussed the matter, they went away leaving the matter

unfinished. When they reported this to the President through the Beadle, the blame was thrown on to an earlier President.[22]

Dr Atkins added more doctors to the team, but at the beginning of 1617 they seemed to be no further forward. On 3 June:

> Fellows were asked to assist also on the pharmacopoeia ... and each of them was to state in addition what they knew of the secret formulae not yet used in the shops, but useful by comparison with the others ... Mr Hewet showed a recipe for chemical oils for the pharmacopoeia now being prepared.[23]

The next February, two months after Dr Atkins had sworn in the new Society of Apothecaries in Francis Bacon's chambers, the *Pharmacopoeia* that he had promised the king was, he hoped, very nearly ready. Four doctors were appointed to see that the new 'Antidotary ... is finally sent to the printers'. But, it was objected, there were many mistakes. Two other doctors were then asked to supervise the corrections. Finally, the *Comitia* decided to bring in the apothecaries to help. 'From the apothecaries Mr Phillips, Mr Higgins, Mr Jones, Mr Darnell, Mr Parkinson and Mr Sherif were asked to assist from day to day'.

The first three of these, the Apothecaries' master and wardens, were asked out of respect only. They were fully occupied defending the existence of their society against the Grocers in the law courts. The task was given to John, Daniell Darnelly and Gabriel Sherriff. These three were dismayed by what they found, and their intervention only threw the doctors into further confusion. The *Comitia* agreed Dr Fludd; Dr Andrews; Dr Baskervill and Dr Rogers 'to consider additions to the Antidotary'.[24]

Early in the new year, the king was told the new *Pharmacopoeia* was ready and he could announce the final cornerstone of his modernized medical system. In a royal proclamation on 26 April the king warned the Grocers and their allies in the City that he would not be turned away from his purpose:

> Wee declared our Royal Pleasure touching a Booke compiled by ye Colledge of Physitians of London (now ye second time reviewed, corrected and reprinted) entituled Pharmacopoeia Londoniensis ... wee required all Apothecaries to compound and make ther medicines ... after those ways and menes only prescribed in ye said Booke.

He threatened anyone 'in contempt of our will' in this matter with the nation's highest and least popular court, the Star Chamber.[25]

Shortly afterwards, on 29 June 1618, the Society of Apothecaries confidently decided that 'all the Company should have the new Dispensatory and Troy weights'. Three months later, on 25 September, the unhappy printer in charge of printing the *Pharmacopoeia* was so exasperated that he turned up in person at the College of Physicians. He was being asked for more corrections and another reprint, but, he said:

he would refuse to proceed unless whatever the Fellows contributed was handed over to him as soon as possible. Then the President and many others promised to him twenty pounds, failing that twenty marks, when the corrected book appeared.[26]

The following January the physicians were still arguing over the epilogue that should appear with the book – whether it should be written by Henry Atkins, or the current president of the college. Dr Atkins won, and the first *London Pharmacopoeia* was finally in print, just over a year after the inauguration of the Society of Apothecaries.

The Apothecaries were not reassured by its appearance. The *Pharmacopoeia* turned out to be old-fashioned and patchy; 'Many of the principall medicines that are of use were left out in the Booke', they agreed amongst themselves.[27] Their faith in doctors as a collective body, never very great, was badly dented. Already the new system they had planned, offering good-quality medicines to the public based on compositions determined by the doctors' knowledge, was foundering.

Even before the *Pharmocopoeia* appeared in its final corrected form, John and his colleagues decided they had to take steps if they wanted to ensure the uniform standards of quality that had been their reason for breaking away from the Grocers. At a meeting on 17 November 1618, they agreed that 'a schedule of all Medicynes proper to the Arte of our Company shall be made by Mr Delaune, Mr Darnelly, Mr Parkinson and Mr Barton'. It was rapidly completed. Four months later, on 22 April 1619, John Parkinson, Daniell Darnelly, Mr Edwards and Mr Cooke were 'appointed to make corrections to the schedule'.

The contrast between this efficient production and the Physicians' performance served to underline Francis Bacon's judgement that the Physicians made up their method as they went along. 'They tie themselves to no receipts [recipes] severely and religiously,' he wrote. The

behaviour of the doctors as a group was so disappointing that it was
already obvious to the most skilled apothecaries that they could not
allow themselves to be guided by them as their royal charter had
intended.

John's expert knowledge of medical herbs was now universally
recognized. He was consistently asked to work on these books of
medical recipes, whether by apothecaries or physicians. Daniell
Darnelly's expertise was in chemical medicines, based on his long association with Dr Mouffet, whose experiments he had shared. Edward
Cooke, though a young man, had his own ideas about a medical
system that would by-pass physicians completely. Why did the people
need physicians when the apothecaries knew the composition of medicines and their effects as well or better? For the time being, however,
particularly in the presence of Sir Francis Bacon, who had helped so
much to bring their society into being, the Apothecaries paid lip
service to the Physicians' *Pharmacopoeia*. Meanwhile their own
Schedule of Medycines became the basis of their commercial practice,
and the standard by which they measured their fellows in the Society.

These Society affairs kept John perpetually busy, attending meetings
almost every day. There were remedies to be discussed with the
Physicians, and the Apothecaries' *Schedule* to prepare. On top of this
there was business arising from the Hearth Day, 11 September, when 'the
Wardens and Assistants made sortie in London, Westminster and the
Southwark for Defective and Bad medicines'. Inspecting the medicines
supplied in London themselves was what the breakaway apothecaries had
fought for, yet John must have found the never-ending affairs of the
society a heavy distraction from the work he loved. As if this was not
enough, he had also been voted joint treasurer for the forthcoming year
at the Apothecaries' election day meeting on 18 August 1618. While
his shop and his garden also demanded attention, John's work was
never-ending.

He can have had no time, even if he had had the inclination, to join
the crowd that stared when Sir Walter Raleigh was led to the scaffold at
the Tower in October 1618. The man's great dream had ended in disaster. He had returned to England at the end of the summer empty-
handed and broken. He had been ill during the trip up the Orinoco
river, his men had attacked the Spanish port of San Thome, reigniting
the Spaniards' hatred of the man they called the 'English pirate', and
his eldest son had been killed. Worse, he had found no gold to placate

the king. James showed no mercy to this old 'pollitician', who openly despised him, and Raleigh used his last words from the scaffold to stir a heady cocktail of nostalgia and disenchantment among the king's subjects.[28] John would have mourned Sir Walter's humiliating fate. He had visited Raleigh and his wife when they were prisoners in the Tower, and admired his ingenious method of curing tobacco, grown from Brazilian seed, which, he said, 'he knew so rightly to cure that it was held almost as good as that which came from the Indies, and fully as good as any other made in England'.[29]

The Apothecaries' dispute with the Grocers came to a head in the Star Chamber on 4 August 1620, and Sir Francis Bacon, who was now lord chancellor, found heavily in the Apothecaries' favour. The Grocers won very few concessions from this protracted legal dispute. The Star Chamber ruling reiterated that only members of the Apothecaries' Society were licensed to make and sell medicines, and approved their ordinances, which was hardly surprising since they had been drawn up by Sir Francis himself.

In the light of the Grocers' objections, and quite a few from physicians who had hitherto made money from selling their own medicines, a schedule of what exactly each was allowed to trade was drawn up. The Grocers were allowed to continue to sell sweets, scents, spices, wax and 'wormed' tobacco. They could also stock painters' and dyers' materials: 'vermillion, ising glass, gum arabick' and 'mastick'. Their claims to the right to sell medical staples such as 'Oyle de Bayes and Nux Vomica' were rejected, but they were allowed to keep 'Mercur. Sublimate; quicksilver [and] arsenicum'.

The Apothecaries, on the other hand, could sell all these staples of their trade, and in addition had the sole licence to sell all the flower seeds and roots that were used for medicines and in gardens; all distilled waters, pills, syrups, conserves and ointments, as well as such rare and expensive medicines as 'argent vivum [silver]' and 'unicornu cornu [unicorn's horn]'. There was nothing in the booming international market of drugs and spices that would be exclusive to the Grocers. 'Things in the Grocers' list to be common to either Company to sell: But with this restraint, nevertheless, that ye Apothecaries shall not sell or utter any of ye same in grosse.'

As for senna, rhubarb and the other drugs 'peculiar to ye Apothecaries', the judges ruled 'that ye apothecaries have ye first offer to buy them of ye Merchants', but if they chose not to buy then the

Interior view of a pharmacy with two apothecaries preparing compounds and another man holding a jar. Shelves to the left contain herbal Galenic medicines with chemical compounds on the right. Engraving by Wolfgang Kilian, in Malachius Geiger, Microcosmus hypochondriacus, *Lucam, Straub, 1652.*

Grocers could handle them as wholesalers. The king, away hunting in Salisbury, endorsed Bacon's judgement with a proclamation that displayed his exasperation at the time it had taken to settle the affair. His Majesty, it concluded, does 'ratify and confirm the said Order....And noe person of what condition soever hereafter presume by Petition or otherwise to mone [moan], or trouble us for alteration of ye said Order, or any part thereof'.[30]

At last the Apothecaries had their victory. More than six years after they had first submitted their petition to the king, they had a realistic prospect of building a strong trade that was separate from that of the

Grocers. The best apothecary shops had become distinctive focal points for the discovery of all the 'vertues' of plants. They were part chemical laboratory, part medical consulting rooms and part garden warehouse. They were places where doctors, painters and botanists would cross paths, perhaps stopping to taste one of the cordial waters or the tobacco that was prepared in the shop. It was in these shops that the latest delicacies could be seen and sometimes tasted: they were the first shops to sell potatoes; the only places to see bananas and, a very short time later, somewhere you could enjoy a new and interesting drink made from a roasted imported bean called coffee.

The dispute with the Grocers was now closed, but not forgotten. It was obvious to all that no apothecary could hope to thrive in the City without joining the new society. After this decision, new members began to come forward. Most of John's old associates gradually came round, and the society steadily grew richer. John Slater joined the Apothecaries' Society in 1620, even though he had been made a member of the Grocers' livery, like his father, in 1618. But Francis Slater stuck doggedly to the Company of Grocers until his death in 1630.

At the next election day, John was chosen to serve as warden, with Thomas Fones and Edmund Phillips, who had held office from the beginning. This extra honour and responsibility meant that he had to attend once a week for every 'court' day, be present for examinations of all the freemen, and swear in apprentices. There were cases between apprentices and their masters, and complaints from the public to sort out.

A week later John was spending his Saturday afternoon at Edmund Phillips' house discussing 'doubts touching the Reformacion of abuses committed by the makers and officers of that water and the makers of Emplasters' with the doctors Henry Atkins and Mr Stone.[31] The Apothecaries intended to prepare such staple medical remedies centrally to a certain standard for the use of all, but so long as they had no premises of their own, this was difficult to get under way.

Once the society was established, John soon decided to leave these matters to other men with a greater taste for the politics of human affairs than his. In general when men became members of the livery of their trade society, they stayed in office until their dying day. Such an appointment was the summit of their careers. Their trade company was their wider family, their brotherhood, and they gave it their lives. But John had already made a dramatic break with tradition when he withdrew from the Grocers, and he was now ready to break with it again.

The Society of Apothecaries was his professional brotherhood in name, but within it John felt he could not fulfil his ambition.

Once the Star Chamber ruling of 1620 had assured the Apothecaries' independent future, John could not wait to get back to his garden and his writing. After his year of service as warden was over, he began to stay away from court meetings. At the end of 1621 he reappeared after a long absence to 'earnestly request and intreat the court that he might leave and give over the said place of an Assistant and that some other fitt man might be elected into his place'.[32]

It was an unusual request but John's colleagues appeared to understand his situation. Without questioning his decision they expressed their gratitude for the 'divers good offices by him done for the good of the Companye', which included his schedule of medicines and hours of work for the physicians. They agreed to repay the money he deposited when he became an assistant five years earlier, and return the bond he had given. John promised to remain a member and 'doe his best' for the company in the future, after which he left the meeting and never again played any further part in the Society of Apothecaries.[33]

As it happened, John was not the only pioneer of the society who dropped out of public office that year. James had reluctantly called another Parliament because he needed to raise money to help his daughter Elizabeth, who had been driven out of the Palatinate in Germany with her young husband by Catholic armies. Parliamentary proceedings did not go well for the king. Fighting the Catholics in Europe was a popular cause, but there was now so much bad feeling between king and Commons after years of James' 'personal rule' that each side was determined to make the other feel their grievance.

High on the king's list of accusations with which he greeted the House of Commons was the City's poor treatment of the apothecaries, which, he complained, was a personal insult.

> I myselfe did devyse this Corporation and doe allow it. The Grocers that compleyned of it are but marchants ... They bring home rotten wares from the Indies, Persia and Greece and herewith their mixtions make watery and sell such as belong to Apothecaries.[34]

In revenge, the Commons made sure the king heard some grievances of their own before they would grant any subsidy. They targeted the corruption of the king's officers, beginning with a minor courtier, Sir

Giles Mompesson, who had made a fortune out of relicensing inns and taverns. They unearthed an ancient law and voted to impeach him.

Flushed with success, they turned their attention to someone much closer to the king. The king's lord chancellor, Sir Francis Bacon, was enjoying the peak of his power. His carelessly flamboyant homosexual lifestyle outraged puritan sensibilities in the country as much as it had upset his mother.

> When his Lordship was at his Country-house at Gorhambury, St Albans seemed as if the court were there, so Nobly did he live.... None of his servants durst appeare before him without Spanish leather bootes; for he would smell the neates leather which offended him.... He was pederastus .... His Ganimeds and Favourites tooke Bribes.[35]

His way of life mirrored the decadence of a royal court that shamed English opinion. If the king was untouchable, Francis Bacon could be made to feel the Commons' wrath. He was accused of sanctioning corrupt patents like Mompesson's and of taking bribes. Details of the case of the apothecaries came back to haunt him. He had, it emerged, taken bribes from all the parties in the dispute. He admitted receiving £200 from the City and the Grocers, a gold taster and ambergris from the loyalist apothecaries, and £100 from the separatists.[36] He would have argued that such even-handed 'persuasion' left his judgement unclouded, but he was impeached in the Lords on 1 May and surrendered the great seal. Sir Francis was barred forever from the public office he craved, and fined the enormous sum of £40,000. The king diverted the money to support him, so that while he continued to live in considerable style at his 'Country-house', he was able to channel his exceptional wit into expressing his bitter sense of betrayal.

> If this is to be a Chancellor ... I think that if the Great Seal lay upon Hounslow Heath, nobody would pick it up.[37]

CHAPTER TWELVE

'PRIDE OF LONDON'

In 1622, had he known it, John was on the verge of the great successes of his life. Yet he seemed at first to be embroiled in personal and financial problems, as far as ever from realizing his dreams.

Within a year of his resignation from the Society of Apothecaries, his son, Richard, turned twenty-one. As the son of a freeman of the City, Richard was automatically entitled to become a freeman apothecary, but he did not. This matter was the first indication to the world at large that the death of John's wife had been a bitter blow with long-lasting effects on his family. John's relationship with his son appeared to have gone badly wrong. He could not persuade Richard to follow in his footsteps and devote his life to the study of plants and medicines that he held so dear.

It might have been possible for Richard to join the Company of Gardeners, which, though not so respectable in John's eyes as the scholarly Society of Apothecaries, would at least have given him freeman status. Richard had learned superior gardening skills at his father's knee, and if he could not buy his way into the company, then a short apprenticeship could easily be arranged.

Even this proved impossible. The problem seemed to be that Richard had grown up openly, defiantly Catholic. The Gardeners' company, like all other City companies, rejected 'papists' who would not swear allegiance to the king's authority above the Pope. Richard's youth had been spent in different circumstances from his father's. He no longer had the option, which amounted to an emollient compromise, of claiming that he had been born into a Catholic community and was therefore a Catholic by tradition. In the fiercely anti-Catholic atmosphere of London, he had been unable to hedge his bets in the tradition of the old English Catholics, loyal to both sovereign and Pope. Faced with the hostility of his contemporaries, he could either reject his father's religion or adopt it more emphatically as his own. He made a choice that must have embarrassed and exasperated his father. Far from channelling his spirituality into the discovery of plants, he preferred to adopt open Catholicism of the kind the Jesuits proclaimed.[1]

From John's point of view, Richard not only lacked his father's scholarship, he also lacked his practical sense. The old man's status in the City and membership of a royal society could no longer protect Richard now that he was an adult.[2] The rift between the two was decisive – the more so because the career that John had dreamed of was beginning to bloom. John could not afford to be tarnished by his son's foolishness now. He believed that his own compromise on religious matters was a perfectly valid path. It was a nice balancing act that was commonplace at court. And John had begun to move in royal circles.

Everyone, including the king and Prince Charles, now accepted John as 'Head botanist in London'. He had proved himself to the royal physicians who were in daily contact with the palace, through his work for the Society of Apothecaries. Dr Henry Atkins was grateful for his efficient assistance on the preparation of the *Pharmacopoeia*. Dr Theodore de Mayerne, whose opinion was immensely valuable, became a friend and colleague. The Frenchman was particularly impressed, as other foreigners had been, by John's honesty and attention to detail. He described him as 'the most skilful [Botanist], the most well practised, the most perceptive, and the [one] with the most discerning nose'.[3]

In 1623, one of John's oldest friends joined the royal household. Matthew Lister, who was appointed royal physician after the death of his elder brother Edward, was born at Thornton in Yorkshire, only a few miles from where John grew up. The Listers were established Yorkshire gentry and mixed in higher social circles than John's family. John Aubrey wrote that Matthew became the *de facto* husband of the notorious Mary Herbert, Countess of Pembroke:

> The Countesse, after her Lord's death, married to Sir Matthew Lister, Knight, one of the colledge of Physitians, London. Jack Markham saies they were not married. He was, they say, a learned and handsome gentleman.[4]

Lister was certainly her retainer until the countess died at the age of sixty in 1621, when he moved on to the court. The countess' sons were in dominant positions there. Her eldest, the Earl of Pembroke, William Herbert, was using his fortune to follow the example set by his mother of entertaining lavishly at Wilton and sponsoring arts and science.

The presence of Matthew Lister at court was important for John because he was one of the few court figures who fully understood

John's Catholic background in the north, and who could vouch for his loyalty to the king. Yet there were other aristocrats to speak for him. Lord Bacon was pursuing his earlier interest in writing and practical experiment while living in political exile, but he was still in social contact with the court. There was also Lord Zouche, who had prospered and remained close to the king, even though he was, in the opinion of Godfrey Goodman, the Bishop of Gloucester, 'the next degree to a fool'.[5]

John's closest friend in this aristocratic milieu was no aristocrat at all. He was John Tradescant, whose work was, like John's, the reason for his influence with these men. Tradescant was about to begin travelling for the all-powerful Buckingham, to whom the king had transferred his affections from Somerset. In 1623 he travelled to 'the Lowe Countries', to do for Buckingham what he had once done for Robert Cecil: find the greatest supply of the best trees for planting up the duke's new estate and garden at Newhall, near Chelmsford in Essex.[6]

Tradescant brought into John's world the vital element of fresh news from abroad. Over the last five years, when John had been bound by the relentless work involved in establishing the Society of Apothecaries, running his apothecary shop on Ludgate Hill and developing his garden in Long Acre, Tradescant had been travelling. He had sailed with Sir Dudley Digges in 1618, on an embassy to Russia that was also an attempt to discover a northern passage to the riches of China. Tradescant was a born sailor, comfortable on a ship when all around him were falling sick. He understood the wind and the tides and was happy to sleep between the decks, complaining only when there was so 'much raine ... that all the decks wear leake, which for my own parte I felt for it rayned doune thourow all my clothes and beds to the spoyll of them all'.[7] He was experienced in dealing with people of all nationalities and curious about their customs. In the three weeks his ship stayed at the Russian port of Archangel, Tradescant noted the houses, carts, boats, cattle and horses, the people's diet and, most of all, their flowers and crops:

> rye the[y] sewe in Jully, ther wheat in June. These two grayens growe
> sume 13 monthes before they be reaped by resin of the snow falling
> in August or September, and so lieth till the May after ... I have bin
> showed oats white, very good, which wer sowne and mowne and
> reapet thrashed in 6 weeks.[8]

This information, which Tradescant wrote in his journal of this first great adventure, would have been eagerly picked over by John when the ship returned home. Tradescant also brought samples of plants that he had gathered in his travels. Gardener that he was, his first thought when the ship finally returned to land at Yarmouth was to find fresh water to tend his plants. He had two little trees 'like a cherry in leafe and beareth a bery les than our Searvis berry' of which ' the wood is wondros pliant and if a twig chance to tuche the ground it will take roote'. There were also '3 or 4 sortes of whorts [berries] red on[e]s and two sorts of blewe on[e]s' which he had taken many samples of, but feared they had suffered from the lack of water and the fact that 'the Boys in the ship befor I pe[r]seved it, eat of the berries' on the way home.[9] He only had a few left from which to preserve the seed.

Tradescant was impressed by how large the fruit grew in the short hot summers of Archangel, and the beauty of acres of white 'helebros ... enough to load a shipe' and jagged wild pinks. These he could describe, though he was forced to ask his companions to smell the single red 'cinnamon rose' he found there, reporting that those 'who have the sence of smelling say they be marvelus sweete'. This rose he brought home, in 'hope that they will growe and beare heere [in England] for amongst many that I brought hom with the roses upon them, yet sume may grow'.[10]

When he finally reached Canterbury, Tradescant planted what samples he could, and sought help to identify others. He sent some berries that he had dried 'muche like a strawbery but of an amber coller. The people eate it fo[r] a medsin against the skurvi'[11] to the man in charge of the royal gardens in Paris, Vespasien Robin, and showed some to John in London.

It must have been disappointing after so much care to find that his plants were already familiar to John. Tradescant's 'Muscovy Rose' was an exception that his son was still growing in 1656. The amber strawberry was cloudberry (*Rubus chamaemorus*). The white 'helebros' was a veratrum which John called 'Neesing roote', used by apothecaries as a strong purgative. John included the plant in his 'Garden of pleasant flowers' 'because their leaves, being faire and large, have a goodly prospect', and because it gave him a chance, one he hardly ever missed, to heap praise on his adventurous friend, and record their companionship. Many people in Europe had the plant from Germany, but John made a point of telling the tale from Tradescant the traveller. This plant is found, he wrote, also in some parts of Russia, in that aboundance, by the relation of that worthy, curious, and diligent searcher and preserver of all nature's rarities, my very good friend John Tradescante, often heretofore remembred, that as hee said, a good ship might be loaden with the rootes hereof, which he saw in an Island there.[12]

While Tradescant was hunting for unusual plants, his companions hunted other curiosities. Sir Dudley Digges found a 'unicorn's horn' on a seashore that he presented as a prize of great value to Prince Charles on his return. For many years it was carefully displayed at Windsor, when royalty were in residence, or kept at the Tower in their absence.[13]

In 1620 Tradescant set off again, this time for the Mediterranean, in the supply ship of an 'expedition to quell the Barbary pirates'. British ships were suffering now from the piracy they had practised so successfully themselves thirty years before. Pirates operating out of Algiers were attacking British merchants even in the Thames. Tradescant sailed as one of 'fourteen gentlemen' who accompanied the king's ships out of curiosity.[14] From the supply ship's decks they witnessed the complete failure of the king's mission to burn the pirate fleet in the port as they planned, but, this time, there were personal triumphs for Tradescant.

John was able to travel down to Lord Wotton's garden in Canterbury where Tradescant entertained him with treasures and tales. He heard that the northern coastal shores of Africa 'had many acres of ground … spread over' with 'Corn Flags' or gladioli. He was told the Spaniards ate an onion 'both long and flat, very sweete … like an apple'. Best of all was Tradescant's little tree, a sight that delighted John. It was a 'greater wilde or double blossom'd Pomegranet tree'. John had seen the pomegranate grown as a cultivated rarity in English gardens like Lord Zouche's. Tradescant had bought some in Paris for Robert Cecil's Hatfield garden. But this little wild pomegranate in Canterbury had branches that 'shoote forth flowers, farre more beautifull then those of the tame or manured sort, because they are double, of an excellent bright crimson colour, tending to a silken carnation'.

John allowed himself another tribute to his friend in his record of this tree, accepting an unusually vague account of its source. 'The wilde [kind of pomegranate tree] I thinke was never seene in England, before John Tradescante my very loving good friend brought it from parts beyond the Seas, and planted it in his Lord's garden at Canterbury'.[15] He did not question John Tradescant as he questioned other men.

Holidays such as this visit to Canterbury were rare for John, even though he no longer had the Society's business to worry about. He was needed every day in the shop, which still generated his income, to teach and supervise. In other circumstances he might have turned to his son for help, but he now depended principally on his assistant, William Orly, who would not qualify as a freeman apothecary until 1626.[16]

The garden part of his business was constantly expanding meanwhile, as John catered to the growing taste for decorative gardens amongst the gentry around London. He not only supplied plants and advised his customers. He was invited to their houses as an equal and a guest. Occasionally, as he was so short of time, he was also uncharacteristically short of temper. When one of his customers, Mistress Geeres, invited him to dinner and was then not at home, John made no attempt to conceal his irritation. He wrote her a curt note:

Good Mres Geeres,

I have by this messenger sent you the ij [two] trees whereof I told when we were last together at your house. I brought them thither on the Saturday you were so earnest with me to come to dinner where I thought to have met with you, but missing you I carried them home again & and laid them in the ground wherein they have been safe without taking any harm.

I do also think that then you would have pleasure and with that you promised and have long expected it. I pray you doe not wearye me with desyre which is worse than denyall, as you please appoint Mr. Codemer to doe it speedily.

So shall ever remaine,

Yors

John Parkinson

In the event John thought better of sending the letter. He turned the paper over and used the back to make some notes on evergreens, information that he shared with Francis Bacon who was preparing his book of *Naturall Historie*, which was published posthumously in 1627.[17]

John's habit of making neat notes and lists on every scrap of paper had recently taken on a new intensity. He stored up Tradescant's stories with a fresh sense of purpose. For decades he had been slowly preparing his account of all the uses and characteristics of the plants known to London apothecaries. It was for this, as much as for the garden that he grew, that his contemporaries knew him as the 'Head botanist'.[18] In his workshop, the roots he was studying lay intermingled with dusty bundles of papers, carefully protected from the water and flame that spread around his stills and the tools of his chemical experiments.

So far not a word of his great project had been published. Now, however, no less than the king encouraged him to finish his great encyclopaedia of plants. King James showed no sign of sharing his courtiers' enthusiasm for the aesthetic aspects of gardens. It is true that he was happiest at Theobalds, and was fond of the fruit his subjects' gardens yielded. Dr Goodman, who visited him during his last illness, believed his immoderate appetite for fruit was a fatal weakness:

> I remember that Mr French of the Spicery, who sometimes did present him with the first strawberries, cherries and other fruits, and kneeling to the King, had some speech to use to him, - that he did desire his Majesty to accept them, and that he was sorry they were no better - with such like complimental words; but the King never had the patience to hear him one word, but his hand was in the basket.[19]

While the king had no interest in the finesse of growing plants, his love of ideas made him extremely sympathetic to John's proposal to write an encyclopaedia of plant medicines in English. It was well known by now that Gerard's book was inadequate in terms of scholarship, and the king wished to be remembered for the initiatives he had taken to further the wellbeing of his people. A reliable and scholarly review of plants and medicines, in English so that it would be available for the common wealth, was exactly the kind of project that appealed to him. His friends informed him that John was the best man to complete this task, and he urged John to do so.

The problem with this flattering commission from John's point of view was that it was unpaid. The king's legendary generosity had run dry since his failure to agree a regular subsidy with Parliament. He was now far more conscious of what he could gain than what he could give. John's circumstances obliged him to keep his business running while struggling to complete his great work. However, there were rewards.

In 1623 he was granted the lease of a house on the east side of St Martin's Lane in what had become an enclave for courtiers. He supplemented his income by subletting to various people. John began to pay rates to the overseers of St Martin's parish, where his garden was, for the first time. The rate was two shillings and two pence, which John shared that year with an apothecary called Thomas Phelps. His neighbour there and fellow apothecary, Stephen Chase, paid two shillings and two pence for his house and shop alone. John must also have been allowed to build a small house in the centre of his garden, and complete the wall around it, so that he could work and study there. The king still took a close interest in the development of the Convent (by now Covent) Garden area, and every new building was scrutinized by the king's council. Finally, John received the right to display a coat of arms, recognized in the rate returns of 1626 when 'John Pirkenson' was dubbed 'esquire'. Like his commission, this right was not officially recorded at the College of Heralds, yet John seems to have been happy with the royal permission, and took no steps to secure any legal document.[20]

John must have been grateful to be so recognized and protected in a political climate that was growing steadily more bitter towards people of his religion. The growing fervour of English Puritans was fanned by the war in Europe, the start of thirty years of hostilities in a continent that had divided along religious lines. In London, John avoided confrontation as much as he could, but he was ready to come to the rescue of friends whose careers were blighted by the religious divide. One of his friends and professional partners was a Catholic doctor called John Moore. While Dr Moore was studying medicine in Padua, John had exchanged seeds with him. Dr Moore sent John the seed of a rare dark pink amaranthus, which he treasured for its rarity and the fact that the flowers would keep their colour for many months if they were carefully picked and dried. Amaranthus takes its name from the Greek word meaning 'non senescens, or never waxing old,' wrote John. 'The Italians, from whom I had it (by the meanes of Mr Doctor John More, as I have had many other rare simples) call it Blito di tre Colori, a three coloured Blite.'[21]

In return, John sent his friend a type of figwort that he called 'sambucifolio' or elder-like because of the shape of its leaves, which he had been given with a collection of other seeds. This figwort had no decorative properties but proved extremely useful for its property of dissolving blood clots and irregular formations of the skin. It was an effective treatment, made into an ointment with butter, for piles, haemorrhoids and 'all rednesse, spots and freckles in the face'.[22]

But when Dr Moore came back from Padua and applied for a licence to practise medicine in London, he was refused. Dr Atkins, who was president at the time, put his case to the college in December 1617, but 'it was objected ... that he had been prohibited by the Archbishop'. The anti-

Catholic laws were now strictly applied. Six months later the college received another letter from Archbishop Abbot warning them against admitting Catholic doctors.

> We are advertised of some yet out of a Puritan vayne and humour, do shew a distaste and unconformity unto the doctrine and discipline established in the Churche of England. Others there are, that are carried away with Popishness and recusancy, who are expressly forbidden to practise by the Lawe. I am to intreat yow to have speciall care and circumspection in this particular, that neither one nor the other have any admittance license or approbation from your College...

Dr Moore's friends made one last attempt to persuade the fellows to accept him if he took the oath of allegiance. 'But this was rejected by fifteen beans when twenty fellows were present.' So the college refused Dr Moore's membership, although it did eventually connive at his unofficial practice in London.[23] John gave his old friend a home in the most fashionable part of the city and the only part where a Catholic doctor could practise because of its proximity to the court. By 1626 Dr Moore was sharing a house with him in Covent Garden.[24]

John's garden there allowed him to bridge the hostilities and make friends in all sections of society. His love of plants inspired him to see the divine in life beyond political divisions and he never lost an opportunity to point out that this was the lesson to be learned from plants. The humble wild or Choke pear, common in 'Woods, Forests, Fields and Hedges', was used to make Perry, 'a drink', John wrote, 'much esteemed as well as Cyder, to be both drunke at home, and carried to the Sea, and found to be of good use in long voyages'. This drink was another proof, John thought, of a world mystically ordered for the help and sustenance of man.

> The Perry made of Choke Peares, notwithstanding the harshenesse, and evill taste, both of the fruit when it is greene, as also of the juice when it is new made, doth yet, after a few moneths, become as milde and pleasant as wine, and will hardly be knowne by the sight or taste from it: this hath been found true by often experience; and therefore wee may admire the goodnesse of God, that hath given such facility to so wilde fruits, altogether thought uselesse, to become usefull, and apply the benefit thereof both to the comfort of our soules and bodies.[25]

In 1625, the conditions were as good as they ever would be for John to complete his great encyclopaedia. His apprentice, William Orly, would soon be fully qualified to take care of the shop, and the favours he had received from the king were enough to give him a bit of extra income. Then, suddenly, he was diverted from his goal by a drastic change at court.

King James' mental powers had been visibly fading for more than two years. In February 1623, the Venetian ambassador reported sadly that

> all good sentiments are clearly dead in the king. He is too blind in disordered self love and his wish for quiet and pleasure, too agitated by constant mistrust of everyone, tyrannized over by perpetual fear for his life, tenacious of his authority as against the parliament and jealous of the prince's obedience.[26]

James drooled over Buckingham, calling himself his 'dear Dad and Husband' and declaring 'he would rather live banished in any part of the world with him'.[27] Buckingham transferred his attentions to Prince Charles as the king declined. Then, in March 1625, King James collapsed at Theobalds from a 'quartan ague', a severe bout of dysentery that induced a stroke and killed him. He was only forty-nine.

His son and heir borrowed £60,000 from the City to bury him with spectacular ceremony, although the old king died owing them £200,000. Nine thousand people were issued with mourning clothes or 'blacks', to watch the king's embalmed corpse carried through the streets in a magnificent Baroque hearse designed by Inigo Jones. 'Recusant papists' were excluded from the list of mourners.[28]

Charles' court seemed to be immediately and deliberately different from his father's. As king, after changing all the locks at Whitehall according to custom, he banished his father's dissolute followers. But in the first of many respects his policies were the same. In the first month of his reign he brought the fifteen-year-old Henrietta Maria to England as his queen, the daughter of Marie de Médicis and Henri IV of France, sister of Louis XIII, and Europe's leading Catholic princess.

She was potentially a highly unpopular choice, bringing with her, as people suspected she did, special concessions for her fellow Catholics in Britain. There was a secret agreement, revealed only in a private letter that Buckingham sent from Paris to the prince and King James. He advised that the Parliament should be silenced, by being prorogued, until the people had a chance to get to know the king's bride: 'for the Princess of France when she shall be here for the virtues and grace that shine in her' would not only prevent 'exorbitant or ungentle motions ... but facilitate those passages, favors, grace and goodness which his Majesty hath promised for the ease of the Romaine Catholicks'.[29]

Henrietta Maria had married her prince by proxy in France. John was one of the few to have a direct account of the splendour of the royal wedding, from his friend John Tradescant who had been there. Buckingham had travelled to France as Charles' personal envoy to bring Henrietta Maria home and Tradescant had been paid to follow on to Paris with 'my Lord's stuff and Trunks'. The duke treated the French court to the greatest display of imperial splendour he could muster. The Duke of Chevreuse, representing Charles in the ceremony, was forced to wear black by King James' sudden death. Next to him stood Buckingham, in a suit 'of purple satin embroidered all over with rich pearl' that was said to have cost £20,000. Buckingham had no fewer than twenty-seven suits to dazzle the French with, including one white velvet suit and cloak, set entirely with diamonds.[30]

Tradescant would have seen the glittering pageant in Paris, how the princess, so covered in jewels that a guard walked behind her to take the weight of her train, had stepped up to a platform in front of Notre Dame, how the great cathedral's walls had been hung with cloth of gold and cloth of silver, and the archbishop's palace with purple satin powdered with gold fleur-de-lys. He had seen her laugh with childish delight the day after the wedding, when the Duke of Buckingham appeared in his dazzling white velvet suit and his mother presented the queen with a pie. When the pie was opened a tiny boy emerged. He was Jeffery, a dwarf, who at once became a part of the new queen's household.

King Charles met his wife for the first time when she arrived with her retinue at Dover. It was immediately noted that she came with 'a Bishop and twenty eight priests, resolute Papists, as are all her servants'.[31] She had also brought a French surgeon called Maurice Aubert, and a German physician called Dr Erlintz. Even 'Jeffery the dwarfe' had his own retinue: a servant, a friend called 'little Sava'; 'Madam Giramir' as his nurse, and Richard Stott who was paid as 'keeper of the Parotts' and for 'keeping the dwarfs'. The queen stood no higher than the king's shoulder, but she was instantly impressive. She was 'of more than ordinary resolution' so that one frown of her brown eyes 'cleared an overcrowded room'.[32]

As it turned out, it was this girl who made John's name for posterity. Because of her he quickly produced a book displaying all the finest beauties of an English garden. It was *Paradisi in sole: Paradisus Terrestris*, and it was this book for which he would remain famous long after modern medicine had nudged his medicinal herbs into oblivion.

Henrietta Maria had spent her life surrounded by lovely gardens. She grew up in the palace of St Germain-en-Laye near Paris, where Salomon de Caus had created a magical grotto and elaborate fountains. After the death of her father, her mother, Marie de Médicis, who herself had grown up beside the finest gardens in Italy, encouraged the work of Jean Robin and his son Vespasien at the Louvre palace.[33] When Henrietta Maria went to live there she found that the garden they created for her father, the Jardin des Plantes, was blossoming. There was nothing of equal splendour in London. The garden at Somerset House was fine in its way, with orange trees on the terrace and a celebrated fountain by Salomon de Caus at its centre. Yet it was too formal to delight a fifteen-year-old girl. The privy garden at Whitehall was clipped and old fashioned, while the garden at the queen's new palace of St James's was small and in shadow much of the time.

The finest gardens in England when she arrived belonged to private citizens, and the finest of these in London was John's. As a lover of plants, an innovator, a scholar, and a Catholic to boot, John Parkinson was called on to show the young queen what great curiosities and beauty the gardens of her new kingdom embraced. Unable to resist such an invitation, John put aside his projected encyclopaedia and began work on a 'garden of pleasant flowers' for the queen. This elegant young lady at the head of her glittering court seemed to release him from dusty medical scholarship and encourage his deep feeling for natural beauty. He completed his task far more quickly than might have been guessed from the progress of his medical encyclopaedia. Within a few years the pages were written, printed and proofed, the illustrations drawn and corrected, and an engraving of the author himself made ready for the flyleaf (see page 12). The black and white lines of this engraving send his message clearly down the ages. In the language of flowers he refers proudly, with just a touch of irony, to the position he holds in the society this young queen has joined. In his hand is a flower that was known to Londoners as a 'Sweet John', but also to most by its other name, 'Pride of London'.

CHAPTER THIRTEEN

'THIS SPEAKING GARDEN'

Sir Theodore de Mayerne, eighteenth-century mezzotint after the portrait, c.1630 by Sir Peter Paul Rubens in the National Portrait Gallery, London.

The king's physician, Sir Theodore de Mayerne, who now lived opposite John's garden in one of the grand new houses on the west side of St Martin's Lane, had become his great friend and admirer. In October 1628, the Frenchman read John's description of his *Paradisus Terrestris*, or Earthly Paradise, in manuscript and wrote an affectionate commendation in his elegant Latin for the front of the book.

De Mayerne congratulated 'my dear Parkinson' on his 'work of untiring labour', which he praised for the 'energetic brevity' of its entries and the clear way that his friend 'loving truth of exposure ... has proclaimed perpetual war with pretence that shades rather than lights up the splendour of nature'. He urged John 'not to be dissatisfied with your work given with difficult labour at night.... It is difficult things that are beautiful. May the sweetness of due praise soften the harshness of the wakeful hours...'.[1]

John had taken upon himself the 'labour and charge' of producing this radical book of the garden. He kept his apothecary shop and his nursery business going and wrote his pages by candlelight late into the night. In the end there were 612 of them, including full-page woodcuts, accurately illustrating nearly 1,000 plants that he had chosen for this garden. He selected plants that were 'the chiefest for choice, and fairest for shew, from among all the severall Tribes and Kindred's of Nature's beauty ... ranked as neere as I could in affinity one unto another'.[2]

The book began with several introductory chapters giving general tips on the secrets of horticulture, an index to the plants in English and Latin, and a table of the medicinal 'Vertues and properties of the hearbes contained in this Booke'. The illustrations caused him most worry and expense. Herbals were generally printed by specialist printers, who owned a set of illustrations that would be reused in works by different authors. A suitable set of illustrations for 'exotic' garden plants was not available to John, so he commissioned specially cut woodblocks, copied mostly from drawings in other Latin herbals. Since each block was the size of a full page and contained images of up to ten plants, the entire block had to be cut again if there were any mistakes. John was so anxious to make his work truthful and accurate that he spent much 'time, paines and charge' on getting these illustrations right. Unwittingly John had chosen an old-fashioned medium. His books of plants would be the last to appear with wooden cuts, which were on their way out in continental Europe, soon to be replaced by copperplate engravings, which were much faster to cut.

Yet the illustrations in the *Paradisus* are part of its charm. Their stiff solid forms are so clearly the plants that grow in our gardens today, the individual shapes of their leaves, fruit and roots picked out with a delicate carver's knife. John was as proud of them in the end as if he had cut them himself, rather than Albert Switzer, the German he employed.

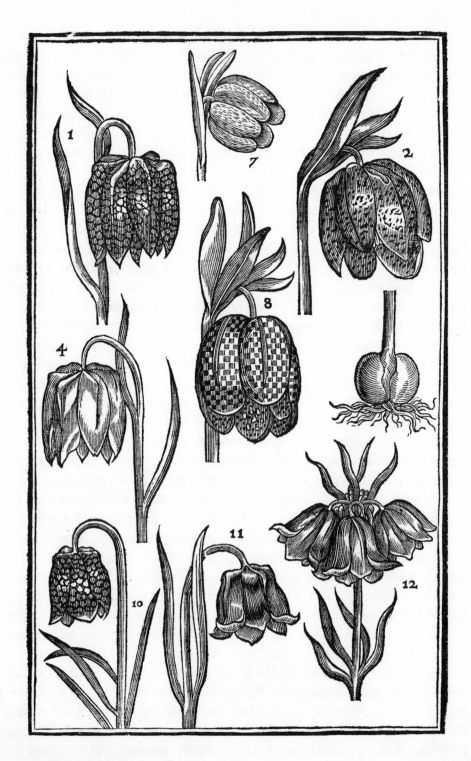

Fritillaries, illustration from Paradisus, *1629.*

I have ... to embellish this Worke set forth the figures of all such plants and flowers as are materiall and different from one another; but not as some other have done, that is a number of the figures of one sort of plant that have nothing to distinguish them but the colour, for that I hold to be superfluous and waste.[3]

Only the frontispiece was pure fantasy. The door into Park-in-sunne's Paradise is Switzer's vision. Apple and orange trees grow alongside date palms and pineapples. Eve runs naked among tropical birds and fritillaries, her long, thick, black hair falling across her dark body as Pocohontas' hair had done. Adam is an African, sheltering behind a tree beside a myriad of cacti, lilies and giant pinks. The wandering stream that runs through Paradise, beside paw-paws, grape vines and climbing roses, encircles the mythical medieval Tartary lamb, with a three-foot tree trunk projecting from its navel (see page 6).

John's book never mentioned the Tartary lamb. Fables had nothing to do with his Park in the sun. His dream was nature, managed by man, so that it yielded God's bounty equally to all the senses. Even a 'Garden of pleasant and delightfull flowers' was incomplete without the food it could produce. After the flowers there was a

Garden ... of Herbes and Rootes, fit to be eaten of the rich and poor as nourishment and food, as sawce or condiment, as sallet or refreshing, for pleasure or profit; where I do as well play the Gardiner, to shew you (in briefe but not at large) the times and manner of sowing, setting, planting and replanting and the like (although all these things and many more then are true, are sett down very largely in the severall bookes that others have written of this subject) as also to shew some of the Kitchen uses ... although I confesse but very sparingly, not intending a treatise of cookery ...; and also the Physicall [medicinal] properties, to shew somewhat that others have not set forth, yet not to play the Empiricke, and give you receipts of medicines for all diseases, but only to shew in some sort the qualities of Herbes, to quicken the mindes of the studious. And lastly an orchard of all sortes of domesticke or forraine, rare and good fruits, fit for this our Land and Countrey.[4]

This description of the feast his book contained for the reader was conventional enough, but in fact his *Paradisus Terrestris* was revolutionary. Nothing quite like it had been written before. John presented each plant he selected with an illustration and a detailed description of its origins and locations, followed by the method of cultivation, and a brief outline of its medical uses or 'vertues'. He deliberately included as much of his professional knowledge, both as an apothecary and a gardener, as he could. This in itself was unusual. Knowledge was generally considered something to be kept from the common people. Those who had knowledge concealed it, honour bound to their secret 'mysteries' or professional companies as John had once been to the Grocers. This age-old argument had protected the rogue apothecaries in the Company of Grocers, held back the appearance of the *Pharmacopoeia* for so long and could even be said to have fuelled the bloody waves of witch trials across the country. It was an argument with which John profoundly disagreed, though he knew that secrets had commercial value, and sharing them with the public could mean professional suicide.[5]

His book was scholarly, in that its information was factual and it was based on research and experience, but it was in English. Here was another novelty. There were, as John wrote: 'many Herbals in Latine, [but] I observed that most of them have eyther neglected or not knowne the many diversities of the flower Plants, and rare fruits that are known to us at this time, and (except Clusius) have made mention but of very few'.[6] He pointed out that the most recent herbal in English was Gerard's, since when 'we have had many more varieties than he ever heard of, as may be perceived by the store I have here produced'. As guides to would-be gardeners the existing books were quite inadequate:

Divers Bookes of Flowers also have been set forth, some in our owne Countrey, and more in others, all which are as it were, but handfulls snatched from the Treasury of Nature.... The greatest hinderance of all men's delight was, that none of them had given any description of them [flowers] but the bare name only.[7]

The most startling feature of the *Paradisus* was that it was the first English book about plants to be devoted above all to their beauty, making this the key purpose of a garden. Several garden books had appeared since the days of Thomas Hyll. Sir Hugh Platt produced the *Floraes Paradise* in 1608, which included 'sundry sorts of delicate fruites and flowers' and a recipe for a 'pleasing remedy in violent Feavers'. Gervase Markham, who was reputed to be the first Englishman to make a living from writing alone, produced *The English Husbandman* in 1613, which included, in its second edition, the 'ordering of the kitchen garden'. But, as John pointed out, no book had so far 'severed those that are beautifull flower plants, fit to store a garden of delight and pleasure, from the wilde and unfit'.

Since John's book referred to the pharmaceutical properties of plants, it was technically a medical book and he needed the approval of the London College of Physicians before he could publish. But de Mayerne, who already knew Henrietta Maria from his days serving her father at the Louvre, had become John Parkinson's champion at court. It was almost certainly he who smoothed the path by which John came to know the queen and her private garden at St James's Palace.

Henrietta Maria's household was mostly young and almost entirely French, so John, who was neither, must have cut a strange figure amongst them. But the queen clearly delighted in curiosity and variety, so much so that she paid the keepers of her dwarves and her parrots a handsome annual salary, which compared very favourably to the sum she paid England's foremost surveyor and architect of the day, Inigo Jones.[8] John's primary motivation cannot have been to make money, since there was so little forthcoming from the court, and his book was an expensive labour of love. Instead, he discovered that the queen shared his fascination with the beauty and properties of plants, and this language of flowers cut through the differences between them. His pleasure in the knowledge he could offer her, which, it seems, he had often spoken of, is reflected in the language with which he dedicated this book to her.

> Knowing your Majestie so much delighted with all the faire Flowers of a Garden, and furnished with them as farre beyond others, as you are eminent before them; this my Worke of a Garden, long before this intended to be published, and but now only finished, seemed as it were destined, to bee first offered into your Highnesse hands.... Accept, I beseech your Majestie, this speaking Garden, that may informe you in all the particulars of your store, as well as wants, when you cannot see any of them fresh upon the ground: and it shall further encourage him to accomplish the remainder; who ... submitteth to be Your Majesties
>
> in all
> humble devotion,
> John Parkinson

John's friends marvelled at the energy he was able to put into his garden at Long Acre, even while writing, so his book was a true reflection of the riches a London garden could yield. 'I do not know whether I admire more such a book or the garden; the whole world that is in the garden is in this book of yours,' wrote one of his apothecary friends, an aspiring young botanist called William Broad, in the front of the completed book. 'Your garden has the plants that Africa produces and India sends.'[9]

When the pages were ready for the printer, Otthovell Meverell, one of the most flamboyant and fashionable physicians in London, dashed off a commendation for the front. He dubbed John the natural successor to the two famous English botanists of the previous century: William Turner and John Gerard. 'Fortunate old man, may you now be the third Hero.' John was sixty-two and obliged to accept this remark as a compliment, but it must have rankled. He would not like to be reminded that he was old, so long as his 'greater' work, his herbal, was still unfinished, and he must have hoped his more perceptive readers would see that his book was significantly different from those of his two predecessors.

Turner and Gerard had both included, for example, a factual description of the plant that produced the barnacle goose. Gerard wrote:

There is a smalle Ilande in Lancashire called the Pile of Foulders, wherein are found the broken peeces of old and brused ships, some whereof have beene cast thither by shipwracke ... whereon is found a certaine spume or froth that in time breedeth unto certaine shells, in shape like those of the muskle ... wherein is contained a thing in forme like a lace of silke finely woven ... which in time commeth into the shape and forme of a Bird; ... bigger than a Mallard, lesser than a Goose.

Even Turner said he had it 'on good authority of a man called Octavian' that such a plant existed. Octavian had even promised to bring him some chicks.[10]

Lancashire was not such a strange remote place for John and he had no time for the barnacle goose. He barely wasted his breath to explain other men's faults, although his own way of working produced quite different results. 'I have only set down those that have come under mine own view and not any by relation,' he wrote about auriculas, 'even as I do with all or most of the things contained in this work.'[11] The new scientific attitude he had learned from Matthias de l'Obel was as important to him when he was speaking of flowers and fruit as it was when he was concerned with medicine.

Another tribute in the front of John's book seems to hint at this relationship with de l'Obel. William Atkins, a grocer who later became an alderman of the City of London, begged John's pardon in his testimony, that he had 'crushed your labours that others extol'. He acknowledged that John's book is a 'Portrait that paints your garden here' and John himself 'our Adam [who] stands there in the middle of that Paradise [his garden] and the species to which he has given his name'. The old quarrel that Atkins refers to is likely to have begun with the Apothecaries' separation from the Grocers. It seems that William Atkins had been one of those who fuelled the gossip that John's work was not original. They said he had copied de l'Obel's unpublished manuscript and repeated Gerard's travesty. Everyone knew he never travelled far from his garden. How could he know so much about the plants of the world? Yet, as Atkins now acknowledged, John carefully cultivated and observed at home what others brought back from afar, distilling the truth from the thunder and glory of their adventure, just as he distilled the essence of plants.

Now, it seemed, the beauty of John's book, of his garden, or the reflected glory of royal favour, had won Atkins round. John's work was universally admired and it must have been sweet to print Atkins' apology.

> You can be believed to have crossed the extremes of India: when this book is just like your garden; You make India itself live with you, you do not seek India. Go now and bring back your things that I have crushed.[12]

Accusations of plagiarism and incompetence were as inevitable as flattery in the London society of the time, given the fierce competition for royal patronage. In fact, though John had learned his method from de l'Obel, no book had been so closely related to personal experience as his. John's defence against the talk was characteristically restrained:

> For my selfe I may well say, that had not mine own paines and studies by a naturall inclination beene more powerfull in mee than any others helpe (although some through an evill disposition and ignorance have so far traduced me as to say this was rather another man's worke than

mine owne, but I leave them to their folly) I had never done so much as I here publish; nor been fit or prepared for a larger [the Herbal he was known to be compiling] as time may suddenly (by God's permission) bring to light, if the malevolent dispositions of degenerate spirits doe not hinder the accomplishment.[13]

The *Paradisus* emerged in an air of courtly splendour, but this was a merely superficial covering, like the court clothes its author wore for special occasions. John spoke directly to ordinary citizens like himself, rather than to aristocrats. His intended audience were men and women obliged to make the best of life, and to them he addressed his first line.

The severall situations of men's dwellings are for the most part unavoideable and unremoveable; for most men cannot appoint forth such a manner of situation for their dwelling as is most fit to avoide all the consequences of winde and weather.[14]

His first readers were his customers and friends, including the wealthier citizens of the nation's capital. Many had only 'Gardens that are small', a tiny enclave to call their own in the expensive and crowded city that London had become, yet each had the potential, John believed, to create a paradise.

Later John would call this book his 'feminine' work, thinking of the 'gentlewomen' among his customers for gynaecological remedies and beautiful plants who shared his love of flowers. He often wrote about women's speech, their desires and their needs. John's garden released feminine aspects of himself in which he revelled, such as his microscopic reverence for colour and detail. Unbound from the labour of scholarly accuracy, he was able to reflect in this book of flowers his deep pleasure in working with nature and the divine beauty he saw in it. When he recommended bulbs to his readers, which 'our English gardeners are all or the most of them utterly ignorant in the ordering [management] of', he gave advice on how to care for them because 'I do wish all Gentlemen and Gentlewomen ... to bee as careful whom they trust with the planting and replanting of these fine flowers as they would be with so many Jewels'. Bulbs were expensive, especially tulip bulbs from Amsterdam, but for John these flowers were more precious than their mercenary value. Working with his plants with the care and devotion that gentlewomen applied to their needlework, John wanted to show that nature could offer an equally satisfying result:

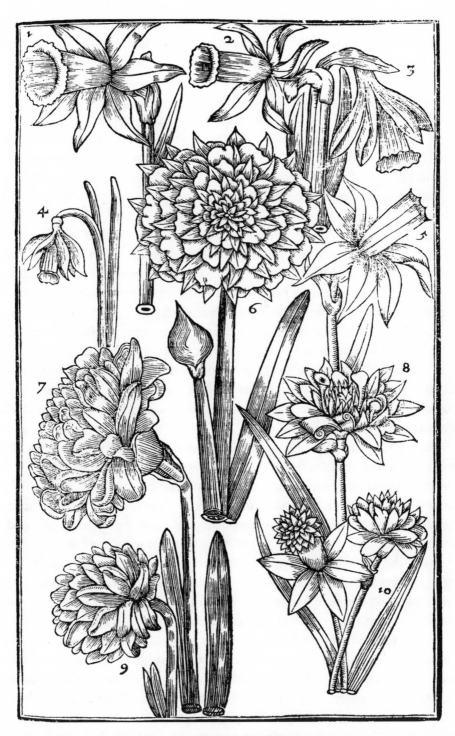

John Parkinson's daffodil (no. 8) and those of his friends, illustration from Paradisus, *1629.*

The Vernall Crocus or Saffron flowers of the Spring, white, purple, yellow and stript [striped], with some Vernall Colchicum or Medow Saffron amongst them, some Deus Caninus or Doggsteeth, and some of the small early Leucoium or Bulbous Violet, all planted in some proportion as neare one unto another as is fit for them, will give such a grace to the Garden, that the place will seeme like peece of tapestry of many glorious colours.... But above and beyond all others, the Tulipas may be so matched, one colour answering and setting of[f] another, that the place where they stand may resemble a peece of curious needleworke, or peece of painting.[15]

The bulbs John loved are described over nearly 200 pages of his book. He unveils in these descriptions many years of investigating his flowers with all his senses. The orange crown imperial lily smells 'strong as it were the savour of a Fox, which is yet not unwholesome' and 'on the inside there lyeth in those hollow bunched places certain clear drops of water, like unto pearls, of a very sweet taste, almost like sugar'. One of the narcissi, the double-headed 'Princess Peerless', has 'a sweet but stuffing scent', and there are three from Africa that he finds too strong for his sensitive nose. The great yellow daffodil of Africa is 'of so exceeding sweet a scent that it doth rather offend the senses by the abundance thereof'.[16]

His own daffodil he calls simply 'Parkinsonia'. 'I think none ever had this kind before myself, nor did I myself ever see it before the year 1618, for it is of mine own raising and flowering first in my garden.' He describes the perfect beauty of its petals as though he saw them artificially enlarged and sparkling before his eyes: 'they seeme to be greenish, whitish, yellow and gold yellow, all mixed one among another'.[17]

From the security of his garden, he cast an indulgent eye on the glittering society around him, a society that had become wild for fashionable display and where people used every means to embellish themselves. The scarlet Flowergentle (*Amaranthus caudatus*) was cultivated with infinite care from seed which would set each year only if the summer was fair, but it was cherished for its long plumes of flower that held their colour so well, 'like unto a feather such as is worn in our gallants and gentlewomen's heads, of an excellent bloody scarlet colour'.[18] One of the eleven different varieties of trefoil (*Medicago*) that he describes as commonly grown in gardens was known as 'snails or barbary buttons'. It has small yellow flowers, but it was grown for its seed heads, which are 'writhen round, almost like a Snaile somewhat like a green button, but afterwards growing whiter and more soft and open'. These were 'pretty toyes for Gentlewomen' who planted the seeds annually to be able to cut and wear the pods. Their husbands were interested in exploring this species as cattle feed.

> The medicas are generally thought to feede cattel fat much more than the medow trefoile or Clover grasse, and therefore I have known divers Gentlemen that have plowed up some of their pasture grounds, and sowen them with the seedes of some of the medicas to make the experience.[19]

Besides the beauty of flowers, the value of plants as food is never far from John's mind. Some new ideas in his 'Kitchen Garden' caught on better than the *Medicago* for cattle. Potatoes were still a delicacy, but Jerusalem artichokes had become very common. John preferred to call these 'Potatoes of Canada' because they were first brought from there to Europe by the French, although he conceded that they were as sweet as artichokes:

> Being put into seething water they are soone boyled tender, which after they bee peeled, sliced and stewed with butter, and a little wine, was a dish for a Queene, beeing as pleasant as the bottom of an Artichoke: but the too frequent use, especially being so plentifull and cheape, hath rather bred a loathing than a liking of them.[20]

These roots grew so well in England that their value declined sharply. 'Even the most vulgar begin to despise them,' lamented John. Yet the English diet was beginning to be permanently changed by the flood of plants that John and his friends had so zealously imported. The chief constituent was still meat, stuffed and flavoured with herbs, but there were new dishes, even for the poor. Pumpkins or 'pompions' grew easily, and were sometimes baked, stuffed with apples once the seeds had been removed. 'The poore of the Citie, as well as the Country people, doe eate thereof, as of a dainty dish'.[21]

For the rich there was the pumpkin's grander relative, the seed of which was also imported from Spain and sometimes Turkey: the melon. Melons needed special care to grow, and as this care was expensive, they became something of a trophy amongst aristocratic gardeners. John

Tradescant was famous for his skill with them, forcing the early growth in beds of hot manure and ripening the fruit with quantities of water. He had used this method so successfully for Lord Wotton that his employer's triumph was envied and emulated throughout the south of the country. By 1629, the method of growing them was widely understood, and they had become quite a common fruit:

> This Countrey hath not had until of late yeares the skill to nourse them up kindly, but nowe there are many that are so well experienced therein, and have their ground so well prepared, as that they will not misse any yeare, if it be not too extreme unkindly, to have many ripe ones in a reasonable time. They have been formerly only eaten by great personages, because the fruit was not only delicate but rare; and therefore divers were brought from France, and since were noursed up by the Kings or Noblemen's Gardiners onely ... but now divers others that have skill and convenience of ground for them, doe plant and make them more common....[22]

With these new additions, John's vegetable and fruit garden now contained most plants that are familiar today. There were some notable absences. The tomato, or love apple, was still grown in the flower garden, for the beauty of its fruit. One kind, with fruit of 'a faire pale reddish colour, or somewhat deeper, like unto an Orenge' at first had fruits the size of an apple, but 'by often sowing it in our Land, is become much smaller then I have here described it', John noted. As the rarity of imported plants and seeds diminished, so did their corresponding share of precious manure and water in the garden. The 'love apple' was found to be a tough survivor. John grew a yellow variety and a small cherry tomato and observed how 'Some years I have knowne them rise of their owne sowing in my garden.' John knew that love apples were naturalized in Spain and Ethiopia, though 'some report them to be first brought from Peru', and also that 'in the hot Countries where they naturally growe, they are much eaten of the people to coole and quench the heate and thirst of their hot stomaches'. In England, however, no one ate tomatoes. The fruit was considered to have an 'amorous aspect' but, unromantically, this derived less from its beauty than for the fact that it was an effective remedy for venereal disease. 'The Apples also boyled, or infused in oyle in the sunne, is thought to be goode to cure the itch.'[23]

Strawberries were wild and native to English woods, from where they had for a long time been transplanted and cultivated in gardens. The English loved to cover the ground under roses with them and their white flowers and tendrils were a familiar theme in needlework. At table, they were eaten with 'claret wine, creame or milke ... and sugar' and their leaves were used 'among other herbes in cooling drinks as also in lotions and gargles for the mouth and throate'. Even so, this age of dedicated gardeners had champions for almost every plant, and John recorded all their triumphs. In his view, the strawberry king of London was his old friend,

> Master Vincent Sion who dwelt on the Banck side [the south bank of the Thames] near the old Paris garden staires, who from seven rootes [of the Bohemia strawberry] as hee affirmed to me, in one yeare and a halfe, planted halfe an acre of ground with the increase from them, besides those he gave away to his friends.[24]

This Bohemia strawberry had recently been imported to England, and it was found that it produced good fruit only when the offshoots were removed. Master Vincent Sion did this so assiduously that he was not only able to fill his ground and supply all his friends, but also produce spectacular fruit. John had seen plants where 'some of the berries have been measured to bee neere five inches about'.[25] Few introductions were so successful. The 'Virginia strawberry', which someone had brought back, never seemed to ripen in England, and the Brussels strawberries that John Tradescant had introduced many years ago had rotted on the plant without ripening every year for the past seven years.

Vines were planted in almost every garden, to give shade in the manner of the old cloisters, and many new aristocrats tried to recreate the great monastic vineyards that had once flourished on their estates. Robert Cecil planted over 30,000 vines at Hatfield, a gift from the French ambassador's wife. It was an expensive gift, since he had to employ two French gardeners to take care of them, but he took his vineyard seriously and sent John Tradescant over to Flanders to buy more vines. The Hatfield vineyard was exceptionally successful long after his death. John Evelyn thought it was 'rarely well watered and well planted' and considered it 'the most considerable Rarity besides the house' when he visited Hatfield in 1642.[26]

Cecil's vineyard was an exception to the general rule. Most vineyards in England eventually failed. Queen Henrietta Maria had vineyards and silkworms at her favourite palace of Oatlands, and intended to add an orangery there. But without being able to match her resources, few ordinary gardeners succeeded with vines at that time. John considered it 'a fruitless labour for any man to strive in these daies to make a good Vineyard in England'. The chief problem was not so much the soil, although it may not have suited the strains of vine that the French brought over, but a run of cool summers and intensely harsh winters: 'Our years in these times do not fall out to be so kindly and hot, to ripen the grapes, to make anie good wine as formerly they have done.'[27]

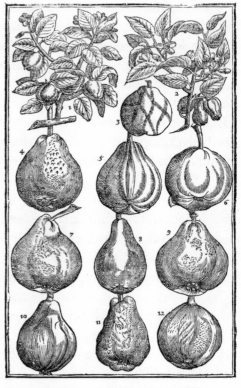

Pears, illustration from Paradisus, *1629.*

Growing orange trees in such a challenging climate was a triumph of hope over experience, but oranges had so many delightful uses besides the beauty of the tree and the smell of the blossom that John thought they were worth the effort. They were popular as 'sawce for many sorts of meates, in respect of their sweet sowernesse, giving a relish of delight'. The rind was dried and put among other things to make sweet powders, or candied and served at banquets and feasts. Orange water was used to wash gloves, leaving its scent on the hands of their wearer. The pulp and juice were considered cooling in fevers and the flowers were used to make an ointment which 'is very comfortable both for the stomache, against the could or cough, or for the head, for paines and disinesse'.[28] So John suggested a way in which even those who could not consider the elaborate preparations for housing orange trees over the English winter could enjoy this fruit:

The kernels or seede beeing cast into the ground in the spring time, will quickely grow up, (but will not abide the winter with us, to bee kept for growing trees) and when they are of a finger length high, being pluckt up and put among the sallats [salads], will give them a marvellous fine aromaticke or spicy taste, very acceptable.[29]

John came at last to the end of his book and so to the orchard, the part of the household garden that was every gentleman's pride. Swapping fine fruit or giving presents of newly grafted trees had become as much a landowner's occupation as hunting and drinking 'the house dry'.[30] The domain of the 'gentlewoman' was 'the garden of pleasure' amongst the fine flowers and the herbs that she tended for household medicines and the kitchen table. The orchard was more manly territory. The trees in John's book were laid out with military precision, but not without thought of beauty. He recommended that the trees be planted diagonally across a square ground, at least sixteen to twenty feet apart, to 'give you way sufficient to passe through them, to pruine, loppe or dresse them ... and may also be brought (if you please) to that gracefull delight, that every alley or distance may be formed like an arch, the branches of either side meeting to be enterlaced together'.[31]

He suggested that the site should be to the north and east of the flower garden, protecting the flowers from the 'strong bitter blasts' of the winds and leaving them exposed to the sun from the south. There should be some sort of wall, even a mud wall if a brick wall proved too expensive, against which apricots, peaches and nectarines could ripen. There were detailed practical notes and illustrations of the tools used for grafting new trees, which John expected to be perfectly familiar to gentlemen throughout the country.

He set down the rules of grafting only for such as 'would faine be taught privately', as though to learn from a 'Gardiner' would be a shameful confession of ignorance for some.[32] The fruit from the garden was a badge of pride for the household, to be shared in companionable hospitality with friends and visitors. 'The figs that grow with us when they are ripe, and fresh gathered, are eaten of divers with a little salt and pepper, as a dainty banquet to entertaine a friend, which seldom passeth without a cup of wine to wash them downe'.[33]

There was an abundance of fruit, all of it treasured by someone. Even the sorbus tree was grown in the orchard for its orange-brown berries, the size of hazelnuts, which were ripened inside in a warm room after the first frosts. Medlars were hung and eaten in the same way, 'for the pleasant sweetnesse of them when they are made mellow', although both were useful binding remedies 'to help stay the fluxe [diarrhoea]'.[34]

Melons and oranges were exceptional, perhaps, but apricots, peaches and nectarines were commonly grown. 'There are so many varieties and differences of Cherries, that I know not well how to expresse them unto you,' wrote John, but he lists and describes thirty-three different kinds.[35] There are over fifty varieties of plum, including damsons and bullaces, and so many kinds of apples that 'I cannot give you the names of all.' Different counties had their own special apples, and their names crowd together like a book of poems, 'The Broading, the Pomewater; the Flower of Kent; the Gilloflower apple; the Marligo; the Blandrill; the Davie Gentle; the Gruntlin; the gray Costerd...'.[36]

> The variety of pears is as much or more then of apples ... for we have in our countrie so manie, as I shall give you the names of ... but verily I believe there be many, both in our country, and in others that we have not yet knowne or heard of; for every yeare almost wee attaine to the knowledge of some, we knew not of before.[37]

Some pears are good for summer eating: 'the greene Chesill is a delicate mellow peare, even melting as it were in the mouth of the eater, although greenish on the outside'; some for winter: 'The Turnep peare is a hard winter peare, not so good to eate rawe, as it is to bake.' Some pears were found in the hedgerows and some had been fetched with great trouble and expense from the further reaches of Europe: 'The ten pound peare, or the hundred pound peare, the truest and the best, is the best Bon Chretien of Syon [a summer pear], so called, because the grafts cost the Master so much the fetching by the messenger's expenses, when he brought nothing else.'[38]

John's friends recommended varieties from all over the country. The chief keeper of the king's granary at Whitehall was Master William Ward, who came from Essex. William Ward was a friend of John Tradescant's to whom Buckingham had now given an honorary post in the granary, as a reward and an extra source of income. John found time for pleasant meetings with both Ward and Tradescant in the autumn sunshine, since the Whitehall granary was so close to Long Acre. They compared notes on plants while they tasted William's 'peare of Jerusalem, or the stript peare, whose barke while it is young is as plainly seene to be stript with greene, red and yellow, as the fruit selfe is also, and is of a very good taste'. William Ward assured John that when it was baked the pear was 'as red as the best Warden [pear]'.[39]

In the end, this very personal book celebrated the wealth of a land basking in newly cultivated riches. There is a stream of optimism running through its pages as John looks forward to a brighter and better society. He cherishes the beauty of English traditions, but he is inspired by the endless promise of new discoveries. Even the smallest import from the New World hints at something of possible value:

> The soon-fading spiderwort of Virginia or Tradescant his spiderwort ... is of late knowledge, and for it the Christian world is indebted to that industrious searcher, and lover of all nature's varieties, John Tradescant ... who first received it of a friend that brought it out of Virginia, thinking it to bee the Silke Grasse that groweth there.

Its discoverer had made a mistake. John could see that this plant was not particularly beautiful or useful, but as a herald from a new continent that his friend was the first to possess, it deserved a place in his garden.[40]

John believed his generation would reward its descendants with the best of legacies. The natural beauty of his country, combined with native skill and ingenuity in discovering the wider world, would reap rich dividends. This *Paradisi in Sole*, John's Park in Sun, was his first contribution to a society that he wanted to see growing along scientific lines, turning its back on the religious bigotry that had already caused him and his family so much pain. His 'Paradise' on Long Acre was like a microcosm of order and possibility that reflected the changing world outside. He could not deny that increasingly bitter arguments over truth and heresy raged outside the garden walls, but he placed his trust in rational observation, and used the flowers themselves to declare his moral truth.

He chose a particularly fashionable new flower from Virginia to invest with a loaded message that had deep personal significance. He described this 'brave and too much desired plant' called 'of the Virginians, Maracoc: of the Spaniards in the West Indies, Granadillo, because of the fruit ... is in some fashion like a small Pomegranate on the outside', and, notwithstanding the fact that his book was dedicated to the young Catholic queen, went on to denounce the popular naming of it.

> Some superstitious Jesuite would faine make men believe, that in the flower of this plant are to be seene all the marks of our Saviour's Passion; and therefore call it Flos Passionis: and to that end have

caused figures to be drawne, and printed, with all the parts proportioned out, as thorne, nailes, speare, whippe, pillar, etc in it, and all as true as the Sea burnes, which you may perceive by the true figure, taken to the life of the plant, and the figure set forth by the Jesuites ... these bee their advantageous lies (which with them are tolerable, or rather pious and meritorious) wherewith they use to instruct their people; but I dare say, God never willed his Priests to instruct his people with lyes: for they come from the Divell, the author of them.[41]

John Parkinson's illustration of the passion flower (right) and (above) the Jesuit illustration of the same plant. Both published in Paradisus, *1629*

For his own sake, and for his son's, John feared the Jesuit extremists. He proposed the innocuous name of 'Virginia climber' for this 'surpassing delight of all flowers', with its purple stamens exotically raised above white petals tinged with violet like the tail feathers of a bird of paradise. He could not have known then the complete legacy of his generation: how their struggle to establish moral truth would sweep everything into ruin, but how sons and grandsons would once again begin to build on the foundations their fathers had laid. The rationality that John championed would soon grow steadily stronger, and as it did so history forgot the pain associated with this exotic bloom. Generations who came after were happy to accept the Jesuits' name, while rejecting their message, so the flower became universally known as 'The Passion Flower'.

CHAPTER FOURTEEN

'INGENIOSE MEN'

With the publication of the *Paradisus*, John became part of the circle of scholars and artists entertained at Charles I's court. The king greeted the book with favour. He gave John a lease on a small parcel of royal land, 'next the Tennis courts in St James Fields,' to use as a garden for plants, at 20 s. a year. John would have the right to enclose the land and 'erect a house there', at his own expense.

This arrangement was similar to the one he already had for his garden in Long Acre. Tempted though he must have been by this direct grant from the throne, there was little immediate advantage in it for him. He could not afford to build there himself and was obliged to involve his neighbour and fellow apothecary, Stephen Chase, who had a lucrative contract supplying the 'chafe' or sealing wax to the court, in raising the capital. Chase offered to put forward £100 to erect a house and a wall around the ground, in exchange for having his name added to this prestigious lease.[1] Still, the king's offer to allow John to build on the other side of the palace remained nothing more than a pleasing prospect. The site Charles offered him in the royal park at St James's was still untouched in 1660.

It is distinctly possible that John considered the king's offer to conceal a threat. In accepting it, he might be obliged to leave his precious garden. His ground on Long Acre was now in the middle of highly desirable real estate. This area had been transformed within fifteen years from a country backwater into a busy suburb. The profits to be had from building houses and renting them to the 'gentlemen and men of ability' who clustered around the court were so great that what was begun by the Earl of Bedford and Thomas Cecil, Earl of Exeter, in 1615 was imitated by others who clubbed together to share the costs and build where they could. The house that John's friend Dr Matthew Lister bought on a twenty-one-year lease in July 1625 had been built by 'Sir Geo. Coppyn Kt, Dame Adeleyne Nevill, wid[ow].; and Roger Houghton Esq'. It was a substantial establishment, 'on grounds late part of Covent Garden pasture, viz: 2 little houses containing 5 rooms beside a stable and hayloft, coach house and drying room; plot or yard used for laying of compost or dung to the said houses'. John's neighbours were now 'the Lord Bishop of Exeter, the Earle of Annandale, the Ladie Levingstone, Sir John Danvers', as well as Dr Matthew Lister and Sir Theodore Turquet de Mayerne.[2]

The royal family attempted to control the development although they did not own the land, arguing that it affected royal journeys to and from the palace at Whitehall. In 1625, Charles repeated his father's decree that new houses were allowed only so long as they were built on old foundations. In spite of this, building went on apace, so he made another attempt to influence development in 1630.

The way called Long Acre... (by reason of the new buildings which cast out their dust, soil and filth into the same) is become so foul and noisome as is both impassable for his Majesty on his way to Tiballs [Theobalds], it is required that some present course be taken for the cleansing of the said passage and the better keeping of it hereafter.

In reply, the Earl of Bedford undertook to convert Long Acre from a muddy country lane into a paved city highway and pay £2,000 for a licence to build. There was too much money at stake for development to be long interrupted (see map, page 266).[3]

John benefited in part from this cluster of new houses. Parish rate returns show that he was a leaseholder of two of them at this time, one in St Martin's Lane and one in a part of the Earl of Bedford's new Covent Garden estate called Round Court. His friend Tradescant had also acquired leases on two houses in the area.[4] They seemed a profitable investment, but their value to John was nothing compared with his Long Acre garden, which was now established as the most famous open laboratory in the country.

When the parliamentary commissioners came to survey the area around Long Acre in the hope of laying claim to it in 1651, shortly after John's death, they found a site there fitting the most likely description that exists of his Long Acre home. Almost on the north-east corner of the junction of St Martin's Lane and Long Acre there was one garden plot, with no tenant named, which they described as 'enclosed by a brick wall in breadth forty foot ... and in midst one small tenement newley built consisting of three rooms, one above the other'.[5] By this time the tenant had gone. Civil war and time had ravaged his garden. The curious plot that remained was hemmed in by buildings on both sides, still green, still a garden, but bearing few other traces of its pre-war fame.[6]

An image of the garden as it had been in the 1630s emerges from the text of the *Paradisus*, rectangular beds near the house, edged with low box hedges, spilling over with tulips, lilies, precious anemones or irises in season, while 'turkey jarres' full of water stood by in the green shade. The path from the garden gate on Long Acre brought in visitors, new friends and customers, many of them attracted by the success of the book. As they passed they could admire the apricots, peaches and nectarines growing against the wall. The wide paths between the beds allowed companionable conversations about the flowers, and a visitor might stray, on one side, to a wooden walkway covered with climbing roses and clematis, honeysuckle and sweet peas. In another direction, a hedge of pyracantha led to the orchard, rich in April and May with the blossoms of many varieties of pear, apple, plum, service, quince and medlar.

The small cottage, standing in the heart of the garden, where its creator lived and worked, was more of a hermitage than a family home. It was a perfect place to study, to entertain and teach the visitors who came, and to carry on the chemical experiments that were part of the great task still before John.[7]

When people met John at his shop or his garden they would be just as likely to see him emerging from his laboratory, with the glass cup from a still in his hand, as they would be to see him holding a root or a flower, or writing careful notes in his close spidery hand. Chemistry was now the fashionable pursuit that alchemy had once been, and, where plants were concerned, John was leading the field. Many plants from the New World offered the 'Christian world' possibilities for the future, and John proposed to chart the discoveries of his generation. Though his *Paradisus* cemented his reputation as a scholar, John could not afford to rest from the task he had set himself. He had proved he was equal to the man from whom he had learned so much, Matthias de l'Obel. He could now call himself a *botanographus* or botanist, as well as a herbalist in the old sense. Like William Turner, he collected plants and accurately detailed their origin and appearance. More assiduously than anyone else, except John Gerard, he grew the plants he studied year after year. His joy in that process was now on record for later generations to discover. Yet John knew that his experiments to develop modern plant medicines had barely scratched the surface. There was much work still to be done.

From his years as an apothecary he had plenty of experience of the damage done to patients by medicine apparently copied from ancient texts. He intended that the great book he had been planning for so long would clarify matters by identifying exactly which varieties of plants used by modern apothecaries were the ones mentioned in the classics. Then he needed to show by his own chemical experiments the most effective method of using those plants for treating illness. Finally, he needed to write about all the new introductions that had been unknown to the Greeks and Romans but were considered effective by modern physicians and apothecaries, and might help combat such episodes as the outbreaks of plague that continually recurred in London and devastated the population.

In the summer of 1630 the plague was back again, after an absence of five years. The aristocrats and the physicians left town, as usual. In November the parish overseers in St Martin's-in-the-Fields, who included Matthias de l'Obel's grandson Abraham, collected a rate for 'the relief of the poor visited with the plague',[8] but neither the Duke of Arundel nor the Countess of Derby was at home when they called. Sir Theodore de Mayerne protected his professional position, like all the other physicians, by keeping his remedy for the plague to himself. He advised his nephew, Sir John Colladon, who became a physician in 1636, 'never to treat plague patients except from a good distance to windward, lest [you] lose form with the "noblesse"', and not to reveal the secret remedy that he had sent him.[9] Meanwhile John protected himself with a remedy he was preparing to publish, 'the juice of small sage drunk with vinegar',[10] and continued working on his radical medical encyclopaedia.

The task he had set himself was mammoth. Just one seed among thousands that came from his garden alone signified how much combined knowledge there was to assimilate in order to explain this changing world. He had a corner dedicated to rhubarb, which he was the first to grow in England. Rhubarb was an important medicinal plant which had been imported to Britain, and the rest of Europe, for hundreds of years. The dried roots used to arrive from a mysterious source:

> brought by Arabian, Turky and other Merchants, in former times from thence, overland by Caravans: as they call them, that is a number of Merchants and others having camels laden with it and all other

manner of drugges and spices there to be had, wherewith they served all this and other parts of the world.[11]

In Cairo and Alexandria in Egypt, in Damascus and Tripoli, the precious drugs were stored in warehouses until merchants transported them for sale in Europe. The long chain of delivery meant that there was considerable confusion about the origin of this plant. Dioscorides and Pliny thought that it came from a place called Barbaria in Ethiopia where, they said, the Troglodytes lived. John's contemporary, Prosper Alpinus, an Italian apothecary from Padua, who had written a study of the plants of Ethiopia, suggested that rhubarb grew above the river Indus, in India. Ironically it was John, an armchair traveller in London, who clarified the plant's true origin:

The Arabians did call it Raved or Raiwand Sceni, or Seni as some write, but I finde it should be rather Cini, which corruptly the Portugalls first pronounced Chini, according to their Language, and from them all our parts of the world doe call that country China.[12]

Through a mixture of linguistics, study and practical experiment, John was gradually unravelling some of the mysteries of the vegetable kingdom. His knowledge of this plant was more than theoretical. Rhubarb is a cousin of native dock, and the variety grown in gardens as a medicine was called 'Monkes Rubarbe' or Garden Patience. This was a common remedy in the countryside.

The leaves of these kindes of Dockes, boyled in broth, doe a little (some more, some lesse) mollify or loosen the belly; but the rootes have a more opening, purging quality in them ... a dramme of the dryed rootes of the ... sort called of some Monkes Rubarbe, with a scruple of Ginger, made into pouder, and taken fasting in a draught or messe of warm broth, purgeth choler and phlegm downward very gently, and safely without danger: the seede thereof contrarily doth bind the belly, and thereby helpeth to stay ... laske [diarrhoea] or bloody fluxe [dysentery].[13]

The true rhubarb, however, or *Rhaponticum verum* as it was known, was a much more powerful remedy prepared by London apothecaries, with many uses. The imported roots of this now travelled directly from

China aboard the ships of the East India Company, bypassing the old caravan routes and arriving more swiftly and certainly in the hands of knowledgeable London merchants. But still they arrived blackened and unrecognizable, often rotten in parts, and were imported at considerable cost. So John was naturally delighted with his discovery that he could easily grow this plant in his garden. With a characteristic tribute to his friends, but unmistakable satisfaction, he later described how it came to him. Prosper Alpinus was growing the plant in Padua:

> from whence some Apothecaryes at Venice had it: and Master Doctor Matthew Lister, one of the King's Physitions, being in Venice, obtained 3 or 4 seedes, which he sent me with some other seedes that he procured; and with me (as I think the first in this Land) they sprung up, grew and seeded within two or three yeares, and from them, both I, and many other my friends, as well in England as beyond Sea have bin furnished.[14]

Rhubarb, illustration from Paradisus, *1629.*

Once he had established that this 'English rubarbe', as he called it, was the same as the *Rhaponticum verum* quoted in the old remedies by Galen and Dioscorides, John began to experiment with the fresh root. He found that the English rhubarb root had exactly half the strength of the dried imported root from China, which he ascribed to the difference in climate. Its moderate strength turned out to be a distinct advantage, however. John was astonished by the power of some of the purgative doses that Dioscorides recommended, which completely overwhelmed the average London patient. He concluded that the English were 'moister bodies' by dint of the climate, and Dioscorides' remedies were only to be used in 'those that are robustious and used to continuall strong labour'.[15]

With this English rhubarb root at his disposal, John distilled an essence that proved especially good 'for the paines and swellings in the head, for those that are troubled with melancholy, and [it] helpeth the Sciatica and Goute and the paines of the Crampe'. His method was to steep

> a sufficient quantity of Rubarbe ... in Cinamon water, which being strongly pressed forth, let it be stilled in a glass limbeck in balneo [narrow-necked glass vessel in a water bath], until the water be drawne forth, and the substance remaining to be of the thicknesse of honey, which keepe in a close covered pot or glasse.[16]

Once this medicine was put into practice by the physicians John worked with, he was able to judge it 'so gentle a medicine that it may be given to all sortes of gentle constitutions ... whether they be children or women with childe, and that safely at all times of the year'.[17] By pleasant coincidence he pioneered a medicine that perfectly matched his character.

The *London Pharmocopoeia* that the physicians had finally produced in 1620 was intended to be a complete guide to useful medicines. Yet it was widely condemned by knowledgeable physicians. Sir Theodore de Mayerne, like John, found it gravely wanting and he urged John to make good the deficit and complete his 'great project', for the sake of the 'Common wealth', for the good of the people. This was the medical encyclopaedia that had been mooted for so long, which would contain details of John's work with rhubarb and other medicines. John's friends knew that much of the book was already complete, although it was still not in print. 'I hear very soon the Medical Garden is going to be dedicated to Apollo [complete and offered to the god of Arts and Sciences],' wrote the French doctor in his literary Latin style. 'No day shall pass by without the stroke of the pen. Thus at length you convey the very abundant fruits of glory ... so that you enjoy fresh and green old age.'[18]

This Frenchman had a talent for encouraging others to do what he would not do himself. De Mayerne was a keen experimental chemist who spent some of his happiest hours in his laboratory in London. He had not given up the fascinating chemical medicines that had got him into so much trouble with the University of Paris in 1603. In 1630 he was corresponding with a Monsieur Maginot in Paris who had sent him a thesis on the 'paradox of the quartan ague', a fever associated with dysentery that revived every four days. He resisted the invitation to endorse M. Maginot's theory, but took the chance to tell tales of his delightful evenings in his workshop.

> I remember one day that I wanted to make some vitriol of mars with acidic essence of sulphur in a big matrass [glass vessel for distilling]. My mixture caught fire, gave off an extremely thick and smelly smoke which itself caught fire when it met the candle flame that was a great distance away. There was an explosion like a canon shot as my vessel shot off, without breaking, and released a phenomenal fart in my face, worse than that of the Pages at the Louvre.[19]

The doctor was enthusiastic about this alarming result, which he considered to be highly significant in the treatment of fevers:

> The same thing happens in our bodies, when a continuous fever forms, when the sulphur of the mass of blood is set alight by meeting some effervescent salt created by matter which will not stop until the sulphur is consumed or extinguished by the completion of the activity of the salts, or until the natural heat is extinguished by a great natural weakness which will lead to the death of the patient.[20]

De Mayerne's treatments were so universally sought after in England that he would have grown rich in London without the patronage of the court. His medical advice to patients, which has survived, shows that his practice was more modest than his experiments suggest. When Lady Rich approached de Mayerne with the problem of her embarrassingly red face, he gave her a commonsense mixture of hope and gentle reprimand which seems likely to have done her some good: 'Since the redness of face which is damaging your beauty and upsetting you comes from inside, especially from the liver, and the stomach plays a part in it, you have every chance of regaining your youth provided you have the patience to do what's necessary.' He suggested she should avoid eating anything that could 'inflame the blood', keep good hours for sleeping and waking, take moderate exercise before meals, and stop using so many pessaries and laxatives.[21]

John's growing bond with Sir Theodore was based on this practical side of the doctor's nature. While de Mayerne bullied John to keep writing, he would not do it himself. He described the activity in general as 'a great disease with which most people, particularly in Germany, are afflicted'. He argued that 'It is easy to swell out books when half is the work of others,' quoting Horace with a characteristic classical flourish, 'Very often in the matter of books "*parturiant montes, nascetur ridiculus mus* [the mountains labour and a ridiculous mouse is born]".'[22] Typically, the only book of de Mayerne's that ever saw the light was a cookbook published after his death. De Mayerne and all his family liked to eat. A patient and neighbour, Sir Henry Slingsby, described him as 'corpulent and unwieldy', and his sister, Mary, as 'a very great lump'. Every Lent the Mayerne household paid the parish a considerable 'fine' so that they could continue in peace with 'the eattinge of ffleshe'.[23] Yet de Mayerne recognized in John's work a valuable fruit derived from observation and skill that he was determined to promote, just as enthusiastically as he promoted the many skilful painters who were his friends.

Practical and proven solutions like John's were a rarity in a nation that was teeming with radical ideas. Many men now claimed the truth, in new and unusual guises. It was, as Sir Francis Bacon had cannily predicted, as though all men felt it their duty independently to seek the will of God in the scriptures, now that truth 'was not confided exclusively to Pope or priest'. From the scriptures it was only a short step to the structure of the natural world. Chemical processes were frequently imbued with divine significance. Many physicians felt they were bound to include philosophy with their cure. Indeed, they often got better results from the preaching than the practice.

Because of the beauty and fame of his garden, and his own chemical experiments, John found himself a part of an influential circle of physician philosophers. His old friend, Dr Robert Fludd, was one who had come a long way since he was rejected by the College of Physicians for boasting 'much about himself and his chemical medicines'. Fludd had become one of London society's most popular doctors, said to use 'a kind of sublime unintelligible cant to his patients, which, by inspiring them with greater faith in his skill, might in some cases contribute to their cure'.[24]

Robert Fludd was influenced by a sixteenth-century German mystic known as Paracelsus, though his real name was Theophrastus Bombastus von Hohenheim. Paracelsus was a doctor who lectured in the vernacular, uniquely for that time, at the university of Basle. In 1538 his

Labyrinthum Medicorum (the Medical Maze) was published. It was a stream of spiritually inspired insight that referred to no other printed work, and was full of visionary claims that bordered on megalomania. 'I shall be the Monarch and mine shall the Monarchy be' was one of his uplifting, if obscure, pronouncements.[25]

This book argued that everything on the earth and indeed the earth itself is a living organism that reflects in its chemical composition the greater universe. He interpreted the creation of the world, as narrated in Genesis, as God's separation of the elements by a chemical process to form matter. This idea, just as fundamental to the alchemists as to the early chemists, suggested that in the processes of chemistry lay the key to understanding the universe. On the other hand, Paracelsus rejected the teachings of Galen and Avicenna, because they were pre-Christian or non-Christian and could not have been divinely inspired. He argued that human health depended not so much on the balance between four elements: earth, air, fire and water, as on three essential chemical elements: sulphur, salt and mercury, representing combustibility, stability and fluidity respectively.

When Robert Fludd left England just over sixty years later to study medicine in different parts of Europe, his country was racked by claims and counterclaims about what constituted the true divine message. He returned convinced of the semi-divine nature of physicians. Their role was to perfect the imperfect in nature, guided by the Holy Scripture and their own observation. In 1617 he published a paper in support of an anonymous group of Parisians who called themselves the 'Rosie Crucians', members of a secret magical society supposed to have been founded by Christian Rosenkreuz in 1484. Fludd's paper became the basis for the complete book of his philosophy, which declared that the key to understanding the universe, the macrocosm, would be revealed through chemical experiment on the microcosm. The book contained a number of experiments to demonstrate this truth. The first, 'the weather glasse', was constructed to tell the time by the degree to which the water inside it evaporated in the heat of the sun, or condensed at night. Fludd used the process to show that 'this experimental Organ [hath] a relation unto the great world, [...] also the Spirit included in this little modell doth resemble and imitate the action of that which is included in the great or macroscosmicall Machin'. The doctor's observations were undermined, however, by his insistence that all the work of the pre-Christian Greeks was 'diabolical'.

A gathering of scientists in the apothecary shop at the Jardin des Plantes, Paris, engraved by Sébastien le Clerc for Mémoire pour servir à l'histoire des plantes, Dodart, Paris, 1676. *It shows how the combination of gardening (seen through the window) with chemistry (illustrated by the furnace and equipment on the right) and discussion (reinforced by volumes of books) had become the most fertile environment for scientific advance in Europe.*

All the plenitude of understanding, consisteth in the revelation and knowledge of the mystery of God, and his son Jesus Christ; because in Christ only is all the treasure of wisdom and science hid. And therefore it is but a folly to seek true and essentiall science, understanding and wisdom from them who had them not.[26]

Some of Fludd's ideas are alive in medical debate today. Paracelsians believed, on the one hand, that disease is a localized abnormality within the body rather than the result of an imbalance in the body as a whole. On the other hand they rejected the Galenic idea that a condition needs to be treated with its opposite to effect a cure, choosing instead an old Germanic folk tradition, later reborn in homeopathy, that like cures like.

Another popular seventeenth-century medical theory was developed out of Paracelsus' work by a Neapolitan follower, Giambattista Porta. Following on from the idea that like cures like, Porta outlined the 'Doctrine of Signatures'. This maintained that the visual form of plants indicated their medical properties. So, it was believed, the walnut was 'very profitable for the brain'. Porta argued that such plants were 'signed' with the mark of God's macrocosm, reflected in every living thing.[27]

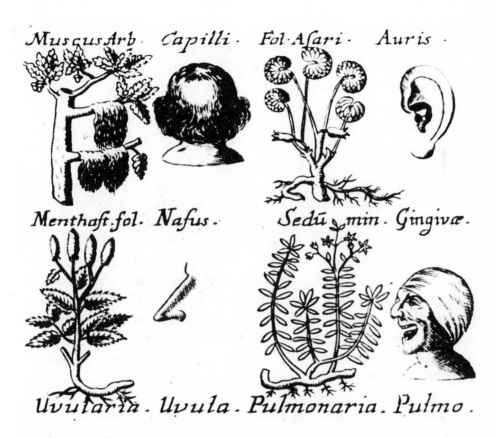

Musqus Arb · Capilli · Fol · Asari · Auris ·

Menthast. fol. Nasus · Sedü min. Gingivæ.

Uvularia · Uvula · Pulmonaria · Pulmo ·

'Plants of medicinal value to particular human body parts,' by Dr Michael Bernhard Valentini, Frankfurt, 1713, indicating the enduring popularity of the doctrine of 'signatures' and how, for example, a moss that looked like hair was prescribed for baldness.

The leading exponent of this doctrine in London was Dr Simon Baskervill, whose practice had also thrived since the days when he had been reproved by the College of Physicians as an unqualified quack. He was another close friend of John's, attracted to his garden by this doctrine and his consequent interest in the structure of plants. Baskervill took the opportunity to press his views in an introductory notice for the book that John was now working on.

Plants not only share company with men because they are both in one family of living things. Most of them have sympathy and resemblance to human parts ... some with eyes, others with lungs, others the liver, others the spleen; each is intended for a specific job ... for ... the physiognomic signature signifies the high parent of nature imprinted in plants....[28]

John allowed this tribute despite the fact that he had no patience at all for this theory, which did not trouble itself with directly observing nature. Its adherents held that some plants were 'signed'. Others with proven medical properties that did not at all resemble the parts of the body for which they were most effective were said to be 'the mysteries and secrets that God meant man to discover, while the "signed" ones were there to encourage him'.[29]

Both Fludd and Baskervill were a great deal more successful than a contemporary who had outlined a theory to his fellow physicians in 1618 that almost halted his career. Dr William Harvey's conclusion from his private experiments and the public dissections held twice a week at the London College of Physicians explained why the bones of cattle fed on rose madder, a plant also used as a red dye, became pink. The only reason the bones changed colour, Dr Harvey maintained, was because the blood travelled through every part of the body, picking up nutrients or infections from one part and spreading them to another. His dissections revealed walls inside the veins that controlled this process. When Harvey published this theory in 1628 as *The Circulation of the Bloode*, his patients abandoned him.

> I have heard him say, that after his Booke of the Circulation of the Blood came-out, that he fell mightily in his Practize, and 'twas believed by the vulgar that he was crack-brained; and all the Physitians were against his Opinion, and envied him; many wrote against him.[30]

So wrote John Aubrey half a century later, when Dr Harvey's theory was accepted and taught throughout Europe.

The social class to which John belonged did not usually presume to argue philosophy. He preferred to devote his life to quietly disproving self-evident fantasies. He had shown that the mandrake root had no 'manlike' resemblance and that the phases of the moon could not change the appearance of plants. As for the walnut, John praised its effectiveness in various preparations for earache, toothache, as 'a dainty junket', and for cooling fevers, but never bothered with the notion that it is good for the brain. He was a pragmatic chemist by nature, as well as by trade. To know that walnut oil is 'farre better for the painters' use to illustrate a white colour than Linseede oyle which deadeth it, and is of singular good use to be layde on guilded [gilded] workes' was more profitable to him than any philosophy could be.[31] Over and above his sense of his social position, John's background made him wary of mystic arguments. He would go no further than to state his belief that the marvellous nature of plants was the manifestation of a divinely ordered universe. It was undoubtedly this characteristic 'energetic brevity' and 'war with pretence' that Sir Theodore so admired.

Preoccupied as he now was with preparing his medical encyclopaedia at the centre of this grand scientific circle, John saw less these days of his old friend Tradescant. Tradescant's career had flourished even after the dramatic demise of his most recent aristocratic employer, the Duke of Buckingham, who had been assassinated in 1628 while having breakfast at a Portsmouth inn. Tradescant had accompanied the duke on the disastrous naval mission that he had led to the Ile de Ré the year before, which proved the nadir of his unpopularity in England. Instead of rescuing the Huguenots besieged in the citadel there, as was the intention, the English ships were forced to retreat ignominiously, leaving the bodies of nearly four thousand men unburied on French soil.

The assassination of the duke meant that King Charles could no longer rely on the judgement of his most influential friend, and Tradescant found himself suddenly without a job. He bought a house in Lambeth, and opened a plant nursery and a 'cabinet of curiosities' there. This collection quickly became a popular new attraction known as 'the Ark', the first public museum in the country. In March 1630, eighteen months later, Tradescant was appointed keeper of His Majesty's 'Gardens, Vines and Silkworms' at Queen Henrietta Maria's palace of Oatlands, on a salary of £100 a year. Meanwhile he kept a copy of John's *Paradisus* in his Lambeth house, using the blank pages at the back to enter the name and the donor of every new plant he acquired. With such characteristic attention to detail, John Parkinson and John Tradescant between them were making a permanent record of the horticultural revolution that was sweeping across England.[32]

The physicians who visited John's garden mixed there with a cluster of younger botanists. Apprentices from the Society of Apothecaries came to learn, just as John had learned in the gardens of Jacques Garret and Hugh Morgan. Thomas Johnson was one of them. As an early apprentice to the society John had worked so hard to establish, Johnson would have made an impression on him from the start. Johnson came from Selby, in North Yorkshire, so his accent was at once familiar to the older man's ear. Deeper similarities to John's younger self would have caught his attention. Thomas Johnson was a boy with a sharp eye and a sharp mind and an exceptionally good command of Latin, who, like John and his own mentor, de l'Obel, had begun his apprenticeship at the relatively late age of sixteen. The spark of ambition in this young man was strikingly familiar, and John took steps to encourage him. Though Johnson was still only twenty-five and had been a free apothecary for just a year, John asked him to write a dedication in Latin for the *Paradisus*. The book's prestige and dedication to the queen made this a flattering opportunity for such a young man. Johnson used it to lavish praise on the Long Acre garden in which he had learned so much.[33]

Johnson's ambition was to claim new ground in the discovery of the vegetable kingdom. While John had looked to Europe and beyond for new plants and horticultural skills, Thomas Johnson had a passion for travelling through his native Britain, realizing that the flora at his feet had never been charted in a systematic way. A few months after the *Paradisus* was published, Johnson set off to explore Kent with nine other young Turks of the botanizing circles who frequented John's garden. Most of them were professional apothecaries. Some were serious amateurs like William Broad or Brodus, who had also written admiring verses for the front of the *Paradisus*, and who was wealthy enough to be the only one of the group to bring his own servant with him. While John was perfecting exotic flowers, Johnson exulted in his discovery of *Stachys arvensis*, a native field variety of betony. This plant was considered 'good whether for the man's soul or for his body', because it had been used since ancient times to shield man from 'visions and dreams' as well as to heal wounds. Johnson noted his find, in a cornfield, 'not far from Greenhive in Kent', and identified it in one of the herbalists' classics, the *Prodromus*, published by the sixteenth-century French scholar Jean Bauhin.[34] This was a way of making dusty scholarship real, tracking and describing the many unrecognized plants that grew wild on the hills and fields of Britain.

When they returned, Johnson dashed off a witty account of their adventures in Latin. He told how their journey into Kent began with a storm, described in true epic style with a quotation from the *Aeneid*, when the boats they boarded at Blackfriars seemed likely to be swept away to sea before they reached Gravesend. Among other adventures, such as being hauled before the Mayor of Queenborough on the Isle of Sheppey, on suspicion of being spies, he interspersed the lists of native plants they had found.

His slim account was eagerly received by a public now literate enough to read such lively Latin prose, and keen to contribute to this popular new science of plants. Johnson glimpsed a possibility of financing further trips through such journals, and turning them eventually into a complete study of the flora of Britain. The band of botanists decided to call itself the 'Socii itinerantes', the society of travellers, shaking off the musty dust of the dried herbs in the apothecaries' shops for the fresh air of discovery on the road. It was around this group of young men, dedicated to innovation, that Johnson chose to build his identity. Already, in the *Paradisus*, he had signed himself 'Thomas Johnson, a member of both societies', allying himself with two radical new movements, the Society of Apothecaries and his own society of travellers.

The study of plants had become so popular that many of John's other visitors were keen amateurs. He had grown close to another student, who had been coming to observe his garden for more than fifteen years. John Goodyer was the youngest son of a wealthy merchant from Mapledurham in Hampshire. He worked as a steward, but he had a private passion for plants. He was familiar with several great gardens, including William Coys' in Essex, but the school where he honed his knowledge was the garden on Long Acre. Goodyer cherished an ambition to write an English translation of Dioscorides' classic, and by the time he was twenty-five, in 1616, he was already collecting curiosities. That year he recorded in his notebook, 'gathered seeds of "Astragalus Lusitanicus" in the garden of my good friend John Parkinson, Apothecary of London'.[35]

This astragalus was no beauty, and was only mildly useful as an astringent medicine, but it played a significant part in one of the scientific puzzles that these men discussed as they wandered along the garden paths. This variety was known as the milk vetch, a white-flowered vetch from Spain that had been recorded by Clusius in his herbal. Probably it was he who had given the first seeds to friends in London because the plant still carried his name. John called it the 'Astragalus Boeticus Clusiis: the Spanish milke Vetch of Clusius' in the *Theatrum*. The question that preoccupied the scholars of the day was which of nine varieties of the species now cultivated in England was the astragalus used by Dioscorides. While medical prescriptions depended upon it, this was more than just an academic question, and no doubt John was happy to chew over the question with his young friend. Goodyer was a methodical man, and this must have endeared him to John. As part of his study, he made a catalogue of all the plants that grew in the Long Acre garden, and this was discovered 300 years later, among John's papers in Magdalen College, Oxford.

In 1630 Goodyer was thirty-eight, and married to Patience Crump from the village of St-Giles-in-the-Fields, just north of Long Acre. He rented a house in the vicinity so that he could be near the company he found most congenial. Johnson and Goodyer had become friends through the Long Acre garden and were often together there. While Johnson was quick-witted and energetic, he was intelligent enough to recognize the value of Goodyer's pedantic habit of making notes on almost everything. In November 1631, Johnson was drinking wine with John Goodyer in Covent Garden.[36] Johnson was preparing another botanists' outing to Kent, this time to Margate, on the eastern tip, which would be paid for by one of the wardens of the Society of Apothecaries. Goodyer would not join the merry band of bachelors in the travelling society. Whatever his inclination, his marriage and his job stood in the way, but Johnson would still have plenty to talk to him about. He was interested in the notes Goodyer had been making of the plants in John's garden since Johnson himself was a child. He seems to have found it useful to have access to John's long years of experiment without showing the old man quite how keen he was.

John was established as the leader in his field. He had reached a pinnacle of his reputation and enjoyed the honour of being at the centre of an eager circle of the most learned men of his day. His great medical encyclopaedia was nearly ready. It would not be long before he could achieve his life's ambition and sit back and enjoy the fruits of the 'fresh and green old age' that Sir Theodore had predicted. Perhaps he rested briefly on his laurels, anticipating that his work was nearly done. If so, it was a costly mistake. Younger men were snapping at his heels.

CHAPTER FIFTEEN

'DISASTROUS TIMES'

Johnson's drawing of bananas. His printer, Thomas Cotes, also used it for John Parkinson's Theatrum, despite the rivalry between the two apothecaries.

Early in the morning of 10 April 1633, Thomas Johnson was busy fixing a special display in the window of his shop. He was delighted with the curious and beautiful hank of green bananas that had been given him as a present by Dr John Argent, the current president of the London College of Physicians. The bananas had come from Bermuda and their properties were still unknown in London, although very many other plants had by that time travelled from the West Indies to Britain.

It was a mark of special distinction to have been chosen to display such an unusual plant, and Johnson proudly made one of his best botanical drawings of it and observed the bunch every day. He kept it hanging in his shop window for as long as he could, attracting admiration and customers in equal measure. With great interest, they watched the bunch turn yellow. '[They] became ripe about the beginning of May and lasted until June: the pulp or meate was very soft and tender and it did eate somewhat like a Muske Melon.'[1] The unveiling of the fruit was a special occasion which Thomas Johnson's closest friends and associates were there to share. John Parkinson was not among them.

In the old days, John would have been the first to taste this strange fruit, but the old manners were passing. The days when the king or queen would be presented at once with any new delicacy had been destroyed by the tensions between the Stuart court and the City of London. The days when younger men deferred to old teachers had been overturned by harsh economic conditions. The traditional sense of fellowship and hierarchy that once prevailed in the City had given way before those who smashed the traditions, like John himself. In its place there had grown up a fierce Calvinist notion of predestined salvation, in which each man fought for his own survival.

John found himself to some extent a victim of his own success. His associates were now the physicians who clustered around the aristocrats at court, no longer the city apothecaries who were in touch with the life of London's busy port. No wonder he was not the first in the city to receive a banana, though the one he tasted probably arrived in the same ship as Thomas Johnson's. He got it from his Long Acre neighbour, Dr Pay, who, like Dr Argent, had it from the London College of Physicians. For many years John had delighted in novelty, but now his long experience was making him seem old-fashioned. When he wrote about his banana he compared it to an almost forgotten treat that long predated the musk melon, reaching further back into history than any of the younger botanists could remember: 'I having tasted one that Doctour Pay gave me did thinke I had tasted of an Orris [scented iris] root preserved with sugar.'[2]

John may have found he was jealous of Thomas Johnson's bananas, but the blow that followed nevertheless stunned him. By this time, Johnson had published two accounts of his botanical journeys, and earned a reputation as a skilled herbalist with a quick and ready style that pleased the public. When three people found they had inherited the rights to Gerard's old *Herball*, Johnson was quite naturally the expert they turned to. The rights were derived through the family of Gerard's printer, John Norton, but Gerard's mistakes were now widely known and the rights were worthless unless someone could be found to correct the original. The new owners asked Thomas Johnson to take on the job.[3]

The problem was that everyone knew that the encyclopaedia of plants on which John Parkinson had been working for so many years was now almost ready for press. If it appeared, it would certainly eclipse another edition of Gerard, so it was necessary to work very fast to get a new edition of Gerard's book out first. No one knew better how fast than Thomas Johnson. As John finished the pages of his encyclopaedia, he would give them to the printer, Thomas Cotes. Johnson was in almost daily contact with that printer, since Cotes had just finished printing his translation of a work by a French surgeon, Ambroise Paré.

Johnson's decision to take on Gerard's herbal was curious. He was already busy with his shop and his own books of British flora, which scarcely overlapped John's work. Although he was ambitious, he had established his reputation far more quickly than most, and he knew that what he was about to do would be a mortal blow to a man who had taught him and generously shared both friends and plants. Perhaps it was Gerard's popular touch and the opportunity to write a book in English, rather than Latin, that tempted Johnson into the job. Whatever his reservations may have been, without pausing to consult his old friend, Johnson took on the task and knuckled down with customary speed and energy. He completed his work in just over a year. By 28 November 1633 'Johnson's Gerard', as it became known, was in print, and Thomas Johnson was able to present a bound copy to the Society of Apothecaries. Ironically, his edition was dedicated to this society that John had helped to found. In his preface, Johnson referred disingenuously to John's work of the last forty years 'which I thinke by this time is fit for the Presse'.

John never got over this betrayal. He felt it all the more deeply because Johnson enlisted his other friends, so that it seemed Johnson was gathering the fruit of John's many years of patient experiment. The old matter of the perennial pea from Spain came back to haunt him. The plants that arrived from Spain when John commissioned William Boel to go there for him now appeared in 'Johnson's Gerard'. Boel had given some of the seed to William Coys 'in love', when John had paid for his trip, and that had rankled. Now, however, they appeared in this new edition of Gerard's herbal. John later complained:

> While I beate the bushe, another catcheth and eateth the bird: for while I with care and cost sowed them yearely, hoping first to publish them, another that never saw them unlesse in my garden, nor knew of them but by a collaterall friend, prevents me whom they knew had their descriptions ready for the presse.[4]

The 'collaterall friend' was John Goodyer. John was horrified to see that Goodyer had not only helped Johnson but actually contributed notes of his own to bring this edition of Gerard up to date. There was the case of the Jerusalem artichoke. Johnson's description of this plant repeats John's assertion in the *Paradisus* that the plant bears no relation to artichokes but is a member of the sunflower family. He refers, slightly coolly, to John, saying that his name for them is far more appropriate than the one by which they have been known ever since:

> Our countryman Mr Parkinson hath exactly delivered the historie of this by the name of Battatas de Canada, Englishing it Potatoes of Canada.... al these that have written and mentioned it bring it from America but from far different places, as from Peru, Brasill and Canada, but this is not much materiall seeing it now growes so well and plentifully in so many places of England.[5]

Johnson was not interested in the history of names, or in the past. He was one of the new breed of botanist apothecaries looking for the potential growing under their feet, in Britain. To save time while hastily completing this edition, he included unedited notes on the Jerusalem Artichoke written by John Goodyer. 'I will ... deliver you the historie as I have received it from my oft mentioned friend Mr Goodyer, who as you may see by the date, took it presently upon the first arrival into England.' Goodyer's description of the Jerusalem artichoke that follows finishes with its 'Vertues', which are its, much despised, uses in the kitchen:

> These roots are dressed divers wayes, some boile them in water, and after stewe them with sacke and butter, adding a little ginger. Others bake them in pies, putting Marrow, Dates, Ginger, Raisons of the Sun, Sacke etc.... But in my judgement, which way so ever they be drest and eaten, they are a meate more fit for swine than men. 17 Octob. 1621. John Goodyer.[6]

The date is significant. Johnson seems to have had this information for twelve years by the time he included it in his book, and Goodyer could quite easily protest to his friend John Parkinson that he had no idea Johnson intended to use it in this way. John had also published the *Paradisus* four years before in which he had described the Jerusalem artichoke, so its mention in Johnson's Gerard was no scoop. Yet

Goodyer's signed and written contributions appear throughout Johnson's edition, and John could quite reasonably ask himself why his friend had been sending Johnson carefully written botanical descriptions, taken from John's own garden, for so many years.

John was now sixty-six. That fact, of course, made Johnson's and Goodyer's behaviour all the more bitter to him. At a time when the span of a man's life was considered to be 'three score and ten' it was reasonable for those about him to ask why, if he had wanted to publish his modern herbal for so many years, he had not yet done so. Could it be that he would never achieve the task he had intended for so long?

In John's experience a proper study of plants was the work of a lifetime. The great European herbalists from whom he had learned each devoted their lives to one chief work that passed on their knowledge. The ready availability of printing, coupled with the profit that could be derived from selling information to an eager and literate public, were beginning to change the landscape under John's feet, however. While John worked with the steady deliberation of the old masters, Johnson's rapid style endeared him to the printers who bore the cost of producing a book. Moving at such speed, Johnson undoubtedly cut corners, but he was young, skilful and witty, and he appeared to be the coming man in a society that had never before so valued youth.

Yet John faced a deeper challenge to the completion of his herbal than the printers' desire for readily saleable works. The truth was that the complexity of the task he contemplated had grown year by year. The first herbals, like William Turner's, had been manuals to identify plants used for medicine, with some accurate comparisons to herbs mentioned in the ancient Greek and Roman texts. This was still an important feature, and one any honest herbalist would want to include. Then the influx of plants from the Americas and the Far East that had been quite unknown to the ancient doctors invited new experiment and study. At the same time, the dramatically increased desire for purely beautiful plants for gardens suggested that far more information about cultivation than was usual in a herbal would be needed. Now, as the countryside changed rapidly beneath new building and farming practices, an interest in native plants was emerging. This aspect of botany valued plants not necessarily as medicine or food, but as native 'curiosities' in a landscape the British had begun to treasure.

The comprehensive knowledge of the apothecary had splintered into multiple facets during John's lifetime. He had been distracted by his great love for cultivating beautiful plants, expressed in the *Paradisus*. This passion prevented him from travelling all over England, like Johnson, or through Europe, like John Tradescant, or to America, like Tradescant's son. He could not then bring back 'rarities' with his own hands and satisfy the eternal public thirst for 'curiosities'. He could only grow them, patiently and slowly, in his own garden. Results from such work took time.

While John had written a book about the cultivation of gardens like none that had gone before, he expected from himself the more 'manlike worke' of his herbal. To those who dared suggest he was slow about producing it, he could reasonably reply that the book would have been published in 1634, had it not been for Johnson's edition of Gerard. In fact John went ahead and registered the book at the Stationers' Hall in that year, but, perhaps on the printer's advice, did not publish. Johnson's Gerard was popular, so popular that another edition was printed in 1636, deepening John's discomfort.[7]

To add insult to injury, Johnson had approached Gerard's original text with a light hand, retaining all the stories, some of which were now distinctly old-fashioned, and others that had been proved to be fantasy. A typical example was Gerard's rambling story advocating Dock or Monk's Rhubarb as a useful purgative in treating fevers.

> A notable experiment I learned of one John Benet, a surgeon of Maidstone in Kent (a man as slenderly learned as my self) which he practised upon a butcher's boy of the said towne.... Being desired to cure the lad of an ague [fever] which did grievously vex him, hee promised him a medicine; and for want of one for the present (for a shift as himselfe confessed unto me) he took out of his garden three or four leaves of this plant of Rubarb [*Rumex alpinus*], which he stamped and strained with a draught of ale and gave it to the lad in the morning to drinke: it wrought extreamely downwarde and upward within one houre after and never ceased until night.[8]

The boy was cured of his fever after this extreme fit of vomiting and diarrhoea and the treatment was counted a success. Johnson quoted this glib story but made no mention, although he must have known about it, of the remedy that John had pioneered as a much gentler, more effective medicine for this purpose, the Chinese rhubarb root or *Rheum rhaponticum*.

John had reason to be grateful at least for this omission, but it did not increase his respect for this work by an apothecary whom he himself had helped to train. There was also Gerard's story about the barnacle goose, which Johnson kept with little comment except the wry remark that 'some Hollanders had found another originall' for the goose than the barnacles that grew on rotting wood. In travelling to find a north-east passage to China they had come across crowds of these geese on some islands, all of them sitting on eggs.[9]

John had waged a lifelong campaign against dangerous myths, and his vigorous views on this subject showed when he came to publish his own account of the barnacle goose in 1640:

Let me bring this admirable tale of untruth to your consideration, that whatsoever hath formerly been related concerning the breeding of these Barnackles, to be from shells growing on trees etc is utterly erronious, their breeding and hatching being found out by the Dutch and others in their navigations to the Northward ... in Anno 1536.

John found Johnson's inclusion of popular but mistaken information inexcusably cynical. Nearly a decade later he was still accusing Johnson of 'extreame covetousnesse', admitting that he was eaten up with 'sharp toothed and tongued selfe-gnawing envy'.[10]

He had no choice now but to watch and see Johnson's edition of Gerard widely approved and admired. Johnson had corrected Gerard's grosser falsehoods, such as his account of the big red-flowered peony, the 'male peiony' (*paeonia mas*), that Gerard said he had found growing wild in Southfleet, near Gravesend in Kent. 'I have been told that our Author himselfe planted that Peionie there, and afterwards seemed to find it there by accident: and I doe believe it was so because none before or since have ever seene or heard of it growing wilde in any parte of this kingdome,'[11] Johnson wrote in one of the corrections that added to the spice and charm of the original rather than detracted from it. In his haste, Johnson left many mistakes unaltered, and scarcely produced a book worthy of the age he lived in, but he won praise subsequently from scientific botanists for his efficient editorial method, with which he clearly marked all his alterations to the original. There is no doubt that Johnson's own methods of plant discovery were a great improvement on Gerard's, but he must have reassured himself privately that much of the quaint material he retained from Gerard's original would soon be updated by his own British flora.

The gulf that opened up between John Parkinson and Thomas Johnson echoed a wider battle that left John alienated from the Society of Apothecaries. The Apothecaries' many simmering disagreements with the Physicians had gradually developed into open warfare. Far from working with the doctors, many of them had begun to work directly against them. Having grown so close to the court, John was now in the position of having more physicians than apothecaries as friends and colleagues.

In early July 1633, while Johnson was still busy preparing his book for the press, the master and wardens of the Society of Apothecaries had made their way, reluctantly, to the Physicians' College in Grenville Street. They would have felt the close heat in the small front room where they stood before the assembled college fellows, and it must have stoked their resentment. Dr Harvey, the president of the college that year, opened the proceedings with a calm appeal to the apothecaries for 'Honesty in the right and well preparing of their medicines'. He declared that doctors could make and dispense what medicines they liked, but apothecaries must stick to the recipes outlined in the *Pharmacopoeia*, now known as 'the Dispensatory'. 'No other medecyne which is not in our dispensatorye shall bee promiscuously sould till itt be allowed and approved by our Colledge,' he affirmed.[12]

This magisterial appeal stirred a hornet's nest of resentments that had been simmering for nearly twenty years. Before the Apothecaries' charter was granted, the Physicians had insisted 'that neither Lac Sulphuris nor any other prescriptions or medicines ought to bee made and sold by the Apothecaries if they bee not conteyned in the Pharmacopoiea Londiniensis'. The Apothecaries argued that they exported medicines all over the world, and could not wait for a doctor's prescription for each. 'Apothecaryes of London doe furnish several partes of the whole world, some the Emperor of Mosco, some the Kings of Poland, other Constantinople ... and many places of the King's dominion.' They insisted particularly on their right to make 'Lac Sulphuris', which was one of the medicines not contained in the *Pharmacopoeia*. It was a mixture of sulphur and tartar salts, and the principal 'chymical medecyne' favoured by the king's physician:

Lac Sulphuris is a medium which the auncient physitians commende of admirable virtues ... even some of their own Colledge prescribing and usinge it, even that famous and honourable Dr Sir Theodore de

Mayerne, Knight, His Majestie's premier Physitian preparing the same medicine and giving it to his patients.[13]

In the event, the Apothecaries' charter had been hurried through on the king's personal command in a way that had left this dispute unresolved. The charter ensured the physicians' rights were not infringed but it failed to limit the apothecaries' powers or make them subordinate to the physicians. Once it became clear the *Dispensatory* to which they were supposed to conform was of poor quality, the apothecaries ignored it. They continued to make and promote their own medicines, approving them internally and, in the case of the volatile 'Lac Sulphuris', making it centrally in their own 'haull'. The physicians still tried to prevent the apothecaries from selling medicines without prescriptions, charging and fining them from time to time for acting as 'empiricks', as they had in John's youth. The more the apothecaries ignored them, the more drastic the penalties the physicians tried to impose. The year before John Buggs, one of Thomas Johnson's companions on the first botanizing trip to Kent, had been sent to prison by the physicians for this offence. The Society of Apothecaries retaliated by paying the prisoner's fines and freeing him. John Buggs left to train as a doctor in Holland. When he returned he was offered a job as physician to Christ Church hospital but the College of Physicians stepped in to prevent it.

The apothecaries had agreed to come to the college this evening for one reason only. They disagreed amongst themselves as to who had the best 'Lac Sulphuris'. Mr Harrison was in charge of making Lac Sulphuris centrally at the Apothecaries' hall. Some apothecaries were making their own, or obtaining it more cheaply from elsewhere, so they had come to ask the doctors to arbitrate. They began by arguing with each other.

> There grewe a great deal of altercation about both that Lac Sulphuris which was formerly made at the Haull; of which Mr Haughton's perished, the glass breaking.... Mr Weale [another apothecary] did pretend that there wear five sortes of Lac Sulphuris secundum only differing in the vessels, and hee sayde it was not necessary to observe any proportion between the sulphur and the salt of Tartar....[14]

The doctors' only interest was to prevent them from making this popular medicine at all, so naturally the meeting broke up with no satisfactory conclusion. When the apothecaries were called to attend another meeting five days later, they failed to turn up. The physicians asked where they were. 'Answear was made it was supposed they were at their HAULL.'[15]

The Physicians then sent the Apothecaries a letter forbidding them from making Lac Sulphuris, and insisting that all existing stocks be turned over. The college censors, who, at the time, included John's friends Dr Fludd and Dr Baskervill, attempted to enforce this rule on 'Hearth day' with a spot check of the apothecaries' stock. But when they visited the shop of the choleric Mr Weale, who had taken the trouble to defend his Lac Sulphuris before the college, the scene rapidly turned into a brawl. The doctors seized Mr Weale's Lac Sulphuris, and 'finding all these compositions different in Colour smell and substance did conceive them all to be unfit and dangerous for the health of man's bodye ... and did condemne them for nought and destroyed them by powring them out in the street'. Meanwhile Mr Weale yelled furiously at the Apothecaries' Society officials who accompanied the doctors to leave his shop or else he would call the constable.[16]

This scene was only the beginning of a bitter battle between the Physicians and the Apothecaries that steadily escalated through the 1630s. The Physicians drew up a case to be heard in the Star Chamber calling for the Apothecaries' charter to be revoked, because they contravened its intention by making their own medicines and selling them direct to the public. While the case was pending and the Apothecaries were vigorously preparing their defence, the doctors tried to drive some of the most obnoxious offenders out of business by blacklisting them. On 23 June 1635 they agreed a list which included some of the cleverest independent apothecaries of the day: 'Discommuned apothecaries: Mr Edwards; Mr Cooke, Mr Weale; Mr Haughton; Mr Holland in Fane church street, and Mr Kendall.'[17]

Meanwhile the fundamental cause of the differences between them was openly spilling out on to the streets of London. The apothecaries considered themselves to be as medically useful as any doctor in London. They saved their patients the doctors' exorbitant charges. Had not Dr Bruart demanded three shillings in advance for a treatment and kept the money even though the patient died before he could receive it, charged sixpence for 'looking on the water' and taken the 'urinall' itself when the patient's servant could only give him fourpence? Such righteous anger swept away the social deference to which the doctors were accustomed. Apothecaries challenged the doctors' authority openly and rudely on the city streets, just as Parliament challenged the authority of the king's ministers. Dr Ramsay hurried to the physicians' *Comitia* with a report of his bruising encounter with one of these uncouth fellows in the street:

> Dr Ramsye reports that one Mr Aierton Apothecarye mett with him before Guild Haull: and said to him the apothecaryes doe as much good as the Doctors, and hee knows not why they may nott have practise as well as the Doctors, with a great many other reproachful speeches.[18]

John was not directly involved in these conflicts, but they must have caused him grief. Two of the blacklisted apothecaries, Richard Edwards and Edward Cooke, had worked with him on the schedule of medicines for the new Society of Apothecaries in 1619. Typically, he tried to steer an honest middle line through the dispute, running the risk of offending both parties. When the Physicians' case to strip the Apothecaries of their charter, the so-called '*quo warranto*', was heard in court in 1635, John was brought in to testify. As one of the apothecaries who had helped the doctors with the *Pharmacopoeia*, he knew better than most how it was put together. His honesty was uncompromising. Notwithstanding the fact that most of his friends and customers were now physicians, he told the court that the *Dispensatory* or *Pharmacopoeia* the apothecaries were expected to rely on was a deeply flawed book for which the doctors had only themselves to blame. If they had consulted the apothecaries sooner instead of bringing them in at the last minute they might have achieved a workable document. As it was the apothecaries had from the beginning relied on their own schedule of medicines.[19]

John's testimony, which undoubtedly strengthened the Apothecaries' case, was all the more surprising because his relationship with the Society of Apothecaries had cooled to freezing by this time. When the Apothecaries sought to raise money from their members in 1634 towards the cost of purchasing their own hall, John was not among the contributors. He had paid no corn money in 1631, the tax levied by the City to which all freemen were expected to contribute, whereas Thomas Johnson paid 10 s., but his exemption from this tax was one of the privileges of his association with the court. The hall was a different matter. As a founding member who had achieved royal recognition and national distinction, John would have been expected to contribute something. Yet his name appears in a list of members of the society 'who have not subscribed at all'.[20]

The resentment John felt towards Thomas Johnson no doubt influenced his decision. Johnson's betrayal finally snapped the thin cord that
still tied John to the free brotherhood for which he had fought. While
John dedicated his work to the crown, Johnson dedicated his to the
society, which was, in turn, now rich enough to sponsor him, perhaps
more generously than John himself was sponsored by the king. It was a
bitter irony.

The Society of Apothecaries was emerging in these years as fiercely
independent from the crown that established it. Gideon de Laune, who
had grown rich selling a single remedy, 'de Laune's pills', was now overwhelmingly the society's main benefactor. He donated the site for their
new hall in his family's heartland at Blackfriars. De Laune's father,
William, had not only been a member of the London College of
Physicians; he was also a Protestant pastor in the city. The society allied
itself with the Puritan fervour that was rapidly gathering strength in
London, reacting powerfully to the perceived influence of Catholics at
court under the protection of Queen Henrietta Maria. As if in emphasis,
society accounts and records now ended with a simple Puritan prayer,
'Praised be God'.[21]

John had avoided letting religious differences come between him and
his friends, but he was naturally uncomfortable in the face of the
growing zeal of the city Puritans. His own background and his son's
behaviour counted against him, and he retreated further into the arms
of friends and admirers around the court.

One last factor influenced John's decision not to give the
Apothecaries money. The court he was associated with had grown to
become one of the most dazzling spectacles in the whole of Europe. The
sums that the richest aristocrats spent on their clothes, their houses,
their jewels and their gardens were matched only by the sumptuous
portraits that the king and the Earl of Pembroke commissioned from
their favourite Dutch painter, Anthony Van Dyke. Yet beneath the glitter
and the gold and the luxurious living, many of the court's adherents
suffered from a common affliction, in which John shared. The affliction
that ailed them was poverty.

CHAPTER SIXTEEN

'GOLDEN RAINS'

Dr Simon Baskervill observed his old friend's growing struggle to muster his resources and complete the task of his life. It was clear to Dr Baskervill that John had denied himself many opportunities for prosperity because he feared they would distract him from his work. 'No golden rains have watered your garden,' he commented, when John's herbal was finally finished. 'You went without in private so that you could be devoted to the public good, so that you could be free for study, and you served the Pharmacopoeia zealously.'[1]

A post in the royal household would have been a lucrative and prestigious sinecure, but there was not a single one that John could have held which would have allowed him time to study, write, and maintain his garden. He knew this only too well from the continual laments of his friend Sir Theodore de Mayerne, who spent much of his time literally following the queen, as she moved from St James's Palace to Oatlands, to Windsor and back to London again. Attendance on the queen was a considerable effort for one of Sir Theodore's corpulent frame.

Even in London, the king might send him hurrying across town to attend a particular patient. When John Donne lay stricken in St Paul's by a mystery illness, the king sent Sir Theodore, as his personal physician, to assist Donne's worried doctor. The patient watched the experts' struggle to describe his symptoms with rueful amusement. 'The names will not serve them which are given from the place affected.... They cannot have names enow, from what it does, nor where it is, but they must extort names from what it is like....'[2] Ultimately, the doctors diagnosed melancholia, brought on by too much thought and study, which caused vapours in the head. Once the poet came out in spots, his physicians were reassured that he was strong enough to be purged. They believed this would put him on the road to recovery, and so it proved.

Sir Theodore could have helped John to gain a royal post if he had wanted one. There were now so many royal households that the number of positions had grown steadily. When the painter Rubens was first presented to King Charles at Greenwich Palace, the stylish gathering he found astonished him.

All the leading nobles live on a sumptuous scale and spend money lavishly, so that the majority of them are hopelessly in debt.... In the first place are the Earl of Carlisle and the Earl of Holland, who, by their fine table, maintain their following and their position among the nobility, since splendour and liberality are of primary consideration at this Court.

In this place I find none of the crudeness that one might expect from a place so remote from Italian elegance.[3]

Just over 300 royal servants provided essential services, such as food, laundry and lighting. But there were also more than 600 others whose role was to create the show of elegance that so impressed foreign visitors. There was an endless list of 'Gentlemen of the Bedchamber, Heralds, Grooms, Trumpeters, Tailors, Barbers, Coachmen, Footmen' and many others on the payroll.[4] The queen had her own establishment of 172 servants in St James's Palace, the great majority of them French Catholics. The princes and princesses had more than 200 personal servants between them. Charles travelled restlessly, as his father had done, from palace to palace, so each palace had its own staff. Every servant in this great royal community was fed, paid and clothed for life out of the royal purse. The winter and summer livery of just one young 'Page of the Bedchamber' required:

8 yards of scarlet for a cloak, jerkin and breeches, 2 and a half yards of baize to line the cloak, six yards of velvet to guard the said cloak, jerkin and breeches and 10 dozen lace for the same, five yards of Fustian for a doublet, eight dozen of silk buttons, two pair of worsted stockings, one pair of silk garters and one hat with a band.[5]

When the king could find no cash in the exchequer for this expensive household, he turned to the tradesmen in the city. Many of them had made their fortunes by catering to the palace's needs, and the king's arbitrary requests were rarely refused for long. Gideon de Laune was one of nineteen of the richest citizens with French or Flemish names who were 'requested' to lend the king 1,000 marks (£667) at the beginning of his reign. By 1650 Gideon de Laune alone was owed more than £2,000 by the late king.

John was loosely a part of the royal household, receiving the king's occasional favours and exempt from taxes, but he was financially independent. He chose to cling to the little niche he had carved out for himself as an unusual creature: an independent scholar. Hitherto all scholars, such as Matthias de l'Obel, William Turner, even John Gerard, had been sponsored by a noble on whom they depended for food and lodging, but John's income came from his apothecary business at first, and his garden. Still, his independence did not come easily. His friends all remarked on how he worked day and night, with remarkable energy for his age.

After the *Paradisus* was published, there is no further record of John in the Apothecaries' books or the parish registers of St Bride's, suggesting that he soon let go of his apothecary shop in Ludgate Hill.[6] Without his son to work beside him, it would have been difficult to keep the shop going. He no longer had a family or a lavish household to maintain, so it was just possible for him to earn enough to live on and work through the sale of plants and medicines from his garden in Long Acre. As Dr Baskervill said, 'after spurning to catch a cheaper small reward, you grow old completely in your little garden'.[7] It would have been a hand-to-mouth existence, particularly as John put everything he could spare into his writing, his experiments and his garden. However, it may have been some comfort for him to see that even those who had grown rich in the king's service were now suffering grim reversals.

The sorry state of affairs at court was apparent in the situation of John's friend and neighbour Lewis Lamere. Lamere and his brother-in-law, John Wolfgang Rumler, were no longer on speaking terms. Rumler had been appointed apothecary to Charles I in 1627, but Lamere felt that Rumler's success had been obtained at his expense. Already, in 1625, while Rumler's wife, Anne, was visiting the continent with her 'four servants', Lamere had served a writ on her husband. The arrangement between the brothers-in-law to 'sublet' John Clavie's appointment as apothecary to James I seemed to work until 1607, when Clavie died. Rumler then won the appointment as apothecary to the king in his own right, while Lamere had the lower-paid place of apothecary to Queen Anne, which he held until she died in 1619. Rumler found favour with King James. He was granted a profitable permit to import Rhenish wine and manufacture 'mercurie sublimate'. But Lamere said his brother-in-law had reneged on a promise to share his royal salary in exchange for Lamere's supply of drugs.

It was not so much the salary, but the potential profit in the rare medicines and perfumes they supplied, that made royal apothecaries rich.

Lamere said he 'had disbursed to druggers and grocers tenne thousand pounds at the least', obtaining these for the court. When Rumler could not get the royal exchequer to pay for them, he allowed Lamere to carry the debt. Lamere said he was paying interest on £8,200, a huge sum that matched the cost of the mansion Sir Francis Bacon had built at Gorhambury. Rumler refused to satisfy his debt, saying that Lamere had accepted money to end their agreement in 1619.

Lamere's difficulties indicated a far more general malaise. Few people expected to have their bills paid promptly, but the burden of debt that Lamere had run up was now killing him. He petitioned Charles for another royal appointment, arguing that he had provided 'all the accomplishments for the embalming of both their Majesties' bodies [James I and Anne of Denmark]', although Rumler had been paid for preparing James I's body to lie in state. In 1630 he was appointed apothecary to Charles and Henrietta Maria's eldest children, the two-year-old Prince Charles and, later, the baby Princess Mary, but in August the same year he made his will. He struggled on with his cause for three more years. Each time he petitioned the king to settle his debt, the king approved the payment, but there was apparently no money in the exchequer. Lamere's last appeal was that 'for God's cause and the love of justice' he should be paid. Then he died. In 1634 his wife took up the cause. She told the court that now her husband was dead she had no money even to pay for his burial and she was starving, while there were debts of more than £1,600. He had had more than £5,000 when he entered royal service, she said, all of which had gone 'in discharge of his calling without any recompense at all'.[8]

John's independence spared him from this kind of situation, yet he was growing increasingly isolated. The rift with his son intensified when Richard chose to work for the Earl of Newport. The earl, who was the illegitimate son of Penelope, Lady Rich, had grown up at court as a companion to Prince Charles. By 1634 he had charge of the king's weaponry and custody of Hyde Park, both significant political positions.[9] Yet for all his public power, the earl could not prevent his wife from following the prevailing fashion at court and converting to Catholicism. Converts were welcomed to worship in Henrietta Maria's chapel in St James's Palace and the French queen dramatically increased the attraction of her style of worship, especially among her female courtiers. For some time the smartest funerals had taken place at the dead of night, leading to a popular suspicion that all the nation's aristocrats had reverted to the faith of their grandfathers and were whispering Mass in the dark. Richard took his gardening skills to this blatantly Catholic household, where he was free to practise his faith openly.[10]

When Richard followed the Jesuits, he seemed to threaten the one prize that John still hoped for: an official appointment as the king's botanist. The king's attitude to Catholics was unmistakable to those who knew him well. His personal taste inclined him towards high ceremony and he found many of the Catholics at court charming and interesting. But he steered a fine line: open Catholicism was a threat to his authority. In 1635 he banished Walter Montague, the son of the Earl of Manchester, for converting to Rome. He had agreed, in secret, to tolerate Catholics, but he would not allow them state influence or be deterred from his historic role as the head of the unique Anglican Church. Nor would he give them public appointments. John felt forced to choose between his work and his son. The greater part of his life and energy had been devoted to his work, and so, of course, he chose to put it before his son, letting it be known at court that he utterly reproved his heir.

The contrast between John's situation and that of his old friend Tradescant was painful. Their interests and their fortunes diverged. Tradescant had a salary, in theory, of £100 a year for his work supervising the queen's gardens at Oatlands. He also had a large family established in his house in Lambeth. While Richard was meeting Jesuits, Tradescant's son, also John, who had had a gentleman's education at King's School in Canterbury, helped his father to produce a scholarly Latin catalogue of all the plants in the Lambeth garden. He looked after his father's nursery and the museum there and was clearly worthy to step into his shoes. Friends and customers came to rely on John Tradescant the younger to do the work his father had done. The young Tradescant even excelled his father's adventurous spirit. In 1637 he set off on his first trip across the Atlantic, to Virginia. He returned the following spring with a triumphant collection of novelties, only to find that his father was no longer there to approve them. John Tradescant the elder had died, his royal salary still owing, just before Easter that year.[11]

John Parkinson was determined to leave the world a legacy of more worth than his son and heir. He worked on, as stubbornly independent in thought as he was financially. The difficulties of the past few years only spurred him to a more ambitious task than he had intended. While Johnson had focused on the European and native plants that had been known to Gerard, John was still spellbound by the possibilities of the wider world. He decided to make his book a 'Theater of plants', which would include all the plants from the New World and the Far East that were now known in London. He would devote it to the medicinal properties of these exotics, as well as of native plants, offering a detailed account of their history and origin to supplement their medicinal uses. He wrote of places to which he had never been and to which he knew he would never travel, but whose riches many hands had brought him. Plants from Constantinople, China, Africa, North and South America and Russia grew in his garden, and he believed that, by understanding them, he could lay bare the essence of their treasure for his countrymen.

In this way his book would surpass the old herbals, particularly Gerard's, which included scant information on the medicinal properties of only the most familiar plants. Inevitably it would break the taboo on giving away professional secrets, since the medical knowledge it offered would be available, in English, to all who took the trouble to read it. Yet, since the rift with his son, John had no one else to whom he could leave his secrets. His solution to the petty disputes and inadequate solutions that continually marred his profession would be a detailed account of the medicinal properties of every substance he knew as an apothecary.

Such a far-reaching ambition committed John to many more years of work. Meanwhile friends and correspondents sustained him by enthusiastically adding their efforts to his own. One of his most faithful contributors was Thomasin Tunstall, who lived 'at Bull-banke, neare Hornby Castle' in Lancashire. She was a relative of one of the royal equerries, Sir John Tunstall, who had a fine garden reputed to be stocked with plants given him by Queen Elizabeth. But the Lancashire branch of the family were all committed Catholics, and locked into battles over their faith. Thomasin's consolation, like John's, was nature. She roamed the dales and crags of John's childhood, keenly searching the ground for a glimpse of an unfamiliar flower. She had already sent him a pale yellow orchid she found on the borders of Yorkshire and Lancashire,

> in a wood ... called the Helkes, which is three miles from Ingleborough, the highest Hill in England, and not far from Ingleton, as I am enformed by a courteous Gentlewoman, a great lover of these delights, called Mistress Thomasin Tunstall ... who hath often sent me up the rootes to London, which have borne faire flowers in my garden.[12]

While John's fame grew, Thomasin Tunstall carried on carefully lifting whole roots and packing them off by messenger to London with her lively, detailed descriptions. She found a pink sedum growing 'upon the mountaines of Pendle and Ingelborough oftentimes on the very raggiest places and most dangerous of them scarce accessible and so steepe that they may soone tumble downe that very warily do not looke to their footing'. John used her words in his description of the plant for the book that he was now preparing.[13]

Thomasin was as well informed as any of his 'professional' botanizing students. She knew what was unusual, and the plants she sent him always arrived in good enough condition to grow in his garden. She kept him in touch with the fashions and tastes of the northern gentry. The scurvy-grass she sent him was grown in gardens there because its salty juice was such a good spring tonic, she said, and it was used to cleanse the skin. So far it had only been found in marshy ground by the sea, but Thomasin Tunstall discovered it on her precious Ingleborough Hill,

which were not knowne to be growing in England, and thereof she sent me some for a manifestation of the truth; I heare also that it groweth nigh unto a castle in the Peake of Derbishire which is 30 miles at the least from the Sea, and that the late Earl of Rutland, and divers other personages of note had some brought from thence for their own use,

wrote John. Its modern botanical name, *Cochlearia alpina*, implies that Thomasin Tunstall was the first to identify a distinct alpine variety.[14]

Since the *Paradisus* had made him famous, John had new connections who could bring him plants from the wider world that so fascinated him. One of them who became a particular friend was the son of a man who had made a fortune as the city of London expanded in John's youth. John Morris' father was a Dutchman who had built the watermills near London Bridge that supplied the city with running water. Peter Morris had been master of the watermills and was able to make his son a gentleman, sending him on a grand tour of Europe that included Florence and Rome. Back in England, John Morris bought a copy of the *Paradisus* for the garden and the library that every gentleman now aspired to own.

He invited John to visit the family home on the Thames at Isleworth, just upstream from London. He lived comfortably there with his wife Lettice, devoting himself entirely to his own interests. These were chiefly

his plants, his books, and his health, about which he was serious enough
to employ the most expensive physician in the country, Sir Theodore de
Mayerne. Morris did have one other interest that made his friendship
particularly helpful to John. He corresponded regularly with a Dutch
merchant from Leyden called Johannes de Laet.

De Laet was a director of the Dutch West India Company, but also a
scholar who published numerous studies of the known and the New
World. He had written geographical accounts of Scotland and Ireland and
recently England, but also of Persia, Turkey, India and Italy, and he was
preparing a work on Brazilian plants and precious stones. De Laet was also
working on a dictionary of Anglo-Saxon law and botany, so he was naturally interested in John. Morris offered to ask de Laet to obtain rare
American plants for John in exchange for some of the precious tulips,
hyacinths and anemones from his garden. John's bulbs were valuable,
especially in Holland. In the early 1630s exotic varieties of tulip were
changing hands there at such high prices that the bubble would soon
burst. Yet the exchange was a good one for John. Dutch traders could
reach places that were barred to the British, and through de Laet, John
had a chance to find plants that no other Englishman had seen.

He began to make lists of the plants he would like to have from
Virginia, keeping a copy of the notes he handed Morris to pass on to de
Laet. 'Melissa Jamaica fl. Albo Coeur; Paleriana Mexicana; Cardus
asphodel radice Monsg. Thorpe if it is not my great Corsind' were some
of the many plants he still wanted to collect. He had heard about them
but still needed to see them to compare with his own and make an exact
record for his theatre of plants.

A couple of months before his sixty-ninth birthday, John's dwindling
fortune was tested by another minor disaster. A gale erupted on 4
November 1636, so fierce that it blew down part of the wall around his
garden. He was forced to employ seven people, some of them for nearly
a week, to build it up again, keeping careful note of every farthing he
paid. Three months later he had reason to be glad he had restored the
security of his garden so promptly. He received the first Virginian seeds
from John Morris and gave him another list of plants for the next
autumn crossing. Slowly he was gathering the information he needed,
but it was a long and expensive business.[15]

He was often distracted these days by flattering requests for his
opinion. Once he was asked to appear before the king and queen at
Windsor with the royal physicians to inspect the king's unicorn's horn.

Charles wished to know if his horn came from a real unicorn or a 'sea unicorn'. 'Real' unicorn's horn was worth a lot of money, because of its legendary powers. It was reputed to be effective against 'plague and other infectious diseases, to expell melancholly likewise, and to cherish, exhilirate and strengthen the vitall spirits and more noble partes'.[16]

John went with Sir Theodore de Mayerne and Dr William Harvey to Windsor and together they bent to inspect the colour and density of the king's horn. The three learned men must have made an odd little group at court. They all wore their hair cropped short, covered with a skullcap in the style of the medical profession, their bare heads contrasting sharply with the flowing locks, hats and feathers that had become the style for young courtiers. Sir Theodore's short round body was a familiar sight but John looked oddly old-fashioned in this crowd. His best satin jerkin and doublet, which the occasion demanded, paraded a style that was now at least twenty years out of date.

These three knew very well which would be the better answer to the king's question. Yet, whatever His Majesty wanted to hear, each was an honest man who knew what the answer had to be. John already knew from Tradescant that Sir Dudley Digges had found the horn he gave Charles on a seashore 'somewhere in the North-West'. He also knew there had been others, one of which found its way into John Tradescant's own collection at 'the Ark'. That was undoubtedly a 'sea unicorn's horn', and so, unquestionably, was the king's.

The myth of the unicorn was so old and so powerful, and there were so many parts of the world still unknown and undiscovered, that even in 1640 John did not feel he could dismiss its existence entirely. As the doctors conveyed their verdict to the king, John could offer, in consolation, his increasing doubt as to the existence of such an animal.

> The received opinion of the unicorne is that it is a beast of the size of a meane [average] horse (but I thinke it cannot be possible but he must be much greater to beare so large, so long and so massie a horne, such as are to be seene in sundry places of Europe, (if such be the horne of any beast).[17]

This would mean that all the seven unicorn's horns, treasured in palaces throughout Europe, were no more valuable than King Charles'. By 1649, when parliamentary forces seized the Tower of London where the king's horn was stored along with his other treasures, its value had slumped. While in 1600 an eight-foot horn stored here had been valued at £10,000, the king's treasure was now listed as 'The unicorn's horne weighing 40 lbs 8 ozs, valued at £600 0s 0d'.[18]

John was much happier being consulted as an expert on plants. His Covent Garden neighbour, Sir John Danvers, was making what John Aubrey considered to be the first in 'the way of Italian gardens' in England, at his other house in Chelsea. Danvers was part of the aristocratic English group who had become dedicated gardeners. One of his elder brothers, Henry Danvers, had given a plot of land to Oxford University in 1621 for the country's first 'Botanical Garden', although there had been little progress so far beyond staking out the plot. Sir John Danvers had made his garden an integral part of the design of his house. The effect so impressed Danvers' 'relation and faithfull Friend', John Aubrey, that he made a detailed description of it in 1691, complete with a rough sketch of its outline. 'As you sitt at Dinner in the Hall, you are entertaind with two delightfull Visto's: one southward over the Thames and to Surrey, the other northward into that curious Garden'.[19] Danvers and his wife, a widow nearly twice his age, made full use of their garden. He was 'wont in fair mornings in the Summer to brush his Beaver-hatt on the Hysop and Thyme, which did perfume it with its naturall Spirit; and would last a morning or longer'. She entertained their many friends and relations there, including her son, the poet George Herbert, and his friend John Donne. When one of their most constant visitors, Sir Francis Bacon, fainted as he walked with them round their garden, she knew at once what to do: 'My Lady Danvers rubbed his face, temples etc., and gave him cordiall water; as soon as he came to himselfe, sayde he, "Madam, I am no good footman".'[20]

The relationship of John Danvers' house to the garden could have been taken straight from the pages of John's own *Paradisus*, 'having the fairest buildings of the house facing the garden ... [you] shall have reciprocally the beautiful prospect into it and have both sight and scent of whatsoever is excellent and worthy to give content out from it'.[21] Evidently a sympathetic friend to consult, John became a part of the Danvers' circle of visitors, often arriving there with new plants he had identified along the way. One day, he made note of a 'Clownes woundwort... by the path ... in the fields going to Chelsea and Kensington', the only species of a plant used to heal flesh wounds caused by iron or steel that was native to Britain. On another occasion he arrived by boat, and noted his finds: 'by the waterside below My Lord of Danvers house at Chelsey'.[22]

This group of friends was distinguished by their close interest in the plants that grew in their gardens. They were distinct from a small group of aristocrats who lavished their fortune on gardens where nature had little part to play. Thomas Howard, Earl of Arundel, set the fashion for Roman carvings, which he imported to fill the garden behind his house in the Strand. Imitating the style of the Venetian princes, he commissioned Inigo Jones to build a 'new Italyan gate' and a stone garden platform beside the River Thames. This he decked with antique sculptures, visible from the house, but also gazing imposingly over the river traffic below. Eventually he imported so many of these statues that when Sir Francis Bacon first came upon them, even though the collection was still incomplete, it prompted his typically scathing mockery. Bacon imagined a visitor chancing on the sight by accident. 'Coming into the ... Garden, where there were a great number of Statues of naked Men and Women, [he] made a stand, and, as astonished, cryed out: the Resurrection!'[23]

King Charles soon followed Arundel in his passion for grand statuary. With hindsight, it seemed to Aubrey that there was more than an element of compensation for other failings in the king's new fancy.

> Ever since his coming to the Crowne, [he has] ... amply testified a Royall liking of ancient statues, by causing a whole army of old Forraine Emperours, Captaines and Senators all at once to land on his coasts, to come and do him homage; and attend upon him in his palace at Saint James, and Somerset House.[24]

Charles and his queen liked the style of the new garden at Wilton. The king's lord chamberlain, Philip Herbert, had inherited the house in 1630, and set about transforming it into a modern European palace. A new garden was laid out in a formal rectangle that swept across all natural features of the landscape, leaving a stream running in an untidy diagonal across its midst. Symmetrical walks laid between the quarters of the rectangle led to fine sculpture and marvellous fountains. The star attraction when the garden was finished was one of de Caus' masterpieces, which took nature as its inspiration and then reconstructed it. Isaac de Caus built a grotto that housed 'a rare water-worke' that could imitate 'the singing, and chirping of Birdes, and other strange rarities, onely by that Element [water]', so that 'the melody of Nightingerlls and all sorts of birds' was heard in one of the side rooms.[25]

Yet, to the discerning eye, it was clear that even here, in these splendid artificial playgrounds for a handful of the country's richest players, John's years of work in his garden were playing a pivotal part. Below the terrace close to the house, scrolls of low growing 'broderie', decorative borders in elaborate patterns copied from Florence, were planted in closely clipped box. Between these, the colour that brought them alive was no longer an assortment of sands and coloured glass, but the living flowers that John had so painstakingly cultivated to extend their growing season for this very purpose. Here was the 'peece of curious needleworke, or peece of painting' that he had described in the pages of the *Paradisus*, brought to life in the garden the king and queen loved best.[26]

CHAPTER SEVENTEEN

INTO THE
LIGHT AT LAST

The drawing John commissioned of the Mimosa
pudica, *published in* Theatrum Botanicum, *1640*

John persisted with what was now to be his 'Theater of Plantes', as the
impact of Thomas Johnson's edition of Gerard's herbal began to
recede. The younger apothecary's betrayal had spurred him to aim
higher in preparing this book, and he was delighted by new discoveries
that constantly interrupted the final stages. He was highly excited when
Sir John Danvers received some seed of the little *Mimosa pudica*, the
sensitive plant that had so fascinated George Clifford's sailors in Puerto
Rico. This plant had never been seen alive in England. One of the dried
specimens brought back by the Earl of Cumberland had ended up in the
hands of 'Mr Job Best at the Trinity House in Ratcliffe', near Oxford, at
whose house Thomas Johnson had seen and drawn the specimen. Yet
John was now able to secure a significant advance, and watch the living
plant unfold.

In a pot at Chelsey ... divers seeds being sowne therein about the middle of May, 1638 and 1639, some of them spreng up to be near half a foote high ... with severall ... paires of winged leaves ... foulding themselves upward close to the middle ribbe upon any touch thereof: this I proved in those two severall yeares.

Triumphantly seizing on this minor living miracle, he arranged to include a drawing of the growing plant, 'that you may see the difference between it and others formerly set forth from the sight of a dried plant'.[1]

John clearly exulted in this triumph over his competitors. Yet though he laboured eagerly to include this exclusive new entry in his book, the tenor of his life's work derived from an entirely different source. John had grown into his knowledge in the company of a circle of men, and a few women, who believed in the free exchange of information for the common good. He was not at ease in the cut-throat commercial world that now dominated London, where information had a monetary value accruing to the first person to bring it to market. John rarely made a point of his triumphs over others, or carped at their faults, in the modern style. His honest pursuit of the Renaissance spirit of inquiry had taken him a long way, albeit slowly, and he was on the verge of taking this principle further than it had ever been taken before, by publishing the fruit of all his skill, in English.

His knowledge at this stage would have been worth a good deal. English apothecaries were now considered among the best in the world, and over sixty years of diligent work John had become the best herbal doctor in England. He was about to break with tradition by making everything he knew available to ordinary men and women who had not been schooled in Latin. He wanted his book to be an accessible champion of logic, study and experiment, and a scientific legacy to the apothecaries and doctors who came after him. 'For finding in my profession many slips and errours crept therein ... it stirred up a desire in me, having rightly weighed them, seriously to consider how such a customary evill could be left off and amended.' He took care not to offend the doctors' vanity by presuming to teach them what they supposed they already knew, but offered himself, with his characteristically deceptive diffidence, as their assistant. 'I goe not about to teach Doctors ... but to helpe their memories, and withal to shew them my judgement, that they mistake not one thing for another, or one man's plant for another.'

Johnson's edition of Gerard, with its mixture of fable and fact, had sharpened John's ambition to persuade his countrymen by reason. He summoned his readers squarely to the truth, 'not doubting of the effect, by the religious inclination of my Country when just reasons shall be shewed therefore ... both to avoid and amend ... [errors]'. Yet he admitted that every day he was faced with examples of stubborn adherence to ignorant myths from the past. 'Some delight to be obstinate, and because they were bred up in errors, they will not be wiser then their Fathers, but together live and dye in them, yea and condemne the light that others have, because they think their darknesse better.'[2]

While his book was still not securely in print, John gave a copy of his mimosa drawing to his new friends John Morris and Johannes de Laet. In return de Laet gave him some information about the plant from a Spanish book about Mexico that he had translated. The South Americans used mimosa as an aphrodisiac, apparently, though John complained that no one explained how. Resolving the loose ends of such new problems to his satisfaction became yet another obstacle that delayed the final completion of his book.

In preparing a guide to the medicinal qualities of plants, John was working in a field whose boundaries appeared to recede the more he sought them. He had acquired Matthias de l'Obel's papers with a view to compiling a modern herbal that would include all the discoveries of recent years and offer a clear method of identifying the plants referred to by the ancient authors. His old mentor's work had turned out to be disappointing, once he had it in his hands. It covered only 835 plants, and many of the notes were repetitive or out of date. John never forgot his debt to de l'Obel, which he recognized in the front of his *Theatrum*, acknowledging his use of 'the chiefe notes of Dr Lobel and Dr Bonham [a friend and collaborator of de l'Obel's] therein'. Yet he had learned so much since his old mentor died. There had been discoveries, not just from America, Canada and Russia, but closer to home. New finds were reported all the time on British soil, and in Ireland, by a young generation of botanists. So many doctors, divines, gentlemen and ladies now took an interest in plants that John could hardly keep track of them. He chose to relax his rigid rule of personal experience which had so far guided his work, and add the reports of the many contacts and friends who sent him descriptions. It was clear he would never live long enough to cover all this ground personally. The infinite variety and complexity of the natural world turned out to be far greater than the limits of his method of discovery. He was aware that he could not be as certain as he had once been that he had not made any mistakes.

Since the *Theatrum* was intended for medical use, John organized his plants according to their physical effects. He began with a chapter on sweet-smelling plants, then 'Purging plants'; 'Venemous, Sleepy and Hurtful Plants and their Counterpoysons' and then Saxifrages, which were used for their ability as internal medicine to 'breake stone', mimicking the way they grow. The chapters that follow are on wound herbs, hot herbs and cooling herbs. After these seven John moved towards modern botanical classification to arrange the huge number of plants that did not fit into the traditional arrangement of a medical cata-logue. A chapter on umbelliferous plants followed, then one on thistles and thorny plants; one called 'Fearnes and Capillary Herbes', and then 'Pulses' and a chapter on 'Cornes'. With two more sections, on grasses and marshy plants, ready in manuscript, the great book was nearly ready. The last-minute entry of the mimosa delayed John a little more. He inserted it into the chapter on ferns that was already at the printer's and, just after Christmas 1638, he showed Morris the pages printed up to page 1142.[3]

Years of study had gone into this 'Manlike worke of Herbes and plants', as John called it when presenting it to the king. He had collated and corrected the existing literature, adding in the results of his own experiments, while collecting new samples to stretch people's understand-ing of plants. He had studied Clusius, and a work called *Pinax* by the French botanist Gaspard Bauhin, published in Basle in 1623. Information on Canadian plants came from Jacques Cornut, another Frenchman, who published in Paris in 1635. He gathered information on Brazilian plants from Johannes de Laet, and drew on numerous modern Italian sources to complete his understanding. These years of dense study were reflected in his writing. The *Theatrum* is swollen with discussions of the derivations of plant names, of earlier mistaken identities, as much as it is crammed with detailed medical uses and remedies. John Parkinson's earlier delight in the minute details of colour and form that he had observed as he worked with his beloved flowers and noted in the *Paradisus*, gave way to a forest of information.

Yet the *Theatrum* shows how far his fascination with the interrelation-ship between plants and man had deepened in the course of his life. As far as he could, he described how newly discovered plants, like the mimosa, were used in their native habitat. But he also showed how the plants in everyday use in his own country were living symbols of ancient history. His chapter on 'Cornes' includes entries for such unusual mixes as 'Ptisana; Mault; Zythum' and 'Curmi'. All these preparations are referred to in the classical medical texts of Galen and Dioscorides or Theophrastus as medicinal drinks. John's research unearthed the exact contents of these drinks and the method of producing them. 'Ptisana' was barley water or cream, which John still considered 'the most praysed and prayse-worthy drink' for treating fevers or weakness. He gave the recipes used by 'our Physitions in these times', who added raisins and liquorice to treat coughs, or almonds, sugar and rosewater to strengthen weak patients. He also described 'the manner of the ancients', based on Hippocrates' recipe, pointing out the variations in soaking and boiling the barley, and the different grains used as a base by various ancient doctors.

True to his purpose as a medical man, John offered practical recipes, just as he had in the *Paradisus*, but this book showed that the inspired gardener who revelled in natural beauty had become a scholar. It was, however, a kind of scholarship forged in his own kitchen, which reflected the daily gossip of the streets and taverns of London. John included 'Zythum' because it was a drink mentioned in the old texts, and weighed it against his own experience of making beer.

> The general Tenet of our times is that it is the same drinke we now call beere or ale, varied according to ... the goodnesse, quantitie and diversity of the graine where it is made and also of the water: for ... it is well knowne that there is no Beere that can be made in the Low Countries by reason of their brackish water, but will taste therof, and be farre inferiour to that is made in England ... it is observed by many that the water of our River Thames about London doth make better and stronger drinke then that which is made of other Spring or River Water elsewhere.[4]

John's intention was to produce 'a more ample and exact History and declaration of the Physicall herbs and Plants than are in other Authors, encreased by the accesse of many hundred of new, rare and strange Plants from all parts of the world'. He included over a thousand more plants than had Johnson in his edition of Gerard seven years before. The effect of his 'Theater of Plantes' was to reach 2,000 years and more back into the medical history of mankind. His book revealed an ancient world whose knowledge and discoveries were then still in daily use. Yet it was also a book of its time, charting the revolution in information and travel that he had seen in his lifetime.

John Morris was delighted with what he saw. He rushed off a report to de Laet:

> As soon as Parkinson's *Theatrum Botanicum* comes out I shall send you a copy, if you would like. It is being published in a folio of ample size, with elegant print, and very nicely drawn images of the plants, with as many woodcuts as it might be possible to include. The work has progressed to page 1142 and it will not fail to be twice as much, as the good old man showed me recently when I went to inspect it with him.[5]

Even at this point, there were, as it turned out, over 500 more pages to go before John considered it finished. He was now past his seventieth birthday. His great work was becoming a burden he could neither finish nor leave alone. Torn between his desire to be comprehensive and his need to find limits to his project, he abandoned some of his habitual methodical care. He rapidly added a chapter called 'The Unordered Tribe' to include all those plants that had somehow escaped his earlier method of classification. A chapter on trees and shrubs followed, and finally John allowed in the temptingly unexplored territory of 'Strange and outlandish plants'. This group was a mixture of exotic substances like musk, myrrh and even 'mummy', still imported by apothecaries and used in remedies, the last being 'the very body of a man or woman … brought chiefly from Egypt or Syria adjoining, and no other part of the world so good'.[6] 'Mummy' was used as an ingredient in treatments for migraine and epilepsy, but was popular also in remedies designed to strengthen the body's immune system. Much of this chapter on 'outlandish' plants gave way, however, to the travellers' tales that fascinated John, but would remain forever beyond his understanding. There was, for example, the story of the 'Chaste Making tree' that he had read of, but he had never come close to a sample that could help him explain its nature. This was a West Indian tree which the natives could not 'be brought to burne … or abide where it was burned, for they said that whosoever came near the fire or flame thereof, or whosoever the smoake onely touched, was made utterly impotent and unabled to any venerous [sexual] acts'.[7]

When at last John decided his book was finished, resorting to an appendix to include entries that had missed the printer's deadline, there were 1,688 pages of text, with clear wood engravings on almost every page. Gerard had given an alphabetical list of each plant's medicinal properties or 'vertues', but John refused to adopt this method, arguing that it would have made his book even longer, and advising his readers that there was unlooked-for benefit in the haphazard. 'In recompense for the time spent looking for what you seek, you may read that which may be more helpful and beneficiall to you.'[8]

Sir Theodore de Mayerne was still John's greatest supporter and advocate. He saw his work as an important advance on previous herbals. De Mayerne poured scorn on the efforts of scholars who 'think that they have done something brilliantly if through surveys and various toils, [they] put into a book the names of simple plants that are already known with perhaps their pictures'. John had done something more profound. He delivered a practical manual that would make a real difference to standard medical treatment. De Mayerne valued the detailed information on the correct preparation of remedies that John had added to his thorough work identifying different species. His book, Sir Theodore said,

> Entered the very marrow of plants and the virtues [medical properties] of each for the good of the public. You reveal the ointment of mortals so skilfully so that your English compatriots (a race born for peace, war, knowledge, arts, fitted to everything) will forever after be intimate with the richest part of nature's treasure chamber.[9]

It was gratifying for John to know that the most respected doctors in the country welcomed the results of his 'long paines and endeavours'. No less than three fellows of the College of Physicians, led by Sir Matthew Lister and Sir Theodore de Mayerne, championed this book, but he had laboured for many years without any direct encouragement from the king. Charles had been distracted from the favours that he and his father had shown John in the early days by his acute political difficulties. In the last eighteen months the king's relationship with his Scots subjects had deteriorated to a point that made average Englishmen shake their heads in disbelief. The king had spent the summer attempting to raise a militia to control the rebellious Scots. In desperation he fell back on the rusty feudal system and asked the Earl of Derby to muster his Lancashire

tenants to defend the north of England. John's Bleasdale cousins would
have been among the first recruits.

In the autumn of 1639, when the king returned briefly to London, Sir
Theodore de Mayerne was able to persuade him to turn his attention to
his country's leading herbalist. The king was in the mood to enjoy the
riches of his civil state, perhaps in defiant reaction to his problems with
the rebels. He found time, amongst other things, to buy for his queen
the beautiful house and garden at Wimbledon that had once belonged
to Thomas Cecil. De Mayerne pointed out that John's completed book
deserved royal recognition, and the king accepted his physician's argument that John had made a significant contribution to the welfare of the
people. At last, John found, the king was ready to award him the title
he had coveted for so long.

Soon after Christmas, John received the news that his official appointment as 'Herbariste' to the king was under way. The lord chamberlain
gave him a place in the new list of the king's 'Establishment', entering
his name on the page below the royal physicians, but above the royal
surgeon and the royal apothecaries. It was the first time there had ever
been such a post in the nation's official records. De l'Obel had had King
James' verbal assent to this title, by his own account, and Gerard's lease
to the land behind Somerset House showed he had also had brief
acknowledgement as something similar. However, this time the title was
included in the official records, so that, after John, a man was regularly
recruited to fill the post.[10]

The appointment was unique, not just because it officially recognized
a science that John had pioneered in England, but for another reason
also. Alone of all the appointments on the king's list, the words 'sans
fee' were entered alongside John's name. This sacrifice was the only
means by which John could win 'the beautiful title' that had been his
goal for a quarter of a century. As a Catholic, he could not be formally
included in the king's household at such a sensitive time in any other
way than by agreeing to dispense with a salary.

John's new title was none the less sweet for the fact that it was a formal
recognition of what had long been the *status quo*. He had been accepted
as part of the court establishment since the days of King James, and only
this had given him the right to dedicate his first book to Queen Henrietta
Maria. However, he had signed that book as 'Apothecary of London'. This
one he would sign as '*Botanicus Regius*' – the royal herbalist. John Morris
beamed with reflected glory and lost no time in telling de Laet the news.

This same Parkinson, because of his work and the recommendation of the Excellent Mayerne, is made Herbalist to the King ['*Botanographum Regium*'], nevertheless without any pay, he should be contented with the gifts of the honour alone, and take pride in the beautiful title.[11]

The *Theatrum Botanicum*, or *Theater of Plantes*, that John had finally completed was the most detailed and accurate herbal there had ever been in English, and would remain unique for hundreds of years. No book before it had attempted to combine correct identification of the plant species known for medicinal use with an explanation of the medical application for each one. No book after it offered such a comprehensive range of material, included for its medicinal purpose rather than its botanical classification, filtered through the working experience of one man. John must have felt the satisfaction of a long job well done when he finally sat down to dedicate this book to the king, in the carefully crafted terms he had learned to use at court.

In matters of religion and politics, the old apothecary found it necessary to dispense with the rigorously logical approach that he applied to medicinal plants. His Catholicism was a peculiar mixture, which it was hardly surprising that his own son found difficult to understand. John could not tolerate the ritual of the Anglican Church, but accepted nevertheless that the British sovereign, and not the Pope, was the chief interpreter of the divine for his people.

As your Majestie is Summus Pater Patriae, the chief of your people under God, that not only provideth for their soules health, that they may have the pure Word of God ... wherein we justly claime the prerogative above any Nation under Heaven ... but many wayes also for their bodily estates, by good and wholesome Laws, that everyone may live obediently and peaceably under their own Vine and Figtree....[12]

John placed his book firmly within the hierarchy that Charles ruled by 'divine right'.

Having by long paines and endeavours, composed this Manlike Worke of Herbes and Plants, Most gracious Soveraigne (as I formerly did a Feminine of Flowers, and presented to the Queenes most excellent

Majesty) I could doe no lesse then submissively lay it at your Majesties feet, to be approved or condemned, and if thought worthy a publique passage, to offer it on the Altar of your Majestyes many favours to me, to be commanded as well as commended unto all for their owne good.[13]

After this courtly overture, the public opened the pages to a voice that had lost its customary gentle tone, deeply scarred by his troubles of the last ten years:

The disastrous times, but much more wretched and perverse men have so far prevailed against my intending purpose, and promise, in exhibiting this Worke to the publicke view of all, that their extreme covetousnesse had well nigh deprived my Country of the fruition: But having at last, though long and with much adoe, broken through all obstacles opposing *'tandem prodiit in lucem'* [into the light at last].

John revealed here the black mood he had suffered after Thomas Johnson's betrayal, admitting that the book he conceived as a young man had almost defeated him as a result. The younger apothecary's shadow still hung low over his horizon. His task, he confessed,

Lay somewhat heavy on me to undergoe ... however Master Johnson's agility could easily wade through with it and his younger yeares carry away greater burdens ... but his quick speed may conclude with this adage: *Canis festinans coecos parit catullos* [the hurrying dog produces blind puppies].[14]

No longer the open-minded enthusiast of his previous work, welcoming friends from every quarter, the scholarly, ageing John Parkinson could not resist a sharp barb here and there. Somewhat wryly, he encapsulated his attitude in the emblem he chose to hold when he presented the fruit of his life's work to the world.

The portrait of the author on the frontispiece of the *Theatrum* shows him as a whitehaired and weatherbeaten seventy-three-year-old in a skullcap (see title page). His whorled nose and cheeks are ruddy beneath the still sharp hooded eyes. His sombre black gown contrasts with the pineapples, the American sunflowers, the cacti, the zebra and the rhinoceros that represent the revolution of discovery he has seen in his lifetime. Yet he holds in his hand one of the oldest medical remedies of all. The plant he has chosen is a thistle, known for its power against plague and pestilence and as a remedy to break through internal obstructions. It is a flattering symbol of his king's Scottish origin, but it also reminds those who care to know of his enemy's errors. Gerard had muddled the 'St Barnabas thistle' with another in his herbal, and given this popular country purgative the wrong illustration. It was one of the mistakes that Johnson had failed to correct. 'Many such faults hath passed Mr Johnson's correction, which I am loth in every place to exhibit, knowing that none of us all can publish anything but there may be slippes and errours in many places thereof'.[15] Yet this little thistle expressed the change that had come over John since he delivered his first book to the public. No longer 'Sweet John' as he had been then, he now saw himself as prickly, awkward and tough.

John launched his life's work on the public with a farewell flourish that hinted at the painful rift with his son.

> Goe forth now therefore thou issue artificiall of mine, and supply the defect of a Naturall, to beare up thy Father's name and memory to succeeding ages...[16]

Anticipating that these would be the last words he would write for publication, he nominated this 'Theater of Plantes' as his legacy to the world, and tagged it with a final statement of the key value in the scientific renaissance that he had pursued faithfully since his first encounter with Matthias de l'Obel at the age of sixteen: 'Some may object that I am somewhat too tart and quick, [but] my Apology to all is *Amicus mihi Plato, Amicus Seneca sed magis Amica mihi veritas* [Plato and Seneca are my friends, but my greatest friend is truth].'[17]

By the spring of 1640, John was able to leave his garden and walk to the palace at Whitehall with the burden of his years of work lifted from his shoulders. He had reason to be joyful. He had completed a unique collection of information, in spite of all the difficulties. His great work was a 'rich Magazin of Soveraigne medicines, physicall experiments and other rarities', in the words of an Oxford university scholar called Dr John Bainbridge. Dr Bainbridge, a lecturer in physic at Oxford and the professor of astronomy there, praised John's 'select Defloration' of the riches of the past, 'the several Botanique monuments of former Ages ... enriched and beautified with new discoveries'. He called John's *Theatrum Botanicum* 'the most compleat and absolute worke (in this

Whitehall and Covent Garden surveyed by Richard Newcourt around 1643–7 and engraved by William Faithorne, published 1662. The detail shows the explosion in decorative gardens in the first half of the seventeenth century.

kind) yet knowne unto the world: [it] will be a perpetuall monument of your Name, Art and Industry'. It must have been particularly sweet for John to receive praises from young scholars he had never met, accustomed as he was to a small world where knowledge was passed from mouth to mouth.

Yet many of the scholars that he did know had now achieve prominent positions. It was as though the world of scientific scholarship had come of age while he watched. Bainbridge's friend and colleague Thomas Clayton had known John since he was a boy. Clayton's uncle Ralph, a Lancastrian like John, had been a royal apothecary and John's neighbour. Now Thomas was 'His Majestie's Professor of Physique' at Oxford, and he thanked John 'for conquering the great enemyes of a civill world, Ignorance and Barbarisme, for saving so many citizens of your own country, from danger, diseases, destruction, by your careful understanding directions, for proper fit remedies, in such a rationall pleasing way'.[18]

John gathered a sheaf of accolades from internationally respected men for the front of the *Theatrum*, including one from Johannes de Laet and two from his friend John Morris. These, and the king's public endorsement, must have encouraged him to anticipate the success of his book, and a sweet revenge on Johnson for his hasty edition of Gerard.

He could now ponder a leisurely future. There could be new schemes that his title as the king's herbalist would help him bring about, including, perhaps, a royal botanical garden. Clayton had referred to the Physic Garden in Oxford with which he and Bainbridge were involved. In twenty years it had made little progress. It was only now at the point of being 'beautifully walled and gated ... in levelling and planting, with the charges and expences of thousands by the many wayes Honourable Earle of Danby [Henry Danvers, Sir John Danvers elder brother.]'[19] Yet, if the nation's capital was to have a fine garden also, then private gardens like John's on Long Acre were no longer the answer. They were too great an expense for one man to maintain. The land next to the tennis courts in St James's Park, where the king had offered a lease of ground, could be a perfect position for a public physic garden to rival the Jardin des Plantes in Paris, if John could kindle the king's enthusiasm.

The hall that the royal surveyor, Inigo Jones, had built for King James, known as the Banqueting House in Whitehall, was where the king now ennobled or honoured his subjects. John could look forward to receiving his beautiful title under the sparkling gaze of Rubens's thronging angels,

Covent Garden, c.1650, by Wenceslaus Hollar.

commissioned by Charles to celebrate his father's reign. The painter's images of peace and creativity had been in place for nearly five years now, and though their detail was hard to see in the dimly lit hall, they generated a thrilling atmosphere of quiet splendour. When the king was in residence the Banqueting House was hung with tapestries that clothed both long sides of the chamber. What little daylight there was shone on the king and queen presiding over their courtly stage at one end. To receive his honour, John would have to step through the doors of this unusually stark white building, go up the stairs and cross the whole length of the darkly glittering hall to kneel at the king's feet.[20]

Outside Whitehall, the images of peace and prosperity the king collected around him were less convincing. Even on the streets of Covent Garden, running right up to the palace gate, it was evident that the 'great enemyes of a civill world' to which Thomas Clayton had referred were not yet conquered. The short walk from John's garden to the court made it only too clear that signs of 'Ignorance and Barbarism' were all around, while 'danger, diseases and destruction'[21] seemed to be growing.

The rich had laid out this parish of St Martin's-in-the-Fields for their pleasure and to show off their wealth. The Earl of Bedford had commissioned Inigo Jones to build a central market in the Italian style and a new church behind his house at Covent Garden. Everyone said that the square, which was now finished, could have been a Florentine piazza, and praised the symmetry of its proportions. The Earls of Newport, Salisbury, Pembroke and Arundel mixed there with the king's servants, who included the cleverest men in the land, amongst whom John could now modestly count himself. Recently, though, the area had become as crowded as the parish of St Bride's against the City walls where John had lived twenty years before. So many 'new bricke buildings' had appeared that it was hard to believe that this was the same country district where a short time ago the aristocracy had chosen to rent garden plots. Many gardens were still there, enclosed like John's by brick walls, but the walls were no longer to keep out stray animals or passers-by. The enemy now was the crowd of insistently drifting scavengers from the countryside.

The poor kept on coming. The churchwardens, who had once collected funds to distribute in times of plague, now collected a 'poor rate' every year, and sometimes an extra 'scavengers' rate', to keep the homeless newcomers from starving on the streets. Sometimes the men picked up casual work in the parish for a while and people knew their Christian name at least before their death, like Godfery who died in February 1639, or Jacobus who was buried a month later. But the sextons had become used to entering *'pauper ignota'*, unknown pauper, in their burial record at least once a month. The new taxes generated a considerable income, with such wealthy households contributing to the pot. Sir Theodore de Mayerne alone had been assessed at £4 in the past. Still, no amount of private or parish charity was enough to keep the poor at bay.[22]

Unquestionably, a dark side was emerging from the great commercial enterprise that John's generation had launched. Men and women were being driven off the land by landowners pushing for a profit. The spirit of independent enterprise that had made many men wealthy had also displaced established customs and duties to protect the poor. Fanatical extremes had taken the place of the one universal Church instead of the hoped-for freedom of conscience in matters of religion. People fought hard to survive in this competitive climate, and the weakest failed. The great discoveries of John's generation had undoubtedly been remarkable, but the changes that fostered them had also brought with them dangerous instability.

CHAPTER EIGHTEEN

'ALL THINGS AS IN A CHAOS'

On the May Day holiday a few weeks after the *Theatrum* was published in 1640, the archbishop was besieged in his palace by a storming mob. A volatile mix of apprentice boys on a day off, fanatical Puritan preachers and the city's paupers attacked Lambeth Palace, calling for an end to the church courts that he had introduced.[1]

The disturbances were an unwelcome distraction for John from the gratifying reaction to his book. On 23 May, John Morris wrote enthusiastically to de Laet: 'Master Parkinson is to be congratulated and earnestly applauded, which he is not unaware of, as he has been surrounded with the well-earned praises of his friends, and he is as grateful to you as could be for your testimony which so honours him.'[2]

Though the rumblings of rebellion in the nation were not at the forefront of their minds, John and his friends observed events with deep disquiet. The king had dissolved Parliament suddenly and travelled north to confront the Scots, who now controlled Edinburgh and were preparing to invade Northumberland and Durham. The militia Charles had ordered to be raised across the country marched to meet him in the north, but news reached London that one levy, recruited in Wiltshire, had turned on its officers and hounded them out of the inn where they were dining. A lieutenant, forced on to a flagpole projecting from the first floor, had been lynched when he fell into the baying crowd. 'I am at a loss', wrote Morris to de Laet, 'to know which faction of this Christian state is the most damnable.'[3]

Fortunately these events occurred a long way from London. In the capital, life continued much as usual. All through the summer, John was occupied with the pleasant business of discussing his great work with friends and readers. The *Theatrum* was a volume that no gentleman who was serious about the science of plants could afford to be without, although its length and the quality of its illustrations made it an expensive addition to their libraries. John Goodyer noted his purchase of a copy in the careful record he kept of all his books. He entered the hefty sum of 36 s. against 'Parkinson, Theatrum', on 24 August 1640, and another 3 s. for the binding.[4]

As the king's herbalist, John was given lodgings in Whitehall Palace, which had become a sprawling village protected from events elsewhere in the country. The 'court is now filled with families of every mean courtier', wrote one such courtier in disgust in 1637.[5] The ancient right of the sovereign to procure food at less than cost price meant that almost every court servant and his family were granted the privilege of eating the three meals a day served in the palace hall, or payment in lieu, the so-called 'bouche of court'. The 'bouche' had become a very attractive perk of royal service since raging inflation and failed harvests had driven up the cost of food outside.

The king's physician had lodgings below the queen's apartments at Whitehall. Other medical members of the royal household had apartments near the main entrance to the court on the south-east side. A plan drawn in 1670 shows the 'Herb house', where herbs were dried and prepared for use in food and medicine, squeezed between the royal apothecary's lodgings and those of the household physician, immediately behind the complex that housed the kitchens, the scullery, the bakehouse and the cellar.[6] John's court lodging would have been near this, the busiest part of Whitehall, although he could still retreat to his house and garden in Long Acre (see map, page 283).

The walls of this part of the palace echoed continually with crashes and cries as delivery carts were loaded and unloaded all through the day. The smells from the kitchen larded the air. Around the dinner hours the noise rose to a crescendo as plates and cups clattered in the scullery, and special wines and delicacies were touted for sale in the courtyard. The frantic pace of life at court was a long way from the solitary peace John had grown used to. The possibility of a new house and garden 'next the tennis courts' that he had been granted by the king must have seemed an attractive prospect for his retirement. The tennis courts were at the other end of the palace grounds, between the privy garden at the north-west end and St James's Park. It would be a challenge to convert open countryside into a garden again at his age, but the peaceful view he would have of the village of Westminster and the beautiful abbey at its heart made an appealing prospect. John could have lived there close to the company he found most congenial – the gamekeepers who looked after the king's deer in the park and the gardener in charge of the privy garden – comfortable in the knowledge that the royal household would now sustain him until his dying day.

Dreams of peaceful retirement grew cold as the summer's heat lessened. At the end of June 1640, Morris promised to send de Laet copies of John's *Theatrum* and *Paradisus*, in the care of Sir William Boswell, who was an ambassador at The Hague. The books were duly delivered. Two months later, Boswell began a secret correspondence with Archbishop Laud that would have serious repercussions for John, not so much for its content as for the suspicion and hostility it fomented against Catholics. John was about to face a grim change of circumstance.

Laud received 'evidence' from a Dutch merchant that neatly brought together the twin enemies of the British state. The king's problems in the north were being fomented by Scottish Jesuits, it said, not, as he supposed, by Scottish Calvinists in London.

'Scarce all Spain France and Italy can yield so great a multitude of Jesuits as London alone; where are found more than fifty Scottish Jesuits', said the intelligence. A detailed plot to poison the king was revealed to have been coordinated by the archdean of the Jesuit College at Cambrai, and the papal legate in London, Count Rosetti, who was a close friend of the queen's.

Every Catholic in London was implicated by association, particularly those who lived, as John did, in the heart of their dark domain.

> Captain Read, a Scot, dwelling in Long acre street, near the Angel Tavern, a secular Jesuit who ... for a recompense, obtained a rent or impost upon butter [an unpopular tax, naturally], which the country-people are bound to render to him.... In his house the business of the whole plot is concluded.... There is in that very house a Jesuit chapel, wherein an ordinary Jesuit consecrates, and dwells there. In the said chapel, masses are daily celebrated by the Jesuits, and it serves for the baptizing of the children of the house and of some of the conspirators. Those who assemble on the aforenamed house come frequently in coaches, or on horseback in layman's habit, and with a great train wherewith they are disguised, that they may not be known....[7]

Many of the king's closest friends were accused.

> The countess of Arundell, a strenuous she-champion of the popish religion ... whatsoever she hears at the King's court ... she presently imparts to the pope's legate, with whom she meets thrice a day ... Mr Porter, of the king's bedchamber [Endymion Porter, a fluent Spanish

speaker, openly Catholic, and Charles' companion on his secret visit
to Madrid] .... Secretary Windebank, a most fierce papist, is the most
unfaithful to the King of all men.... He sent his son expressly to Rome
... the Countess of Newport [John's son's employer], the Duchess of
Buckingham, and many others....[8]

Nothing could have expressed more clearly than these letters the
power of the popular conviction that Catholics were to blame for every
evil threatening the kingdom. The Scots were now occupying the two
most northern English counties, having humiliated the king's levies.
Charles concluded an unsatisfactory peace that entailed paying them a
subsidy of £860 a day. He returned to London in October 1640, a month
after Boswell's letters arrived, urgently needing another Parliament to
vote him the money he had agreed to pay the Scots.

The members of parliament who travelled to London from the
country brought the sense of a hidden Catholic enemy in the capital to
fever pitch. The king was only too willing, in the light of this most
recent plot, to ditch his Catholic friends to get what he wanted out of
the House of Commons. On 11 November, Parliament passed a motion
ordering all Catholic recusants to leave London and the court. The same
day Thomas Wentworth, recently named Earl of Strafford for his services to the king in Ireland, was impeached on suspicion of seeking to
raise an Irish Catholic army to wage war on the king's subjects on the
mainland. Three weeks later, the Commons accused the king's personal
secretary, Sir Francis Windebank, of selling pardons to recusants. Sir
Francis did not stay to argue the matter but fled to France the same
night. At last members of parliament and merchants were in a position
to use the king's desperation for money to press their point home.
When Charles agreed to his wife's request that he pardon an English
Jesuit priest, John Goodman, the City aldermen refused him the loan
they had been about to make.

In such an atmosphere, recusants left London swiftly for their own
safety, complying with the new laws of the land. John's son, Richard,
was one of those who melted away, leaving no trace of where he had
gone. Those who could afford it fled to France like Secretary Windebank.
Others headed for Ireland, where the sheer number of English Catholics
offered protection, and there was work to be had managing the English
'plantations'. Others returned to the north-western counties of
Shropshire and Lancashire, where a robust Catholic society could still

absorb them. Six years later John Morris lamented Richard's disappearance in a letter to Johannes de Laet. 'They have driven out this young
man, very skilled in this Art [of Botany], who before the Civil Wars was
gardener to the Earl of Newport, on account of his papism.'[9]

Richard's father did not forget him, of course. John's fears for his son's
open Catholicism had proved correct, and now Richard was not only
entirely lost to him, but a liability. It could be hard to put yourself above
suspicion, whatever you said in public. Many people were damned by
association, like Endymion Porter's sons, said to be 'secretly instructed in
the popish religion; [although] openly they profess the reformed'.[10]

This wave of anti-Catholic fervour cost John more than just his son.
He also lost the confidence and respect of the public to whom he had
dedicated his life's work. He had openly professed his loyalty to the king
above all other authorities, and to the king's father before him, so as the
king's servant he should have felt protected. Yet as a member of no parish
church, as a northerner, and the father of a papist, he was vulnerable.
For safety's sake, he left the little house and his beautiful garden in Long
Acre. When the parish overseers came to collect the poor rate on 24
December 1640, there was no sign of John.[11]

The king's herbalist could retreat to the safety of the palace in
Whitehall, but even here there was a sense of unimaginable chaos. It
quickly became apparent that the king was in a mood to sacrifice many
loyal servants. Suspicion of Catholics rapidly spread to include the High
Anglican Church, the church the king had moulded exactly to his taste.
Parliament impeached Archbishop Laud and sent him to join Strafford
in the Tower. Laud's office was ransacked and the 'plot' by Scottish
Jesuits was revealed among his papers, adding fuel to the anti-Catholic
fervour. A few months later, in May 1641, Strafford was executed in front
of a jeering crowd of more than 100,000.

It seemed impossible that the great advances in the civil state that had
been achieved in the last fifty years, in commerce and trade, in education
and arts, in medicine and science, could collapse because of disagreements
about the placing of an altar and the language of prayer. John had
devoted his life to building a rational society where the benefits of
greater understanding could be spread to all. This was his contribution
to his country, his way of replacing the social service and charity that
had once been dispensed by the monasteries. The one benefit of the
monks' disappearance had been to open up knowledge to all curious
men. Such wisdom, scientifically gained and honestly communicated,

was the greatest virtue he could see in this brave new English society. Yet the 'Common Wealth' could only flourish in a state of order. All living things need stability to grow, and in John's view, the stability of the state depended on accepting the sovereign's connection to God. It was for the king to interpret the word of God, and for his subjects to labour 'obediently and peaceably under their owne Vine and Figtree'.

John was not alone in clinging to the belief that year that the king would effectively reassert his authority so that life could go on. His friends and acquaintances continued with their plans, confidently anticipating that the present crisis would pass. Edward Cooke offered the Society of Apothecaries £500 in 1641, out of the great fortune he had amassed from selling 'Cooke's pills', to build a laboratory. The society must have been delighted that at last it had the funds to build a facility planned for so long, but the laboratory was not to be built for a long time.[12] The same year, the German botanist Jacob Bobart arrived to take up his appointment to manage the Physic Garden in Oxford, expecting to find a peaceful refuge there from the Thirty Years' War that still ravaged Europe. Thomas Johnson published the second part of his catalogue of native British flora, based on a journey through Wales in 1639, but even his customary rapid style could not outrun the impending disaster.[13]

In the autumn, the Irish launched a rebellion. Protestant English believed Catholics would overrun them from the west. Trade in the nation's capital slowed to a trickle in the tense state of affairs and London grew dismal. In a single month, as many as twenty-two unknown paupers died on the streets of Covent Garden and were buried in the churchyard. By Christmas, most of the grand houses of the gentry in the parish were locked and empty. The churchwardens recorded only 'arrearages' in their customary book of receipts.[14]

All through the winter, Parliament struggled with the king for control of the army. Every tactic the king tried to exert authority over the House of Commons increased its opposition to him. In the spring, Charles appealed directly to the mayor and aldermen of the City for support, and when he received only a mute response he decided to abandon his capital. A summer of hope and disappointment passed before John and his friends understood that their precious rational society had indeed irrevocably dissolved. On 12 August, in a field near Nottingham, the king raised his standard and called on all his subjects good and true to join him. Charles had chosen to declare war on those subjects who opposed his God-given rights.

The king moved his court to Oxford and called for his courtiers to join him there. John had never been a fighter and was now certainly too old, and probably too poor, to establish a footing in Oxford. He had nowhere safe to go but the stretch of land between Whitehall and St James's Palace, where the king's remaining authority offered him thin protection. It was a cruel irony that a man whose imagination had been fired by his generation's discovery of the wide world would live the rest of his life in the narrow horizons of a field or two.

There were now at least two supreme authorities in the nation: the king, who was a long way away, and Parliament, whose instruments of power were soldiers roaming the streets of London. The city's population blamed these military men for ruining their trade. A band of apprentices gathered 'at the Piazzas in Covent-Garden' to petition Parliament against the soldiers who 'suck [our] whole subsistence and fix their hopes to repair their breaches and decays upon the ruin of others; fearing that the settling of our trades will be the decay of theirs...'. They begged Parliament to sue for peace with the king, but Parliament was much alarmed by this crowd of 'mean quality', and refused to allow them near the Houses of Parliament. Humbly, the apprentices pleaded their 'want of experience in parliament courses' but maintained their right to be heard:

> foreseeing the face of our own ruin, in our masters' present condition, as also prizing our parents' and friends' lives and livelihoods , [we] hold ourselves engaged by laws of conscience and nature to be no less solicitous for the bleeding condition of this church and state....[15]

The London citizens' sense of alarm deepened with the eerie silence that had crept over the Palace of Whitehall. An anonymous pamphlet sang a double-edged lament at the loss of the court:

> a Pallace without a Presence! A Whitehall clad in sable vestments. A court without a court! These are misteries and miseries, which the silken ages of this peacefull island have not beene acquainted with ... Majesty had wont to sit inthrone'd within these glorious Walls ... creating to those Favourites on whom their beames of grace reflected, names of honour and estates to maintain it till world's end, and now all things as in a Chaos, involv'd and wrap't up in the black mists of confusion, and desolation.[16]

The city's population wandered freely through Whitehall's yards and halls, disturbed that this seat of national power lay abandoned and open to all comers. They gaped at the empty chambers, where

> there had wont to be a continuall throng, either of Gallants standing to ravish themselves with the sight of Ladies hansome Legs and Insteps as they tooke Coach; Or of the tribe of guarded Liveries, by whom you could scarce passe without a jeare or a fancy answer to your question; now if you would ask a question there is nobody to make answer.[17]

A nation accustomed to hierarchies was shocked by the absence of authority. In the 'Presence Chamber', where the king once sat to conduct state business, no respect or obeisance was called for. You could walk 'without your Hat, spurres and Sword on, And if you will presume to be so unmannerly, you may sit downe in the Chair of State ... for now a dayes common men do sit in the Chaire of State'. Even the young courtiers who 'used to shew their new brought over French cringes [bows]' were missed, since the innkeepers and tradesmen of the city could hardly survive without their custom.[18]

The king's departure had been so sudden that those who followed him had no time to arrange their affairs. Looters roamed through the palace, harvesting anything they could find of value. Dr William Harvey, the king's physician, had his Whitehall quarters turned upside down and lost the records of insects, frogs and toads he had dissected over the years. 'He often sayd ... no griefe was so crucifying to him as the losse of these papers, which for love or money he could never retrieve or obtaine', remembered Aubrey.[19]

In Oxford, the newly formed court squeezed into whatever lodgings it could find. For a while the men and women of the court brought an atmosphere of wit and glamour with them that lit up the city. It was there that John Aubrey first met William Harvey. 'He came several times to Trinity College to George Bathurst B.D., who had a Hen to hatch Egges in his chamber, which they dayly opened to discern the progress and way of Generation'.[20] Oxford's apothecary shops became places where this new scientific information was exchanged, just as it had once been in the apothecary shops of London. Some Oxford apothecaries even served coffee to sustain these agreeable gatherings, as they did in London.[21] Normal university discipline evaporated in the king's presence. Only five months after he arrived, the university begged him to stop awarding so many honorary degrees. In less than three months the king had created more than forty new bachelors or doctors of physic, giving the honours in exchange for loyalty, when he had nothing else to give.[22]

By the end of July 1643, news filtered through to London that one of those new doctors of physic was Thomas Johnson, who had abandoned the city to fight for the king. Here was another stab from the demon of 'sharp-toothed envy' that gnawed at John. Such an honour, which he could reasonably believe he had earned at least as much as had his rival, would have cemented his reputation and made him the equal of his doctor friends. Bitter circumstance had seen the younger man vault over his head once more. Yet John would not envy Thomas Johnson much longer. Now a lieutenant-colonel, Johnson had been posted to help the Marquis of Winchester defend one of the few remaining medieval castles, Basing House in Hampshire, which was suddenly useful in a way no one had foreseen. After months under siege by Parliament's army, royalist forces relieved the castle, but in the sequel to the battle Johnson was shot in the shoulder. He died from his wound a fortnight later, and his ambitious plan to be the first to record all the native plants of England and Wales died with him.[23]

The situation in London was becoming desperate, and it is unlikely that John had much time to thank fate for allowing him to complete his own legacy to the world. The city's population had begun to be squeezed by both sides, in a fierce bid to raise money. The royalists imposed an economic blockade on the port, their privateers harassing merchant ships in the Thames. Meanwhile Parliament tightened its grip on civilians. A gun was set up between Inigo Jones's Banqueting House and Holbein Gate, the old gateway from Whitehall to Westminster, to protect the Houses of Parliament from any royalist advance. Plans to encircle the new wealthy suburbs as well as the old city with a defensive wall, proposed in 1642, were never actually carried out, but London was still, effectively, a fortress. Soldiers guarded every road out of the city and no one could travel without a pass.[24]

Parliament now described royalists as 'Malignants and Delinquents', and royal servants who were both loyal and Catholic, like John, were considered the lowest enemy. Still, the problems of John's past were now, in one sense, a blessing. He had so little of the one commodity that everyone wanted, money, that he was at least allowed the peace of being ignored. Parliament had formed a 'Committee for the Advance of

Money', in an effort to raise funds for the war. 'Malignants' and 'Delinquents' were their key targets, but only if their property was worth more than £100.

John's wealthy doctor friends were obliged to make a statement of their capital to the committee. 'Discoverers' were appointed who were allowed to claim up to a third of any assets they could prove that another possessed. Sir Theodore received a notice assessing him as worth £1,000 at St James's Palace in the summer of 1643, and expostulated that 'he had nothing to do with it [the war], neither did any man know the half of his estate'. Eventually, however, he was forced to pay Parliament half this sum. Sir Matthew Lister grappled with a similar problem all year. The notice that assessed him as worth £800 was based on his property in the parish of St Martin's-in-the-Fields, the house in Covent Garden he had rented from the Duke of Bedford for many years. It was a substantial household. His garden was more than double the size of most, nearly 150 feet long and 40 feet wide, with another 32-foot-square formal garden near the house. Besides the main building, there was a 'banquetting house', a stable block, an independent cottage, a coach house and a workshop on the property. But the old doctor got away with giving only £250. One of his many nephews was on his way to becoming an officer in General Fairfax's army, and this protected him from the committee.[25]

In the summer of 1644 there seemed to be no hiding places left. A Mr Whitlocke was appointed to pay informants to 'make Searche for the Discovery of Ten Thousande pounds informed to belong unto Malignants and Delinquents: and it is left to Mr Whitlocke to compound with the Party that shall discover the same, for a fit allowance for every one thousand pounds he shall discover.'[26]

Anyone who could denounce a neighbour's religious or political deviance, and so make his property liable to seizure, was promised a reward. John's friend Stephen Chase, the apothecary supplier of chafe wax for the royal seals, was taken with his wife and sent to Newgate prison. Their property was either confiscated or plundered. By July 1646 both had died in prison, and their eldest son and daughter, John and Anne Chase, were petitioning Parliament to be granted what was left of their goods.[27]

The last bastion of the royal establishment in London was yet to be plundered. The parliamentary force that killed Thomas Johnson marched to Oxford on money seized from the queen's apartments in St James's Palace. Hitherto Parliament had protected royal property in the palaces, but in June 1644 they took the queen's treasure for the specific purpose of ousting her husband from Oxford. The Commons Journal recorded, 'The Cabinet, Jewels, Money and Plate found at St James and ordered by the House of Commons 13 Junii 1644 to be engaged for the advance of Monies, for setting forth of forces into Oxfordshire and the parts adjoining'.[28]

The queen was in Exeter, pregnant, anxious and thin. She had failed to raise money in France for the king. She returned to England via Yorkshire, where she was forced to take cover in a ditch from a parliamentary bombardment before she could join her husband in Oxford. Within months the fighting came too close even to that city for her advanced state of pregnancy. She fled to the temporary haven of Exeter in such a state of nervous collapse that no one thought she would survive the birth. Charles sent the royal doctors in London a desperate letter from Oxford: 'Mayerne, pour l'Amour de moy alle trover ma Femme. C.R.' [Mayerne, for the love of me, go find my wife.][29]

Sir Theodore de Mayerne and Sir Matthew Lister took the queen's coach from London and covered the 170 miles in seven days, although Sir Matthew Lister was now eighty, and Sir Theodore, still corpulent, had never been a good traveller. The queen greeted Mayerne with the confession that she was afraid she would go mad. 'Madame,' he replied, 'you already are'.[30] Nevertheless with the doctors' help she was able to give birth safely to her last child, a day after Parliament's order to seize her property in London, and, soon afterwards, to escape back to France.

Once the doctors had left London, John was entirely alone in a desolate city. For some time the last inhabitants of Whitehall had been reduced to a shadowy existence, eking out survival on what remained of the palace stores, like the monks of a century before, who clung to the remains of their abbeys.

> If at any time you desire to see any body in, or neere the court, that belongs to it; goe just about the shutting in of evening, And then perhaps, you may see one creeping away with a Sack of Coles on his back, another with a bundle of Fagots, another with botells of Wine, another bartering with a Vinegar man about certaine Vessells of decaied beere, etc, for everything would live by its own element as long as it can: But when it's all gone, they'll be all gone too, and will be within a very short time if the times doe not alter.[31]

When he returned to London from Exeter, Sir Theodore moved away from the city to his house in Chelsea. London, he noted, had become a place where it was dangerous to see or speak too much. 'We cannot hinder children from growing nor people from talking, but in these times one should leave the mouth shut and the ears long and wide.'[32] The College of Physicians dropped the royal doctors from their list of fellows. De Mayerne's wealthy patients, such as John Morris, retreated behind locked doors, opening them from time to time for a visit from their doctor. Hunkered in his library in Isleworth, a few miles further west along the Thames from Chelsea, fretting about his health and protecting his property, Morris continued to write to de Laet once a month. He could speak more freely to him than to his neighbours, because he wrote in Latin, and though his letters were mostly about plants, there were rare forays into politics.

Curiously, one of Morris's neighbours in the little village of Isleworth was the king's royal apothecary and de l'Obel's son-in-law, the aged John Rumler, whose long streak of luck had come to an end. Rumler had been allowed to take 'several parcels of medicine' from London to the king in Oxford in 1642. He had then followed Charles around in the time-honoured manner of the royal apothecary in war until the king's ingenious midnight escape from Shrewsbury, where parliamentary forces had trapped him. Rumler was obliged to abandon 'two cart loads of possessions, including plate, trunks of medicines, provisions and money to the value of £800'. After that he was 'forced to leave his attendance on his Majesty, and to return to his habitation at Isleworth ... in fear of utter ruin of himself and his family'.[33]

It is unlikely that Morris saw much of his notable neighbour. Such associations, which would have been highly desirable before the war, were now potentially dangerous. As for his old friend John Parkinson, Morris believed he was dead. He wrote to de Laet in June 1646, complaining that he was making no headway with the copy of a catalogue of plants he had promised, because there were no longer any experts he could consult.

I fear very much that the crop of true Botanists nowadays is thin, with the death of Johnson, [and] of Parkinson ...Tradescant [the younger] is quite exiled from the art, indeed he has almost abandoned these literary works, and now carries on as a merchant in the Canary Islands. The best and only hope left to us is the gardener to the young

Duke of Buckingham, who is skilled enough, but entirely ignorant of the literature.[34]

Morris's doctor, Sir Theodore, was in no position to correct him. These men lived quite cut off from the city that had once been the centre of their world. Yet, though John was nearly eighty, he was not dead. He was holding on somehow in the place he had loved so much, a stone's throw from his old garden. He had a powerful friend on the parliamentary side. Sir John Danvers, whose town house was in Covent Garden, was with Parliament against the king. One of John's friends, perhaps Sir Matthew Lister, perhaps Sir John Danvers, fed and sheltered him near his old haunts in Covent Garden.

Old though he was, John Parkinson was a tough survivor who could still be useful at a time when people preserved their precious gardens where they could. John's knowledge was vital to people who found that, with trade at a standstill, their gardens were once again the essential source of food and medicine for the household, in the way, although not the circumstances, that Richard Gardiner, the draper from Shrewsbury, had predicted all those years before. It was a bitter consolation for the state of their nation that now, at least, they could boast new roots for the pot: potatoes, Jerusalem artichokes, and rhubarb to add to the carrots and coleworts. Even the wealthy like John Morris, who scorned to 'eate herbes', found more time to devote to their curious bulbs, now that they scarcely dared step outside. No doubt that John found a useful niche in Covent Garden where he could live quietly while the king's forces were hammered into surrender.

By 24 July 1646, the royalist cause was lost. The king put himself at the mercy of the Scots, and soon became a prisoner of the Puritan New Model Army. Parliament took Oxford, and gradually the king's remaining friends drifted back to London. People who had fled to France to escape the fighting came back to check on their property. In London, pleasures and habits from before the Civil War re-emerged irrepressibly, in spite of parliamentary laws designed to suppress them. An ordinance forbidding plays, first introduced in 1642, lapsed briefly at the very beginning of 1648. Four theatres opened instantly, to flourishing trade, before the ordinance could be renewed. A young man called John Evelyn had just returned from France and managed to see a 'Tragie-Comedie acted at the Cockpit' at the beginning of February. Evelyn began to keep a journal of his interesting experiences in London. Three weeks later he

was in Isleworth, that popular riverside village close to London, where
so many of John's old acquaintances had washed up. He saw 'curious
flowers' that had survived the war in a garden that belonged to Gilbert
Barrell, and also 'some good medals and pictures'. On 1 July he sat for
a portrait by Robert Walker, while ten miles away, at the village of
Kingston, the Duke of Buckingham's second son, Francis, was killed in
the last royalist uprising of the civil wars.[35]

Whitehall Palace became an army barracks. The privy gardens were a
wilderness, their dismal disarray expressing the utter overthrow of the
state. Sir John Danvers put his name to the document that decided the
fate of the king, so that at the beginning of January 1649, a winter so
hard that sudden frost had iced the Thames for the first time in fifteen
years, King Charles stepped on to the scaffold erected outside his own
Banqueting House in Whitehall.[36] He worried most that the crowd would
think him afraid if he shivered in the cold, so he wore two shirts to keep
himself warm for his public execution.

Who can say whether John was in that crowd? He had marked his
eighty-second birthday a few days before. His age and health alone
would not keep him from witnessing the king's humiliation, yet it is hard
to conceive of an event that would have caused him more pain. In John's

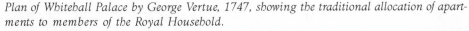

Plan of Whitehall Palace by George Vertue, 1747, showing the traditional allocation of apartments to members of the Royal Household.

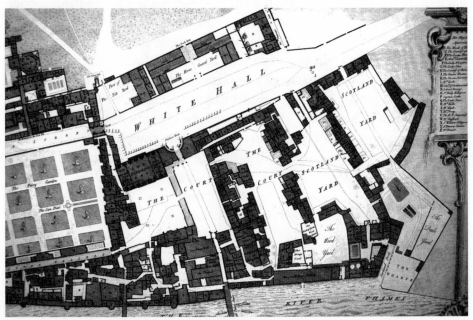

eyes, the king was the state and this execution was the end of everything
that had given his life purpose. He had dedicated his life's energy to
rational process so as to unravel function and beauty from nature's wild
bounty. He had found miracles of potential in cultivating and crossing
seed, and he had laid his work at the feet of his society for its benefit
and prosperity. Now even men he had counted as friends had destroyed
everything, including the figurehead and root of the state, the king
himself. This little kingdom, which once held such promise, lay in pieces
around him. Scotland and Ireland were at war with England, while
England was at war with itself.

John had aimed to serve the 'Common Wealth', but the very term
had been hijacked to describe the wreckage of a state that soldiers and
regicides now argued over. All his life John had believed that his countrymen would use their God-given common sense to create a better
society. Clearly he had been wrong. There was no civil order in the
nation any more. Chaos was the only king. Black despair was reflected
in a bitterly cold spring that year. In the wet summer that followed,
John's tough old body began to decline. The ten years since he had
reached the pinnacle of his ambition and become the king's herbalist
had borne bitter fruit. He had lost his home, his garden, his family, his
king and his country.

At the beginning of August the following year, John gave up the struggle to live. He died in the parish where he had made his beautiful garden
into an echo of paradise on earth, now engulfed by a mass of city
dwellings. His friends carried his body along the streets to the parish
church of St Martin's-in-the-Fields for burial. He had nothing left when
he died except a small package of notes and papers that John Goodyer
collected and took away. But, even in those troubled times, he still had
his reputation. The parish clerk entered an exceptional note alongside
the name that appears for the first time in this church's records. In the
burial register for 6 August 1650 he wrote: 'John Parkinson: A Famous
Botanist'.[37]

EPILOGUE

It was not long before John Evelyn bought a copy of Parkinson's *Paradisus* and put it to use as he set to work improving his father-in-law's garden at Sayes Court in Deptford. Evelyn was only eight when the *Paradisus* was published, so he did not discover it until after its author was dead. Yet he had seen many fascinating gardens during his exile in France in the Civil War, and came back to England with a lively interest in plants. When he began to read John's book, he found a source of inspiration.

The *Paradisus* was an expensive and beautiful volume to own, compared to the other books about gardens and husbandry that Evelyn acquired for his library. Eventually he gave it a gold-tooled leather binding, with his initials stamped on the spine, and on the front his family crest with the motto in Latin: 'Explore everything, retain the best'. From the first, however, Evelyn treated this book as his practical guide and teacher. He underlined the most valuable information and made copious notes in the margins.

He took careful note of John's practical gardening methods – the best way to propagate plants, for instance: 'When you have cut off your slippes [cuttings], you may either set [plant] them by and by, or else <u>as the best Gardiners use to doe, cast them into a tubb or pot with water for a day or two</u>...'. Evelyn underlined the words with several other precious pieces of advice, such as how to stop the roots of French box spreading sideways. Further on he noted carefully the best stock to use to propagate 'red nectorins' and 'apricockes' and his exclamation mark seemed to endorse John's comment that although a bed of horse manure was an effective method of forcing early vegetables in the kitchen garden, it had a damaging effect on their 'naturall vigour and quickenesse of taste'.

Evelyn was as fascinated by bulbs as John had been and the process of growing them from seed captivated him. He noted especially carefully each stage and season of the procedure for growing tulips and the particular variety that John said produced the best new forms: '<u>whitish spotted edged or straked</u>'. John's experiments to see whether the form of plants could be affected by the phases of the Moon were taken gravely to heart. Evelyn liberally marked the text with 'n.b.', underlining the author's dry conclusion. 'I have made tryall at many times, and in many sorts of plants, accordingly ... by planting and transplanting them, but I could never see the effect desired but rather in many of them <u>the losse of my plants.</u>'[1]

While the Puritan army was dominant and the weather hostile, John Evelyn shut himself away in his library and 'wentt through a Course of Chymistrie'. Meanwhile the shattered society that John had surveyed at his death gradually began to revive. The passions of the pre-war period, apparently lifeless in the hostile climate of Oliver Cromwell's Protectorate, which slowly imposed order on the country after 1652, survived underground like dormant roots in the winter. If you knew where to look, traces of the old culture could still be found. Endymion Porter, the 'papist' courtier and friend of the king, was to be seen at the London home of the painter George Geldorp, being entertained only months after the king's death with 'wine and hams, and other curious eatables'.[2]

Gardens were, as always, a refuge from politics. The radical experiments in civil government in the years of Cromwell's Protectorate only enhanced John's message that nature was an open path to God. His reverence for the marriage of beauty and function in plants began to resonate with ever more adherents from the moment of his death. No man emphasized more than he that the vegetable kingdom was a divine gift to every man, whether Puritan or Royalist. The *Paradisus* went into a second edition in 1656, in spite of its dedication to a queen who was still a figure of hostile suspicion to the ruling Protectorate.

While both sides in the conflict jockeyed to retain or acquire property that was forfeit after the battles, they continued to sow and improve their gardens. The nation's Protector, Oliver Cromwell, had little time for such frivolities. The privy gardens at Whitehall were simply ploughed up and returfed to prepare for his family's move into the palace, but his commander-in-chief was proud of his beautiful garden. Sir Thomas Fairfax retired to Nunappleton House in Yorkshire after the fighting. He engaged the poet Andrew Marvell as tutor to his daughter, and the beauty of both the garden and the girl was immortalized in beguiling poetry. Fairfax' friend and fellow Yorkshireman John Lambert bought Wimbledon Manor, whose gardens bore the mark of the succession of aristocratic and royal gardeners who had owned it before him. They were stocked with a collection of the very best 'rootes' or bulbs that had survived the war and which Lambert prized highly.

Yet the scientific approach John favoured suffered in the social upheaval that followed the Civil War. There was much talk of reason, but the revolutionary atmosphere was at odds with a patient search for truth based on observation. At the beginning of the war a young gentleman, trained as an apothecary, set up a practice in Spitalfields, on the east side of the city of London. Nicholas Culpeper's fame grew rapidly, because he proclaimed himself as a political alternative to doctors, and treated the poor for free.

Culpeper castigated physicians for growing rich on the back of people's sickness. 'Is it hansome and wel-beseeming a Common-wealth to see a Doctor ride in State, in Plush with a footcloathe...?' He accused the doctors of relying on authorities so ancient they were no longer relevant: 'A company of proud, insulting domineering Doctors, whose wits were born five hundred years before themselves'. He rejected the ancient Greek doctors, Hippocrates and Galen, as 'homicides who were ignorant of astrology'. As for the famous English authorities, Gerard and Parkinson, Culpeper dismissed them as though he had never read them:

neither GERARD or PARKINSON ... ever gave one wise reason for what they wrote, and so did nothing else but train up young novices in Physic in the school of tradition, and teach them just as a parrot is taught to speak.... But in mine, if you view it with the eye of reason you shall see a reason for everything that is written.[3]

Culpeper's notion of reason was very different from John's. 'Meer idle tales and fancies' that John had disproved by experiment, Culpeper revived. Culpeper's method of curing the sick was to determine which planet was the root cause of the disease. Then he would use either the plant that 'belonged' to an opposing planet, or the one indicated 'by sympathy' of its resemblance to the part of the body affected.

'Wormwood is an Herb of Mars, I prove it thus: What delights in martial place is a Martial Herb; but Wormwood delights in Martial places, (for about forges and Iron works you may gather a Cart load of it) Ergo it is a Martial Herb.'[4] Culpeper's arguments show how power-fully the philosophies of Dr Fludd and Dr Simon Baskervill had diverted the practical experimental method that John had used. The despair of his final days would have deepened had he known how popular such theories would become.

Nicholas Culpeper ensured his appeal by publishing, among other works, an unauthorized English translation of the physicians' Latin *Pharmacopoeia*, opening up the doctors' secrets to an impoverished population. It was ironic that he should have chosen as his original a work that the city apothecaries' practical experience had led them to condemn so roundly. As it turned out, Culpeper's medical remedies could not prolong his own life. He died in 1654 at the age of thirty-eight. His *Herbal*, in which medicinal plants came a poor second to astrology, remained popular, even though his contemporaries acknowledged that he knew very little about plants: 'for aught I can gather, either by his books or learn from the report of others, he was a man very ignorant in the forme of Simples', wrote a botanist called William Cole by way of obituary.[5] It is an even greater irony that Culpeper's herbal, published in 1653, is still in print, whereas John Parkinson's long and careful study of the essence of plants has been forgotten. It is as though, to prove our habitual presumption that old knowledge is inferior to our own, we deliberately select the most quaint.

In his day, Culpeper was so detached from the medical mainstream that he had no impact on John Parkinson's immediate legacy. The value of John's scientific work was accepted for longer than most modern scholars could dream of. His *Theatrum Botanicum* held its place as a textbook for doctors and apothecaries for about 120 years. Dr Richard Pulteney, who in 1790 wrote a book tracing the *Progress of Botany in England* from its origins, recalled, 'Many now living ... can recollect that when they were young in science there was no better source of botanical intelligence (in English) than the herbals of Gerard and Parkinson.' Dr Pulteney acknowledged that the *Theatrum* in which John had 'endeavoured to comprehend all the Botany of his time' was 'a work of much more originality than that of Gerard and it contains abundantly more matter than the last edition of that author, with all Johnson's augmentations'.[6]

Yet as the society that John had worked for gradually came back from the ashes, and Parliament considered whether they could seize the valuable land he had cultivated, the life of this modest man was forgotten. When he lived, John's habitually sharp honesty had been softened by an inclusive humanity that bridged all divisions of nationality, class or creed. Such an expansive style could not survive the deep divisions left by civil war. After he died, there were few men prepared to champion a northern Catholic royalist.

The study of plants continued at the Physic Garden in Oxford, and in 1655, a graduate of these studies and doctor of physic named William How published a section of de l'Obel's unpublished Latin manuscript

Stirpium Illustrationes (*Illustrations of Plants*), accusing John of having plagiarized it. In the foreword, he thundered that Parkinson had 'plundered from this Treasury and but one ravish'd Plant acknowledged ... whose Volumes were compleat. The title! Epistle! And Diploma affixed'.[7] The accusation was hardly justified, since John had acknowledged de l'Obel's help and the manuscript had been severely out of date even by the time John finished his *Theatrum* in 1640. Still no scholar leaped to defend John from this blatant marketing manoeuvre, until, in the second half of the seventeenth century, a blacksmith's son named John Ray began to develop his work.

After Charles I's son was restored to the British throne in 1660, the 'ingeniose men' of the apothecary and coffee shops were formally inaugurated into a Royal Society. A founder member was the physician and naturalist Dr Martin Lister, a great-nephew of John's friend Sir Matthew Lister. Dr Martin Lister's second wife was Anna Parkinson, from Craven in West Yorkshire, one of the large network of Parkinson kin still living on the borders of Yorkshire and Lancashire.[8] Charles II incorporated the new sciences into his household more enthusiastically than his father had done. Each study John had embraced in his work was now dignified with the appointment of a Royal Professor. John Evelyn accompanied His Majesty to a demonstration by Nicholas le Fèvre, the new French 'Professor of Chymicks', who was the son of an apothecary and had once taught Evelyn in Paris. They watched while le Fèvre made 'an accurate preparation of Sir Walter Raleigh's rare Cordial, he making a learned discussion before his Majestie on each ingredient'.[9]

Charles appointed Dr Robert Morrison as 'Botanic Professor', with a salary of £200 a year and the right to occupy a house and ground in the royal Physic Garden. This was handsome treatment that John might have envied, but the conditions of royal service had hardly changed. By 1669 Robert Morrison was forced to surrender the house and grounds where he lived and in 1693 his widow was petitioning the crown for unpaid salary and pension amounting to £4,400.[10] With the creation of a Physic Garden in 1670 on Sir John Danvers' land in Chelsea by the Society of Apothecaries, the seeds that John Parkinson had sown could be seen to blossom.[11]

The man who made the greatest contribution to the modern understanding of plants was John Ray, who, like John, devoted himself to the study of nature after his early brushes with the Church. When Ray was forced to give up his post as a church minister in Cambridge in 1662, because he refused to accept the Act of Uniformity, he set out to compile a complete history of plants. Initially he toyed with the idea of publishing an updated edition of John's *Theatrum*. Yet his interest served only to underline the fact that the comprehensive herbal had had its day.

It was not just the size of the *Theatrum* and the number of illustrations in it that made any proposal to reproduce it prohibitive. John's work had depended on the unity of sciences which took separate paths after his death. The perspective on plants began to change, due in part to John's own work as a gardener, which highlighted plants as objects of great beauty and potential regardless of their medicinal properties. So plant studies were no longer indissolubly linked to medicine. Doctors began to focus more and more on the mechanics of the body, while botanists learned about the structure of plants.

Classification and identification, rather than cultivation, became the core skills for botanists. The groups that John had adopted as a medical man, classing plants according to their healing effects, became too unwieldy for modern scholars. Though John's insistence on the evidence before his eyes meant that he had made some advances in classification, distinguishing between plants with a single or double leaf structure at seed, he had not fully understood the difference between species and variety of plant. In his anxiety to include everything, he had been unnecessarily repetitive at times. Later botanists left the garden and roamed the hillsides to extend their science. They were offended at the number of species in which John had not made a clear distinction between plants in their natural situation and the effects of cultivation, although, considering the number of plants he cultivated in order to study them, this is hardly surprising.

John Ray eventually rejected John Parkinson's comprehensive enthusiasm, and focused instead on compiling the first detailed British flora, *Synopsis Stirpium Britannicarum*, which he published in 1670. It was far more rigorous than the *Theatrum* in its classification of plants according to their form, and differentiated more clearly between species. John Ray fully established the system of dividing plants into single or double leaf at seed, the two classes known as monocotyledons and dicotyledons into which flowering plants are still divided. Then, in the middle of the eighteenth century, a Swedish professor of botany at Uppsala University, Carl Linnaeus, published a method of naming plants so easy to use that it has been the universal system ever since. The Linnean names supplanted the old herbalists' personal favourites. They papered over all the discussions about the origin of a species, about who had given the plant to whom, and the means by which it had come to be cultivated in Europe, to which John had devoted so many hours. The study of plants was reborn as a reliable, impersonal science. The impact of the personalities who had made it their own in the time of the European Renaissance receded into the mists of history.[12]

So the *Theatrum Botanicum* proved to be the first and the last great herbal in English. It was a work that involved study, practice and personal observation of a kind that took a lifetime to complete. Gaspard Bauhin's *Pinax*, published in 1623, had taken him forty years. The *Theatrum* had taken John fifty.

Yet the Renaissance method that John had learned from his Flemish mentors, that of using the old to re-examine the new, lived on to create a scientific revolution. It was exactly the approach adopted by Ray and the host of other 'ingeniose men' in the king's Royal Society, from Newton to Hooke, who made such critical discoveries about the nature of the material world in the second half of the seventeenth century. While Ray criticized the repetitiveness of his predecessor, he so valued his 'industry' that he awarded him a place in the plantsmen's roll of honour that would have thrilled the old apothecary. No longer a rival of John Gerard, Thomas Johnson or even Nicholas Culpeper, John Parkinson was the first Englishman who in Ray's opinion rightly belonged with the great European herbalists of the day.

> I suppose that [Bauhin's] history, together with what Fabius Columna, Prosper Alpinus, Cornutus, our Parkinson, Geor. Marggravius, Dr Morrison, & Paulo Boccone have written concerning plants, doth compleat the history of all yet extant, except with some few stragglers, whose descriptions are scattered heer and there.... Our Parkinson I put into ye number because there be many plants in his work not elsewhere described.[13]

The country boy from Lancashire, who never left his home shores, would have considered himself well rewarded for his lifetime's labour by his place in this list of seventeenth-century scholars.

Outside the scientific world, in the gardens that the British now cultivated enthusiastically wherever they could, John Parkinson was never forgotten. The wilderness of the countryside in John's youth continued to recede rapidly, so gardeners no longer sought to shut it out.

By the eighteenth century it had been tamed to a point that fashionable designers like William Kent and Capability Brown deliberately created gardens to look out on a picturesque manicured landscape, often artificially altered to improve the view. Even an admiring student of John's work like Richard Pulteney was by this time describing his *Paradisus* as 'a valuable curiosity'. The small, enclosed 'Paradise' of John Parkinson's day was out of favour until, in the twentieth century, gardeners began once more to close out the wider world.

While gardens evolve and the number of beautiful plants increases in a way that would have delighted John, people who love plants have continued through the generations to turn to him for inspiration, relishing the fresh vitality of his common sense as much as John Evelyn did in the 1650s. Evelyn's descendants, who inherited his copy of John's *Paradisus*, continued to make notes in the margin on the correct seasons for planting and methods for propagation, even though Evelyn's generation developed designs for heated greenhouses that made much of John Parkinson's advice redundant. My own family's copies have similar marks and underlinings, revealing how someone planted his orchard or planned her vegetable garden with the voice of this great old gardener ringing in their ears.[14]

I have been inspired to uncover his trail by this same voice. As I said at the beginning, this is a story that is universal as well as intensely personal to me. Universal, because we can all share John Parkinson's love of plants and reproduce the benefits he uncovered. Personal, because I would never have begun this story if my father had not dangled John's book in front of my eyes. It might never have interested me so much if I had not felt the way I did about my father. You might never have read it if I did not have the same last name as the man whose story it is. So the question that remains to be resolved is whether, in fact, I am directly descended from Britain's first royal herbalist, John Parkinson, as my father believed.

The smoke thrown up by the destructive phases in history was particularly thick when John died. If he wrote a will, it has never been discovered, and was not among the papers that John Goodyer left to Magdalen College in Oxford when he died. The church courts that proved all the wills in the country had been suspended, remaining so until two years after John's death. His children had disappeared from London. His friends, Lister, Mayerne and Goodyer, retired to their country homes and lived the rest of their lives in quiet obscurity.[15] Only one small echo suggests that someone was watching. Three months after John was buried in St Martin's-in-the-Fields, a note was entered in the parish register in Whalley of the death of a John Parkinson. This could have been one of the Parkinson clan still left in the area, some of them still clinging to their Catholicism, others now converted and working for the Anglican state. Yet no other Parkinsons then remained in the parish of Whalley itself, and three months was about the time it took for news to travel across the war-torn country. The coincidence suggests the possibility that someone, perhaps his married daughter, Katherine, may have given him a Catholic burial in the parish where he was born.[16]

John's children left no traces to make it possible to prove decisively my father's claim. John's son Richard could have gone to Ireland, where several Parkinson families appeared after the middle of the seventeenth century. English Catholics migrated to the west after Cromwell's brutal suppression of the Irish rebellion in 1649. Richard would have been easily absorbed amongst these Catholic Anglo-Irish families whose religion gave them a strong bond with the Gaelic people of Ireland. But if he did go to Ireland, his presence is untraceable. The Catholic Irish parishes at the time kept no records and anyway most Irish civic records were destroyed in a fire at the Dublin Record Office in 1922.[17]

The only clue that bridges a gap of two generations before my father's direct line is documented is a curious accident. My father's great-great-grandfather was James Parkinson, born in Shrewsbury in Shropshire. James was christened at the church of St Mary's there on 28 February 1730, the only son of 'parents who settled in Ireland in the time of Charles I'.[18] This man's father was also called James, but could his grandfather have been John's son Richard who brought up his family in Ireland after the death of Charles I?

The Shrewsbury-born James Parkinson became a 'law-stationer' or solicitor, and would have lived and died in respectable obscurity had it not been for a chance event. He was a steady sort, not given to flights of fancy, 'employed by many noblemen and gentlemen in management of their estates, being an excellent accountant, with the clearest head, frequently of great use in arranging their concerns'. However, when he was fifty-three, on a whim he bought a couple of lottery tickets, and one of them changed his life.

The passion for collecting curiosities that had begun in John Parkinson's day had grown into a mania with English gentlemen. The largest collection open to the public in 1770 belonged to a Manchester squire called Sir Ashton Lever. It had reached by then 'a bulk incredible almost', including stuffed animals from around the world, stones from the Giant's Causeway in Ireland and a cloak of green feathers given to Captain Cook by King Owhyhee during his journey to Australia. In 1774 Sir Ashton transferred the collection from his home in Alkrington to the prestigious new position of Leicester House, in London's Trafalgar Square. However, the cost of renting Leicester House was threatening to ruin him, so in 1784 he decided to auction his collection by public lottery. James Parkinson bought two tickets and gave one away. By dint of the other, he became the new owner of the remarkable 'Leverian Museum'.

For the next twenty years this collection completely absorbed him. Having failed to sell it, he moved it to the Rotunda, a curious round building at the south end of Blackfriars Bridge in London. He took 'great pains to study' all the branches of natural history that had developed since the time of John Parkinson, 'in which he not only succeeded to a wonderful degree, to the great surprise of his friends, but enriched the collection with many additional and valuable specimens both of Nature and Art'.

He wrote and published two catalogues of the collection, dedicating the first to George III and the second to Sir Joseph Banks. His friends attributed his ultimate failure to make money from it only to 'his singular modesty', which set the price of admission too low. So after twenty years of struggle, and, curiously, when James reached seventy-three, the age that John Parkinson had been when he published his *Theatrum*, he decided to break up the collection. It was sold at a public auction in 1806 that lasted over a week and many of the pieces were acquired for the present British and Natural History Museums.[19]

So it was by accident, rather than design, that this modest man made a mark on his country's understanding of the natural world. The unassuming curiosity and dedication that his friends remarked in him carry a distinct echo of his supposed ancestor, the king's herbalist. It is as if he was guided by forces stronger than he knew to help reveal the intricacies of nature to his countrymen, making exactly the kind of contribution that John Parkinson would have wished for his son.

APPENDIX

PLANTS IN JOHN PARKINSON'S GARDEN ON LONG ACRE

This list is based on a compilation of plants specifically mentioned as growing in John Parkinson's garden in his work or by contemporaries, originally assembled by the late Dr John Riddell of Wadham College, Oxford (*Journal of Garden History*, Vol.6, No. 2). I have not attempted to add other references to plants beyond those that Dr Riddell noted. It therefore serves as an indication of what John Parkinson grew, rather than an exhaustive list. I have added the modern common names and the botanical name for each plant, based on the listing in the RHS plant finder directory (www.rhs.org.uk). Plants marked with an * are not found in the RHS directory but named in accordance with one of the sources quoted by the International Organization for Plant Information (IOPI). Occasionally the description given by John's contemporaries, particularly John Goodyer, is unclear, or duplicates a plant that appears elsewhere in the list under John Parkinson's more botanically accurate name. I have retained those duplications for information. Sometimes the botanical name I have given refers to a plant cultivated more recently than the seventeenth century. Decorative innovations in John's garden that had no established medicinal function are the most difficult to identify with their modern equivalent. They would have been extremely rare in John's day, if not exclusive to his garden, and between their fragile existence in Long Acre in the early seventeenth century and the varieties in our gardens today lie generations of plant breeding.

A note on the Sources:

'Goodyer' refers to the list made by John Goodyer, now in Magdalen College Oxford.

'Johnson' refers to Johnson's edition of Gerard's Herbal, London, 1633.

'De Lobel: Stirpium' refers to the revised edition of de l'Obel's *Stirpium Adversaria Nova in Opera Omnia*, London, 1605; 'Animad.' refers to 'Animadversione' in that edition.

Ps. is John Parkinson's *Paradisi in Sole Paradisus Terrestris*, London, 1629 and *Th.* is his *Theatrum Botanicum*, London, 1640.

Modern common name	Seventeenth-century name	Botanical name	Source
Wormwood	Absinthium folio Lavendulae	*Artemisia absinthium*	Goodyer
	A. Insipidum	*A. santonicum**	ibid.
	A. marinum repens	*Seriphidium maritimum*	Johnson p.1099
Bear's breeches	Acanthus Sativus Brahca Ursina	*Acanthus mollis*	*Ps.* p.330
Yarrow	Achillea Sideritis/Nobilis odorata	*Achillea nobilis*	*Tb.* p.695
English wild basil	Acinos Anglica Clusii	*Acinos arvensis*	*Tb.* p.22
Winter aconite	Aconitum hyemale	*Eranthis hyemalis*	Goodyer
Wolfsbane	A. luteum Ponticum,	*Aconitum lycoctonum* subsp. *vulparia*	ibid.
	A. lycoctonum flore Dripinii	*A. lycoctonum*	ibid.
Sweet flag	Acorum legittimum	*Acorus calamus*	*Tb.* p.140
Marvel of Peru	Admirabilis	*Mirabilis jalapa*	*Ps.* p.364
Privet	Alaternus	*Rhamnus alaternus*	Goodyer
Hollyhock	Alcea peregrine (foreign)	*Alcea*	Goodyer
	A. vulgaris (common)		ibid.
Chickweed/	Alsine repens major baccifera,	*Stellaria media**	Goodyer
Greater stitchwort	A. maior	*S. holostea*	ibid.
Love lies bleeding	Amaranthus purpureus	*Amaranthus caudatus*	Goodyer
Joseph's coat	Amaranthus tricolor	*A. tricolor**	*Ps.* p.372
Bullwort	Ammi vulgatius	*Ammi majus*	*Tb.* p.913
Winter cherry	Amomum Plinii	*Solanum pseudocapsicum*	Goodyer
Scarlet pimpernel/	Anagallis flore carneo,	*Anagallis arvensis*	*Tb.* p.559
blue	A. foemina cerulea	*A. arvensis* var. *caerulea*	Goodyer
Laburnum	Anagyris	*Laburnum anagyroides*	*Tb.* p.244
Yellow alkanet	Anchusa lutea	*Anchusa ochroleuca**	Goodyer
Anenome	Anemone flore pallido	*Anemone pavonina*	Goodyer
	A. tenuifolia flore coccineo pleno vulgare	*A. coronaria*	*Ps.* p.213
	A.tenuifolia flore pleno suaveruhente	ibid.	ibid.
	A. tenuifolia purpurea vulgaris	ibid.	ibid. p.208
Indian gourd	Anguina Americana versicolore pelle		*Tb.* p.773
Yellow monkshood	Anthora	*Aconitum anthora*	Goodyer
Kidney vetch	Anthyllis leguminosa marina Boetica	*Anthyllis hermanniae*	*Tb.* p.1094
Lady's fingers	A. leguminosa vesicaria Hispanica	*A. montana*	ibid.
False pimpernel	Antirrhinum minus	*Chaenorhinum minus*	Goodyer
Columbine	Aquilegia	*Aquilegia*	Goodyer
Sweet woodruff	Aparine leavis	*Galium odoratum*	*Tb.* p.567
Swamp milkweed	Apocynum rectum latifolium	*Asclepias incarnata*	*Tb.* p.1679
Everlasting pea	Arachus sub terrae siliquafera Lusit.	*Vicia atropurpurea*	*Tb.* p.1070
from Portugal	A. maior Baeticus	*V. grandiflora*	ibid.
Spanish vetch	A. minor Lusitanicus	*V. hybrida*	ibid.
Judas tree	Arbor Vitae	*Cercis siliquastrum*	Goodyer
Strawberry tree	Arbutus	*Arbutus unedo*	*Tb.* p.1489
Mousetail	Arisarum latifolium	*Arisarum proboscideum*	Goodyer

Birthroot	Aristolochia clematitis	*Aristolochia clematitis*	Goodyer
Smearwort	A. rotunda	*A. rotunda*	ibid.
European wild ginger	Asarum	*Asarum europaeum*	ibid.
Swallow-wort	Asclepias flore albo	*Vincetoxicum hirundinaria*	ibid.
Milkweed	A. flore nigro	*Vincetoxicum nigrum*	ibid.
Blue woodruff	Asperula flore caeruleo	*Asperula orientalis*	ibid.
Asphodel	Asphodelus bulbosus Galeni	*Asphodelus albus*	*Ps.* p.138
Aster	Aster conizoides ex Virginia	*Aster tradescantii*	Goodyer
	A. Italorum	*A. amellus*	ibid.
Maryland goldenaster	A. Virgineus angustifolius scrotinus		*Th.* p.133
	A. Virgineus latifolia luteus repens	*?Chrysopsis mariana*	ibid.
	A. Virgineus latifolia praeccocior purp.		ibid.
	A. Virgineus luteus alter minor		ibid.
	Astragalus	*Astragalus cicer*	Goodyer
Iberian milk vetch	A. marinus	*A. lusitanicus*	ibid.
Yellow milk-vetch	A. marinus Boeticus	*A. boeticus**	*Th.* p.1084
Bayonne astragalus	A. marinus Boeticus supinus	*A. baionensis**	ibid.
Masterwort	Astrantia nigra	*Astrantia major*	Goodyer
Distaffe thistle	Atractylis flore luteo	*Carthamus lanatus*	ibid.
Goosefoot	Atriplex baccifera	*Chenopodium rubrum*	Johnson p.325
Stinking arrach	A. olida	*C. vulvaria*	Goodyer
Bear's ear (red)	Auricula ursi flore rubro	*Primula auricula*	Goodyer
Great fleabane	Baccharis Monspeliensium	*Inula conyza*	Goodyer
Arnica	Bellis major spinosa flore lutea nudo	*?Arnica angustifolia*	*Th.* p.531 Animad. p.508. De l'Obel
Wood betony	Betonica flore albo	*Stachys betonica*	Goodyer
Snakeroot / Bistort	Bistorta major	*Persicaria bistorta*	ibid.
	B. minor	*P. vivipara*	ibid.
Moth mullein	Blattaria flore luteo	*Verbascum blattaria*	ibid.
Ambrosia	Botrys	*Chenopodium botrys*	ibid.
Viper's bugloss	Buglossum scorpioides	*Echium vulgare*	ibid.
Yellow ox eye	Buphthalmum Dodonaei	*Buphthalmum salicifolium*	ibid.
Hare's ear	Bupleurum angustifolium	*Bupleurum tenuissimum*	*Th.* p.578
	B. latifolium	*B. fruticosum*	ibid.
Pale Indian plantain	Cacalia Americana	*Cacalia atriplicifolia*	*Th.* p.1222
Frankincense	Cachris Verior	*Cachrys libanotis*	Goodyer
Gt mountain calamint	Calamintha Montana praestantior	*Calaminta grandiflora*	ibid.
Yellow lady's slipper orchid	Calceolus Mariae	*Cypripedium calceolus*	*Ps.* p 348
Marigold	Calendula simplex	*Calendula officinalis*	ibid. p.298
Marsh marigold	Caltha palustris multiplex	*Caltha palustris* 'Multiplex'	Goodyer
Bellflower – blue & white	Campanula persicifolia flore albo et ceruleo	*Campanula persicifolia* var. *alba* 'Caerulea Plena'	ibid.
Indian hemp	Cannabis sativa Virginensis major	*Cannabis sativa**	*Th.* p.598
Arrowroot/ Indian shot – red	Canna Indica flore rubro	*Canna indica*	*Ps.* p.376

Fumitory	Capnos altera fabacea radice	*Fumaria officinalis* *Corydalis bulbosa*	Goodyer
Lady's smock	Cardamine flore pleno C. trifolia	*Cardamine pratensis* *C. trifolia**	*Ps.* p 389 ibid.
Blessed milk thistle Great globe thistle Tall globe thistle	Carduus Mariae lacteus C. glubosus maior C. glubosus minor	*Silybum marianum* *Echinops sphaerocephalus* *E. exaltatus*	Goodyer ibid. ibid.
Herb Bennet	Caryophyllata vulgaris	*Geum urbanum*	Goodyer
Thrift	Caryophyllus Mediterraneus C. minimus muscosus nostras	*Armeria maritima* *A. maritima* subsp. *sibirica*	*Ps.* p.317 *Th.* p.1340
Burr chervil	Caucalis pumila Hispanica	*Anthriscus caucalis*	Goodyer
Cornflower Knapweed	Centaurium majus C. maius flore luteo	*Centaurea cyanus* *C. macrocephala* *	Goodyer ibid.
Flowering cherry	Cerasus recemosa putida Padus Theophrasti C. Virginianus	*Prunus padus* *P. virginiana*	*Th.* p.1520 Goodyer
Honeywort Cerinthe Wax flower	Cerinthe flore luteo C. Major flore purpurante C. Minor flavo flore	*Cerinthe major* *C. major* 'Purpurascens' *C. minor* 'Aurea'	Goodyer *Th.* p.521 ibid.
Dwarf cherry	Chamaecerasus	*Lonicera alpigena*	Goodyer
Bay rosemary	Chamaedaphne vera Dioscoridis	*Chamaedaphne calyculata*	*Th.* p.701
Germander	Chamaedrys laciniatis foliis C. Spinosa Cretica	*Teucrium chamaedrys* *T. fruticans* (see *Teucrium*)	ibid. p.107 ibid.
Spurge laurel	Chamelaea tricoccos	*Daphne laureola*	Goodyer
Camomile	Chamaemelium nudum odoratum	*Chamaemelum nobile*	ibid.
Cotoneaster	Chamaemespilus Gesneri	*Cotoneaster franchetti*	ibid.
Unidentified of Montpelier!	Characias monspel	*Euphorbia*	ibid.
Blue lettuce	Chondrilla semine deciduas purpurante	*Lactuca perennis*	ibid
Herb Christopher	Christophoriana	*Actaea spicata*	ibid.
Sweet pea (blue fl.)	Cicercula Clusii	*Lathyrus odoratus*	ibid.
Chicory (red fl.) Lamb's succory	Cichorium flore rubella C. Sylvestre Hispanicum pumilum	? *Cichorium intybus* cultivar *Arnoseris minima**	*Th.* p.775 *Th.* p.778
Spotted hemlock	Cicutaria latifolia foetidissima maxima	*Conium maculatum*	*Th.* p.932
Enchanter's night- shade	Circaea lutetiana	*Circaea lutetiana*	Goodyer
Melancholy thistle Tuberous thistle	Cirsium maius C. Maximum Asphodeli radice	?*Cirsium heterophyllum** *Cirsium tuberosum*	ibid. Johnson p.1181
Rock rose	Cistus annuus folio Ledi	*Tuberaria lignosa*	*Th.* p.662
Clematis (white) Clematis (blue) Clematis (purple)	Clematis alterafurens flore albo C. Coerulea Pannonica C. Flore purpurea	*Clematis flammula* *C. integrifolia* *C. viticella*	*Ps.* p.392 Goodyer ibid.
False saffron	Cnicus flore caeruleo	*Carthamus tinctorius* cultivar	Goodyer
Danish scurvygrass	Cochlearia rotundifolia maior	*Cochlearia officinalis*	*Th.* p.286

Meadow saffron	Colchicum atropurpureum variegatum	*Colchicum atropurpureum* variegated	*Ps.* p.157 ff.
	C. Versicolor	*Crocus versicolor**	ibid.
	C. Variegatum pleno flore	*Colchicum variegatum* double-flowered	ibid.
Bitter gourd	Colocynthis pyriformis	*Citrullus colocynthis*	*Tb.* p.160
Scorpion vetch	Colutea scorpioides	*Coronilla scorpioides**	Goodyer
False senna	Colutea Theophrastii	*Hippocrepis emerus*	ibid.
Larkspur	Consolida regalis	*Consolida ajacis*	ibid.
Blue bindweed	Convolvulus coeruleus minor Hisp.	*Convolvulus humilis*	*Ps.* p.359
Cornelian cherry	Cornus Mas	*Cornus mas*	Goodyer
Crown Imperial	Corona fratrum	*Fritillaria imperialis*	ibid.
Bear's ear sanicle	Cortusa Mathioli	*Cortusa matthioli*	ibid.
Virginian hazel	Corylus Virginiensis	*Corylus americana**	*Tb.* p.1416
Wild Byzantine crocus	Crocus sylvestris Byzantinus scrotinus	?*Crocus banaticus*	De l'Obel *Animad.*
Cypress	Cupressus	*Cupressus sempervirens*	Goodyer
Dodder	Cuscuta	*Cuscuta*	Th. p10
Bluebottle	Cyanus Boeticus supinus	*Centaurea montana*	*Tb.* p.483
Cyclamen/ Sow bread	Cyclamen folio hederae	*Cyclamen hederifolium*	ibid.
	C. Romanum orbiculato folio	*C. purpurascens*	ibid.
Ivy leaved toadflax	Cymbalaria Italica Hederaceae	*Cymbalaria muralis*	*Tb.* p.681
Coco grass; nutgrass	Cyperus rotundus odoratus vulgatior	*Cyperus rotundus*	ibid.
	True Cyperus of Diosocorides	?*C. papyrus*	*Ps* p.446
Broom	Cytisus maior sempervirens	*Cytisus ? praecox* 'Albus'	Goodyer
Winter daphne	Daphnoides maior	*Daphne odora*	Goodyer
Spanish larkspur	Delphinium Hispanicum parvum	*Delphinium halteratum**	*Ps.* p.278
Toothwort	Dentaria bulbifera	*Cardamine bulbifera*	Goodyer
Rusty foxglove	Digitalis ferruginea	*Digitalis ferruginea*	ibid.
Straw foxglove	D. Flore pallido luteo	*D. lutea*	ibid.
Cone flower	Doronicum Americanum	*Rudbeckia laciniata*	*Tb.* p.323
Leopard's bane	D. Romanum	*Doronicum plantagineum*	Goodyer
Shrub trefoil of Montpelier	Dorycnium suppositium Monspeliense	*Lotus pentaphyllus*	*Tb.* p.360
Dwarf elder	Ebulus	*Sambucus ebulus*	Goodyer
Broad leaved helleborine	Elleborine minor flore albo	*Epipactis helleborine*	*Ps.* p.348
Barrenwort	Epimedium	*Epimedium alpinum*	Goodyer
American variety	E. alterum Americanum	?	*Tb.* p.1365
Bitter vetch	Ervilia	*Vicia ervilia*	Goodyer
Everlasting pea	Ervum sylvestre	*Lathyrus sylvestris*	*Tb.* p 1365
Red sweetpea	E. Catananse	*L. clymenum**	
Alpine eryngo	Eryngium caerulae alpinum	*Eryngium alpinum*	Goodyer
	E. Luteum Monspel.	? *E. amethystinum*	*Tb.* p.972
Dark fl. stock	Erysimum Italicum & Matthioli	*Matthiola frutticulosa*	Johnson p.254
Spurge laurel	Esula maior	*Daphne laureola*	Goodyer
Swamp agrimony	Eupatorium aquaticum Americanum	*Agrimonia parviflora**	*Tb.* p.596
Hemp agrimony	E. Cannabium Americanum angustifol.	*Eupatorium cannabinum*	ibid.

'Greek' bean	Faba sylvestris Graecorum veterum	*Vicia narbonensis*	Goodyer/ Th.p.1055
Giant fennel	Ferula Tenuiore folio	*Ferula communis*	Goodyer/ Th. p.875
Indian fig	Ficus Indica	*Opuntia ficus-indica*	Goodyer
Dropwort / Spiraea	Filipendula	*Filipendula vulgaris*	Goodyer
Ground clematis	Flammula Iovis subiecta	*Clematis recta* 'Purpurea'	ibid.
Pheasant's eye	Flos Adonis flore rubro	*Adonis annua*	ibid.
French marigold	Flos Africanus	*Tagetes patula*	ibid.
Sunflower	Flos solis	*Helianthus annuus*	ibid.
Jerusalem artichoke	F. solis Peruvianus	*H. tuberosus*	ibid.
Fennel	Foeniculum sylvestre	*Foeniculum vulgare*	Th. p.885
Fenugreek	Foenugraecum	*Trigonella foenum-graecum*	Goodyer
Burning bush	Fraxinella	*Dictamnus albus*	Ps. p.334
Balsam of Peru (fruit)	Fructus / theca Balsami Occidentalis	*Myroxylon balsamum* var. *pereirae**	Th. p.1570
Goat's rue	Galega	*Galega officinalis*	Goodyer
Stinking deadnettle	Galeopsis altera pallida	*Lamium maculatum*	Th. p.609
Oak apple from Virginia	Galla Echinata		ibid. p.1390
Carolina jasmine	Gelseminum luteum odoratum Virg.	*Gelsemium sempervirens*	ibid. p.1465
Spanish gorse	Genista Hispanica	*Genista hispanica*	Goodyer
Trumpet gentian	Gentiana concave	*?Gentiana clusii*	ibid.
Gt. yellow gentian	G. Maior	*G. lutea*	ibid.
Cross gentian	G. Minor / Cruciata	*G. cruciata*	ibid.
Spring gentian	Gentianella verna major	*Gentiana verna*	Johnson p.437
Cranesbill	Geranium Alceae versicariae foliis	*Geranium sanguineum* var. *striatum*	Th. p.707
	G. althaeodes minus	*G. ibericum*	ibid. p.708
	G. flore caeruleo	*G. pratense*	Goodyer
	G. haemotodes	*G. sanguineum*	ibid.
	G. malacoides lacintium	*G. pyrenaicum*	Th. p.707
	G. maluoides	*G. malviflorum*	Goodyer
	G. saxatile	*G. saxatile*	Th. p.708
Cotton grass	Gramen plumosum	*Eriophorum angustifolium*	Goodyer
Great quaking grass	G. tremulum maximum albus Hisp	*Briza maxima*	Th. p.1166
Hedge hyssop	Gratiola	*Gratiola officinalis*	Goodyer
Lignum vitae	Guaiacum Patavinum	*Guaiacum officinale**	Th. p.1522
Tree purslane	Halymus vulgaris	*Atriplex halimus*	Goodyer
French honeysuckle	Hedysarum clypeatum	*Hedysarum coronarium*	ibid.
Hatchet vetch	H. sive securidaca	*Securigera securidaca**	ibid. Th. p.1090
Bear's foot	Helleborastum	*Helleborus foetidus*	Goodyer
Hellebore	Helleborus albus	*Helleborus argutifolius*	ibid.
	H. alb. flore atrorubente	*H. atrorubens*	ibid.
Christmas rose	H. niger verus	*H. niger*	ibid.
Large blue hepatica/	Hepatica exhalido flore	*Hepatica transsilvanica*	Goodyer
Liverleaf	H. Polyanthos	*H. nobilis*	De l'Obel, *Stirp*
	Hepatica minor flore pallido caeruleo	*H. nobilis*	Ps. p.225

Goldenrod	Herba Doria (see below: Saracen's compound)	*Solidago virgaurea*	Goodyer,
Woundwort	H. Doria altera serrate folio	*S. graminea**	*Th.* p.538
Canadian goldenrod	H. Doria minor Americana (1)	*S. canadensis*	*Th.* p.541
Herb Paris	Herba Paris	*Paris quadrifolia*	Goodyer
Rupturewort	Herniaria	*Herniaria glabra*	ibid.
Sweet rocket/	Hesperis flore pleno purpurante	*Hesperis matronalis*	*Th.*p.628
Dame's violet	H. Sylvestris latifolio flore albo parvo	*H. matronalis* var. *albiflora*	ibid.
Hawkweed	Hieracium medionigrum Boeticum majus	*Hieracium spilophaeum*	*Th.* p.792
	H. med. Boet, minus	*H. spilophaeum* 'Leopard'	ibid.
	H. montanum tomentosum	*H. lanatum*	ibid.
Horsetongue	Hippoglossum bonifacia	*Ruscus hippoglossum*	Goodyer
Garden patience	Hippolapathum rotundifolium	*Rumex patientia*	*Ps.* p.484
Lovage/Alexanders	Hipposelinum/Smyrnium vulgare	*Smyrnium olusatrum*	*Th.* p.930
Pearl barley	Hordeum distichum minus	*Hordeum distichon**	*Th.* p.1129
	H. hexastichum vernum	*H. vulgare* var. *hexastichum*	*Th.* p.1130
Wild clary sage	Horminum sylvestre Pannonicum	*Salvia sclarea*	Goodyer
Hyacinth	Hyacinthus Autumnalis minor	*Scilla autumnalis*	*Ps.* p.132
	H. Eriophorus	*Scilla hyacinthoides*	ibid.
	H. Stellatus Boeticus maior vulgo	*Scilla peruviana*	*Ps.* p.126
Henbane	Hyosciamus albus	*Hyoscyamus niger*	Goodyer
	H. Creticus	*H. albus**	*Th.* p.363
St John's wort	Hypericum	*Hypericum perforatum*	Goodyer
Holm oak	Ilex glandifera	*Quercus ilex*	Goodyer
Masterwort	Imperatoria	*Peucedanum ostruthium*	ibid.
Indigo (seed & root)	Indigo semen	*Indigofera tinctoria*	*Th.* p.601
Spanish iris (blue)	Iris bulbosa prima	*Iris xiphium*	*Ps.* p.172 ff.
English iris	I. Latifolia Clusii	*Iris latifolia*	
Camel grass	Iuncus odoratus tenuoir	*Cymbopogon schoenanthus**	*Th.* p.144
Brown knapweed	Jacoa marina Boetica	*Centaurea jacea*	Goodyer, *Ps.* p.328
Wallflower	Keiri / Leucium sylvestre Clusii	*Erysimum chieri*	*Th.* p.626
Laburnum/ Trefoil	Laburnum	*Laburnum anagyroides*	Goodyer
Lamb's lettuce	Lactuca angnina	*Valerianella locusta*	ibid.
Endive	L. Sylvestris Endiviae foliae	*Cichorium endivia**	*Th.* p.813
Opium lettuce	L. Sylvestre maior odore opii	*Lactuca virosa*	Johnson p.309
Narrow clover	Lagopus angustifolius Hispanicus	*Trifolium angustifolium*	*Th.* p.1106
Red clover	L. flore ruberrimo	*T. pratense*	ibid. p.1107
Creeping clover	L. vulgaris	*T. repens*	ibid.
Hungary deadnettle	Lamium Pannonicum	*Lamium orvala*	Goodyer
Annual sweet pea	Lathyrus annuus maior Boeticus	*Lathyrus odoratus*	*Th.* p.1064
	L. annuus siliquis orobi	*L .odoratus* purple-white-flowered	*Ps.* p.340 *Th.* p.1064
	L. Boeticus elegans siliquis orobi	*L.odoratus* orange-yellow-flowered	ibid. ibid.
Mountain e'lasting	L. Boeticus flore luteo	*L. luteus*	ibid.
	L. maior angustissimo flori	*L. odoratus*	ibid.

Chichling vetch	L. maior siliqua brevi	*L. sativus*	ibid.
	L. minor angustissimo folio	*?L. clymenum*	
Perennial pea	L. minor siliqua brevi	*L. latifolius*	
Cherry laurel	Laurocerasus	*Prunus laurocerasus*	*Ps.*p.401
Alexandrian laurel	Laurus Alexandrina genuine	*Danae racemosa*	*Tb.* p.701
Oleander	L. rosea /Oleander	*Nerium oleander*	*Ps.* p.401
Laurustinus	L. Tinus/sylvestris	*Vibernum tinus*	ibid.
Black radish	Leontopetalon	*?Raphanus sativus* var. *niger**	*Tb.* p.682
Dittander	Lepidium Monspeliacum Dentellaria	*Lepidium latifolium*	*Tb.* p.855
Summer snowflake	Leucojum bulbosum autumnale	*Leucojum aestivum*	*Ps.* p.110
Spring snowflake	L. Bulb. Vernum minimum	*L. vernum*	ibid.
	L. Patavinum marinum	*L. vernum* var. *carpathicum*	Goodyer
Lovage	Levisiticum	*Levisticum officinale*	*Tb.* p.936
Lily of the Valley	Lilium Convallium	*Convallaria majalis*	Goodyer
Sea lavender	Limonium Africanum Guil. Boelii	*Limonium bellidifolium*	*Stirp.*p.92
American var.	L. Ferrulae folio	*L. carolinianum*	*Tb.* p.1235
Graymile	Lithospermum maius	*Lithospermum officinale*	Goodyer
Princess pea	Lotus siliquosus/Pisum quadratum	*Psophocarpus tetragonolobus*	ibid.
White lupin	Lupinus Arabicus	*Lupinus albus**	*Tb.* p.1075, 396
	L. Flore obsoleto	*?L. hirsutus**	ibid.
	L. Gadensis marinus flore caeruleo	*L. littoralis*	Goodyer
	L. Minimus caeruleus	*L. nootkatensis*	*Tb.* p.1075
Yellow lupin	L. Sativus flore luteo	*L. luteus**	Goodyer
Cretan hemp	Lutea maxima Cretica feocunda	*Datisca cannabina*	*Tb.* p.603
Maltese cross	Lychnis Chalcedonica	*Lychnis chalcedonica*	Goodyer
Rose campion	Lychnides Coronoriae folio	*Lychnis coronaria* cultivar	*Tb.* p.629
Yellow loosestrife	Lysimachia lutea	*Lysimachia vulgaris*	Goodyer
Purple loosestrife	L. Flore Delphinii	*Lythrum salicaria*	ibid.
Evening primrose	L. Siliquosa ex Borealibus Virginia	*Oenothera biennis*	ibid.
Common mandrake	Mandragoras mas	*Mandragora officinarum*	*Ps.* p.377
	M. Femina		Goodyer
Passion flower	Maracoc Virginiana	*Passiflora* white-flowered	*Ps.* p.393
Scarlet turk's cap	Martagon Pomponeum	*Lilium chalcedonicum*	*Ps.* p.34
Ribbed melilot	Melilotus Germanica flore albo	*Melilotus officinalis* subsp. *albus*	Goodyer
Lemon balm (white)	Melissa Turcica flore albo	*Melissa officinalis* cultivar	*Tb.* p.40
	Mentastrum tuberosum Clusii	*Nepeta tuberosa*	*Tb.* p.34
Catmint	Mentha Cattaria	*Nepeta tuberosa*	Goodyer
Dog's mercury	Mercurialis mas	*Mercurialis perennis*	ibid.
	M. foemina		ibid.
Spignel (Alpine)	Meum Alpinum Germanicum	*Meum athamanticum*	ibid. *Tb.* p.889
Mezereon	Mezereon Germanorum	*Daphne mezereum*	Goodyer
Showy milfoil	Millefolium odoratum sive nobile	*Achillea nobilis*	ibid.
Woolly yarrow	M. luteum	*A. tomentosa*	ibid.
Marvel of Peru	Mirabilis Peruviana	*Mirabilis jalapa*	Goodyer

Onion	Moly Dioscorideum Hispanicum	*Allium campanulatum* (white-pale blue-flowered)	*Ps.* p.145
	M. Indicum	*A.* (green flowered)	*Ps.* p.141
	M. Pyxidatum argenteum Hisp.	*A.* (silvery white-flowered)	*Ps.* p.145
	M. serotinum Coniferum	*A. neapolitanum*	ibid.
Banana	Musa arbor	*Musa* × *paradisiaca*	*Tb.* p.1496
Sticky catchfly	Muscipula	*Lychnis viscaria*	Goodyer
Catchfly	M. altera flore albo	*L. viscaria* var. *alba*	*Tb.* p.637
Lichen – Liverwort	Muscus aridus crustatis	*Trametes* or *Peltigera*	*Tb.* p.1313
Gold-of-pleasure	Myagrum thlaspi facie	*Camelina sativa**	Goodyer
Common myrtle	Myrrhis	*Myrtus communis*	Goodyer
Daffodil dble. white	Narcissus albus multiplex	*Narcissus* Div. 4, white-flowered	*Ps.* p. 83
Daff. large cup white	N. Latifolius totus albus	*N. tazetta Div.* 2, white-flowered	*Ps.* p. 80
Sea Lily	N. Marinus/ tertius Matthioli	*Pancratium maritimum*	*Ps.* p. 96
Miniature purple ringed daffodil	N. Minimus mediopurpureus	*Narcissus minor*	*Ps.* p. 88
Mountain daffodil	N. Montanus albus apophysibus	*N.* × *poculiformis** Div. 2, white-flowered	*Ps.* p. 72
White polyanthus	N. Totus albus polanthos	*N. tazetta*	*Ps.* p. 80
Constantinople daff	N. Trapezunticus flore luteo	*N. tazetta* subsp. *lacticolor*	*Ps.* p. 70
A nasturtium he discovered	Nasturtium indicum	*Tropaeolum*	Goodyer
Catmint	Nepeta media	*Nepeta cataria*	*Ps.* p.479
Oleander	Nerium Oleander	*Nerium oleander*	Goodyer
Roman coriander	Nigella Romana flore albo	*Nigella sativa*	Goodyer
Parsley water dropwort	Oenanthe aquatica	*Oenanthe lachenalii**	*Tb.* p.1233
Fine leaved water dropwort	O. aquatica minor	*O. aquatica**	ibid.
Winter marjoram	Origanum Heracleoticum Veniis	*Origanum vulgare* subsp. *Hirtum*	*Tb.* p.15
Arabian star flower	Ornithogalum Arabicum	*Ornithogalum arabicum*	*Ps.* p.135
Star of Bethlehem	O. luteum	?*O. dubium*	*Ps.* p.140
Bitter vetch	Orobus recept. herbariorum	?*Lathyrus vernus*	Goodyer
Royal fern	Osmunda regalis / Filix florida	*Osmunda regalis*	*Tb.* p.1039
French sorrell	Oxalis franca	*Rumex scutatus**	Goodyer
Coral peony	Paeonia mas	*Paeonia mascula*	Goodyer
Common peony	P. foemina	*P. officinalis*	ibid.
American cow parsnip	Panax Heracleum alterum Americanum	*Heracleum lanatum*	*Tb.* p.950
Cow parsnip	P. Her. alterum Dodonaei	*H. sphondylium* subsp. *alpine*	*Tb.* p.948
	P. Her. alterum recentiorum	?	Goodyer
	P. Her. verum ficulneo folio	*H. sphondylium* subsp. *pyrenaicum*	*Tb.* p.948
Bladder campion	Papaver spumum	*Silene vulgaris*	Goodyer
Horned poppy	P. spinosum Clusii	*Glaucium corniculatum*	ibid.
	Paradise/dwarf apple tree	*Malus*	*Ps.* p.587
Cowslip	Paralysis altera odorata flore pallido	*Primula veris* cultivar	*Ps.* p.244

Cinquefoil	Pentaphyllum maius/Quinquefolium	*Potentilla fruticosa*	Goodyer
	P. Minus argenteum	*P. argentea*	*Th.* p.398
Arab sp. (pink/wh.)	P. Siliquosum Arabicum	*Potentilla fruticosa* cultivar e.g 'Abbotswood'	*Th.* p.397
Hare's ear	Perfoliatum vulgatius	*Bupleurum rotundifolium*	Goodyer
Honeysuckle	Periclymenum rectum	*Lonicera periclymenum*	ibid.
Silk vine	Periploca recta Virginiana	*Periploca graeca*	*Ps.* p.444
	P. Repens folio angustiore	*P. purpurea*	Goodyer
Stone parsley	Petroselinum Macedonicum quibusdam	*Sison amomum*	*Th.* p.924
Hog's fennel	Peucedanum	*Peucedanum officinale*	Goodyer
Spiderwort	Phalangium Ephemerum Virginiarum	*Tradescantia virginiana*	*Ps.* p.152
St Bruno's lily	P. Majus Italicum album	*Paradisea liliastrum* 'Major'	ibid.
Lima bean	Phasiolus siliqua hirsuta	*Phaseolus lunatus**	*Th.* p.1058
Spider brake fern	Phyllitis multifidio folio	*Pteris multifida**	Goodyer
Rampion	Phyteuma monspel.	*Phyteuma betonicifolium*	ibid.
Mousear hawkweed	Pilosella maior	*Pilosella officinarum*	ibid.
Greater burnet	Pimpinella maior Fuchii	*Pimpinella major*	ibid.
Burnet saxifrage	P. Saxifraga minor	*Pimpinella saxifraga*	ibid.
Salad burnet	P. hortensis	*Sanguisorba minor*	ibid.
Hackberry (tree from Virginia)	Pishamin prunus Virginiana	*Celtis occidentalis*	*Th.* p.1523
Suffolk sea peas	Pisum aliud maritimum Britanicum	*Pisum sativum* cultivar*	*Th.* p.1059
Chinese lantern	P. cordatum vesicarium	*Physalis alkakengi*	*Th.* p.1377
Saw leafed plantain	Plantago angustifolia serrata	*Plantago serraria**	*Th.* p.497
Coastal plantain	P. Rosea spicata	*P. subnuda**	ibid.
Mithridate	Plumbago Plinii/ Dentaria Rondeletii	*Lepidium campestre*	Goodyer
Golden germander	Polium montanum	*Teucrium polium* subsp. *aureum*	Goodyer
	P. montanum.pumilum Africum	*T. montanum*	*Th.* p.25
Great Solomon's seal	Polygonatum Virginianum	*Polygonatum biflorum*	*Th.* p.698
Tomato	Pomum amoris minus	*Lycopersicon esculentum**	*Ps.* p.379
Purslane	Portulaca Cretica	*Portulaca oleracea*	*Th.* p.722
American flytrap	Pseudopocymum Virginianum	*Apocynum androsaemifolium*	*Th.* p.386
English marjoram	Pseudodictammus	*Origanum vulgare*	*Th.* p.27
Wild daffodil	Pseudonarcissus aureus Anglicus	*Narcissus pseudonarcissus*	*Ps.* p.104
	P. Aureus Hispanicus	*N. nevadensis*	*Ps.* p.103
Sea daffodil	P. Marinus albus	*Pancratium maritimum*	*Ps.* p.108
Spanish sneezewort	Ptarmica Imperati	*Achillea ptarmica* The Pearl Group	*Th.* p.480
Pennyroyal	Pulegium cervinum	*Mentha cervina*	Goodyer
Pasque flower	Pulsatilla Danica	*Pulsatilla vulgaris* subsp. *grandis*	*Ps.* p.200
Firethorn	Pyracantha	*Pyracantha coccinea*	Goodyer

A remarkable oak near Malwood, Hampshire, said to come into leaf at Christmas	Quercus natalitiis Di virens	Acorns and leaves were collected and given to John Parkinson by John Goodyer	*Th.* p.1646
Fumitory	Radix cava flore albo	*Fumaria capreolata**	Goodyer
Field buttercup	Ranunculus arvorum	*Ranunculus arvensis* cultivar	ibid.
Bulbous buttercup	R. Asphodeli radice flore luteo	*R. bulbosus*	*Th.* p.339
Grassleaved b'cup	R. Gramineus	*R. gramineus*	Goodyer
	R. Illyricus maior	*R. illyricus*	ibid.
	R. llyricus minor	*R. illyricus*	ibid.
Persian buttercup	R. Omnium maximus	? *R. asiaticus*	ibid.
	R. Pyrenaeus folio plantaginis	*R. pyrenaeus/ platanifolius?*	ibid.
Black radish	Raphanus niger	*Raphanus sativus* var. *niger**	ibid.
Horseradish	R. rusticaniis	*Armoracia rusticana*	ibid.
Rampion	Rapuntium parvum	*Phyteuma humile*	ibid.
Knapweed	Rha capitatum folio Enulae	*Stemmacantha rhapontica*	ibid.
Rhubarb	R. Ponticum verum	*Rheum rhaponticum*	ibid.
Buckthorn	Rhamnus primus Clusii	*?Rhamnus* red-flowered dwarf	ibid.
Mignonette	Rheseda	*Reseda alba; R. lutea; R. luteola*	ibid.
Leedy's stonecrop	Rhodia radix	*Rhodiola integrifolia*	*Th.* p.729
Redoul	Rhus Plinii myrtifolia	*Coriaria myrtifolia*	Goodyer
Staghorn sumach	R. Coriaria Virginia Sumach	*Rhus typhina*	ibid.
Double yellow rose	Rosa lutea multiplex	*Rosa chinensis*	*Ps.* p.417
Eglantine	R. Pomifera major	*R. rubiginosa*	ibid. p.418
Lancashire red rose	R. Rubra humilis/pumilio	*R. gallica* var. *officinalis*	ibid. p.414
Rosemary (naturalized)	Rosmarinum sylvestre minus nostras	*Rosmarinus officinalis*	*Th.* p.75
Long leaved sundew	Ros Solis sylvestris longifolium	*Drosera capillaries*	*Th.* p.1053
Pineapple sage	Salvia minor alt. flore rubente	*Salvia elegans* prostrate	*Th.* p.53
Wood sanicle	Sanicula	*Sanicula europaea*	Goodyer
Lifelong saxifrage	S. guttata	*Saxifraga paniculata* (*?S. hirsuta*)	ibid.
Saxifrage	Saxifraga vera Diosciridis Matthioli	*?Saxifraga iranica*	*Th.* p.426
Pale yellow scabious	Scabiosa Montana flore luteo	*Scabiosa colombaria* subsp. *ochroleuca*	Goodyer
Egyptian rose	S. rubra Indica	*Scabiosa atropurpurea*	*Ps.* p.324
Scammony, Syrian bindweed	Scammonia Syriaca legitima	*Convolvulus scammonia**	*Th.* p.164
Sea squill	Scilla alba	*Urginea maritima*	*Ps.* p.133
False salsify	Scorsonera latifolia	*Scorzonera laciniata**	Goodyer
Salsify	S. minima tuberosa Hispanica	*S. hispanica*	*Th.* p.410
Carpenter's square	Scrophularia Indica	*Scrophularia marilandica*	*Th.* p.612
Yellow figwort	S. lutea Bauhinii	*S. vernalis*	Johnson p.717
	S. peregrina altera	*S. vernalis* from Italy	*Th.* p.612
	S. sambuci folio	*S. sambucifolia*	ibid.
Vetch	Securidaca peregrina Clusii	*Biserrula pelecinus*	*Th.* p.1091
Milk parsley	Selinum segetale	*Selinum carvifolium*	*Th.* p.931

Moon carrot	Seseli	*Seseli*	Goodyer
65 sp. Biennial &	S. species a D. Franqueville	? De Franqueville's sesily	ibid.
perennial herbs	S. Aethiopicum	*Seseli libanotis*	ibid.
	S. A. Matthioli	? Mattiolus' sesily	ibid.
	S. Cretense nodosum	*Seseli gummiferum*	*Th.* p.908
	S. Creticum	*?Seseli libanotis*	Goodyer
Ironwort	Sideritis Hederulae folio	*Impatiens noli-tangere*	*Th.* p.588
St Mary's thistle	Silybum majus annuum	*Silybum marianum*	*Th.* p.976
Spanish varieties	S. minus Boeticum		ibid.
Lesser water parsnip	Sium minimum/Noli me tangere	*Berula erecta*	*Th.* p.1241
Alexanders (Cretan)	Smirnium Creticum	*Smyrnium rotundifolium*	*Th.* p.930
Carolina horsenettle	Solanum halicabum	*Solanum carolinense**	Goodyer
Red ink plant	S. magnum rubrum Virginianum	*Phytolacca americana*	*Th.* p.348
Deadly nightshade	S. somniferum et lethale	*Atropa belladonna*	Goodyer
Sea bindweed	Soldanella marina	*Calystegia soldanella*	ibid.
Saracen's compound	Solidago Sarracenica germanica	*Solidago virgaurea*	*Th.* p.539
Cow parsley	Sphondylium majus aliud lacinatis foliis	*Anthriscus sylvestris*	*Th.* p.953
God's flower	Stachys	*Helichrysum stoechas*	Goodyer
Spanish cornflower	Stoebe Salmantica	*Mantisalca salmantica**	ibid.
Tuberous comfrey	Symphytum tuberosum	*Symphytum tuberosum*	ibid.
Mock orange	Syringa Italica alba	*Philadelphus coronarius*	ibid.
Lilac/ Pipe tree	S. caerulea	*Syringa vulgaris* (blue-flowered)	ibid.
Mountain tea	Tetrahit	*Sideritis syriaca*	ibid.
Tree germander	Teucrium majus vulgare	*Teucrium fruticans*	*Th.* p.109
Meadow rue	Thalictrum pratensis	*Thalictrum flavum*	Goodyer
	T. tenuifolium	*T. simplex* subsp. *tenuifolium**	ibid.
Spanish tuft	T. Hispanicum aquilinae folio	*T. aquilegiifolium*	ibid.
Cretan carrot	Thapsia	*Athamanta cretensis*	ibid.
Baldmoney	T. tuberosa radice	*Meum athamanticum*	*Th.* p.879
Pennycress	Thlaspi Dioscorides	*Thlaspi montanum*	Goodyer
	T. incanum Mechliniense	*T. bulbosum*	*Th.* p.835
	T. vulgatissimum	*T. arvense*	Goodyer
Woolly thyme	Thymum durius Candidus	*Thymus pseuodolanuginosus*	*Th.* p.6
	T. d. vulgare	*T. vulgaris*	ibid.
Cardinal flower	Trachelium Americanum flore ruberrimo	*Lobelia cardinalis*	*Ps.* p.356
Canterbury bells	T. flore albo	*Campanula trachelium*	ibid.
Giant throatwort	T. Giganteum	*C. latifolia*	ibid.
Giant bellflower	T. maius flore duplici albo & caeruleo	*C. trachelium*	ibid.
Creeping bellflower	T. serotinum	*C. rapunculoides*	*Th.* p.646
Gum Tragacanth	Tragacantha / Goat's Thorn	*Astragalus gummifer**	Goodyer
Goatsbeard	Tragopogon aestivum	*Tragopogon pratensis*	*Th.* p.413
	T. laciniatum maius	*T. dubius**	ibid.
	T. flore caeruleo	*T. crocifolius*	*Ps.* p.302
	T. purpureum	ibid.	ibid.

Clover: American bituminous	Trifolium Bituminosum Americanum	*Bituminaria bituminosa*	*Tb.* p.716
	T. Burgundiarum	*? T. rubens*	Goodyer
Strawberry clover	T. fragiferum alterum	*T. fragiferum*	*Tb.* p.1108
Another	T. fragiferum Frisicum	ibid.	ibid.
Woolly trefoil	T. fragiferum Lusitanicum tomentosum	*T. tomentosum* *	ibid.
Sea aster	Tripolium alterum Ferulae folio	*Aster tripolium*	*Tb.* p.673
	T. Lychnidis Coronariae folio	*Ageratum corymbosum*	ibid.
Tulips	Tulipae	*Tulipa*	Goodyer
Tower cress	Turritis major	*Turritis glabra* *	Johnson p.272
Whortlebery	Vaccinia rubra	*Vaccinium vitis-idaea*	Goodyer
Mountain valerian	Valeriana petraea	*Valeriana montana*	ibid.
Honesty	Viola lunaris	*Lunaria annua*	*Ps.* p.265
Violet	V. Mariana	*Viola odorata*	Goodyer
	V simplex Martia	*V. odorata*	*Ps.* p.282
Goldenrod	Virga aurea serrate folio	*Solidago virgaurea*	Goodyer
Foxgrape	Vitis Virginiana	*Vitis labrusca*	De l'Obel, *Stirp.* p.129
Dark eye sunflower	Wosaran Virginianum(2)	*Helianthus atrorubens*	Goodyer
Spoonleaf yucca	Yucca	*Yucca filamentosa*	*Ps.* p.434
Bead tree / Ceylon mahogany	Zizypha Candida Azadarach avicenne (JP)	*Melia azedarach*	Johnson p.1492 *Tb.* p.1443

Notes:

1. J.P. received this as a gift from the French Royal Gardener, Vespasian Robin.

2. According to J.P.(Theatrum p.130), many, including presumably Goodyer, mistakenly gave this American plant the Indian name 'wosacan' or ' wisanck' which J.P. thought belonged properly to the Silk vine (Pericploca purpurea).

NOTES

Abbreviations

BL: British Library
CPA: Annals of the Comitia of Physicians, Royal
    College of Physicians, London
PRO: Public Record Office, Kew
SOG: Society of Genealogists, London
SP: State Papers

Prologue, pages 7–11
1 *Paradisi in Sole: Paradisus Terrestris*, 1st edn,
   pub. Tho. Cotes, London, 1629.
2 The sheep-wolf is the 'Tartary Lamb' or
   'Borametz' of fifteenth-century legend, described
   in the Ashmolean Catalogue 1836 as 'Lamb of
   Tartary', 1498 ff.
3 *Paradisus*, p.2.
4 Rohde, p.66.

Chapter 1 The Blessed Place, pages 13–23
1 Albert Switzer had done the cuts for Speed's
   History of Britain, printed in 1611, and is
   described in the preface in this way.
2 Ainsworth, p.11, refers to a deed in Edward III's
   reign 1362–3, 'in connection with land at
   Farringdon near Preston in Lancashire, when
   Perkin's name is mentioned and that of his son
   John-le-Perkynson'.
3 Humphery-Smith, C., *Armigerous Ancestors:
   Catalogue of sources for C16th and C17th
   Visitations of Heralds*, 1928, p.13, SOG;
   Ainsworth, p.137: St George, Richard, *Visitation
   of Lancaster*, 1613.
4 Farrar and Brownbill, Vol. 6.
5 See details in surviving sixteenth-century
   Parkinson wills, Richmond Wills, Lancashire
   Record Office.
6 See Hoskins. See also Ziegler, P., *Study of the
   Black Death. Losses in Lancashire*: 'In the ten
   parishes of Amounderness it was claimed 13,180
   people died between 8 September 1349 and 11
   January 1350. In the parish of Preston 3,000 died,
   in Lancaster 3,000, in Garstang 2,000, and in
   Kirkham 3,000.'
7 Richmond Wills, Lancashire Record Office.
8 Ainsworth, p.38.
9 Richmond Wills: WRW A Robert Parkynson
   1562, Lancashire Record Office.
10 Parish Register of St Mary and All Saints,
   Whalley. See Lancashire Parish Register Society
   edition.
11 See Whitaker, Book II, p.211.
12 *Paradisus*, p.468.
13 Ibid., pp.521–2. Sixteenth-century English
   sailors who ate this diet suffered far less from
   scurvy than the sailors of the Royal Navy who
   came after them. The Navy ration of salt beef

and biscuit had none of the vitamin C
contained in dried peas.
14 Ibid., p.509.
15 Ibid., p.512.
16 Ibid., p.483.
17 This is *Tragopogon porrifolius*, also known as
   scorzonera. For modern recipes see Spoczynska,
   J., *The Wildfood Cookbook*, Robert Hale, 1985.
   John Parkinson cultivated purple varieties of this
   plant in his garden: *Paradisus*, pp.302, 514–15.
   Not to be confused with ground elder,
   Aegopodium podagraria, sometimes called
   goatweed but really known as goutweed for its
   medicinal use against gout.
18 *Paradisus*, p.483.
19 *Paradisus*, p.479, refers to the variety cultivated
   in gardens as a household medicine: *Horminum
   sativum*. *Theatrum*, pp.55–9, describes twelve
   varieties of clary, *Salvia verbanaca*, from all
   parts of the world.
20 Ibid., pp.474, 478.
21 Fuller, Thomas, *The Holy State and the Profane
   State*, 1642.
22 *Paradisus*, p.477.
23 Kildwick-in-Craven: St Andrew, Church
   Registers, pub. Yorkshire Parish Register Society,
   Jan. 1600/1601.

Chapter 2 'The rude people of the North', pages
24–33
1 Farrar and Brownbill, Vol. 6, p.369.
2 For further details of the influence of the great
   abbeys in the north of England see Watkins, P.,
   Bolton Priory and its Church, pub. Bolton Priory
   Parochial Church Council, 1989, available from
   Bolton Abbey; Williams.
3 Inventory of the goods of the monastery,
   Whitaker, Book II, p.82.
4 From a letter to Thomas Cromwell, 4 June 1535,
   quoted in Whitaker.
5 See Ellis, H., *Letters & Papers of the Reign of
   King Henry VIII*, ed. Gairdner, J., Longman, xi,
   pp.504, 531–4. See also Ridley, J., *Henry VIII*,
   Constable, 1984, Chapter 21.
6 Ibid., pp.856–7, 1251.
7 Letter from Henry VIII to Norfolk, Jan./Feb. 1537,
   SP i 537–40, PRO.
8 Letter 10 March 1537 from Robert de Radcliffe,
   Earl of Sussex, to Thomas Cromwell. See
   Williams.
9 Notes of Thomas Talbot, who lived at Salesbury
   near Whalley, and graduated from Brasenose
   College, Oxford, in 1523. He records that John
   Paslew had dreamed the appearance of the ghost
   of a brother monk that predicted to him he would
   live for another sixteen years and no more. Talbot
   remembered this when Paslew pleaded guilty. He

thought the abbot felt his 'time' had come. See Williams, pp.105–8.

10   Inventory of Whalley Abbey taken by the Earl of Sussex in residence after the execution of John Paslew, April 1537. See Whitaker, Book II, p.185.

11   Letter from Henry VIII to the Earl of Sussex at Whalley, 17 March 1537. Williams, p.110.

12   Whitaker found evidence that monks still lived in the old abbey as late as 1553; Book II, p.211.

13   Kildwick-in-Craven: St Andrew, Church Registers pub. Yorkshire Parish Register Society.

14   John Bradyll's will reproduced by the Chetham Society, Vol. 51, p.109, and Whitaker, Vol. 3, p.4.

15   The Act of Six Articles, 1539.

16   The second Chantry Act of 1547 dissolved all remaining chantries. For Whalley Grammar school see Whitaker, Book IV, p.17.

17   Farrar and Brownbill, Vol. 7.

18   Letter to Archbishop Parker, 1564, in *Correspondence of Matthew Parker, 1535–1575*, ed. Bruce & Perowne, Cambridge 1853, p.221; also Whitaker, p.212.

19   See Morison, J., *Burghley's Land and Domestic Following*, Ph.D., St John's College, Oxford, 1990, for a description of how William Cecil increased Protestant power in the north; pp.29ff.

20   The original of Burghley's beautiful map is in the British Library: BL Roy 18 D III.

Chapter 3 'Idle Tales', pages 34–44

1   Letter to Archbishop Parker, 1564, see Chapter 2, note 18.

2   As late as 1719 this was the job specified for the schoolmaster in a school endowed in Hazlewood, Yorkshire, by Sylvester Petyt. See Watkins, p.106, cited in Chapter 2, note 2.

3   Description given with the order for printing. See English Short Title Catalogue, British Library.

4   See Raven, pp.13–21: an excellent account of medieval science.

5   Ibid.

6   Ibid., pp 27–30. Later anonymous additions turned the book into a kind of sportsman's guide. It was popular, reprinted many times in the sixteenth century, but still owned by few. In the foreword its authors say they have expressly made it so large and expensive that it should appeal only to 'gentyl and noble men'. Idle persons, who might have been inclined to buy a 'pamphlet' on the subject, could 'utterly destroye' the sport of fishing.

7   From *Rosa Angelica* by John of Gaddesden, c.1314, printed Pavia, Italy, 1492; Venice 1502, 1517; Augsburg, 1595. See Sanecki, K., *History of the English Herb Garden*, Ward Lock, 1994, p.18.

8   *Paradisus*, p.377.

9   Margaret Clifford's letter to Dr Layfield, quoted in Williamson, G.C., *George, 3rd Earl of Cumberland*, Cambridge University Press, Cambridge 1920, but since lost.

10   See Spence, R.T., *Lady Anne Clifford*. This Puritan resistance to foreign languages, typical of English xenophobia of the time, was later spelled out in a book dedicated to Francis Russell's son, the 3rd Earl of Bedford. *Epistola de Peregrinatione Italia* by Justus Lipsius, distinguished Latinist of the University of Leyden, was translated into English by Sir John Stradling in 1592, warning the English against association with foreigners.

11   See Clifford, D.J.H., ed., *The Diaries of Lady Anne Clifford*, Sutton, Stroud 1990. See also Spence, *Lady Anne Clifford*, p.8.

12   *A Catalogue of the Books in the Closset in the Passage Room next the Pantry in Skipton Castle, 28th August, 1739*, Yorkshire Archaeological Society, DD121/111. Also Spence, *Lady Anne Clifford*, Appendix II, p.257.

13   John Dee's Preface to the first English translation of Euclid's *Elements*, published by Sir Henry Billingsley in 1570.

14   See Lawson-Dick, p.90.

15   Letter from William Cecil quoted by Sitwell, Appendix A, p.484. Details of Dr Dee's later life in Comitia proceedings of College of Physicians, 13 January 1614.

16   Anne Clifford's *Great Boke of Record*, 1648/9. Anne Clifford was Margaret's only surviving child, and lived long enough to reclaim her father's estates, which had been entailed against her. She celebrated by compiling these fascinating records of her family history which are now all in the possession of Cumbria County Record Office, Kendal (WD/Hoth/A988/10/1). She also commissioned the Appleby Triptych in 1646, a revealing family portrait which now belongs to Abbot Hall in Kendal, Cumbria. See Spence, *Lady Anne Clifford*, Chapter 9.

17   See Jacques.

18   See Ainsworth for history of the Bleasdale Parkinsons. Also Farrar & Brownbill, Vol. 7; Houghton's early seventeenth-century accounts: MS Salisbury Box U 14-17, also MS Salisbury 35.24,109; 143.25; HMC Salisbury 8.280.

Chapter 4 'The New Found World', pages 45–56

1   Towneley transcripts No. 99. Lancashire Record Office, Preston, Lancs.

2   See William Camden's *Britannia*, 1526, tr. Gibson, E., London 1753, Vol. 2, p.966.

3   Lord Burghley's Map. Roy 18 D III, BL.

4   Hoskins, p.118.

5   See Bagley, J.J., and Hodgkiss, A.G., *Notes from Lancashire: A History of the County Palatine in Early Maps*, Neil Richardson, 1995, p.10, for description of Lancashire building.

6   Harrison, William, *The Description of England, 1587*, Folger Shakespeare Library/Dover, 1994, p.199. See also Girouard, M., *Robert Smythson and the Elizabethan Country House*, York University Press, 1983, p.4.

7 *Paradisus*, p.470.

8 The earliest record of kitchen gardens in English: *Profitable Instructions for the Manuring, Sowing and planting of Kitchen Gardens. Very profitable for the common wealth and greatly to the help and comfort of poore people. Gathered by Richard Gardiner of Shrewsburie. Imprinted at London by Edward Allde for Edward White dwelling at the little North doore of Paules at the Signe of the Gunne. 1603. Preface by Edward Thorne, gentleman.* British Library. See Rohde, p.29.

9 Ibid.

10 Bacon, F., *History of Henry VII* in *A Complete History of England*, Vol. I, pp.93–5. See also Spedding, Vol. III, p.14.

11 Hoskins, p.125.

12 John Spencer's petition to the Royal Commission, 1517, PRO. See also Hoskins, p.122.

13 See Hentzner, p.82.

14 See reproduction of Agas map in St Bride's Church, Fleet Street, and Guildhall.

15 Ibid.

16 Details from Stow, Vol. II, p.83.

17 As quoted in Taylor, p.45.

18 Stow, p.81.

19 Ibid., p.19.

20 See Charterhouse survey, Guildhall Library, London, for the four-storey building on the approach to London Bridge, the tallest in London.

21 Rees, p.116.

22 Ibid. The Grocers' Hall had once been a synagogue, hence the name given to the area: 'Old Jewry'.

23 *A Short History of the Grocers' Company*.

24 Details from Inventory in Grocers' Company wardens' accounts for 1584/5, MS 11571–7, Guildhall.

25 One master they elected would later address them on quarter-day like a preacher addressing his flock: 'It was once with me, as now it is with you; I was as negligent, remiss and careless of the duty of coming to these assemblies as any. But God hath his end in human things as in divine, for once I came hither on a quarter day as peradventure some of you have not been here twice, and then by hearing of a grave, wise and religious exhortation made by the then Father of our Company, Sir John Harte, Knight, tending to my obedience, I was caught and then my conscience told me I had not done well in neglecting my duty in not coming upon these occasions.' See Rees, p.109.

26 *A Short History of the Grocers' Company*.

27 Ordinance of 1562 at the inauguration of Sir Thomas Lodge as master. See Herbert, W., *The History of the Twelve Great Livery Companies of London*, 1834, David & Charles, 1968, Vol. 2, p.334.

28 Rees, pp.79–80, from Henrician ordinances, later modified.

29 Grocers' wardens' accounts, 1584/5, Guildhall.

Chapter 5 Weapons for the New Age, pages 57–72

1 Minutes of the Worshipful Company of Grocers. See also Calendar of Minutes Vol. 1, Part II, and Grocers' wardens' accounts, 1584/5, Guildhall.

2 Sitwell, p.342.

3 Minutes of the Worshipful Company of Grocers. See also Calendar of Minutes Vol. 1, Part II, and Grocers' wardens' accounts, 1584/5, Guildhall.

4 Ibid.

5 Ibid.

6 Ibid.

7 Ibid.

8 Ibid.

9 *A Short History of the Grocers' Company*, p.8.

10 London Port Book 1567/8, see Dietz, B., *Port and Trade of Elizabethan London*, London Record Society, 1972. See also *A survey of the Legal Quays drawn up in 1584*, PRO, E 178/7075.

11 Stow, Vol. I, p.206.

12 Gunther, *Dioscorides*.

13 Turner, *Herbal*, Vol. II, p.18.

14 Turner, *Libellus de re herbaria*, p.F, i.

15 Raven, p.93: correspondence between Coudenberg and Conrad Gesner. For a full discussion of Turner and his influence see Raven, Chapters IV–VIII.

16 Bacon, F., *The Advancement of Learning*, 1605, in Bacon, *Essays*.

17 Gerard, p.1308. See also Legré, Vol. 3, pp.8–9. The diaries these German physicians kept give a delightful insight into the tradition of hospitality that was common amongst scientific men of the day. Felix Platter learned his trade in Montpellier and travelled to Arles, where a well-known local doctor, Francois Valleriola, opened his house to Platter and his companion. He *...nous fit bon accueil, nous montra sa bibliothèque, ses propres écrits, des poissons de mers empaillés, entre autres un Orbis marinus etc. Après avoir pris nos noms et nous avoir recommandé de lui écrire souvent, il se mit à notre disposition pour visiter la ville* ('he made us very welcome, showed us his library, his own writing, some stuffed fish, including a sea urchin. After taking our names and enjoining us to write to him frequently, he offered to show us the town').

18 *Paradisus*, p.86.

19 Morren, E., *Matthias de l'Obel: Sa vie et ses Oeuvres*, Bulletin de la Fédération des Sociétés d'horticulture de Belgique, University of Liège, 1875.

20 Lawson-Dick, p.254.

21 Ibid., p.138.

22 De l'Obel, *Stirpium Adversaria Nova*, p.395. See also Raven, p.168.

23 *Observationes S. Stirpium Historiae*. John Parkinson's heavily annotated copy of this book, recognizable from his tiny neat handwriting, is part of the small bundle of his personal papers that has survived. It is in a collection left to Magdalen College, Oxford, by John Goodyer

and catalogued by Robert Gunther in the 1920s as a Goodyer Manuscript MS 327; 328. See also Gunther, *Early British Botanists*.

24 Parish Registers of St Mary and All Saints, Whalley, 1587, Lancashire Parish Register Society.

Chapter 6 Elizabethan Gold, pages 73–87

1 Calendar of Minutes, Worshipful Company of Grocers, Vol.1, Part II, 8 May 1582, Guildhall.

2 Foster, J., ed., *London Marriage Licences*, 1887.

3 Parkinson, *Theatrum Botanicum*, preface.

4 Letter purporting to be an accurate description of Florida, sent to the English ambassador by Robert Thorne. He was a Bristol merchant living in Seville, whose father had sailed to Newfoundland. See Foss, M., *Undreamed Shores*, Harrap, 1974, p.63.

5 Ibid., p.120.

6 Ibid., p.124.

7 The land was mostly in present-day North Carolina between Cape Fear and Cape Henry: 33° 50' N to 36° 56' N.

8 Hakluyt. John Parkinson in the *Theatrum*, p.1624, describes cassava root which 'was used by all the people of America, from Florida to Peru' to make bread. The juice from the root, which was poisonous unless it was boiled, was thickened, dried, ground into a powder and made into small cakes which would 'abide good ... twenty years without corrupting'.

9 See De Bry, foreword.

10 Nichols, P., *Sir Francis Drake Revived*, London, 1626. Drake's letter to the queen in the introductory pages. See also Kelsey, H., *Sir Francis Drake, The Queen's Pirate*, Yale University Press, 1998, p.108. Francis Drake had been sailing since boyhood in the 1550s. He had learnt his ruthless brilliance as a captain from his uncle, John Hawkins, a Devon merchant who was an occasional pirate and stumbled upon a lucrative trade in slaves. Carrying Africans to sell as slave labour to Spanish merchants in the West Indies was so profitable that the route from West Africa to the Caribbean became Hawkins' staple business.

11 See Spence, *The Privateering Earl*, p.64. An excellent, detailed study of the relationship between George Clifford's sailing expeditions and his finances. The queen eventually made him her champion, but this great honour cost him more money than it earned him. From November 1590, it appeared every year in the lists at Whitehall Palace, wearing a glittering suit of armour that had cost £3,000, riding a beautiful white charger to joust in the pageant that was held to mark the anniversary of her accession.

12 Introduction by V. Sackville-West to *The Diary of the Lady Anne Clifford*.

13 Hakluyt, Vol. 3, p.211.

14 HMC Salisbury, X, 138-9. Spence, *The Privateering Earl*, p.65, gives a full account of this sea battle, in the aftermath of which one of the English ships' surgeons recorded that there were so many dead on the Portuguese ship that 'no man could almost steppe but on a dead carkase or a bloody floore but specially about the helme where very many of them fell suddenly from stirring to dying'.

15 Ibid.

16 Minutes of the Worshipful Company of Grocers, Guildhall. Memoranda for 29 September 1597 show that by this date George Clifford owed the daughter of the grocer apothecary Peter Houghton over £5,000. His expeditions were expensive to mount, and, glorious though the prizes were, only two of them proved profitable.

17 *Theatrum*, p.1592.

18 Ibid.

19 John could not relate ambergris to any of the plants he understood so well. He thought it most likely to be 'a kind of Bitumen (as the yellow amber is before said to be...) whose springs are in the rocks of the sea', *Theatrum*, p.1566. Ambergris is in fact secreted in the intestines of sick or dying sperm whales.

20 *Theatrum*, p.1575.

21 Ibid.

22 Ibid., p.1576.

23 Ibid.

24 Ibid., p.1572.

25 Ibid., p.1602. He called it *Olibanum sive Thus* or White Frankincense.

26 *Paradisus*, p.578.

27 *Theatrum*, p.1614.

28 Woodward, p.93.

29 Henztner, p.42.

30 *Paradisus*, p.364.

31 This oath comes from the forty-five ordinances agreed on 26 November, 15 Henry VIII (1524). See Rees, p.79. There is nothing to suggest an alteration in the oath before 1592, in spite of the religious upheavals that had occurred. In fact the Grocers' Company oath today has barely changed: 'I, [Name], solemnly and truly declare that I will be good and true to our Sovereign Lady Queen Elizabeth II and be obedient to the Wardens of this Company in lawful manner. I will also keep secret all the lawful counsels of this Fellowship. And all manner of rules, impositions, and ordinances that are now or hereafter shall be made and lawfully ordained for the ordering and well governing of the said fellowship, I will truly observe and obey to my power.'

32 Grocers' wardens' accounts, 1579-1892, Guildhall.

33 *Theatrum*, p.1569.

34 Ibid., p.1592. See also Spence, *The Privateering Earl*, p.172, and Purchas, S., ed., *Hakluytus Posthumus or Purchas his pilgrims*, 20 vols, Maclehose, Glasgow, 1905-7: San Juan expedition, Vol XVI, 29-42, 43-106, which includes an abridged version of the account in BL Sloane MS 3289.

35 *Theatrum*, Introduction.

Chapter 7 Brotherhood, pages 88–102

1 For details of the Grocers' dinners and furnishings see the wardens' accounts, 1579–1892, Guildhall.
2 Calendar of Minutes of the Worshipful Company of Grocers, Vol. 1, Part II, 1569–83, 18 March 1574, Guildhall.
3 St Antholin's was in Budge Row in the heart of the Grocers' district of Bucklesbury. The document 'to accorde and clere the suspicions conceived of Edmond Campion and one of this Companie's scollers, that he may utter his mind in favoring the religion now authorized; it is agreed that, between this and Candlemas next, he shall com and preache at Pawll's Crosse in London, or ells the Companie's exhibitions to cease and be apoynted to another...' is in the Guildhall, MS 11571/7.
4 Ordinances of the Grocers. MS 11570/A, Guildhall.
5 Jacques, Chapter 2, p.1.
6 Ordinances of the Grocers, MS 11570/A, Guildhall.
7 Stow, 'This whole street called Bucklesbury on both sides throughout is possessed of Grocers and Apothecaries.'
8 Hentzner, pp.12, 44.
9 Ibid.
10 Grocers' wardens' accounts, Guildhall. Richard Bragge was freed in 1603.
11 Stow, p.260.
12 Ibid., p.263.
13 Stow, Vol. 2, pp.43, 260, 263. Fleet Street pavement was relaid in 1595, when Stow noted the existence of a much better pavement four feet below the existing one.
14 Foster, J., ed., *London Marriage Licences*, 1887: 'Dr Henry Atkyns Nov. 13 1591, Dr of Medicine, of Christ Church, Newgate, London and Mary Piggot, Spinster of St Lawrence's, Old Jewry, daughter of Thomas Pigott of Dodershall, Co Bucks, esq., Gen Licence', p.291. 'Nov. 24 1604, Dr William Harvey, Dr of Physic, Bach. 26, of St Martin's Ludgate and Elizabeth Browne, Maiden, 24 of St Sepulchre's, daughter of Lancelot Browne, of same, Dr of Physic, who consents; consent also of Thomas Harvey, one of the jurats of the town of Folkestone in Kent, father of said William, at St Sepulchre's Newgate'.
15 Diary of Felix Platter, pp.8–9.
16 CPA, College of Physicians, London, November 1585. See also 4 July 1595, Vol. II, Fol. 112a: 'Dr Edward Jordan appeared and was examined. It was decided that he should be given verbal authority to practise provided he read Galen's books, De Temperamentis, De Elementis (ex Hippocrate), De [naturalibus] Facultatibus, De [Causis] Morborum, De Symptomatum Causis, de Symptomatum diferentiis, and de locis Affectis, before next Michaelmas'.
17 Grocers' wardens' accounts, 1591–2, MS 11570, Guildhall. This annual event was sometimes known as 'the Apothecaries' dinner'.
18 CPA, 3 July 1596.
19 Jacques, Chapter 1, p.4.
20 CPA, 10 May 1594.
21 CPA, 25 February, 21 May 1596.
22 CPA, Vol. 2, Fol. 134b, 19 August 1598.
23 CPA, 18 May 1589.
24 Grocers' wardens' accounts, October 1598, notes: 'Thomas Niccol, from the Feast of All Saints last, presented the same day. 2s 11d'. John was obviously tardy about registering his new apprentice.
25 Grocers wardens' accounts, October 1598.
26 CPA, 1602.
27 Calendar of Minutes of the Worshipful Company of Grocers, 17 February 1588, p.735. The four were Anthony Soda, Robert Morer, John Nashe and Humphrey Wembs.
28 *Paradisus*, pp.132–4.
29 CPA, October 1589.
30 Ibid., November 1589.
31 Ibid., December 1589. The College dropped the Dispensatory in 1590 because one of the Fellows responsible for it, Dr Taylior, 'had very frequently been summoned by the Beadle to come to the President and bring with him his notes and those of Dr Smith which he had in his possession, relating to our public Pharmacopoeia, but he refused to come. Moreover he had even replied openly with some insolence that he did not have sufficient free time at his disposal either to consider college affairs or to come to the President.'
32 *Paradisus*, pp.202–12.
33 Naunton, R., *Fragmentia Regalia*, c.1630, in *Travels in England*, Cassells National Library, 1889, pp.132–3.
34 Churchwardens' accounts for St Antholin, MS 1046 1, 1574–1702, Guildhall.

Chapter 8 The Garden Laboratory, pages 103–21

1 Gunther, *Dioscorides*, p.1.
2 Ibid.
3 Stow.
4 Hentzner, P., p.56.
5 Rye, W.B., ed., *England as seen by Foreigners in the Days of Queen Elizabeth and James I*, London, 1865.
6 Ibid.
7 Hyll, T., *The Profytable Arte of Gardyning*. See also Rohde.
8 Ibid.
9 Ibid.
10 From *Anti prognosticon contra inutiles astrologorum preadictiones Nostradami*, Hilli by Fulke (1566); Rohde, p.22.
11 *Paradisus*, pp.63–4.
12 Ibid., p.206.
13 Ibid., p.213.
14 De l'Obel, *Opera Omnia*, p.508. See also Morren, Chapter 5, note 19 above.
15 Hentzner, p.52.
16 Ibid., p.53.

17 Peck, F., Antiquary, *The Complete Statesman*, in *Desiderata Curiosa*, Vol. 1, 1779.

18 Hentzner, p.53.

19 De l'Obel, *Animadversione*. This volume, which de l'Obel printed at his own expense, contains a supplement with many personal references to the people who changed the face of English gardens. The scant surviving details of Lord Zouche's garden are in de l'Obel's references to the plants he had. See p.434 for references to *mala transplanta*: transplanted apples.

20 Ibid.

21 Woodward, p.x.

22 Allison, A.F., *John Gerard and the Gunpowder Plot*, Catholic Record Society, Vol. 5, 1959.

23 Woodward, p.221.

24 Ibid., p.222.

25 Ibid., 'The Epistle Dedicatorie', p.3.

26 Gerard, dedication by George Baker.

27 Gerard; Woodward, p.100.

28 Gerard, dedication by George Baker.

29 De l'Obel, M., *Adversaria*, 1605, BL, Sloane MS 2346 f.68, p.1, Line 11. Preface in Latin, trans. R. Pulteney, *Sketches of the Progress of Botany in England*, London 1790, p.120.

30 *Paradisus*, p.392.

31 Ibid., p.213.

32 Ibid., p.437.

33 Stow.

34 For a history of Elmfield see Imray, J., *History of Mercers' Company, Covent Garden*, unpublished MS. I am indebted to the Mercers' Company, London, for making it available.

35 Gillow, J., *Notes on the Burghley Map of Lancashire*, Catholic Record Society, 1907, p.17.

Chapter 9 The World in a Garden, pages 122–43

1   *Paradisus*, p.1.

2   Ibid., p.7.

3   Ibid., p.8.

4   Ibid., p.2.

5   Grocers' wardens' accounts, October 1598, MS 11571/7, Guildhall. This green oasis in the centre of the city had always been important to the Grocers. Wardens who were candidates to be master for the year walked there while the choice was considered. The garland of bay that was placed on the head of the victor was cut from the tree in this garden before the other wardens accompanied him home in triumph. There had been a lead cistern under a shady vine and a great old bench where grocers could sit and watch games of bowls on the close-clipped lawn. But in 1597 the company decided they needed something more showy. The garden was remade to create 'a bowling alley and a new room at the end', with long beds for flowers and wide paths.

6   See Van Albroeck, M., trans. W.L. Rham, *Outline of Flemish Husbandry*, 1841, and Swarbrick, J., ed. A. Crosby, *Lancashire Local Studies*, 1993, Carnegie Pub. Ltd., pp.88–9.

6a *Paradisus*, p.2.

7   *Paradisus*, p.100.

8   Ibid., pp.39–42.

9   Ibid., p.6.

10 Ibid.

11 Ibid.

12 *Theatrum*, p.124.

13 St Martin's Ludgate Parish Register; St Bride's Parish Register, September 1603; Guildhall.

14 Sackville-West, p.21; Chapter 3, note 11 above.

15 Lawson-Dick, pp.253–60.

16 James I Chancery Patent Rolls, PRO C66/1656.

17 Woodward, Introduction, pp.xii–xiii, taken from R. Benjamin Daydon Jackson, *Life of Gerard*, private printing, 1876. The discussions with the Physicians were not raised again after July 1587, when negotiations with a Dr Sackford seem to have foundered. See CPA, College of Physicians, for that date. Vespasien Robin was appointed Herbarist to Henry IV in 1597.

18 Ibid.

19 Lawson-Dick, p.263.

20 *Paradisus*, p.596.

21 Nicholas Geffe translated an account of silk-worm cultivation from French. *The Perfect use of silke wormes and their benefit* by Olivier de Serres was published in London in 1607 and dedicated to the king. For a good discussion of the attempt to start the industry in England see Potter, J., *Strange Blooms*, Atlantic Books, 2006, p.211.

22 De l'Obel, M., Sloane MS 2346 fol.68, BL.

23 De L'Obel, M., *Animadversione*, pp.508–9. See also *Paradisus*, p.323. De l'Obel's 'Bellis Spinosa' becomes 'Globularia luteamontana' (*sp. Trollius*). See also p.400. John describes de l'Obel's 'Lauri Alexandrina' as 'The Rose Bay', grown from a seed sent by his friend Dr John Moore, but the picture makes clear that it was *Nerium oleander*.

24 Lewis Lamere was born in Flanders and was granted a 'patent of denization' on 17 August 1599. He had been in London for some time, and learned part of his trade as apprentice to the grocer Henry Ockerman from 1576. Lamere was married to Matthias de l'Obel's daughter Mary, and had helped him revise the *Adversaria* for publication in 1605. His partner, John Wolfgang Rumler, was already part of the royal court, but still not fully established in London when the agreement with Clavie was made. He secured an early appointment as Queen Anne's apothecary to supply her with 'sweet powders, waters and perfumes', on 26 November 1604. She was said to have once consulted his father, a famous apothecary in Augsburg. Rumler had married Anne, another of de l'Obel's daughters, who was born in Middelburg in Zetland. See Matthews, L., *The Royal Apothecaries*, Wellcome Historical Pub., 1967, pp.87ff.

25 *Paradisus*, p.401. The tree was *Prunus laurocerasus*.

26 Ibid., pp.123, 124.

27 Hentzner, p.42, described seeing 'one of these

theatres which are all built of wood [where] English actors represent almost every day tragedies and comedies and to very numerous audiences; these are concluded with excellent music, variety of dances, and the excessive applause of those that are present'.

28 *Paradisus*, p.104.

29 Ibid., p.63.

30 See Glanville, P., *London in Maps*, The Connoisseur, 1971, p.90.

31 Lawson-Dick, pp.138–9.

32 Taylor, J., *A new Discovery by Sea, with a Wherry from London to Salisbury*, London 1623, in Hindley, C., *Miscellanea Antiqua Anglicana*, London 1873. Note the early evidence of a maze in this description of Gilbert's garden at Wilton: 'Moreover, he hath made his walks most rarely round and spaceous, one walk without another (as the rinds of an onion are greatest without and less towards the centre), and withal the hedges betwixt each walk are so thickly set one cannot see through from one walk who walks in the other; that, in conclusion, the work seems endless, and I think that in England it is not to be followed, or in haste will be followed.' See also Tipping, H. A., *Gardens Old and New, the Country House and its Garden Environments*, Country Life, n.d., London, i, pp.41–2; Strong, p.122.

33 Gilbert, W., *De Magnete*, London 1600. The doctor discovered that the magnetic quality thought peculiar to amber when it was rubbed could be generated from nearly every other natural substance. Dr Gilbert also happened to be one of the six doctors who had been entrusted by the College of Physicians with creating the new Pharmacopoeia, sharing 'the task of examining all the work so that the final form in which it appeared to the public would be more complete and more elegant'. This task evidently occupied him less than his experiments with magnetism.

34 Thomson, p.61.

35 The Worshipful Company of Gardeners' royal charter, 1607. See Gardeners' records, Guildhall.

36 Thomson.

37 Ibid. At the beginning of August, John Chamberlain wrote: 'We are busied with new works which have succeeded so well that we have a fine fountain with a pool in the lower garden where the fort was, and a running stream (from the river) in the upper garden, between the knots and ranks of trees in the broad walk or alley, wherein we hope to have plenty of trouts fed by hand: the works with industry and cost are brought almost to perfection, and when they are well and come to the highest, I would there might be an end, for else there is no end of new inventions, for hither came yesterday Signor Fabritio [Henry Wotton] and as he is ignorant in nothing, so he takes upon him many new devices, and would fain be a director where there is no need of his help.'

38 Wotton, H., *Elements of Architecture*, 1624, Somers collection of tracts, ed. W. Scott, London 1810, Vol. 3, p.267.

39 Ibid.

40 *Paradisus*, p.8.

41 Ibid.

42 Ibid., p.67.

43 Ibid., p.434.

44 Ibid., p.339.

45 Ibid., p.88.

46 Ibid., p.126.

47 Ibid., p.365. It was called 'Mirabilia Peruviana' (*Mirabilis jalapa*).

48 *Theatrum*, p.1064.

49 *Paradisus*, pp.339–40. The satin flower was *Hedysarum coronarium*, which John called a 'red flowred Fitchling', or 'Hedysarum clypeatum'.

50 Ibid., p.96. See also CPA, 1605: 'Dr Flud of Oxford examined November 8 1605: "in both galenical and spagyrical medicines, he was not satisfactory enough in either ... advised to apply himself more diligently to his studies".' On 7 February 1605 he was examined again and 'he did not fully satisfy the inquiries, yet he was considered be not uneducated: so he was given permission to practise medicine'; 2 May 1606, 'A report was brought to the college that Dr Fludd had boasted much about himself and his chemical medicines and looked down with contempt on galenical medicines.' He denied it and 'was sent away with a warning to think and speak modestly about himself.'

51 Gerard, J., A Herball, ed. Johnson, T., p.766.

52 See Tradescant's diary of his visit to Russia in 1618. The journal was discovered in the Bodleian, Oxford, in 1814, and is reproduced in full in Leith-Ross, p.26.

Chapter 10 'The Art and Mystery of Apothecaries', pages 144–63

1 See Robert Parkinson, Chester Wills, 1600–1620.

2 An Act of 1606 made it compulsory for children to be christened at an Anglican church within a month of their birth. Although this is what John had done with his own children, even before the Act, the new law was widely flouted by ardent Catholics.

3 Witch hunters were paid £1 each, and thus in some county courts there were more cases of witchcraft than any other crime. This was true of Essex, where Calvinism was particularly strong. The last witch was hanged in 1727.

4 From the Assizes accounts of Lancashire, reprinted in Hird, F., *Lancashire Stories*, T.C. & E.C. Jack, London, 1912. Grace Sowerbutts said that she had been going 'toward Salmesbury bote [the boat on the Ribble that plied the route to the market town] to meet her mother coming from Preston, [when] she saw ... Jennet Bierley [one of the accused] who met [her] at a place called the Two Brigges, first in her own shape and afterwards in the likeness of a black Dog,

with two legges ... and the said Dog spake, and persuaded the Examinate to drown herself there, saying it was a fair and easie death'. Jane Southworth, Grace said, had several times come to her father's house and carried her off, leaving her robbed of her speech and senses. She was one of the three women who had been with Grace by the river 'every Thursday and Sunday at night by the space of a fortnight, and at the waterside there came unto them four black things, going upright yet not like men in the face' that had carried them across to a place where they 'found something ... which they did eat.... And after they had eaten, the said three women and (witness) [Grace] danced every one of them.'

5 The separatists' leader was Anthony Soda, who was now a warden and so a senior member of the Grocers' Company, but still committed to the case for reform, after failing to bring about change within the company for twenty years.

6 Grocers' Orders 29 June 1611, MS 8286, Guildhall.

7 Ibid.

8 Ibid.

9 These medicines are mentioned in the *Charter Act and Ordinance Book*, MS 8251, Society of Apothecaries, London. The leading English exponent of them, Dr Mouffet, died in 1601, but the apothecary he worked with, Daniel Darnelly, kept his notes and handed them eventually to a newcomer, Dr Theodore de Mayerne, who was eager to take this work forward.

10 Spedding, Vol. 1, p.38. Francis's mother was a sister of the 'learned lady' Catherine Killigrew, who sent the beans she found in Cornwall to Matthias de l'Obel. Her other sister, Mildred, had been William Cecil's second wife.

11 Ibid., October 1584. Francis Bacon was twenty-five and MP for Melcombe in Dorset. A majority of the Commons was in direct opposition to the queen regarding her government of the Church and the authority of the bishops.

12 Nichols, *Progresses*, 23 July 1603.

13 *The Advancement of Learning*, in Bacon, *Essays*. Details of Francis Bacon's medical treatment appear in the accounts of Thomas Whitgift, the Cambridge tutor he shared with George Clifford. See Maitland, S. R., 'Archbishop Whitgift's College Pupils', *British Magazine and Monthly Register of Religious and Ecclesiastical Information*, Vol. 33, 1848, p.444, and Spence, *The Privateering Earl*. For himself Sir Francis employed only the best. His own household physician was Dr William Harvey, whose scientific experiments were leading him to a novel theory that the blood circulated through every part of the body by means of a system of valves in the veins.

13a CPA 10 January 1594.

14 'The usual and splendid feast was given by Dr Poe to entertain the fellows and their wives', CPA, June 1616. See also 10 January 1594; ibid., 11 January 1598; ibid., 11 December 1606.

15 'Cosmetics prescribed by me for the Queens of Great Britain, Ann & Henrietta Maria, 1612–1643', College of Physicians, London, MS 444.

16 CPA, 5 July 1616.

17 Accounts of Gray's Inn for 1597, 1598 and 1600. See Taylor, pp.37ff.

18 Lawson-Dick, p.9.

19 2 April 1614, MS 8251, Fol. 68a. Society of Apothecaries, London.

20 Ibid.

21 Ibid.

22 Ibid.

23 CPA, 23 May and 3 June 1614.

24 Grocers' Orders, 29 June 1611. MS 8286, Guildhall.

25 Ibid.

26 Grocers' Court Minutes, 22 June 1614, Guildhall. A mark was 13 shillings and 4 pence, so this was about £333 sterling.

27 MS 8256, Society of Apothecaries, London. This document, which may be a later copy, is called 'The Charter granted to the Apothecaries of London' and dated at the beginning, confusingly, 30 May 1614, 13 Jac. I. The thirteenth year of James' reign was 1615, bearing in mind that the year began on 25 March, and this seems a more likely date given the sequence of petitions from the City and the Grocers (MS 8251, fol. 84) which were presented on 27 January 1614, and replied to three months later on 24 April 1615. However, the Apothecaries' charter was not witnessed and completed until 6 December in the fifteenth year of James' reign, or 1617. This and the text of it make it likely that there were further objections after it was first made public.

28 Ibid.

29 Thomson, p.113, no.177.

30 Details of the trial in Abbot, G., *The Case of Impotency*, London 1715.

31 Thomson, p.114, no.188, 23 June 1613.

32 Ibid., p.116, no.182.

33 Ibid., p.115, 14 October 1613.

34 Ibid.

35 Ibid., p.135, no.236.

36 SP 14, PRO, Dom. 1615, vol. LXX XIII. Examination by Edward Ryder.

37 Thomson, p.118, no.238, 6 April 1616.

38 Schomburgk.

Chapter 11 A New Family, pages 164–81

1 See Chapter 10, note 24 above.

2 The unpublished notes and papers of Matthias de l'Obel that John acquired found their way eventually into the library at Magdalen College, Oxford. See Chapter 5, note 23 above.

3 Smith, J., *Generall Historie of Virginia*, London 1624.

4 Register of Burials 1595–1653, Parish of St Bride's, TS 65471/2/3x, Guildhall: '1617 April 29th Mary, w. to (blank) Parkinson'. Alys, the widow of Thomas Hutchins, lived in the area

until 10 March 1608. Samuel Hutchins lived there – his son, Nicholas, died in May 1625, and Jane Hutchins, who was 'a widdowe', lived there until her death in January 1626. The names Hutchins and Hutchens were generally interchangeable at this date.

5   See Calendar of Patent Rolls and Calendar of State Papers, 1604–25, PRO, and Matthews, Chapter 5, pp.83–97.

6   *List of Freemen and Freemen Admissions*, Gardeners' Records, MS 21128, Guildhall.

7   In 1585 Helena Ruckher was appointed court apothecary in Württemberg. She was succeeded by another woman, Anna Blos. See introduction to Matthews, and *Grundriss der Geschichte der Deutschen Pharmazie*, Adheng & Urdang, Berlin 1935, pp.45–7.

8   CPA, College of Physicians, 3 January 1605.

9   English Short Title Catalogue 53479, 'Given at Theobalds the 10th day of November in the seventeenth year of our reign', 1619, Society of Antiquaries Library, London. See also SP 17/C/5: *A proclamation concerning the viewing and distinguishing of tobacco in England and Ireland*, PRO, for reference to the 'suppression of the planting'.

10 Leith-Ross, p.72, gives details of Tradescant's investment. For conduct of the Virginia company see HMC, 8th Report, Appendix, Part II, 1881, p.41, PRO.

11 Spence, *The Privateering Earl*, p.178.

12 Middleton, T., *The Pageant of Nations*, 1617. Reproduced in Appendix of Heath, B., *Some Account of the Grocers' Company*, London, 1869. Twenty-eight pensioners of the company were dressed in azure-coloured gowns, 'with sleves of crimson mechados', while the beadles of the four royal hospitals wore blue coats with long caps and ribbons. Eight drummers and four fifes were paid to 'furnish themselves with black hats, white doublets, black hose and white stockings, and scarfs of the company's colours' and make as much noise as they could in the streets.

13 Record kept by Anne Clifford. See Sackville-West, Appendix: *A Catalogue of the Household and family of the Right honourable Richard, Earl of Dorset in the year of our lord 1613; and so continued until the year 1624, at Knole, in Kent.*

14 Register of Burials in the parish of St Bride's, 19 December 1610, Guildhall.

15 *Paradisus*, p.365.

16 Leith-Ross, p.37: Hatfield House accounts.

17 *Paradisus*, p.584.

18 *Theatrum*, p.9.

19 Ordinance Book, MS 8251, Society of Apothecaries, London. See also MS 8202. 'The Oath of Allegiance and Supremacie' required John Parkinson to swear that the king was 'the supreme governor' of all his realms 'as well in all spirituall, or ecclesiasticall things or Causes; as in temporall'.

20 MS 8202, Fol. 71, Court Minutes Book 1617–1651, Society of Apothecaries, London. On John's departure from the livery of the Apothecaries in 1621, this money was repaid.

21 MS 8251, Society of Apothecaries, London.

22 CPA, 13 September 1616.

23 CPA, 3 June 1617.

24 CPA, 20 February 1617.

25 MS 8251, Society of Apothecaries, London.

26 CPA, 25 September 1618.

27 Underwood, pp.289–90. This statement was made in the course of the case in the Star Chamber between the Apothecaries and the Physicians in 1634, see Chapter 16 of this book. The original records have been lost, except for some lawyer's notes in Latin, MS 8286, Guildhall.

28 *The Life of Sir Walter Raleigh* by William Oldys, London, 1740, pp.517ff.

29 *Theatrum*, p.712.

30 Copied into the Apothecaries' Ordinance book, MS 8251, Fol. 81, Society of Apothecaries, London.

31 MS 8202, 30 August 1621, Society of Apothecaries, London.

32 Ibid., 28 January 1621.

33 Ibid.

34 Copied into the Apothecaries' Ordinance book, MS 8251, Fol. 81, Society of Apothecaries, London.

35 Lawson-Dick, p.8.

36 Jacques, Chapter 4, p.14; Spedding.

37 Lawson-Dick, p.11.

Chapter 12 'Pride of London', pages 182–93

1   This is the inference I have drawn from the comments of John Morris to Johannes de Laet in a letter, June 1646, see Chapter 18, notes 9 and 34 below. The conclusion that the 'younger' he refers to is John Parkinson's son is reinforced by circumstantial evidence: John's own Catholicism, the absence of Richard Parkinson in any trade or parish records of the day, and John's lamentation of the defects of his 'natural' issue in his note 'To the reader' in the *Theatrum*. See Chapter 17, note 16 below.

2   *List of Freemen and Freedom Admissions*, Records of the Gardeners' Company 1618–58, MS 21128, Guildhall, e.g. 'Robert Atkyns, a papist, not admitted, 1618'.

3   *Paradisus*, titles and dedications.

4   Lawson-Dick, p.139. Lister was formally appointed to the Court 20 May 1623. Calendar of Patent Rolls 1–19 James, Vol. 1, 128, List and Index Society, and PRO, E 403/2542.

5   Goodman, G., Bishop of Gloucester, *The Court of King James I*, ed. J. Brewer, 1839.

6   *Book of Accompts containing the Receipts and Disbursements on behalf of the Duke of Buckingham* by Sir Sackville Crowe, quoted by Allen, M., *The Tradescants*, Michael Joseph, 1964, p.109: 'Paid to John Tradescant by his

L'ship's order for his journey into the Lowe Countries, for his charges, and Trees bought for his L'ship there, etc, £124 14. 0d'.

7 Tradescant J., *A Viag of Ambusad*, in Leith-Ross, pp.53ff., and Bodleian Library, Oxford.

8 Ibid.

9 Ibid.

10 Ibid

11 Ibid.

12 *Paradisus*, p.346. John was not very impressed with Tradescant's Russian rose. He later called it the 'wild bryer of Muscovia', mentioning its 'deepe incarnate colour' but not his friend Tradescant when describing it. He did record a Muscovy geranium, found 'in Muscovy' and 'brought to us by Mr John Tradescant', 'about two foote high with sundry tufts of large purplish blew flowers tending to red'. After both Johns were dead, even this was agreed to be the same as the British native *Geranium pratense*. See *Theatrum*, pp.1027 and 706 respectively.

13 *Theatrum*, p.1611.

14 Sir Robert Mansell commanded a mission to give the 'Grand Signior' a letter from the king, and demand the surrender of captured ships and the release of English captives. These negotiations yielded nothing, and the secondary strategy of setting fire to the pirate ships in harbour proved a failure also. See Leith-Ross, pp.69ff.

15 *Paradisus*, pp.430, 190, 512.

16 Accounts, 1626–, Society of Apothecaries, London.

17 This note was discovered by R.W.T. Gunther amongst the Goodyer papers in Magdalen College. The letter was never sent, since the paper has been turned over and used again. It cannot be dated precisely but it is unlikely to have been written earlier than 1620. Gunther speculates, *Early British Botanists*, p.266, that John might have copied Francis Bacon's notes on evergreens, from his *Naturall Historie*. This is possible, but although Bacon conducted many practical experiments for the book himself, John was the greater expert in this field and Bacon is just as likely to have consulted him.

18 *Paradisus*, dedication.

19 Goodman, G., Bishop of Gloucester, *The Court of King James I*, ed. J. Brewer, 1839.

20 St Martin's-in-the-Fields Parish accounts giving a list of householders in the parish and their annual rate, 1623, F350; 1626, F 3354; 1630, F 356. Westminster Archive, London.

21 *Paradisus*, p.372, 'Amaranthus Carnea Spica'. This is different from the modern variety, *Amaranthus tricolor*, which has scarlet, green and yellow leaves, which John's contemporaries also grew and which he describes.

22 *Theatrum*, pp.612–13. The seed was *Scrophularia sambucifolio*. Some of these figworts are grown as garden plants today for their evergreen or semi-evergreen foliage.

23 CPA, December 1617–July 1618, College of Physicians. Dr Moore was magnanimous in defeat. He wrote to Dr Atkins urging him to accept his present of £20: 'I brought you not my mony upon conditions'. The college voted in favour of taking the money, by 'ten beans and twelve peas'. In contrast Dr Dee was allowed to practise: now old and poverty-stricken, he was summoned for practising without a licence. He turned to medicine to make a living after his lifetime study of alchemy failed to yield results, and he defied the college. He pointed out that their statutes were widely flouted, naming two Catholic doctors who practised in spite of being refused a licence by the Bishop of London because of their religion. In reality, he said, medicine in the capital was practised by 'Drs Moore and Turner [Catholics] and the apothecaries who were all condemned. But because he [Dee] was burdened by a family he was now sent away more mercifully and he was informed that unless he came back to us and made peace, he would be indicted'. In the end he said he practised medicine 'by the royal prerogative'. And 'thus he went away'.

24 St Martins-in-the-Fields Parish accounts. In 1626 John Parkinson and John Moore paid 20s. together in rates collected by the churchwardens.

25 *Paradisus*, pp.593–4.

26 Alvise Valaresso, see Ashton, p.260.

27 King James in December 1624, quoted by Bowle, J., *Charles the First*, Weidenfeld & Nicolson, 1975, p.84.

28 See Nichols.

29 Ellis, Vol. III, p.180.

30 Harleian MS 1576, f.642, BL.

31 Ashton, p.242, and Henrietta Maria's Household 1629: National Archives/ PRO, LR5/63/580.

32 The Venetian Ambassador, Zuane Pesaro, to the Doge and Senate. Cal. SP Venetian, Vol. 19, p.87.

33 Sandys, George, *A Relation of a Journey begun Anno Dom. 1610*, London, 1615, p.272, describes the garden of the Cardinal of Florence, Ferdinando de Medici: 'In the garden, a cage wherein are all kinds of birds making sweet harmony, divers rare water-works, and plentifully planted with cypress trees, yielding a savour so admirable sweet, as the body therewith may be ravished.... [He] caused a hill to be made, and one hundred and fifty stairs to go up; on the top is built an excellent pleasant summer house.... The hill is overgrown from the bottom to the top with cypress trees, which is as pleasant a prospect as a man can imagine. The garden is adorned with such and so many artificial and rare waterworks, plants and statues, as would drive a man to admire...'. For a discussion of the influence of Italian gardens on English nobles, see Strong.

Chapter 13 'This Speaking Garden', pages 194–213

1 *Paradisus*, dedication, trans. from Latin.
2 Ibid., 'Epistle to the Reader', 1st edn, 1629.
3 Ibid.
4 Ibid.
5 John had witnessed this very recently when Dr William Harvey published his explanation of how blood moves in the body. See Lawson-Dick, p.131.
6 *Paradisus*, 'Epistle to the Reader'.
7 See note 2 above.
8 Madam Giramir, Jeffery the dwarf's nurse, was paid £100 a year. See *Household of Henrietta Maria: a copy of the establishment, 1629*, LR5/63/580, PRO.
9 *Paradisus*, dedication, trans. from Latin.
10 See Gerard, p.282, Lib. 3, Chapter 188, and Raven, p.130, ref. William Turner's herbal of 1568.
11 *Paradisus*, p.240.
12 Ibid., dedication, trans. from Latin.
13 Ibid., Epistle to the Reader.
14 Ibid., Chapter 1, p.1.
15 Ibid., p.14.
16 Ibid., pp.27, 74, 78.
17 Ibid., p.103.
18 Ibid., p.371. John Parkinson called this plant *Amaranthus coccinus*, in reference to its cochineal colour. It was an import from the West Indies.
19 Ibid., pp.338ff (moon trefoil: *Medicago arborea*).
20 Ibid., p.518.
21 Ibid., p.526.
22 Ibid., p.525.
23 Ibid., p.379.
24 Ibid., pp.526–8.
25 Ibid.
26 De Beer, Vol. 1.
27 *Paradisus*, p.564.
28 Ibid., p.586.
29 Ibid.
30 See *Journal of Nicholas Assheton of Downham*, ed. Raines, F. R., Chetam Society, Manchester, 1848, p.122. Assheton was a young gentleman who grew up in the country of John's origin. He even borrowed money from John's cousin, Christopher Parkinson, who was steward of Bowland Forest, as well as from the local vicar, Mr Ormerod, to whom he owed a 'desperate' amount of money by 1631. Assheton spent his days drinking, hunting, gardening and going to church. He particularly enjoyed otter hunting. 2 May 1617: 'Hunting the otter; killed one, taken another, quick at Salley.' The reference to 'drinking the house dry' actually comes from a journal written a hundred years later by Thomas Tyldesley of the local Myerscough Lodge, showing not much had changed. 28 August 1713: 'Went an otter hunting – killed an otter near New Mill ... we eatte the whole otter.... We drank the house dry.' On 14 February 1618, Nicholas Assheton was grafting fruit 'which came from Holker' (the house in the parish of Cartmel that belonged to his cousin Elizabeth Assheton and her husband George Preston).
31 *Paradisus*, p.537.
32 Ibid., p.547.
33 Ibid., p.566.
34 Ibid., p.568.
35 Ibid., p.571.
36 Ibid., pp.587–8.
37 Ibid., p.590.
38 Ibid., p.592.
39 Ibid., p.593.
40 Ibid., p.152.
41 Ibid., pp.393–4.

Chapter 14 'Ingeniose Men', pages 214–30

1 SP Dom. 1660–1, p.290, PRO. The official record of this is in the form of a petition from Stephen Chase's son John to Charles II after the Restoration. John Chase asked for an extension of the lease on the land in St James's Fields at 20s. a year, 'granted by the late King to John Parkinson, his herbalist, as a garden for plants, towards the enclosing of which and erecting a house there, the petitioner's father advanced £100 on condition of joining John Parkinson in the grant'.
2 Overseers of the Parish Rate Books, St Martin's-in-the-Fields: 1623, 1625, 1629, 1632, in Westminster Archive, London, and Bedford Estate Rental Returns, 1625, in London Metropolitan Archives, London.
3 SP Dom. 1630. See also Imray, J., *History of the Mercers' Company, Covent Garden*, Mercers' Company, London.
4 John Tradescant's will, January 1637. PCC, Lee, 63, quoted in full in Leith-Ross, p.104.
5 1651 Parliamentary Survey of 'a close called Elm Close alias Long Acre', Mercers' Company, London. John's garden could not have been on the south side of Long Acre, because the Bedford Estate owned this land, and he does not appear in the Bedford Estate rent returns with a Long Acre address. See Bedford Estate rent books, London Metropolitan Archives.
6 Next door to the garden plot were 'five large tenements' in 1651, each of two storeys with a cellar below and a garret above, 36 ft north/south in breadth and 86 ft east/west along Long Acre. On the other side was an inn called the 'Eight Legged Lamb' with a small garden and a stable behind. See Parliamentary Survey, note 5 above.
7 John Evelyn left an account of a French naturalist of this period, René Morin, who lived in a similar kind of hermitage in Paris: 'A person who from an ordinary Gardner, is arriv'd to be one of the most skillfull and Curious persons of France for his rare collection of Shells, Flowers and Insects: His Garden is of an exact Oval figure planted with Cypresse, cutt flat and set even as a Wall could have formed it: the Tulips, Anemonies and Ranunculus's, Crocus etc.,

being of the most exquisite; were held for the rarest in the World, which constantly drew all the Virtuosi of that kind to his house during the season; even Persons of the most illustrious quality: He lived in a kind of hermitage at one side of his Garden where his Collection ... is greatly esteemed'. De Beer, Vol. II, pp.132–3 (April 1644).

8   Overseer's accounts, St Martin's-in-the-Fields, 1630. Westminster Archive, London.
9   De Mayerne's notebooks at the College of Physicians, MS 444, pp.317–60. See also Nance, B., *Turquet de Mayerne as Baroque Physician. The Art of Medical Portraiture*, Wellcome Series, 2001. Sir Theodore believed this ravaging disease could and should be managed. He shared the Calvinist belief that it was largely a matter of fate whether or not a person succumbed, but 'when naturall and ordinarie causes do conspire to the destruction of mankind ... the physitians who are the assistants and ministers of nature must put themseves in a posture and with courage, learninge and presence oppose this devouring Monster, which cannot bee, but by an exceeding exact order and Politique government for the prevention of it, and by generous and powerfull remeadyes to strangle it in the birth and extinguish it'.
10 *Theatrum*, pp.124, 54.
11 Ibid., pp.155–9.
12 Ibid.
13 Ibid.
14 Ibid.
15 Ibid.
16 Ibid.
17 Ibid.
18 *Paradisus*, dedication by Sir Theodore de Mayerne, trans. from Latin.
19 MS 444, pp.59ff., Royal College of Physicians: *Il me souviens qu'un jour voulant faire le vitriol de mars avec l'esprit acide du souffre dans un grand matras, ma matière s'inflamma, exhala une fumée très épaiise et for puant qui rencontrant la chandelle fort éloignée prit fire donna un coup comme de canon par le vol de mon vaisseau sans le romper et me bailla un furieux camoufflet pire que ceux des pages qui sont au Louvre....*
20 Ibid.: *Il s'en fait de même dans nos corps, ou les fièvres continues se forment, quand le soulfre de la masse du sang allumé par la rencontre de quelque sel éxuberant fournit de la matière à cette flame qui ne cesse pas juisque à tant que les soulfre soit ou consumé ou estinct par le retouchement de l'activité des sels, ou que la chaleur naturelle estant estinguée elle mesme par une plus grande conne nature, la mort du sujet ne s'ensuira.*
21 *Puisque la rougeur du visage, qui fait tort à votre beauté, et vous travaille l'esprit, venent du dedans, spécialement du foye, et que l'estomac y prend sa part ... vous faites très bien d'y pour-*

voir estant jeune pourveu que vous ayez la patience de faire ce qu'il faut.... MS 444, pp.52 ff, Royal College of Physicians. Many of de Mayerne's patients suffered from 'melancholia', like Lady Carteret for whom he sent remedies for 'melancholia and hysteria' to the Isle of Wight. This condition required purging and a long subsequent course of medicines that included herbal pills, 'treakle' and a course of tablets made from ground minerals. Sadly, he doesn't record the outcome.
22 SP, Dom. xvi, 57, 8 October 1651, 470–1, and Horace, *Ars Poetica*, I: 139, from a letter to Viscount Conway. See also Nicholson, M., *The Conway Letters*, Oxford University Press, 1930, introduction, p.xiii.
23 The cook-book was *Archmagirus Anglo-Gallicus, or Excellent and Approved Receipts and Experiments in Cookery*. For comments on Sir Theodore's family see Parson, D., ed., *The Diary of Sir Henry Slingsby*, Longman, 1836, p.70. Also St Martin's-in-the-Fields, Overseer's accounts, 1621 and 1622, Westminster Archive, London.
24 Attributed to one of Fludd's contemporary physicians, Aiken. See Munk, R., *Roll of the Royal College of Physicians*, Vol. I, p.151.
25 See *Labyrinthum* in Arber, p.254.
26 '*The Mosaicall Philosophy grounded upon the Essential Truth or Eternal Sapience*, written first in Latin and afterwards thus rendred into English, By Robert Fludd esq. and Doctor of Physick', London, 1659, pp.7, 12.
27 Arber, p.254: 'All things by immortal power, Near or far, Hiddenly, To each other linked are, That thou canst not stir a flower, Without troubling of a star'.
28 *Theatrum*, dedication by Simon Baskervill, trans. from Latin.
29 Arber, p.254.
30 Lawson-Dick, p.131.
31 *Theatrum*, pp.1414–15.
32 See Leith-Ross, Chapter 7, and Allen, Chapter 16. John Tradescant's copy of the *Paradisus* is in the Bodleian Library, Oxford.
33 Thomas Johnson's shop was on Snow Hill in the parish of St Sepulchre's.
34 *De Plantiis Absinthii*, Montbéliard, 1593. Notes on *Stachys arvensis* from writing of Aurelius, reproduced in Grieve, M., and Leyel, C., ed., *A Modern Herbal*, Jonathan Cape, 1931. Reprint of *Iter Plantarum*, Hunt Botanical Library, 1972.
35 Record in Goodyer MSS, Magdalen College, Oxford. See also Gunther, *Early British Botanists*, p.56.
36 Ibid. On 8 November 1631 Goodyer notes 'wyne with Johnson 6d'.

Chapter 15 'Disastrous Times', pages 231–242
1   Johnson, *Gerard's Herbal*, p.1515.
2   *Theatrum*, p.1496.
3   The rights passed through the printer John Norton's family to his cousin, Bonham, who

assigned them in 1632 to Adam Islip, Joice Norton and a Mr Whitaker.

4   *Theatrum*, p.1064.
5   Woodward, p.172.
6   Ibid.
7   Details from the Stationers' Company Archives, Stationers' Company, London.
8   Woodward, p.100. *Rumex alpinus* is a species of dock that was originally cultivated for use in medicine and has since naturalized. Dock and cultivated rhubarb (*rheum*) were so closely associated by common name and medical use that John classified them together in his *Theatrum*, even though they are different species.
9   Woodward, p.282 and notes, p.299.
10 *Theatrum*, p.1306 and 'Epistle To the Reader'.
11 Woodward, p.234.
12 CPA, College of Physicians, 4 July 1633 to 23 March 1634.
13 Society of Apothecaries, MS 8251, fol. 68, 2 April 1614. Copy of *The Humble Petition of the Apothecaryes of this the Citty of London*, replying to the Physicians.
14 CPA, College of Physicians, 9 July 1633.
15 Ibid.
16 Ibid., 'two of which apothecaryes ... he excepted against and caused them to goe downe upon the peril of calling for the Constable, terming those men his enemyes'.
17 Ibid., 23 June 1635.
18 Ibid., 23 March 1634.
19 MS 8286, Guildhall. The record of the proceedings is reported in lawyers' notes of the case in Latin. See also Underwood, pp.289–90.
20 MS 8230, Society of Apothecaries, London. No date given for this list.
21 Accounts, 1626–, Society of Apothecaries, London.

Chapter 16 'Golden rains', pages 243–54

1   *Theatrum*, dedication by Simon Baskervill, trans. from Latin.
2   Hayward, J., ed., *John Donne, Complete Poetry and Selected Prose*, Nonesuch Press, 1945. Devotions IX, p.521.
3   Letter from Rubens to the Count-Duke of Olivares, dated London, 22 July 1629, and his letter to Pieresc, London, 9 August 1629. See Magurn, R., trans. & ed., *The Letters of Peter Paul Rubens*, Harvard University Press, 1955, pp.314, 322.
4   PRO, LC3/31, 7 October 1626, the records of the King's Establishment from 1626 onwards. As specified in this document, all 'his Majesty's servants' had 'privilege of not being subject to arrest without the authority of the Lord Chamberlain, never to be charged for anything except in Court, not called to Assizes or Sessions, Inquests or Jury service, not charged towards any furnishing of ships or setting forth of soldiers, keeping of watch and ward contributions, not to be chosen in any office, either of constable, churchwarden or scavenger'.

5   Ibid.
6   The last precise records of the shop relate to his apprentice William Orly in 1626. No individual records of shops were kept in the company accounts after that time. Thereafter, 'shop money' which each shopkeeper paid the society was lumped together in the accounts. See MS 8202, Accounts 1626–, Society of Apothecaries, London.
7   *Theatrum*, dedication by Simon Baskervill, trans. from Latin.
8   Exchequer Bills: E112/203/33, PRO, London. See Matthews, pp.91ff. Lamere's petitions to the king are recorded in the State Papers in June 1632, March and November 1633. CSP Dom. 1633–4, pp.303, 344, 556. His wife's petition is in SP 15/39, Nos. 66/67, PRO, and CSP Dom. Addl., 1580–1625, p.512. Lamere made his will on 20 August 1630, although he did not die for several years afterwards and it was proved on 6 June 1635 (PCC, Wills, Sadler, fol. 63). It was unusual to make a will so long before death unless some dangerous event was expected.
9   Appointed 'Master of the Ordinance' for life in 1634, a position he used *against* the king in the Civil Wars.
10 See Chapter 18, note 34 below, for the text of a letter from James Morris to Johannes de Laet in June 1646 which refers to the young Parkinson working for the Earl of Newport. See Bekkers.
11 See Leith-Ross, Chapter 7, and Allen, Chapter 16. The catalogue of plants in Tradescant's garden, *Plantarum in Horto*, was published in 1634, ESTC S95558.
12 *Paradisus*, p.348. This is the Lady's Slipper orchid (*Cypripedium calceolus*), though John calls it a 'helleborine' for the similarity of its leaves to the 'hellebore' or Lenten rose.
13 *Theatrum*, p.729, lists *Sedum roseum* as 'rose-wort'
14 *Theatrum*, p. 286, it is called *Cochlearia minor rotundifolia* or 'Small Dutch scurviegrasse'.
15 There are several of these lists in John Parkinson's close, careful handwriting among the Goodyer MSS at Magdalen College, Oxford, as well as the account for the repair of his wall at Long Acre, with which the handwriting may be compared. See also Gunther, *Early British Botanists*.
16 *Theatrum*, p.1611.
17 *Theatrum*, p.1611. This horn seems to have been the only one belonging to the king at that time, even though Paul Hentzner had seen one at Windsor in 1598 which he said was 'above eight spans and a half in length, valued at above £10,000' (Hentzner (op. cit., p.53). It is not clear what happened to that. It may have been sold in a bid to raise money by King James, or Paul Hentzner exaggerated its size. Three or four decades later there were thought to be about twenty horns kept in the various capitals of Europe, of which the largest was the one in the church of St-Denis in Paris. This was

'7 foot long at the leaste so that a tall man can hardly reache the toppe thereof with his hand', according to John's account. *Theatrum*, ibid.

18 Parliamentary Survey 1949.

19 From Bodleian Aubrey MS 2, fols. 53–56 and 59: *Plan of Sir John Danvers Garden at Chelsea*, repr. in Charles, A., *A Life of George Herbert*, Cornell University Press, 1977, pp.61–5. For further details of Danvers' garden see also Strong, pp.176–85; Hadfield.

20 Lawson-Dick, pp.81, 12.

21 *Paradisus*, p.1.

22 *Theatrum*, p.588. 'Clownes Woundwort' (*Stachys palustris*), *Paradisus*, p.348.

23 Tenison, T., *Baconiana*, London, 1679, p.57. For the full story of Arundel's collection see Hervey, M., *The Life, Correspondence and Collections of the Earl of Arundel*, Cambridge 1921.

24 Lawson-Dick, pp.144–6.

25 See Wickham Legg, L., ed., *A Relation of a Short Survey of the Western Counties by a Lieutenant of the Military Co. in Norwich in 1635*, Camden Miscellany XVI, 1936, p.67.

26 *Paradisus*. Introductory Chapter 6 describing 'How to plant and replant all the Outlandish flowers'.

Chapter 17 Into the Light at Last, pages 255–69

1 *Theatrum*, pp.1617–18.

2 Ibid., Epistle To the Reader.

3 Bekkers, *Correspondence*, 12 January 1638. See note 5 below.

4 *Theatrum* pp.1132–3.

5 Bekkers, *Correspondence*, see note 3 above: *Quandocumque prodierit Theatrum Botanicum Parkinsonii mittam tibi, ni nolis, exemplar unum. Prodit in folio satis grandi, et charactere eleganti, figurisque plantarum perbellis, quantum tabellis ligneis fieri potest. Progressae sunt operae usque ad pad 1142 deestque fere alterum tantum ut mihi bonus senex nuper, cum eum invisi, monstravit.*

6 *Theatrum*, p.1592.

7 Ibid., p.1646.

8 Ibid., 'Epistle to the Reader'.

9 Ibid., dedication by Sir Theodore de Mayerne, trans. from Latin.

10 LC3/1, 'A list of His Majesty's servants in Ordinary of the Chamber, compiled by the Lord Chamberlain', 1641, PRO.

11 Bekkers, *Correspondence*, 27.2.39 (February 1640): *Non possum omittere, quod mihi certe posthas literas exaratas primum innotuit ex ore ipsius Parkinsonii, eum opera et commendatione Excell. Mayernii Botanographum Regium factum esse, sine tamen stipendio, honore solo muneris contentum esse oportet, tituloque specioso superbire.*

12 *Theatrum*, author's dedication to King Charles I.

13 Ibid.

14 Ibid., Epistle To the Reader.

15 Ibid., p.990.

16 Ibid., Epistle To the Reader.

17 Ibid.

18 Dedications in English from the front of the *Theatrum Plantarum*, London, 1640.

19 The date of these dedications, written in the spring of 1640, suggests that John Tradescant the Elder could have played very little practical part in the Oxford Physic Garden, with which he has been connected, since he had been dead for three years before the dedication began.

20 See Thurley, pp.82ff. for details of the only seventeenth-century building in Whitehall that has survived. Rubens was first asked to paint the ceiling of Inigo Jones' Banqueting House in 1621, although not actually commissioned until 1629. The commission was a gesture from King Charles grieving for his assassinated friend and councillor, Buckingham. After an eight-month visit to England to measure up and create the designs for the site, Rubens finished the paintings in Brussels some time before August 1634, when the ambassador sent the king a message saying he was awaiting payment. In the end the paintings were despatched late in 1635 and paid for in June 1636.

21 *Theatrum*, dedication by Thomas Clayton.

22 Details from the Parish Registers and rate books of St Martin's-in-the-Fields, Mf 3 and Mf 1546–9 respectively at Westminster Archives, London.

Chapter 18 'All things as in a Chaos', pages 270–84

1 SP 16/454/39.

2 Bekkers, *Correspondence*, 23 May 1640.

3 Ibid.

4 Goodyer MSS, Magdalen College, Oxford. See Gunther, *Early British Botanists*, p.199.

5 Letter from George Gerrard, quoted in Thurley, p.93.

6 Vertue's plan of Whitehall, 1670. Guildhall and British Library.

7 *The Grand designs of the Papists in the reign of our late sovereign Charles I*, Harleian Society, Vol. 8. Sir William Boswell's first letter to the archbishop concerning the plot was dated 9 September 1640. The information became public when the archbishop himself had fallen victim to the anti-Catholic hysteria the papers expressed. They were discovered in Laud's office when it was ransacked less than eighteen months later.

8 Ibid.

9 Bekkers, *Correspondence*, 11 June 1646: *exulantque iam iuvene eius artis peritissimo ob papismum, qui hortulanus fuit ante hoc bellum civile Comitis Neoportensis.*

10 See note 7 above.

11 Parish accounts of St Martin's-in-the-Fields, Rate books, F366/MF 1547, Westminster Archives.

12 See Jacques, Chapter 3, note 42. Edward Cooke died in 1644.

13 The second part of *Mercurius Botanicus*, published in 1641 by Thomas Cotes, was a

thirty-seven-page Latin account of Johnson's itinerary through Wales with his friends, followed by an alphabetical catalogue of the plants they found. In the introduction, Johnson stated his intention eventually to produce an illustrated history of plants jointly with John Goodyer. See Ralph, T., ed., *Opuscula Omnia Botanica Thomas Johnson*, London, 1847.

14 See note 11 above.

15 *A Humble Declaration of the Apprentices and other Young Men of the City of London, who were the petitioners for Peace, shewing the Causes of their Petitioning*, 1642, Harleian Society, Vol. 8. On Monday 2 January 1642/3 a 'very considerable number' of 'Apprentices and other young men of the City of London' gathered in Covent Garden piazza.

16 *A deep sigh breath'd though the lodgings At Whitehall deploring the absence of the court, and the miseries of the Pallace*. Anon., London, 1642, BL 100.d.29.

17 Ibid.

18 Ibid.

19 Lawson-Dick, p.129.

20 Ibid.

21 The impact of the London medical community on study in Oxford carried on even after the court was gone. John Wallis was a doctor who remembered how the court scholars had brought the habit of experiment and discussion with them: 'About the year 1648/9 some of our company being removed to Oxford ... our company divided. Those in London continued to meet there as before ... and those of us in Oxford ... continued meetings in Oxford and brought those studies into fashion there; meeting first at Dr Petty's lodgings (in an apothecarie's house), because of the convenience of inspecting Drugs, and the like, as there was occasion.' This group entertained themselves with chemical experiments: '1649–59: the Royal Societie at Oxon and of Chemistrie. They did in Clerk's house an apothecaries in St Marie's Parish exercise themselves in some chemical extracts, which were carried on and much improved before the King's restauration, in so much that several scholars had private elaboratories and did perform those things which the memory of man could not reach.' See Druce, *Foundation of the Oxford Botanic Garden*, Report, Botanic Society, 1923, p.344.

22 See Wood, Anthony A, *Athenae Oxoniensis to which are added the Fasti or Annals of the said University*, 1691, pp.692, 717.

23 See Powell, H., and Wallis-Kew, H., *Thomas Johnson – Botanist and Royalist*, Longman, 1932, p.110; the *Wednesday Mercury*, 28 July 1643, reported: 'It is thought M. Johnson the malignant [royalist] Apothecary (a man formerly of great esteem and eminency in the City of London) shall be made President of the Physicians Garden, a great place and of small

profit considering the estimation, which hee hath lost in this City, by professing himselfe so open an Enemy to the liberty of his Country.' *Wednesday's Mercury or the Speciall Passages Continued*, No.3, E.62.8 Thomason Tracts, BL.

24 Thurley, pp.161, 162.

25 *Record of the Committee for the Advance of Money*, 4 July 1643, PSO 6/1,Vol. 79, p.107, PRO. See also London Metropolitan Archive Rent Roll of the Bedford Estate. Survey, May 1635, 'undertaken by vertue of a commission under his L'ship's hand', E/BER/CG/E/04/01/003, p.3, describes Sir Matthew Lister's Covent Garden establishment.

26 *The Parliamentary History of England*, 12 vols., 1763, BL, Vol. XII, 38.

27 CSP Dom. 1660–61, p.290. It was many years before Anne Chase could complain openly about her parents' fate. After the Restoration, she and her brother, John, petitioned Charles II for the restitution of what had belonged to their father. Anne asked for the reversion of the office of controller of customs in Devonshire for herself and her two sisters, because although both her parents had served Charles II while prince they had suffered imprisonment, sequestration and plunder in the war. See also Chapter 14, note 1 above.

28 Commons Journal, iii, p.533: Monday 17 June 1644.

29 See Green, M., ed., *Letters of Queen Henrietta Maria*, 1857, p.167.

30 See Nance, p.15: Chapter 14, note 9 above.

31 See note 16 above.

32 CSP Dom. 1651–2, p.508.

33 See petition from Rumler, Journal of the House of Lords, 18 Car. I, v, 503b and 22 Car. I, viii, 690b. See also Matthews, pp.96, 97.

34 Bekkers, *Correspondence*, 66, fol. 368, p.117, 11 June 1646: *Catalogum istum tuum seminum bis terve iamdudum exscripsi, ut possim eum cum amicis liberius communicare, in eum scilicet finem, ut tibi amicoque tuo quam primum satisfiat. Vereor enim quam plene, Botanicorum enim nuper quam rara seges est, mortuis Johnsonio, Parkinsonio, ... ipseque Tradescantius ab arte fere exulat, adeo haec studia fere negligit, et iam in insulis Canariis mercaturum exerc et. Solus nobis restat opt. Spei iuvenis Ducis Buckingamiae, hortulanus satis peritus, sed literarum omnino rudis.*

35 De Beer.

36 See Thurley; Easton.

37 St Martin's-in-the-Fields Parish Register, Westminster Archives, London.

Epilogue, pages 285–94

1 *Paradisus*, BL Eve b. 49.

2 De Beer.

3 *Culpeper's Complete Herbal*, Wordsworth, 1995, Epistle to the Reader, p.vi.

4 Ibid.

5   Ibid.

6   See Pulteney, p.142. Pulteney dedicated his
    book to Dr Joseph Banks who was by this time
    presiding over the spoils of the greatest century
    of expansion and discovery in British history.

7   Goodyer MSS, Magdalen College, Oxford.

8   See Ainsworth, pp.269ff. This chapter about the
    'Parkinsons of Yorkshire' contains a putative
    family tree of 'Parkinsons of Craven and
    Accrington'. Ainsworth's reference to John
    Parkinson married to Anne Hyde and 'said to be
    Royal Botanist' is wrong. Neither the dates nor
    the parish registers agree with this assertion.

9   De Beer.

10 Matthews, p.114.

11 For details of the beginning of the Chelsea
    Physic Garden see Hunting, P., *History of the
    Society of Apothecaries*, Worshipful Society of
    Apothecaries, 2000.

12 Carl Linnaeus published *Philosophia Botanica*
    in 1751, followed by *Species Plantarum* in 1753.

13 Ray to John Aubrey from Falbourn, 3 March
    1677: Bodleian MS Aubrey 13 in Gunther,
    R.W.T., ed., *Further Correspondence of John
    Ray*, Ray Society, 1928, p.159.

14 Early in the twentieth century, Mary Ewing was
    inspired to found a short-lived Parkinson Society
    and the *Paradisus* was republished in a limited
    vellum-bound edition by the Folio Society in
    1904, and as a facsimile by Dover Publications
    in 1976.

15 Sir Matthew Lister was reported by John Aubrey
    to have retired to his estate in Lincolnshire
    where he lived into his nineties; Lawson-Dick,
    p.138. The supple survivor, De Mayerne, at his
    death in 1655 was mourned as 'a stranger in
    point of birth but not of affection to this nation

... so well known and of so clear fame amongst
all degrees and with all persons who had any
esteem for worth', Nance, p.15: see Chapter 14,
note 9 above. John Goodyer never published his
translation of Dioscorides, although he finished
it at his home in Petersfield, Hampshire, and left
all his papers to Magdalen College, Oxford. His
Dioscorides was published privately by R.W.T.
Gunther in 1929; see bibliography.

16 Parish Register of St Mary and All Saints,
    Whalley, Lancashire Parish Register Society.

17 See *County Louth Society Archaeological
    Journal*, Vol. 6, p.234. Some of the Parkinsons
    were good Protestants who had helped in
    Cromwell's suppression, such as Edward
    Parkinson who was given the confiscated estate
    of an Ulster English lord called John Bellew as a
    reward. John Bellew's fate was typical of
    Catholic royalists who survived the fighting. He
    was a career soldier who joined the royalist
    army under Lord Ormonde in 1648. After 1650
    the Commissioners confiscated his land and
    offered him land in Galway 'to the value of third
    of his estates'. Bellew was deported west with
    his family to Connaught, while 197 acres in the
    east at Nicholstown were allowed to Protestants
    Edward Parkinson and William Armitage.

18 Anon., *Gentleman's Magazine*, 1813, for biogra-
    phical detail of James Parkinson. See also Parish
    Registers of St Mary's, Shrewsbury. Births:
    February 1730, 'Christened: Feb. 28, 1730
    (1731), St Mary's: Son of James Parkinson,
    Mother: Jane Birch'. Mother, Jane, married his
    father, James, 11 December 1723. Father, James,
    died in the parish 14 October 1736.

19 Mullens, W., *The Leverian Museum*, Museums
    Journal, Vol. 15, no.4, October 1915.

SELECT BIBLIOGRAPHY

All published in London unless otherwise indicated

Ainsworth, R., *The Parkinson Family of Lancashire*, Wardleworth, 1936

Allen, M., *The Tradescants*, Michael Joseph, 1964

Arber, A., *Herbals, Their Origin and Evolution*, Cambridge University Press, Cambridge, 1938

Ashton, R., ed., *James I by his Contemporaries*, Hutchinson, 1969

Aubrey, J. *see* Lawson-Dick

Bacon, F., *Essays*, Dent/Dutton, London & New York, 1906

De Beer, E.S., ed., *Kalendarium. The Diary of John Evelyn*, Clarendon Press, Oxford, 1955

Bekkers, J., ed., *Correspondence of John Morris with Johannes de Laet (1634–1649)*, based on letters in Latin in Utrecht, MS 986x, Van Gorcum & Co., Netherlands, 1970

De Bry, T., ed., *Thomas Hariot's A brief and true Report of the New Found land of Virginia*, trans. from Latin by R. Hakluyt, Frankfurt, 1590

Chamberlain, John *see* Thomson

Clifford, Anne *see* Sackville-West

Easton, C., *Les hivers dans l'Europe Occidentale*, Leiden, 1928

Ellis, H., *Original Letters Illustrative of English History*, Vol. 11, Dawsons of Pall Mall, 1969

Emberry, J., trans., *CPA Comitia Proceedings*, unpublished MS, Royal College of Physicians, 1954

Evelyn, John *see* De Beer

Farrer, W., and Brownbill, J., eds., *The Victoria History of the County of Lancashire*, Vol. 6, 1911 and Vol. 7, 1912, Constable & Co.

Gerard, J., *A Herball*, 1597

Gunther, R.W.T., *Early British Botanists*, Oxford University Press, Oxford, 1922

Gunther, R.W.T., ed., *The Greek Herbal of Dioscorides, illustrated by a Byzantine AD 512, Englished by John Goodyer AD 1655*, Oxford University Press, Oxford, 1934

Hadfield, M., *A History of British Gardening*, John Murray, 1979

Hakluyt, R., *Collection of the Early Voyages, Travels and Discoveries of the English Nation*, 1810

Harriot, Thomas *see* De Bry

Hentzner, P., *Travels in England during the reign of Queen Elizabeth*, trans. from Latin by R. Bentley, 220 copies commissioned and printed by Horace Walpole; repr. Cassell, 1889

Hoskins, W.G., *The Making of the English Landscape*, ed. C. Taylor, Hodder & Stoughton, 1988

Jacques, D., *Essential to the Practick Part of Phisick: The London Apothecaries*, The Worshipful Society of Apothecaries, 1992

Johnson, T., ed., *Gerard's Herbal*, 1633

Johnson, T., *Iter Plantarum*, in *Botanical Journeys in Kent & Hampstead*, facs., ed. J. Gilmour, trans. C. Raven *et al.*, Hunt Botanical Library, 1972

Lawson-Dick, O., ed., *Aubrey's Brief Lives*, Secker & Warburg, 1971

Legré, L., *La Botanique en Provence en XVI siècle: Felix et Thomas Platter*, Vol. 3, Marseilles, 1900

Leith-Ross, P., *The John Tradescants: Gardeners to the Rose and Lily Queen*, Peter Owen, 1998

Lodge, E., *Illustrations of British History, Original Papers selected from the Manuscripts of the noble families of Howard, Talbot and Cecil*, Vol. 2, 1568–89; Vol. 3, 1590–1618, G. Nicol, 1791

Matthews, L., *The Royal Apothecaries*, Wellcome Historical Pub., 1967

Nichols, J., *The progresses and public processions of Queen Elizabeth ... to which are subjoined some of the early progresses of King James etc.*, 1788–1821

De l'Obel, M., *Opera Omnia*, Thomas Purfoot, 1605

De l'Obel, M., *Stirpium Adversaria Nova*, 1571

Parkinson, J., *Paradisi in Sole, Paradisus Terrestris*, 1629, 2nd edn 1656

Parkinson, J., *Theatrum Botanicum, The Theater of Plants*, 1640

Pulteney, R., *Sketches of the Progress of Botany in England*, 1790

Raleigh, W. *see* Schomburgk

Raven, C.E., *English Naturalists from Neckam to Ray*, Cambridge University Press, Cambridge, 1947

Rees, J.A., *The Company of Grocers*, Chapman & Dodd, 1923

Rohde, E.S., *Old English Gardening Books*, The New Aldine Library, 1924

Sackville-West, V., ed., *The Diary of the Lady Anne Clifford*, Heinemann, 1913

Schomburgk, R., ed., *The discovery of the large, rich, and beautiful empire of Guiana ... performed in the year 1595 by Sir W. Raleigh, reprinted from the edition of 1596*, 1848

Sitwell, E., *The Queens and the Hive*, Macmillan, 1962

Spedding, F., ed., *Letters and Life of Francis Bacon*, Longman, 1861

Spence, R.T., *Lady Anne Clifford*, Sutton, Stroud, 1997

Spence, R.T., *The Privateering Earl, George Clifford, 3rd Earl of Cumberland*, Sutton, Stroud, 1995

Stow, J., *A Survey of London*, 1603; ed. C.L. Kingsford, Clarendon Press, Oxford, 1908

Strong, R., *The Renaissance Garden in England*, Thames & Hudson, 1979

Taylor, G., *Old London Gardens*, Ian Henry Pub., 1977

Thomson, E., ed., *The Chamberlain Letters*, John Murray, 1965

Thurley, S., *Whitehall Palace*, Yale University Press, 1999

Turner, W., *A Herball*, Cologne, 1568

Turner, W., *Libellus de re herbaria 1538, The names of herbes 1548*, facs., ed. Britten, Jackson, Stearn, Ray Society, 1965

Underwood, E., *A History of the Worshipful Society of Apothecaries of London*, Wellcome Historical Medical Museum Pub., 1963

Whitaker, T.D., *History of Whalley*, ed. Nicholls and Lyons, Lancashire, 1872

Williams, G.A., *Locus Benedictus*, Whalley Abbey Fellowship, Lancashire, 1995

Woodward, M., ed., *Gerard's Herbal*, Studio Editions, 1990

Worshipful Company of Grocers, *A Short History of the Grocers' Company, based on original Grocers' Records in Guildhall Library*, Guildhall, 1980

INDEX

The abbreviation JP refers to John Parkinson. Subentries under the entries for John and Mary Parkinson are in chronological rather than alphabetical order. Page numbers in *italic* refer to illustrations.

A

Abbot, Archbishop 189, 190
Agas, Ralph, map of London 50-1
alchemy 40-3, 44, 69, 136, 216
'Alexandrian bay' tree (oleander) 131
Alpinus, Prosper 218, 219
Althorp (Northamptonshire) 50
amaranthus 189
Amaranthus caudatus (flowergentle) 204
amaryllis lily 143
ambergris 81-2
America 75-7, 116
    see also Virginia
anemones, JP grows 108, 110, 216, 250
Anne of Denmark, Queen 127, 128, 128-9, 147, 151, 152, 170, 246
anti-Catholic feeling 120-1, 144-5, 182, 189-90, 191-2, 242, 272-4
Antwerp 64, 81
apothecaries 42, 43, 93-4, 115, 126, 146
    charged with 'practising' 95-8
    and College of Physicians 95-8, 99-100
    and Company of Grocers 98-9
    professional knowledge 63-6, 235-6
    see also Society of Apothecaries
apothecary shops 81, *89*, *178*, 179, *224*, 277
    JP's income from 101, 245
    JP's shop 92, 126, 165, 167-8, 184, 187, 191
apples 62, 210, 216
apricots 210, 216, 285
Archangel (Russia) 184-5
Argall, Captain Sam 168-9
Argent, Dr John 155, 231
Aristotle (384-322 BC) 35
Armeria maritima (thrift) 125
Artemisia arborescens 64-5
Arundel, Earl of *see* Howard, Thomas
Assheton, Sir Richard 24, 31
Astralagus lusitanicus (Spanish milk vetch) 229
astrology 107, 134, 287-8
Atkins, Dr Henry 172, 179, 189-90
    Censor of College of Physicians 93, 95
    and *Pharmacopoeia* 173-4, 175, 183
    and reform of Company of Grocers 146, 151, 153-5
Atkins, William 201
Aubrey, John 69, 183, 226, 252, 253, 277
Augustine, St 35
'auncient' Catholics 121, 144, 172, 182

B

Babington, Antony, 1584 plot 58
Bacon, Anthony 70, 149
Bacon, Lady Anne (Francis Bacon's mother) 149, 150
Bacon, Sir Francis (1561-1626) 49, 66, 70, 149-51, *150*, 184, 252, 253
    and creation of Society of Apothecaries 151, 153-4,

155-6, 156-7, 172, 176, 177-9
    downfall 181
    garden at Gray's Inn 153
    Naturall Historie (1627) 187
    views on physicians and medicine 151, 175-6
Bainbridge, Dr John 265-6, 267
Baker, George 116-17, 118
bananas 179, 231-2, *231*
Banqueting House (Whitehall) 267-8, 278
barbary buttons 204-5
barber-surgeons 93, 94, 115, 146
    see also Company of Barber-Surgeons
barnacle goose 200, 237
Barnes, Juliana, *Boke of St Albans* 36-7
Barnsley, Richard 131-2, 139
Bartholomew (Franciscan monk) 35, 36
Basilicon Doron (James I, 1598) 127
Basing House 278
Baskervill, Dr Simon 174, 225-6, 240, 243, 287
Bathurst, George 277
Bauhin, Gaspard, *Pinax* (1623) 258, 291
Bauhin, Jean 228
bay laurel 131
bay trees 51, 52
beans 20
Bedford, Earls of *see* Russell
beer 259
'Benjamin' (benzoin) 80, 83
Bess, William 99
betony (*Stachys arvensis*) 228
Bleasdale Moors (Lancashire) 15-16, *16-17*
bloodwort 21
Blount, Mountjoy, 1st Earl of Newport 246-7
Bobart, Jacob 275
Boel, Dr William 139-42, 170, 233
Boke of St Albans (Juliana Barnes) 36-7
Bolton Priory (Yorkshire) 29, 40, 42
Bonham, Dr 257
borage 104
Boswell, Sir William 272
'*botanographum*', role of 166
botany, development 290-1
box edging 125, 134, 216, 254
Braddyll, John 30
Bragge, Richard (JP's apprentice) 92
Bredwell, Stephen 95-6
Broad, William 200, 228
'broderie' (in gardens) 254
Brown, Lancelot 'Capability' 292
Buckingham, Duke of *see* Villiers, George
Bucklesbury (City of London) 91, 92, 126
Buggs, John 239
bulbs 113, 202-4, *203*, 250, 282, 285
Burghley, Lord *see* Cecil, William

C

Calvin, John 30, 38
Calvinism 43, 232
Camden, William 45
camphor resin 82, *82*
Campion, Edmund 89-90
cardomom seeds 83

ACKNOWLEDGMENTS

This book has come slowly into being with help and encouragement of many friends at critical moments. I am grateful to Jonathan Mantle for his incisive and useful support in the early stages. Catherine Clarke and the staff at Felicity Bryan's agency offered valuable advice at the beginning of the project, and Sally Montgomery gave me helpful comments on an early draft of the manuscript. Helena Attlee generously offered her wide knowledge and excellent judgement to steer the book on the right path. I would especially like to thank my cousin Robert Yeatman for his painstaking advice and enthusiastic support. I am grateful to my friend Gail Pirkis for her skilful comments, and likewise to Christopher Sinclair Stevenson. Julian Dickens, Jane Carr and Tim Binding rallied round to my rescue when there was a danger the book would be crushed by a publishing industry in turmoil. I would also like to thank my friends and former colleagues at the BBC, Gwyneth Williams, Dennis Sewell, Simon Coates, Jill Pack and Marcel Berlins for their early encouragement. My editor Jane Crawley has given me a generous dose of her steady confidence and a sure touch throughout the final stages, which has been an invaluable asset. I owe a particular debt to her patience and persistence, and also to Elisabeth Ingles, the designer Michael Brunström and of course, to my publisher, John Nicoll.

I would like to thank Danielle Parker for her assistance with the Latin translations, and James Armitage of the Royal Horticultural Society for expert advice on the list of plants in the appendix.

For help with the illustrations I am particularly indebted to the generous assistance of the Stanley Smith Horticultural Trust. Also I would like to thank Nick Baker and Michael Meredith of Eton College Library for permission to reproduce images from their collection. The extract from the Collection of Early Maps of London is reproduced by kind permission of the publishers, Harry Margary at www.harrymargary.com in association with the Guildhall Library, Aldermanbury, London, and at http:collage.cityoflondon.gov.uk.

The slow evolution of this book could never have taken place without the support and loyalty of my wonderful family, and the steady encouragement of my mother. To her, and to Russell, and to all my family, my love and thanks.